# Enterprise: Entrepreneurship and Innovation

*To Sylvia, Catherine and Jonathan*
– Robin

*To Andrew, Ian and bouncebackability*
– Sue

# Enterprise: Entrepreneurship and Innovation

## Concepts, Contexts and Commercialization

**Robin Lowe and Sue Marriott**

AMSTERDAM • BOSTON • HEIDELBERG • LONDON • NEW YORK • OXFORD
PARIS • SAN DIEGO • SAN FRANCISCO • SINGAPORE • SYDNEY • TOKYO

Butterworth-Heinemann is an imprint of Elsevier

Butterworth-Heinemann is an imprint of Elsevier
Linacre House, Jordan Hill, Oxford OX2 8DP, UK
30 Corporate Drive, Suite 400, Burlington, MA 01803, USA

First edition 2006
Reprinted 2007

**British Library Cataloguing in Publication Data**
A catalogue record for this book is available from the British Library

**Library of Congress Cataloging-in-Publication Data**
A catalog record for this book is available from the Library of Congress

ISBN: 978-0-7506-6920-7

For information on all Butterworth-Heinemann publications
visit our website at books.elsevier.com

Printed and bound in *China*

07 08 09 10   10 9 8 7 6 5 4 3 2

# Contents

# Introduction

Enterprise is the art – or science – of not standing still. Whether you are reading this as an individual or as a manager with organizational responsibilities you are faced with a stark choice. You can accept being carried along 'with the flow' and risk being flattened by the juggernaut of change or you can try to take charge – or at least influence – your own or your organization's destiny through being enterprising. Enterprise embraces many diverse themes including:

- entrepreneurship, starting up your own company and becoming self-employed;
- intrapreneurship, being an entrepreneur in an existing organization;
- being innovative in exploiting personal and organization opportunities, by adopting a particular approach to work, study or life in general; and
- being enterprising and becoming more independent and self-reliant throughout life, by gaining the necessary knowledge, skills and attitudes.

In today's competitive environment enterprising organizations must innovate in order to establish themselves, survive and grow. The traditional view of innovation, expressed by the majority of business textbooks is that strategies must be developed, and processes and systems established to encourage the generation of new or improved products, services, processes and ideas necessary for organizational growth and development. But it is the motivated, skilled and knowledgeable individual owners, managers and staff that are the innovators. They have the choice of whether to be innovative or not and must be encouraged if the organization is to succeed.

The traditional view of entrepreneurship is that there are a small number of exceptional people, such as Bill Gates, Richard Branson and James Dyson, who are the charismatic individuals who successfully commercialize new ideas, manage their own organizations and are incapable of working for anyone else.

In practice, however, many people are entrepreneurial and succeed in implementing new ideas. They can be found in virtually every type of organization and in every aspect of life. They aim to be self-reliant and keen to pursue their goals using the organization for which they work as their vehicle. These people will seek to be innovative, wherever they work and, if an organization does not allow them to be entrepreneurial, they will move on.

Entrepreneurs and innovators are creative in diverse areas, such as design, science, technology, the arts and organizational development and they work for many different types of organizations. Commercial success comes from innovations that are embedded within a product, service, process or an idea that fulfils the market requirements by providing value for customers, whether they be consumers, clients or patients, and maintains the organization's viability. This is market innovation but it is not confined to 'for profit innovation'. There are social entrepreneurs, too, that add value in the 'not-for-profit' sector by embracing new techniques and challenging the way things have always been done.

In this book we focus on enterprising behaviour, and on those individuals who make a difference, whether as entrepreneurs, as employees, as volunteers, or as active members of the communities in which they live. Irrespective of context, they introduce new perspectives, and have the self-confidence to back their judgement with action.

## Skills, knowledge, attitudes and techniques

New products and services must be developed and delivered to fulfil the new needs and desires of ever-more demanding customers and clients. New processes must be developed in order for organizations to more cost-effectively deliver their offer to customers and clients. The pace of change is accelerating as competitors copy new ideas and make alternatives to existing products and services available more quickly. As a result organizations grow if they have the right formula but decline more quickly if they do not. Hence there is more uncertainty in employment and so individuals must gain the skills of self-reliance, enterprise and entrepreneurship in order to survive and progress throughout their career.

The consequence of this is an increasing interest in how entrepreneurs, with their apparently special skills, knowledge and attitudes, are able to identify new opportunities, have the motivation to obtain the necessary resources and knowledge to exploit their ideas and make them commercial successes. By identifying, understanding and acquiring the entrepreneur's skills, attitudes and knowledge, and the techniques needed to generate new business and, if necessary, create a new organization it is possible to learn how to become more innovative, self-reliant, and opportunistic.

The key, however, is not simply to study the highest-profile, most successful entrepreneurs because their unique set of skills and circumstances may not be reproducible. Instead, by considering a broader range of situations, more modest levels of innovation and entrepreneurial achievement, entrepreneurship characteristics can be identified, acquired and applied to many situations: new starts; small and large firms; private, public and not-for-profit sectors. Associated with the introduction of new products, services and processes and new business start-ups, there is a high failure rate. By obtaining a better understanding of the entrepreneurial processes and gaining the relevant skills it seems reasonable to assume that better success rates can be achieved.

For large organizations the need for entrepreneurship and an understanding of the processes of innovation are just as great. Over a period of time large firms often become complacent and rely on their existing successful strategies, products and services. As competition increases they need to respond to the new demands of their customers and clients by harnessing the innovative capability of their staff to offer new products and services that their customers and clients will value. However, many fail to do this quickly enough, and reach a crisis point where the organization needs an entrepreneurial leader to turn it around.

The increasing emphasis on enterprise has spilled over into the public and not-for-profit sectors over the last two decades. Contracting out and public–private sector partnerships are two examples of this. Although time has proven that the private sector has not been particularly effective in tackling the public or social agenda, enterprise has remained a strong value in both, and is evident in the current trend to encourage the participation of the voluntary and community sectors in supporting the delivery of public sector services. This presents new challenges, and demands different capabilities if the opportunities are to be effectively exploited.

## The target audience

*Enterprise: Entrepreneurship and Innovation* aims to meet the needs of students and practitioners who wish to study enterprise, entrepreneurship and innovation in different contexts. It is primarily targeted at undergraduates and masters students taking a module in entrepreneurship and innovation who are interested in how entrepreneurship can be applied to new business starts, large private sector businesses, and public sector and social enterprises. Many students who are interested in entrepreneurship, and ultimately wish to run their own business, are often not ready to start their own business immediately but need to learn the dynamics of innovative business and management first. Many basic mistakes can be avoided by reflecting upon and, thus, learning the lessons of entrepreneurship in different contexts.

Many practitioners consider the options of self-employment, while others work in the area of business support policy or delivery or are consultants in a wide range of business situations and, for them, a more comprehensive conceptual underpinning is needed to prepare them for developing solutions in many different scenarios. In fact many practising managers try self-employment at some point in their career but return to employment to pursue their innovative approach to management. Others give up 'conventional management' positions for the challenge of starting up or running a social enterprise, not for their own personal benefit but rather for the good of the community.

This book discusses the factors that should be taken into account when starting up a new business, but this is not the primary focus of the book. In fact there are already many good practical guides to 'How to start a new business'. Therefore, a key aspect of this book is the emphasis on the learning and decision-making processes of entrepreneurs. Through encouraging students to practise enterprising skills, and to reflect on their learning, the hope and expectation is that they will gain the experience and self-confidence to believe that they can be more enterprising themselves. As a consequence, they will be able to realize their potential in whichever way they feel is right for them.

### Outline of the book

The following is an outline of the book.

| Chapter | Chapter title |
|---|---|
| **Part I Concepts** | |
| 1 | What is enterprise and where do we find it? |
| 2 | What entrepreneurs are like, and what they do |
| 3 | Innovation and its management |
| 4 | Learning, decision-making and leadership |
| **Part II Contexts** | |
| 5 | The personal enterprise environment |
| 6 | The enterprise environment and the entrepreneurial response |
| 7 | The social, public and not-for-profit context |
| 8 | Multicultural entrepreneurship |
| **Part III Commercialization** | |
| 9 | Opportunity identification and solution development |
| 10 | Enterprise planning and risk management |
| 11 | Getting started: creating the organization, obtaining resources and reaching break-even |
| 12 | Enterprise strategies and fast growth |

## How to study using this book

The aim of the book is to provide readers with an accessible and readable introduction to the various dimensions of entrepreneurship and market innovation.

It has a clear structure that is easy for the reader to follow.

## Part I Concepts

Part I of the book is concerned with the concepts of enterprise, entrepreneurship and innovation and we begin by introducing the topics. We start by discussing the characteristics of entrepreneurship and particularly the skills, knowledge and attitudes that define the way that entrepreneurs behave, explaining that it is not our intention to describe entrepreneurs as an elite species but rather the most visible tip of an iceberg of innovative and creative people.

Many people are innovative and we suggest that there is an entrepreneurial continuum with the 'archetypal' entrepreneurs at one extreme and, at the other, the 'followers' who show few of the characteristics of entrepreneurship. It is useful to study the characteristics of 'archetypal entrepreneurs' so that it is possible for the reader to understand what they are like and compare their own motivations and capabilities. We explain what entrepreneurs do and explore how they work to identify and exploit opportunities. Of particular interest is how entrepreneurs address the key challenges, such as the management of risk.

We then go on to discuss the nature and role of innovation and how it can be managed within the organization, including some of the lessons of good practice as well as some of the reasons for the failure of innovation. For large organizations initiating and managing innovation can be particularly problematic and, often, such firms develop very bureaucratic cultures that stifle ideas.

In the final chapter of Part I we discuss the alternative approaches to learning and emphasize the importance of learning in developing a more entrepreneurial and innovative approach. Sustainable innovation depends on effective learning processes being embedded in the strategic decision-making processes of organizations. This means that there is a need to foster a climate in which creativity can flourish, and where individuals can experiment and learn. We suggest that building learning capability is crucial to entrepreneurial success. We conclude that it is possible to build entrepreneurial capacity through reflective practice at both individual and organizational level.

## Part II Contexts

Right from the start we have emphasized that entrepreneurship occurs in many different contexts, and in this second part of the book we explore how enterprise appears in many facets of life, in the context of the individual and the organization, in small and large businesses, and in the commercial and 'not-for-profit' sectors. Individual entrepreneurs experience different challenges, depending upon their own set of circumstances and we set out to understand some of the difficulties they face and how they overcome them.

We start with the entrepreneur's personal circumstances and support environment and consider the challenges facing female, ethnic minority, and young and older entrepreneurs. We then go on to explore the nature of the broader market environment and the entrepreneurial response to the changes that take place.

In the chapter on social and community enterprise in the not-for-profit sector we focus on its role in social and economic regeneration.

Often social and community enterprise fills the gap in supply of services and frequently operates at the interface between the public and private sectors and this frequently sets different challenges for entrepreneurs.

We finish Part II by exploring what we consider to be a significant facet of entrepreneurship – the nature of multicultural entrepreneurship. We look at this from the perspective of the success of ethnic minorities in developed economies, international exploitation of innovation and also the problems of the informal economy and the significant influence of entrepreneurs in economic regeneration in different economies, but particularly in emerging markets.

## Part III Commercialization

In Part III, we focus on the elements of the commercialization process starting with the various ways in which opportunities are identified and solutions are developed, going on to planning the venture, gathering the necessary resources and finally discussing the strategies that are needed to ensure the start up venture becomes a sustainable organization.

We start by discussing the specific approaches to identifying market opportunities and ensuring that they might be feasible projects to pursue in the competitive market. To do this it is necessary to develop an offering that will appeal to customers.

We then go on to explore the role and benefits of planning at the different stages in the development of the organization and assessing the feasibility of the initial idea. Of particular importance is developing a viable business model and sustainable supply chain position.

Having identified an innovative project the entrepreneur must gather the resources and other support necessary to establish the idea as a sustainable product, service or process. This includes forming and legally protecting the organization, securing finance and a team to deliver the proposition, and finding customers that will generate the necessary revenue.

While establishing one innovative idea provides a sound basis for a new business it rarely guarantees a long-term, sustainable future for the business and, therefore, in this chapter we discuss the strategies that will ensure survival and lead to growth. Of particular interest is to identify the strategies and tactics of those organizations that achieve fast growth.

## Chapters

Before the introduction to each chapter the learning objectives for the chapter are set out and these should provide the focus for the study of the topic. A strong emphasis has been placed upon the practical application of the concepts, frameworks and academic research in order to enable the reader to appreciate the key lessons. To help to reinforce the learning and encourage the reader to explore the issues more fully the chapters contain a number of additional aids to learning.

## Enterprise in Action

The Enterprise in Action boxes provide examples of the practical application of the concepts of enterprise, entrepreneurship and innovation. The aim has been for the settings for these illustrations to be as diverse as possible, on the basis of business sector, and size and type of organization and its market situation as well as different geographies and cultures, to try to help the reader consider the situations described from alternative perspectives. They often highlight the decisions made at a critical time that ultimately prove to be crucial for successful entrepreneurship or innovation. We have not attempted to tell the 'life stories' of successful entrepreneurs but, rather, identify decisions at critical moments that offer lessons for students and practitioners. However, many of the examples provided are worthy of further investigation by the reader using online information, or newspaper or library sources.

## Spotlights

The Spotlights that have been provided are intended to reinforce a key issue or learning point that has been presented within the chapter. The questions provided should help to encourage further discussion or information search.

## Pause and Reflect

Many of the situations that occur in the Enterprise in Action examples do not have a clear-cut solution. Often it is necessary for the entrepreneur or innovator to pause and reflect on the information they have available before making their decision. The Pause and Reflect boxes are included within the chapter to emphasize the point that there are few simple and straightforward decisions. Organizations and entrepreneurs often face difficult situations that require a decision. However, they often fail to fully consider the various factors and so reach a lower quality decision, and therefore these boxes aim to encourage the reader to pause and reflect upon the deeper and broader implications of the individual scenarios, which is often necessary in 'real life'.

### Case studies

The 12 case studies provide the opportunity for the reader to carry out more comprehensive analysis of the key chapter topics. These short cases provide only limited information on the scenario in question and, where possible, readers should supplement the information provided using appropriate online and library sources in order to complete the tasks. The reader should start with the questions that have been supplied in order to help guide the analysis or discussion. Thereafter, however, the reader should think more broadly around the issues raised and decide whether these are indeed the right questions to ask and answer.

### Key words

Key words are listed at the end of the chapter and highlighted in the text.

### Chapter summary

A bullet point chapter summary is provided at the end of the chapter.

### Chapter questions

Five questions are provided at the end of the chapter to reinforce the chapter learning.

## Integrated personal development activities

After each part of the book we have included an integrative personal development activity that provides a basis for readers to reflect on the learning of the chapters and develop a personal development strategy to increase their ability to become more entrepreneurial and improve their ability to manage market innovation.

Essentially the chapters provide knowledge about the skills, attitudes and techniques that are central to the processes of entrepreneurship and market innovation and so the activities focus on how the reader might apply that knowledge to their own context by analysing what is needed to succeed in their own situation, reflecting on their own skills, attitudes and techniques and identifying the steps that might lead to improvement in their own personal performance.

We address this in three stages. At the end of Part I we focus on entrepreneurial characteristics, skills, motivations and actions. We emphasize the need to learn from the examples of entrepreneurs from a range of other contexts. At the end of Part II we focus on the skills, attitudes and techniques associated with the process of market innovation and its strategic and operational management. At the end of Part III the focus is on the development of a new start up business or turning around an established company.

In practice, long-term organizational success requires an effective combination of all enterprise skills, attitudes and techniques. It is unlikely that any one person can be effective in all of these areas and so having a grasp of one's own capabilities is an essential starting point in building a high performance team, from members with complementary attributes.

## Web support

An accompanying website (www.textbooks.elsevier.com) is provided for this textbook to enable students and lecturers to access additional resources in order to explore the subject further. A full set of Powerpoint slides is provided plus exercises, and suggestions for the use in class of the case studies and other illustrations. Students can access further learning resources to build up their knowledge of innovation situations using the hotlinks to useful websites that will add further depth and bring up to date the case studies and illustrations. Support is also provided that will enable students to assess and reflect on their own skills and attitudes to entrepreneurship and innovation through the provision of exercises and links to appropriate websites.

# Acknowledgements

In writing a book that brings together a diverse range of situations, challenges and actions under the umbrella of entrepreneurship and innovation we have drawn not only on our own experiences and the literature but on our encounters with a large number of enterprising people. We would like to thank our colleagues at Sheffield Hallam University, at other universities and in many businesses for their formal and informal contributions over the years.

Our students are a constant source of inspiration by sharing with us their learning experiences and their creative ideas for innovation and new business starts. This has helped us to develop the pedagogical elements of the book that are explained in the Introduction.

We have drawn extensively on the knowledge and experience of the owners and managers from organizations that we have worked with, who have provided insights and examples of the many dimensions of enterprise.

We are particularly indebted to Maggie Smith and the team at Elsevier in supporting us in presenting a broader view of entrepreneurship and innovation.

Robin Lowe
Sue Marriott

# PART I

# Concepts

The words enterprise and entrepreneurship appear so frequently in newspapers, radio and TV programmes, and everyday conversation that we pay very little attention to what the words actually mean. The academic literature helps us very little in coming to a clear understanding of the concepts, as there are so many different definitions/perspectives, and they carry both positive and negative connotations.

It is surprising perhaps that 'enterprise' is the word associated with the very largest firms – multinational enterprises, and at the same time is associated with individual endeavour; an enterprising individual might not be associated with any organization at all. The UK government, for example, has an initiative to encourage enterprise in schoolchildren. Individual enterprise is almost always seen positively as relating to individual creativity and pursuit of opportunity, innovation and development backed up by the individual's determination to succeed. However, when applied to a large organization, the word 'enterprise' is by no means always used positively. Often it is associated with a large, lumbering and rather bureaucratic organization.

Perhaps all enterprises should be enterprising but unfortunately they are often not, and this brings us to the fundamental idea that runs right through this book. Large and small enterprises are not spontaneously enterprising. They need enterprising people, individually or collectively to be innovative, creative and capable of developing and successfully exploiting new and exciting opportunities. This applies whether the firm is a commercial enterprise or operating in the public, voluntary or community sectors.

Part I of this book focuses on enterprise concepts. Chapter 1 introduces enterprise in its broadest sense, exploring how conceptual perspectives have developed over time, comparing definitions, and beginning to identify the contexts in which it emerges (this latter aspect being explored in much greater depth in Part II). Chapter 2 looks at the individuals themselves – what entrepreneurs are like and what they do. We consider what it is that distinguishes them from managers in general, what their motivations are, and where we tend to find them. The concepts introduced here relate to entrepreneurial personality, characteristics, and behaviour, and consider how far 'received wisdom' is accurate in helping policy makers to 'pick winners'. In Chapter 3 we shift our focus from the individual to the organization, and consider the sources of innovation in organizations and the process through which advantage is created. Finally, in Chapter 4 we bring individuals and organizations together again, looking at how organizations can develop their innovative capacity through learning and leadership.

# What is enterprise and where do we find it?

Learning objectives

By the end of this chapter the reader will be able to:

- appreciate the different conceptual perspectives on entrepreneurship and innovation;
- compare narrow and broad definitions, and evaluate their usefulness and purpose;
- understand the relationship between individual and organizational enterprise;
- recognize the different contexts in which enterprise skills and behaviours arise;
- assess whether initiatives to support the development of an 'enterprise culture' have the impact they intend.

## Introduction

Over time, there have been a variety of writers who have offered views on what enterprise means and the role that entrepreneurs play in economic and, more recently, social regeneration. They have highlighted examples of how individuals, and the organizations that they establish, have contributed to the prosperity of communities, regions, and nations. Whether you see these elusive characters that we call entrepreneurs as saints or as villains, it is difficult to argue that they make no difference to the world in which we live. Many governments see them as vital in growing economies, and seek to encourage more enterprise and innovation at all levels in society. This means that they would like to see individuals and organizations being able to achieve their full potential, and contribute as much as they can to society in general. By 'organizations' we do not just mean businesses – we mean any group of people that come together with a shared purpose. This can be as simple as your local gardening group or as complicated as a multinational firm. It can be private sector, but it can also be public sector, or not-for-profit.

Our view is that defining enterprise just as something that happens within businesses would be a very narrow way to approach the subject. Individuals can be enterprising in how they live their lives and those that are enterprising create and pursue more opportunities for themselves and, perhaps, get more enjoyment out of life. Unfortunately, not all enterprising people are successful, however they choose to measure success. Success to some means social standing or self-esteem, while to others it might mean artistic excellence; to some it might mean financial gain, while for others it might mean more time at home with their family. Enterprising behaviour inevitably includes taking risks, and where there is risk there can also be failure. Not many people write about failure, but maybe they should. Enterprising people often see failure as an opportunity to learn – it tells them something that helps them do things differently next time.

In this first chapter we will explore what we mean by enterprise for both individuals and organizations (whatever their size or sector), and where it can be found. Is enterprise really the prerogative of small and medium-sized businesses, or is it found more broadly? We will consider the various approaches to entrepreneurship and innovation that have evolved over time, and how innovative organizations rely on individual enterprise to maintain their competitive edge. We then go on to consider issues of enterprise policy: why might governments want to encourage a more enterprising culture, how might they go about it if they did, and what might the implications of intervention be?

## The evolving conceptual perspectives of entrepreneurship

Over time, various authors have taken different perspectives on entrepreneurs and their role in the economy. Some focus on their contribution to economic change, some on their creativity and innovation, some on the way they organize the factors of production, or resources, to add value, and some on their propensity for risk and its consummate reward. Deakins and Freel (2003: 3–10) offer a useful analysis of these, which is briefly summarized below.

## The physiocrats

Theories of **entrepreneurship** had their origins in economics. Cantillon and Say belonged to a French school of thought known as the 'physio-crats'. Cantillon saw entrepreneurs as having a key role in economic development by virtue of their having individual property rights as capitalists. He saw entrepreneurs as the key group, the other two that he recognized being landowners and workers. However, should we take it for granted that the entrepreneur is always the capitalist? We see entrepreneurs acting within a social and community context where they own little tangible capital but nevertheless add value in terms of social and economic regeneration. Also, in today's knowledge-based businesses, the distinction between who holds the capital and who does the work is less clear cut than it was, for example, during the Industrial Revolution. Where the capitalist owned the factory and the machines and the workers were employed by them to produce physical products the distinction between capitalist entrepreneur and worker was obvious. By way of contrast, if we consider a small company involved in research and development, the premises may be rented and the capital is the skills and expertise of the company as a whole, not only of the founder. In this case, the intangible capital belongs to each of the workers as the expertise is personal to them, although they may achieve synergy from working collaboratively. As a team of professional people, they may have equal status and run the company on more democratic lines, making it difficult to distinguish one individual as the leader (although it is common to identify senior partners, as, for example, in accounting firms). Each of them may act in an entrepreneurial way, and the distinction between entrepreneur, capitalist, and worker becomes somewhat more complicated to make.

Cantillon saw the entrepreneur as someone who consciously makes decisions about resource allocation, in that they choose to pay a certain price for a product to resell it at an uncertain price, consequently also bearing the risks of enterprise.

Cantillon did not believe that entrepreneurs must be innovators. Although they are expected to estimate demand for a product or service they do not have to be the ones who first create it.

Say also saw the entrepreneur as a **catalyst for economic development**, viewing their role as one of bringing together the different factors of production, moving resources from less to more productive areas. He did differentiate between the entrepreneur and the capitalist, separating the profits of the entrepreneur from the profits of capital. He did not see risk or uncertainty as a central issue, or as a force for change.

## The Austrian School

Some of these views were developed by the Austrian School. Kirzner did not feel that ownership was a necessary condition of entrepreneurship. Wherever disequilibrium exists in a market there will be frustrated buyers or sellers who are willing to accept or pay higher or lower prices. The entrepreneur, being alert to an opportunity for profitable exchange, can facilitate the deal. The market has imperfect knowledge, and anybody can be in a position where they know something that others do not. They do not necessarily have to own anything in order to make a profit. There is an element of creativity in making the match, however.

Schumpeter did not agree that anyone can perform the function. He sees the entrepreneur as someone special, an innovator, who brings something new to the process. Entrepreneurs change things, and challenge constraints suggesting greater proactivity, but they are not entrepreneurial all of the time. Such activity gets mixed up with other kinds of non-entrepreneurial activity, for example, 'management'.

## Risk taking

Schumpeter is adamant that entrepreneurs are not risk bearers unless they fund themselves. If someone else invests in a business, then they carry some of the burden of risk. At certain times, the element of risk is less than at others; for example, if the economy is relatively stable it is easier to predict what might happen in the future. Being first in a market carries more risk than being second or third, and entrepreneurs who are successful innovators are a rare and talented breed, in Schumpeter's opinion.

Other writers agree that entrepreneurs are risk takers, although some, like Knight, qualify this by saying that the risks they take are calculated. Knight also distinguishes between risk and uncertainty. When we do not know how things will turn out, we have to take risks. Some types of risk can be calculated and, indeed, insurance companies make a business out of it. But not all of the risk can be covered in this way and we cannot always calculate with any degree of precision the odds of many events occurring. Entrepreneurs are willing to go the extra mile and accept the risk of the uninsurable element but expect profit to be their reward for bearing this uncertainty. But of course, risk does not always result in profit and sometimes can result in serious loss. Wickham (2004: 13) refers to this as a 'market for risk'. Many people are risk averse and are not prepared to take uncalculated risks but are willing to pay a price which allows an element of profit to the entrepreneur who has borne the risk on their behalf.

---

## Enterprise in Action 1.1

### What risk?

Martin Whealey, age 53, and Fred Deakin, age 40, worked for a company who decided to change their product focus, and as a result they had either to find a new job or to buy out the failing manufacturing company. They took the biggest gamble of their working lives, setting up Stetfield Separators, which produces a range of equipment for the environmental market to treat oily waste and rainwater run-off at sites such as power stations, rail yards, and transport and storage depots.

They bought out the design rights, sales leads and enquiries, investing their own money and taking an overdraft from HSBC. They say the most nerve wracking part was turning the order book into sales and convincing people of their credibility as a company. Because of the sale negotiations, there had been a six week gap in work, and picking up work after the gap and keeping customers on their side was a tense process. The work is low volume and high value, so losing a lead was critical. Repeat business is low, and so maintaining a stream of new customers is vital.

They are pleased that the export side of the business is healthy, with a recent £49 600 sale to China, and just 11 months after starting up forecast turnover has doubled to £470 000. They have improved cash-flow control, and focused on developing good relationships with the key suppliers who carry out most of their manufacturing. With the support of their families, they are now (cautiously!) optimistic about the future.

*Adapted from*: Maisha Frost, 'Gamble pays off', *The Express*, 10 August 2005

**Question:** What risks did Whealey and Deakin actually take?

---

As we said earlier, not all risk is financial. Even where the investor is separate from the entrepreneur and therefore sharing the financial risk, they may not be sharing the same degree of personal risk. For example, the stigma of failure may be felt much more keenly by the entrepreneur as they may feel that their personal credibility is on the line. It may be argued that a manager becomes an entrepreneur when they are willing to stand up and be counted. Taking personal responsibility means accepting that their judgement is liable to error but they must still assume responsibility for its correctness. To be more right than wrong in making critical decisions requires knowledge, judgement, foresight and competence. Some managers might be performing activities that we generally attribute to entrepreneurs so can we argue that entrepreneurship has some connection with superior management ability? We might hypothesize that entrepreneurs can be found anywhere, so organizations could be described as pools of potential entrepreneurs. These potential entrepreneurs may choose to remain employed, but if they feel they can achieve more, and fulfil their potential through self-employment, they might take that opportunity.

## Entrepreneurship as a multifaceted activity

Casson tries to bring some of these issues together, seeing entrepreneurship as a **multifaceted activity**. Entrepreneurs have different skills; they coordinate scarce resources, make judgements and decisions and take risks. He looks at issues of supply and demand. Some economies seem to encourage entrepreneurship more than others, and he gives consideration to how far this is attributable to a predisposition towards enterprise and environmental circumstances. He sees change going hand-in-hand with entrepreneurship as it provides opportunities and choices for the entrepreneur as to which they will pursue.

## The social dimension to entrepreneurship

Although we can clearly see that entrepreneurs operate in an economic context, they also operate in a social one. They do make the economic system more competitive but they also drive changes in the structure of society – they enrich life, challenging the status quo, and changing perceptions.

For some entrepreneurs, the motive is primarily social; for example, Trevor Baylis (Handy 1999: 70) invented a clockwork radio, which is the only way in which health information and education can be spread in many parts of Africa. We see examples every day of the achievements of enterprising people in all walks of life. Kirby (2003: 29) suggests that the Beatles were cultural entrepreneurs; it could be similarly argued that Live 8 is an example of Bob Geldof's entrepreneurial ability. Julia Middleton (Handy 1999: 180) set up Common Purpose in 1988 (she held the view that by bringing key decision-makers within cities together, they could be educated and encouraged to collaborate in the regeneration of the areas in which they live and work). There are other people who are less well known, but who make a significant difference in their local communities by their dedication, hard work and determination. We can all think of such people: the person who single-handedly keeps the local brass brand solvent; the person who campaigns for community facilities, etc.

The balance between the **economic, cultural or social motive**, and its ultimate impact, varies. It would be naïve, however, to assume that economic impact is all that we should look for today. Indeed, the popular press is quick to use the word entrepreneur negatively to describe the individual who has got rich quickly by using unethical business methods to defraud his or her customers.

This suggests that, over time, and in different circumstances, our understanding of the role played by entrepreneurs can change. If we accept that entrepreneurs play a social as well as an economic role and that managers can sometimes perform entrepreneurial activities, this has consequences for how we define entrepreneurship and innovation.

## Pause and Reflect 1.1

### Reviving National Savings

Alan Cook is 51, lives in Milton Keynes, worked for the Prudential for 30 years working his way up to be their number 2, and took a 30 per cent pay cut almost three years ago to become chief executive of National Savings, an organization seen to be something of a dinosaur in the Financial Services industry. Despite what seems like a pretty uneventful employment background, he has turned the organization around. Today 23 million Britons invest £27 billion in Premium Bonds, compared to £5 bn in 1995. Total savings at National Savings have increased by £6 bn to £69 bn in just over 2 years.

How did he do this? He admits that there were external forces that supported the turnaround. The stock market was weak, and corporate scandals eroded the public's faith in business, making National Savings seem like a port in a storm, with its watertight Treasury Guarantees. This is something that their competitors complain about, as the protected status skews the market in their view. Cook doesn't accept this criticism, pointing out that only 5 of his 12 products enjoy tax-free status and that their interest rates are lower as a consequence of that. Without tax-free status it would be almost impossible to operate premium bonds.

Financial products are quite complicated, and savers are also growing tired of being lured by higher rates only to find that a month after they move their money the rate comes down again.

Over the last two years Cook has introduced direct debits for the public to build up savings, and swipe cards to access them, doing away with 13 million of those familiar little blue savings books in the process. He has just launched an advertising campaign with Alan Sugar to publicize a second million-pound prize for premium bonds.

There are plans for new longer-term savings products and a deal with a leading supermarket that will enable customers to buy their premium bonds and index-linked savings certificates when they are doing their shopping.

Although there were fears that its market would be undermined by the National Lottery, the opposite seems to be the case, as customers seem to be influenced more by the frequency of winning than by the amounts they win. Cook does express some concern about the public's increasing interest in gambling, but says that they spend their money on other luxuries like expensive holidays too. He would like to encourage them to save rather than spend, so that they can provide for their future.

With two years left on his five-year contract, his career prospects certainly haven't suffered from the move; a top job in financial services or the running of a government agency may well be likely at the end of Cook's contract.

*Adapted from*: Nick Mathiason, 'The man who saved Premium Bonds', *The Observer*, 14 August 2005

**Questions:** Would you describe Cook as an entrepreneur? Why/Why not?

## Some definitions of entrepreneurship

Although the literature recognizes the importance of entrepreneurs, it provides such a broad range of definitions that it becomes difficult to pin down what the term actually means. The word entrepreneurship derives from the French *entreprendre*, which translates literally as 'between taker', or 'go-between', the verb meaning 'to undertake'. This implies that it is action based – not something that we just think about or theorize about, but something that has meaning in what is actually done in practice.

There are both **narrow and broad definitions**.

## Narrow definitions of entrepreneurship

For some people, the word entrepreneur is defined quite narrowly, meaning the same as 'capitalist employer' or 'business owner/manager'. Others see it as a phenomenon of small businesses rather than large ones, of the private sector rather than the public, social or not-for-profit sectors. Some see entrepreneurship in terms of business creation and development, and there are many textbooks on the subject that focus almost entirely on how ideas are generated, business plans written, resources acquired and business concepts brought to realization. Some writers argue that 'true' entrepreneurship exists only where there is potential for high growth, and many public sector support programmes reinforce this view, prioritizing scarce resources in such sectors where, they argue, the potential return is greater.

## Broader definitions

Other writers take a broader view, still focusing on organizations, but recognizing that people can be creative and innovative as employees as well as in a self-employed capacity. These people are labelled 'intrapreneurs', and organizations that wish to remain competitive in fast-moving or complex and competitive environments need to nurture such individuals and harness their creative capacity in order to achieve sustainable competitive advantage.

How we define the term sets the parameters for our understanding of the concept and has implications for the way society sees entrepreneurship, and for the way policy makers and businesses themselves relate to it. For example, Wickham (2004: 3) argues that 'entrepreneurs are just *managers* who make *entrepreneurial* decisions'. This would imply that entrepreneurs are not born, but made. If we agree with this definition we might then accept that it is possible to learn the skill of entrepreneurial decision-making. Within organizations, if we want to adopt a more innovative culture, we could perhaps encourage our managers to learn to be more creative and to be less risk averse in their day-to-day decision-making. Policy makers might choose to look at the way we educate our children in schools to encourage more autonomy and self-reliance. However, if we believed the opposite, and defined the entrepreneur in terms of personality characteristics, our actions would be different. In organizations we might choose not to invest in skills development but recruit certain personality types. Rather than investing in skills development, public sector training might then concentrate on picking out individuals with potential, and investing in their ideas or matching them with investors.

## Focusing on skills or attitudes

Lord Young, in his role as UK Secretary of State for Employment in 1993 said that enterprise was about 'Get up and go – not sitting back and accepting it. Think positive and things can happen; think negative and nothing happens. It's a mental attitude'. Almost a decade later, the Davies Review (2002) defined '**enterprise capability**' broadly as 'the capacity to handle uncertainty and respond positively to change, to create and implement new ideas and ways of doing things, to make reasonable risk/reward assessments and act upon them in one's personal and working life'.

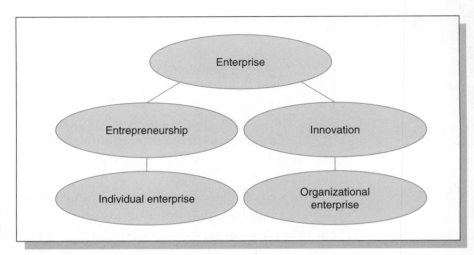

**Figure 1.1**
Enterprise:
entrepreneurship
and innovation.

Our view is that the term should be broadly defined. To understand how innovation and entrepreneurship can impact on organizations, communities, and economies, we do need to look at people themselves and ask a number of questions:

- Why is it that some people appear to be more enterprising than others?
- What is different about them as people, their experiences, their motivations, their circumstances?

But this is only part of the equation.

- People do not always choose to act in entrepreneurial ways despite being enterprising people, so what prevents them from expressing their creativity, from following their hunches, from taking a little bit more risk, from developing enterprise skills?
- Do some cultures and some environments inhibit enterprise, and why?

Organizations are simply vehicles for the creativity and enthusiasm of individuals, the context in which enterprising behaviour finds expression. If we are to describe an organization as enterprising, it needs both entrepreneurship (individual enterprise) and innovation (organizational enterprise) (Figure 1.1).

## The characteristics of individual enterprise

We have seen that enterprising people are often labelled 'entrepreneurs'. If they behave in enterprising ways within the organizations that employ them, they are labelled '**intrapreneurs**'. Often a business is the personification of the entrepreneur; for example, it is difficult to think about Virgin without Richard Branson popping into your thoughts.

## Self-managed or -employed

If we are looking to encourage people to be more enterprising, these labels may not always be helpful. Perceptions of 'entrepreneurs' differ from one culture to another. Stereotypical images sometimes lead people to disassociate themselves from the concept, feeling that perhaps the idea of creating wealth is inappropriate to them; or perhaps they link it to the idea that to be entrepreneurial means running your own business, which seems too great a risk. Being an employee does not debar you from being enterprising. Ask any teacher who has helped to turn around a school described as 'failing'. The growing interest in social entrepreneurship, and the idea that enterprise can be directed towards generating social capital rather than economic capital might give encouragement to those who are motivated more by 'making a difference' than by accruing personal wealth and achieving independence from the organization.

It is easy to exclude yourself from this band of enterprising people – the truth is that many of us are more enterprising than we realize, and that this 'spark' lies dormant in many of us, just waiting for the opportunity to show itself.

## Knowledge and learning

Entrepreneurs have a personal store of knowledge of an area of activity – the business, the people, the customers, the competition – and they apply it to a new situation. As they make decisions they learn, build on their existing knowledge and recognize its value, identify gaps in that knowledge and fill them. They adapt, and make the changes that are necessary to pursue an opportunity in a single-minded way.

Learning is a central aspect of entrepreneurship but learning comes in many guises, largely because individuals learn in different ways. It is not all about formal learning although theory and knowledge have their place. However, entrepreneurs are often action-oriented and **learn by doing**. They analyse and decide, reflect and revise, and consider what went right/wrong. They retain detailed knowledge of subjects that are important and store the lessons of good and bad practice for future reference.

If learning is so important, this begs the question of whether the education system encourages individuals to be enterprising. The statistics do not really help, although there is evidence to suggest that people who have degrees, for example, tend to be less likely to fail in business than those who do not; successful entrepreneurs come from all educational levels, following different educational experiences (SBS, 2003). There are some unexpected findings, for example, a higher than expected number of entrepreneurs have dyslexia.

## The family connection

Looking back through history, in pre-industrial societies family and working life were highly integrated; the separation of the two is a fairly recent phenomenon. According to the BDO Centre for Family Businesses (2005) up to 76 per cent of UK businesses are family owned. Furthermore, it is, perhaps, only natural that having built a business one would want to 'pass it on' and so retain the accumulated wealth in the family. But one of the most difficult issues faced by such firms is that of succession. There is an old, probably true, adage which says 'clogs to clogs in three generations'. Around four out of five family businesses are managed by the first generation. Only 15 per cent ever reach the third generation of family management. This might suggest that having an entrepreneurial family background does not predispose the offspring to being entrepreneurial. However, there is evidence to suggest the opposite (SBS, 2003); whether it is genetic, or because you are exposed to certain attitudes and experiences early in life, because you have role models, or because you make useful contacts, coming from an enterprising family does help and encourage people to become an entrepreneur. Perhaps the conclusion to be reached from this is: beware of working for the family business!

## Personality drivers

Our personalities predispose us to see things in certain ways. Gareth Morgan (1997) talks about 'psychic prisons' and how people and organizations can become trapped in favoured ways of thinking. Some of us are more optimistic than others and see opportunities where others see only problems. Our personal history and experiences lead us to expect certain things to happen as a result of something else, and so we narrow our perspective and sometimes fail to see the bigger picture, the chance that things will turn out differently next time. If you have never experienced being involved in a business, for example, your perceptions of what it would actually be like may be quite wrong (it may be too rosy, or too gloomy, a perspective!). If we are to nurture the spark of enterprise within us, we need to challenge our preconceptions.

## Life circumstances

The current life circumstances of individuals might also influence their willingness to be more enterprising. When a person is young and without responsibilities the risks may seem less than when they have a family to look after and a mortgage to pay, or if they have aged parents to take care of. Responsibilities can make the individual feel as if they have less freedom to start a business, diversify into new markets, or take on more staff. In Enterprise in Action 1.2, being made redundant might have made the decision to set up easier, as the responsibility for the decision to give up paid employment was made for Gemma, and the redundancy payment meant that she was able to fund the start-up independently.

### Enterprise in Action 1.2

#### Rock and Ruby

When Granada and ITV merged, Gemma Stone was made redundant. Having 10 years' experience in event management, she decided to use her redundancy money to set up Rock and Ruby. She admits that she did this with some trepidation, and that the process of registering the company and even deciding on its name seemed difficult at the time. The company is funded entirely by her partner, Steve, and herself, from their savings and the redundancy money because they did not want the added stress of repaying loans. As a 30-year-old, a female, and a mother of two, without a degree she does not see herself as a typical entrepreneur. Despite the long hours and hard work, she says that running her own company is very satisfying and she strives to maintain an appropriate work-life balance. 'Owning my own company has given me the opportunity to do what I do best and that is what motivates and inspires me.'

*Adapted from*: www.startups.co.uk

**Question:** Do you think that a trigger is needed for an employed individual to start a new business?

# Perceptions of risk

The self-esteem and status of an employed person is often linked to their job and the perks it provides, e.g. the expensive company car, private healthcare or first class train travel. It may appear to be too much of a risk to give up steady income, promotion prospects or the retirement package.

There are also professional risks. People from specialist professions may find that the more generic management approach of running their own business means that they fail to keep up with developments in their profession, and might no longer be able to compete with their peers should they later wish to return to their former occupation.

Sometimes it comes down to confidence in an ability to analyse or 'sense' the environment. The individual must decide whether he or she is the sort of person who will trust their intuition, and have confidence in their own assessment of trends, the market and customer needs.

# The cultural dimension

These issues vary from culture to culture. Some cultures appear to be more naturally predisposed towards enterprise than others. Some writers argue that dislocation and hardship can lead to enterprise. The very experience of surviving in a new and hostile environment requires certain qualities. Certainly it would appear that in troubled times, some minority groups have had little to lose and much to gain from enterprise, leading in some cases to the global organizations of today.

Prior to the growth of interest in the small business sector in the 1980s, there had been little recognition of the role that women played in enterprise, either as business owners in their own right or as contributors to family-owned firms. As women have engaged more in the labour market in general, there has also been a growth in the numbers of women entering self-employment. For many it can be a positive lifestyle choice allowing the flexibility to balance responsibilities; for others it is a reaction against the inability to make progress in employment when they realize that their nose is pressed right up to the glass ceiling. They may well be tempted by an alternative way of living that provides more control over their own destiny and rewards that are more appropriate to their contribution to the organization.

Recently, there has been much interest in 'grey entrepreneurs'. As their family responsibilities diminish, and with experience in management and knowledge of the market, many people are tempted to 'retire' early and set up on their own.

Although creative people are often said to be driven by the need to 'make a difference', for many, being seen as 'different' is the last thing they want. We can only imagine what a society that consisted wholly of stereotypical entrepreneurs would be like. But if you are so inclined, it *could* be you at some point in time, in some circumstances. Many successful entrepreneurs never imagined they could attain to where they have reached. There are many ways to be entrepreneurial and, as we discuss in this book they do not all involve featuring on television programmes. The chosen way will never be absolutely right and there is likely to be a defining moment when it is necessary to choose to take the risk. The years after the decision will involve many obstacles but the rewards are there for those who have the courage.

## The continuum of enterprise

Rather than categorizing people as entrepreneurial or not, it may be more useful to think in terms of a **continuum of enterprise** (Figure 1.2).

Wherever they sit on that continuum, there is a role to be played. But if the road to economic and social prosperity depends on more individuals becoming more enterprising, people need to be encouraged to

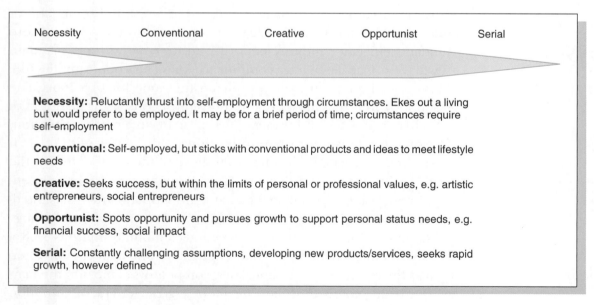

Necessity      Conventional      Creative      Opportunist      Serial

**Necessity:** Reluctantly thrust into self-employment through circumstances. Ekes out a living but would prefer to be employed. It may be for a brief period of time; circumstances require self-employment

**Conventional:** Self-employed, but sticks with conventional products and ideas to meet lifestyle needs

**Creative:** Seeks success, but within the limits of personal or professional values, e.g. artistic entrepreneurs, social entrepreneurs

**Opportunist:** Spots opportunity and pursues growth to support personal status needs, e.g. financial success, social impact

**Serial:** Constantly challenging assumptions, developing new products/services, seeks rapid growth, however defined

**Figure 1.2**
Continuum of entrepreneurial activity.

consider whether they might be able to improve their chances of realizing their personal or professional aspirations in life by developing certain skills or attributes, or by actively seeking out opportunities to practise and develop enterprise skills.

Furthermore, in an increasingly competitive and over supplied world, organizations must differentiate their offerings from those of the competitors and become more enterprising if they are to survive and grow. To do this they must become more innovative, but if organizations are to be more innovative, they have to be able to harness the potential for individuals to be more enterprising on their behalf.

## Organizational enterprise

At the heart of enterprise is the identification and exploitation of opportunities that will benefit the stakeholders of the organization. Stakeholders are all those individuals, groups and organizations that have an interest in what the organization does, and includes the partners, owners, managers, staff, trades union, customers, competitors, suppliers, government and community in general.

## Innovation

Many organizations are initially established as a result of some kind of **innovation** whether the initial idea is new to the world or a rather more mundane efficiency improvement. To ensure survival and maintain growth the organization must continue to exploit new opportunities too.

Few organizations are able to remain the same for very long. The reason for this is that most organizations must constantly adapt to the ever changing external business environment and market situation. Most organizations must strive to do things differently and better in order to differentiate their offer from those of the competitors in the minds of the customers and clients. In this way they can gain competitive advantage and so maintain the loyalty and support of their stakeholders. This is essential for survival and growth. For example, technology constantly develops, legislation changes and community interests evolve. Market dynamics change as consumer demands and expectations alter, often as the result of new fashions; new competitors come into the market; or existing competitors become more aggressive. The organization itself learns from its collective experience of success and failure and develops good practice in the management of its processes and systems.

Opportunities constantly emerge from the changes but it is the organization's speed in identifying them and its effectiveness in exploiting them that is critical for success.

In defining innovation, it is not surprising that new technology and new products are often the first things that spring to mind. It is natural to think about invention as a key aspect of innovation.

But invention is only part of the process – these ideas need to be commercialized if they are to achieve impact. The Sinclair C5 is a good example of how an invention can fail to find a market. A highly economical, powered vehicle met its technological design specification fully but was perceived by potential customers to be too near to the ground and dangerous on busy roads. On the other hand the Sony Walkman tapped into a latent demand for mobile personal entertainment.

Innovation can be driven by technological advancement, referred to as science push, or it can be market pull, a response to the changing demands from customers and consumers or the changing bases of competition within markets.

It is also about new processes and new ways of doing things that may not be obvious to customers but add significant value in delivering the services and products that our (increasingly sophisticated) customers require, e.g. online banking, or the no-frills airlines. So innovation is not just about high-technology firms, and high-tech does not always mean high growth.

Innovation is broader than just technological advancements; it is a process of creating, experimenting, transforming not only what is offered but the way in which it is offered – the business model. Successful innovators are not foolhardy. They are in many ways conservative. They are not focused on risk, but on opportunity and its potential for exploitation.

Although some innovations do arise from a flash of genius, the successful ones tend to be born of a conscious, purposeful search for opportunity which involves taking a hard look at customer preferences, the way the industry currently competes, and the way a business is configured. Sometimes the new ideas, the new opportunities start small, but some are ultimately transformational.

## Creative destruction or incremental change

Schumpeter (1934) identified five principal sources of what he referred to as '**creative destruction**' that often underpin innovation:

- introduction of a new good (or a significant improvement in the quality of an existing good);

- introduction of a new method of production (i.e. innovation in processes);
- the opening of a new market (in particular an export market in a new territory);
- the 'conquest of a new source of supply of raw materials or half-manufactured goods';
- the creation of a new type of industrial organization (i.e. an administrative innovation).

Although the quantum leaps are the ones that often have immediate significance and impact, it is sometimes the smaller adjustments that reinforce changes in attitudes and behaviour. It is important not to dismiss **incremental innovation**, or fall into the trap of restricting our discussion of the context in which innovation arises as being the prerogative of the private sector. For example, governments can be innovators and also facilitators of innovation. Government-sponsored research may lead to industry innovations, but there also may be innovation in the process of governance itself.

Although a significant innovation is possible, and in line with customer needs, commercial considerations sometimes inhibit its exploitation. An example of this can be seen in Enterprise in Action 1.3, where an opportunity has not been fully exploited because it may undermine the existing business of a number of stakeholders.

## Enterprise in Action 1.3

### Rokr – innovation (or not!)

Apple undeniably exploited online music extremely successfully with the iPod, transforming expectations of the way the industry competed as it linked to the first legal online music business (iTunes). The possibility of combining this technology with a mobile phone opened up numerous possibilities for further exploitation of the concept. So why might the Rokr (a mobile phone designed by Motorola with an iPod inside) fail to live up to its hype?

It seems to be quite a good phone, having reasonable battery life, a camera, Bluetooth, speaker and voice dialling, but it isn't unique in that. The music player works like an iPod, but without the clickwheel, so maybe it doesn't score as high on user-friendliness as it could. Its memory card is configured to act like an iPod shuffle, but it can only hold a hundred songs.

It could have exploited the synergies between the technologies. There is no technological reason why it shouldn't hold a thousand songs, but that might undermine existing iPod sales. It would be possible to download iTunes tracks from the Internet direct to the phone, but instead you have to download to a computer and get songs from the music library just as iPod works now. It would be possible to use songs stored on the phone as ringtones, except that the mobile operator's very profitable trade in ringtones would be hit.

Apple scored a winner in exploiting online music, but its assets (tangible and intangible) are now so valuable that it would be foolish to undermine them. Another quantum leap innovation would do just that. So Apple has settled for the half-way house to retain its current market – victims of its own success. It remains to be seen whether competitors might now exploit the gap that Apple have identified, but barely exploited.

*Adapted from:* John Naughton, 'Why the iPhone won't rock your world', *The Observer*, 11 September 2005

**Question:** What are the critical success factors for an innovative new product?

In summary, innovation is, we argue, the process by which opportunities are identified and exploited. These opportunities are often radical, and potentially disruptive. The key elements in developing successful innovation are:

- creativity that challenges the taken-for-granted assumptions and unsettles the status quo;
- entrepreneurial capability that will drive the commercialization of the idea;
- management of the process, the staff and other resources, both from within and outside the organization;
- the motivation and ambition of the individuals to identify and exploit the opportunities.

## Contexts – where do we find enterprise?

Much of the literature refers to the economic role of entrepreneurs. In creating wealth, they add value, providing employment and contributing through taxation to the provision of social benefits. But this is a restricted view given that, by our broader definition, there are some entrepreneurs whose motives are more social than economic.

The received wisdom is that we need more entrepreneurs to lead the economy, and more enterprise to liven up all industry. Small firms create economic development, and there is an implicit assumption of a positive connection between jobs and entrepreneurship. But do the facts bear this out?

## Size of businesses

According to the Small Business Service (statistics published 25/8/05), there were 4.3 million **private business enterprises** in the UK at the start of 2004. These enterprises employed an estimated 22 million people, and had an estimated combined annual turnover of £2400 billion. Almost all of these enterprises (99.3 per cent) were small (0 to 49 employees). Only 26 000 (0.6 per cent) were medium-sized (50 to 249 employees) and 6000 (0.1 per cent) were large (250 or more employees).

## Creating jobs and turnover

Small and medium-sized enterprises (SMEs) together accounted for more than half of the employment (58.5 per cent) and turnover (51.3 per cent) in the UK. Small enterprises alone (0 to 49 employees) accounted for 46.8 per cent of employment and 37 per cent of turnover.

But, very few businesses actually employ many people. The number of businesses with no employees at all was 3.1 million, equivalent to 72.8 per cent of all enterprises. They had an estimated combined turnover of £190 billion. The number of businesses with employees was 1.2 million. They had an estimated combined turnover of £2160 billion.

The pattern in the UK is broadly typical of that of most developed countries. In countries that previously had a command economy there often remains an over-representation of large organizations and in underdeveloped countries there are often even larger numbers of small businesses.

## The types of organizations

### Small and medium-sized enterprises (SMEs)

Smaller entrepreneurial businesses have been seen as the source of new ideas and are considered to be particularly effective in exploiting new market opportunities. In order to defend their competitive position they increasingly have to operate in global niche markets.

Rather than categorizing by size it is useful to use innovativeness and potential for growth as criteria.

#### Marginal/lifestyle firms

The vast majority of SMEs only provide a basic income for the family and it is often lower in terms of £/hour than is possible from employment. It is not the basis of dreams!

### Attractive small company

There is a group of organizations with stable inputs and revenues and the potential to provide significant salaries, perks and a flexible lifestyle for the owners. Professional services, such as accountants and legal and medical services, fall into this category. Their innovations are often limited to what is necessary to maintain a competitive position.

### High growth potential firms

There are a limited number of organizations that have the potential for rapid growth of sales and profits to become a large corporation. They may be start-ups or established companies. The really fast-growing firms, often referred to as hypergrowth firms, tend to focus on being unique, with the vast majority of them exploiting a niche market that they can defend, with products or services that are perceived to be 'leading edge' by customers. They compete in areas that require speed, flexibility and customer service. They diversify into related products and adjacent markets, often leaving the industry before the window of opportunity closes.

## Enterprise in Action 1.4

### Grippling with growth

Success doesn't always have to be about trying to be big; many small firms turn their size to commercial advantage. Small firms can be more flexible, closer to their customers, and have a more personal relationship with their staff. Their employees are often more motivated, because it is easier for them to see how their contribution makes a difference in the company. They often thrive on doing things differently.

Hugh Facey is Chairman and Founder of Gripple, a Sheffield-based engineering firm. The company was formed in 1988, and was based on a new invention for joining and tensioning wire and rope. It has sold over 130 m units worldwide, and its products are now available in over 50 countries. Doing things differently is embedded in the business model. There are no job descriptions, and no personnel department or planning department. Hugh says that everybody knows what they need to do, and job descriptions inhibit people from doing anything else. Most of the 150 employees own shares in the company. They own 38 per cent of Gripple and 48 per cent of its sister company, Loadhog. They invest in the shares themselves – they aren't given them, although the company will lend them up to £10 000 (at commercial rates of interest) to buy shares, which they repay from their monthly salary. There is a target of between 20 and 25 per cent of turnover coming from new products which have been launched in the previous three years. Gripple only ever manufactures products that it can patent. To do this it invests 7 per cent of turnover in product development every year. Gripple acknowledges that, being small, it can't do everything itself and so it works with research partners such as specialist engineering teams at Sheffield's two universities, Cardiff University for rapid proto-typing and Cambridge University for cutting-edge research.

Growth means a company might run the risk of losing flexibility, and get more set in its ways. The challenge is to make sure that the constant questioning becomes so ingrained in the way things are done that it cannot be turned off.

*Adapted from:* Gareth Chadwick, 'Small in size but big in profits and innovation',
*Independent on Sunday*, 24 July 2005

**Question:** What initiates innovation in a small firm?

## Large organizations

There are arguments as to the relative importance of these different categories of organizations to the economy. Beck and Demirguc-Kunt (2004) question the widely held belief that SMEs are the drivers of economic growth, and point out that large enterprises may exploit economies of scale and more easily secure the resources to support the research and development that underpins innovation.

Economies go through phases. The largest firms always have the power and influence to change markets and are the drivers of global trade. Many however are:

- not growing organically but by acquisition;
- focusing on core business;
- outsourcing components and services.

Although this effects a change in the structure of the economy, the large organizations are still in a position to influence innovation and entrepreneurial activity through their trading networks, particularly their supply chains.

## Public sector organizations

**Public sector organizations** are not immune from the effects of changing environmental circumstances, and also need enterprising people working within them if they are to meet stakeholder expectations.

Despite periodic restructuring the public sector organizations continue to grow and offer employment to large proportions of the working population. Closer public scrutiny on efficiency and accountability have driven innovation in the delivery of many public services, leading to closer working with both the private and **not-for-profit sectors**.

The public sector also plays a role in encouraging innovation through intervention, for example grants to support innovation and research; funding to encourage technology transfer; or advice and guidance for potential start-up businesses.

---

### Spotlight 1.1

**Taking risks in the public sector**

Although the need for accountability is ever-present, the past few years have seen a shift in the way that public sector participants do business. From being risk-averse, they are now beginning to talk of the value of risk in offering creative solutions as they try to deliver more efficient and effective services.

The PFI (private finance initiative) programme is one example of this trend. This involves creating direct partnerships with the private sector to build capital projects such as hospitals. The hospital (or other capital project) is then leased back to a public authority such as a health trust or a council. The government sees this as a way to accelerate capital developments, but the initiative has aroused controversy, as there have been some high-profile failures. For example, this summer the government abandoned a project for a new hospital in Paddington before building had even started, having already spent £14m on lawyers, consultants and architects. The projected cost had risen from £360m to £1.1 billion.

Successes include the Highways Agencies contract for the recent A1–M1 link road. The Audit Commission praised this contract for encouraging innovation, as contractors were allowed to develop alternative techniques which did not necessarily conform to standard specifications, so long as they delivered to certain standards, for example that they designed the road in a way that would cut the need for future maintenance.

*Adapted from*: Gareth Huw Davies, 'Public sector goes more boldly', *Sunday Times*, 4 September 2005

**Question:** The public sector has to accept some level of risk if it is to meet the modernization agenda. How might the expectations of all stakeholders be managed in this new environment?

---

## The myths of entrepreneurship

It is important to remember that although **high-growth firms** sound like the epitome of entrepreneurship, they are comparatively rare. Although there is much talk, particularly in terms of public policy, of the need to encourage more of these types of firm, they are not sufficient in themselves. And despite sometimes being very profitable, they often do not provide very many jobs. A healthy economy needs innovative organizations in all sectors, and of all sizes. Roure (1997) drew our attention to the myths and realities of entrepreneurship, which are summarized in Table1.1.

**Table 1.1**
Myths of entrepreneurship

| Myth | Reality |
|------|---------|
| SMEs are the job creators | Only some SMEs create jobs and are high growth |
| New companies are the source of employment | High job growth comes in old and new companies |
| Growing firms come from new and high-growth sectors | Dynamic companies come from all sectors |
| Entrepreneurs of growing companies are young and well educated | Dynamic entrepreneurs come from all ages and education levels |
| Growing companies are built by an energetic and self-sufficient entrepreneur | Built by teams with a professional management approach |
| Target large and growing markets | Target sectors where they can be leaders or strong challengers |
| Target domestic markets that they can dominate | Often use exports to learn and grow |
| Growing companies use low-cost strategies to compete | Compete with high quality products and superior service |
| Growing companies rely primarily on unique technology | Rely primarily on recruiting, training and developing people |
| Growing companies use sophisticated sources of finance | Predominantly self-funded with assistance from bank loans |

Adapted from Juan Roure, Ten myths about entrepreneurship. In: Birley and Muzyka (2000), *Mastering Entrepreneurship*. Harlow: Pearson

# Individual propensity to entrepreneurship

In terms of individual propensity to entrepreneurship, the Small Business Service (SBS) Household Survey of Entrepreneurship 2003 shows that:

■ almost a quarter of adults in England are either already involved in entrepreneurial activity (13 per cent) or thinking about it (11 per cent);

■ men are twice as likely as women to be involved in entrepreneurial activity or to be thinking about it;

■ while young people are more likely to be thinking about starting their own enterprise they are less likely to be entrepreneurs than older people;

- ethnic minority groups are more likely to be considering starting a business but there are low levels of actual entrepreneurial activity among the black population;
- there is a north–south divide in the UK, with participation rates being higher in London, the South-West, East of England (all 15 per cent), and the South-East (14 per cent), than in the North-West (11 per cent), the West Midlands (10 per cent) and the North-East (9 per cent);
- those with a higher degree or degree are more likely than average to be entrepreneurs (15 per cent compared to 13 per cent);
- only 5 per cent of those who rent from local authorities and housing associations are engaged in entrepreneurial activity compared to 15 per cent of those who own or are buying their own properties.

But although the statistics show where active entrepreneurs are currently found, they say nothing about future potential. If it is believed that there is a need to encourage entrepreneurial activity at both individual and organizational level, then it is necessary to explore individual and organizational barriers to enterprise, and consider how we might actually develop a more enterprising culture.

## Enterprise in Action 1.5

### Getting a Flying Start

Flying Start is a government-sponsored initiative which brings together recent graduates so that they can test out their business ideas, get some business advice, and develop commercialization strategies with mentors. The idea is to get them to focus on who needs their product, rather than its features. The mentors also benefit, as they get a chance to see the good ideas early, and can choose to invest.

It will also begin to test whether government initiatives in this area are cost-effective. More entrepreneurship does lead to more economic growth, but there is no firm evidence of the degree to which one generates the other. Some free-marketeers argue that government interference actually stifles entrepreneurship.

The events organizer, Ian Robertson, has entrepreneurial experience himself. He founded a distance learning company called Vektor in 1989, which became a joint venture with Sony in 2001, and has a turnover of £9 m. When questioned as to whether graduates are an appropriate group to encourage to set up their own business, Robertson said 'Why should they work for a couple of years first? Does seeing how a bureaucracy works help you? It might dull your entrepreneurial senses'. He also points out that the average age of the founders of Google, Microsoft, and Yahoo when they started was 24.

Shaid Luqman graduated from Manchester University in 1991, already owning 24 houses. He would persuade banks to lend him most of the purchase price, then barter the vendors down at the last minute, effectively meaning that the banks were financing the whole purchase. He then rented the properties to students, using the university's accommodation service. The rent was higher than the mortgage. Today he is worth around £125 m. He did this without any scheme like Flying Start. He says that he thinks entrepreneurship should be encouraged, but that 'a lot of it is about instinct, and how you are yourself, not government policies'.

*Adapted from*: Guy Dennis, 'The wealth creation college', *Sunday Telegraph*, 24 July 2005

**Question:** The success of the initiative will come down to whether it has attracted the right people, with the right ideas. Do you think it will?

## Developing an enterprise culture

The British government is committed to making the UK the best place in the world to set up and grow a new business (SBS, 2004). Although recognizing that it is the dynamism of individual entrepreneurs that drives small business success, the government believes it can help to stimulate enterprise and overcome barriers to growth. A range of measures are proposed, including addressing the perceived bureaucracy of the regulatory framework and supporting better access to finance. However, it also recognizes that policy needs to address a broader range of issues than merely those specific to businesses that are trying to start up or trying to grow.

## Government support for enterprise

Governments have, over time, taken many different approaches in attempting to embody the spirit and ideals of enterprise. The Davies Review (2002) talks about the role of education in developing an **enterprise culture**, for example including enterprise projects in schools and developing a more positive view of business in careers advice. Government recognizes the part that it needs to play in supporting enterprise not only in education but across all departments. For example, there is an interest now in public–private partnerships and how the two sectors can work together in stimulating enterprise in the health service. In terms of public procurement, the government is looking to the voluntary and community sector (often referred to as the 'third sector') to deliver more services, valuing its flexibility and responsiveness to local needs. In recognizing the need for innovation, links between universities, research institutions and business are encouraged to support technology transfer and encourage spin-outs. Training programmes are offered free of charge to individuals looking to start a business, and business advisers are available to assist with business planning and a wide range of other practical issues relating to setting up a business. The range of interventions can be seen by referring to the websites of some of the key business support agencies such as the Small Business Service and the local Business Links, the Regional Development Agencies, Chambers of Commerce, and Local Enterprise Agencies.

## Enterprise in Action 1.6

### Growing the next generation of entrepreneurs

The Learning and Skills Council are providing funding for Enterprise Advisers, who are working with schools to encourage young people to develop business skills, including innovation and risk management. All 15- and 16-year-olds will be entitled to five days of 'enterprise activity'.

At Holywells High School in Ipswich, groups of 10 students were asked to form companies, each student playing a specific role, e.g. managing director, accountant, marketing manager, or business adviser to the group. The first task they were given was to create 50 origami ducks and ship them over to France to sell. The process involved them in many of the practical skills involved in running a business, including designing a logo, sourcing and costing supplies, making the ducks, costing the shipping to France, organizing the distribution and so on.

The intention was to encourage the young people to use their imagination and initiative and develop enterprise skills, not only to encourage more of them to consider setting up a business later in life, but to allow them to be better placed to compete in the world of work. The project helps them to learn about the world around them and how business impacts upon their lives, and equips them with skills, such as teamworking and resourcefulness, which employers value. Also, having fewer preconceived ideas, the young people can offer ideas that adults may not think of, which is a resource that businesses could profitably tap into.

*Source*: adapted from 'Pupils taught to be enterprising', BBC News Online, 17 November 2004

**Question:** What specific skills, attitude, and knowledge can students gain in this type of programme?

## Cause and effect of intervention

There are arguments that support **government intervention** of this kind, i.e. that where free market principles leave gaps in provision it is valid for government to 'level the playing field'. Others argue that intervention can lead to dependency, and that adversity can often be the spur for innovation and creativity. Sometimes this might arise from unexpected sources. For example, the UK pharmaceutical industry is highly regulated and yet it is notably more innovative than less regulated national competitors, such as the French. It could be argued that by not providing the industry with an easy life, government regulation has, in fact, acted as a catalyst.

It is difficult to prove the case one way or the other, as, for example, if the number of start-ups improve in an area it would be difficult to prove that this had been caused by a specific initiative (say, for example, a training programme) or environmental factors that would have occurred in any event (for example an upturn in the economy or an inward investor creating supply chain opportunities).

Opinions have changed with time. In the 1970s the route to competitiveness was seen in terms of large companies who could secure economies of scale; in the 1980s small firms became the focus of attention, being seen as more flexible and responsive. This view still predominates although it is clear that small businesses do not have a monopoly on enterprise and many of them are lifestyle firms.

In looking for the cause and effect linkages it is possible to see indicators, but to some degree governments also have to take risks and take a leap of faith in investing in initiatives, in the hope that the desired impact will indeed result. Unfortunately the greater degree of accountability that we expect from public sector agencies as opposed to private sector organizations makes this type of 'risk-taking' more difficult for those with the responsibility of negotiating the contracts, but it may be necessary in order to foster greater innovation and creativity in the economy in general.

## Learning the lessons

There are undoubtedly lessons to be learned. There are lessons that can be drawn from international comparisons, helping the analysis of how the context in which entrepreneurial activity takes place can influence the likelihood that it will do so. Changing attitudes to risk at an individual level may have a knock-on effect. The Household Survey of Entrepreneurship (2003) suggests that attitudes to risk have become more negative, that a dependency culture is being created and that people are more fearful of debt than they were in 2002. It will be interesting to see whether this affects levels of entrepreneurial activity over time.

Patterns of ethnic minority involvement in enterprise, for example, might offer us insight into best practice where it is flourishing as well as identifying the barriers that need to be overcome if greater success is to be achieved. As well as generic approaches (e.g. changes in the education system, or fiscal or legislative changes that apply across the board) intervention is sometimes targeted. For example, funding is often given to support under-represented groups such as women, or specific sectors that are perceived to have growth potential such as high-technology firms. These are driven by laudable objectives – encouraging diversity in the former and encouraging structural change in the economy to improve competitiveness in the latter – but again these assume that there are causal links between such intervention and the desired outcome. One would think that in a fully fledged enterprise culture the role of government would be minimalist, but history suggests that governments do continue to intervene in various ways, and economic and political commentators continue to argue about whether there is adequate return on the investments made. One of the central issues of debate is whether it is indeed possible to 'pick winners' and whether it is individuals who are more likely to be entrepreneurial, the type of business that is most likely to grow and create wealth, sectors that can drive economic prosperity, or cities/regions that can act as catalysts for regeneration, as discussed in Pause and Reflect 1.2.

## Pause and Reflect 1.2

### Diamonds are an economy's best friend

In South Africa, the African National Congress are intent on reversing the inequalities of the apartheid era, and that includes addressing the racially skewed economy. There is much talk of socialism, but rather than banishing capitalism there is much support for a market-based system, with social responsibilities taken very seriously. Legislation has been introduced to oblige large firms to recruit black employees, procure goods from suppliers with a sizeable black workforce, and sell off equity stakes to black businesses in an attempt to spread wealth more widely.

Nicky Oppenheimer is the head of De Beers, who control half of the world's diamond supply. The company will comply with this rule, selling off at least 15 per cent of their equity to black economic empowerment groups, saying that in the South African context this is fair, although it may not be thought so in a different context.

He and his family have always held liberal views, and are more popular than most with the new black elite. They are at the heart of what could be described as a unique and bold experiment in South Africa. De Beers and ministers talk about the urgent need for investment in training and education, and policies designed to encourage black entrepreneurs to set up their own businesses.

However, there are tensions. De Beers are involved in discussions about how the company can help to boost employment (40 per cent of the population is out of work), but at the same time, several of De Beers mines are running at a loss, and job cuts seem unavoidable. South Africa's President wants De Beers to give more business to indigenous manufacturers who cut and polish the rough diamonds that the company extracts, and although Oppenheimer is sympathetic in principle he is concerned that this will add to costs and consequently prices, making them less competitive in world markets.

Demand for diamonds is high, and growing rapidly in India and China. Early in 2005, De Beers announced after-tax profits of $500 million. The family get $180 million as 40 per cent shareholders, the other shareholders being Anglo-American (a gold-mining colossus) and the Botswana government. De Beers stress that they have been long-standing supporters of corporate social responsibility, opening orphanages, maintaining hospitals and offering free AIDS treatment to workers who are HIV positive. However, it has been in their interests to do so, and now the ministers would like De Beers to do more to help close the gap between rich and poor.

*Adapted from*: Richard Wackman, 'King of the Diamond Dealers', *The Observer*, 6 February 2005

**Question:** Evaluate the advantages and disadvantages of this policy in terms of developing enterprise in the South African economy.

## Summary

- Perspectives on entrepreneurship have changed over time, and are influenced by context.
- There is no single definition, but personal qualities and attributes such as intuition, insight, inspiration, ingenuity, innovation, flair, boldness, courage, daring, drive, determination, resilience and passion often arise.
- Motivations do not have to be economic; many entrepreneurs are driven by social and aesthetic goals as well as, or indeed instead of, economic ones.
- If we are to describe an organization as enterprising, it needs both entrepreneurship (individual enterprise) and innovation (organizational enterprise).
- Innovation is a process by which opportunities are identified and exploited and it requires the commitment of enterprising people.
- Much of the received wisdom about where we find enterprising companies and enterprising people turns out to be myth. Enterprise arises wherever you look for it. You can be enterprising in:
  - large firms as well as small firms;
  - lifestyle and fast growth organizations;
  - public, voluntary and community sector organizations as well as the private sector;
  - economies; and
  - communities.
- There is a willingness from governments to stimulate an enterprise culture, but there is little empirical evidence to prove whether such investment actually generates the impact it intends.

## Chapter questions

1. How would you define entrepreneurship? Does it matter that we have a definition? Why/Why not?
2. Do you think that entrepreneurs are calculated risk-takers? Give examples to illustrate your views.
3. What factors influence the decision to become self-employed?

4.  Is a region's low level of enterprise due to a lack of entrepreneurs or an inappropriate or inadequate support infrastructure?
5.  Argue the case for and against public sector support being given to people wanting to start up their own business.

## Case study

### Podcasting

A podcast is a recorded broadcast that can be downloaded, usually for free, from the Internet to a portable device such as an MP3 player or an iPod. Podcasting arrived in the Autumn of 2004, and was first used by amateur radio enthusiasts. Podcasts are inexpensive to produce as all you need is a computer, a microphone, and the necessary (free) software.

The concept was very quickly adopted by conventional radio companies, such as Virgin Radio and the BBC. They want to appeal to the younger audience, who take their music around with them. From a customer point of view the appeal is obvious – for example, you can listen to the main interview from the Today programme anytime, anywhere.

### Skipping ads

We have all been irritated by our favourite TV programmes being interrupted by adverts, and taken pleasure in fast-forwarding the video through them, or skipping through them with Sky+. Now we have the opportunity to do the same with commercial radio. This means that the advertising industry is needing to take a long hard look at the way it operates. For a start, its audience becomes fragmented – local radio promotes local services, which might not be quite so interesting if you are listening on holiday in the Algarve.

### Copyright issues

The podcast is stripped of the news, weather and travel information that might date it. Unfortunately for Virgin, for copyright reasons, they have to take the music out too. Despite this, the Pete and Geoff show is one of the most popular podcasts in Britain, with 85 000 downloads a month. James Cridland, the head of new media strategic development at Virgin Radio, believes that the appeal lies in the entertaining and wry observations on the world, and sees podcasts as a great marketing tool, which will mean that many people who would not otherwise have listened to Virgin Radio will now give it a try. They have also been able to sell advertising specifically for the podcast, which go out at the start of the programme. Apparently customers are not fast-forwarding through them.

### Developing the software

Podcast development was interesting. The original software was written by 'the Podfather', Adam Curry. By his own admission it wasn't very good. He made the first podcast in August 2004, and used it to get help in improving the iPodder programme – people began to improve his code, and to build iPodders of their own. These all contributed to the public domain and as a consequence the original programme was developed and improved. People developed a liking for making their own radio, and a community was born.

### Democratizing radio

Hundreds of amateur talk shows sprang up, first in America and then in Britain, about everything from pig-rearing to spoof celebrity interviews. Colleges are using podcasting to make lectures available to students, and a vicar in Surrey is podcasting his sermons.

### Enter Apple

In June 2005, Apple added 3000 podcasts to its iTunes music downloading site, and within two days customers had subscribed to more than 1 million pod casts. That number is now more than 5000, and Apple are publishing a chart which shows the 100 most popular downloads. Although the talk was about democratizing radio, in fact the traditional media companies feature strongly. In the last week in July, the BBC had 8 in the top 10, with the Chris Moyles show at No. 1. Virgin, LBC, CNN, Newsweek, and the Wall Street Journal are all in the top 100. However, it is an ideal way of reaching a minority audience anywhere in the world.

### Challenges

Apple has certainly upped the ante in the competition. One of the challenges will be to sort out the digital rights issue, so allowing music to be legally included in the podcasts, and allowing artists and record companies to be paid. One approach could be to replicate the model used by iTunes, limiting the number of times that songs in a podcast can be played, or to render the podcast itself unplayable after a certain time. But the industry will be more receptive this time around, and the various stakeholders are trying to find a business model that will work fairly for everyone.

*Adapted from*: Paul Durman 'Will podcasts kill the radio ads?', *The Sunday Times*, 7 August 2005 and Catherine Elsworth, 'Homemade Internet broadcasts pull the plug on mainstream radio', *Daily Telegraph*, 30 July 2005

### Questions

1. Analyse the threats and opportunities for enterprise that podcasting presents for either:
   (a) Local commercial radio;
   (b) The BBC; or
   (c) Higher Education.

## References and further reading

Beck T. and Demirguc-Kunt A. (2004) SMEs, Growth and Poverty: Do pro-SME Policies Work? *Public Policy for the Private Sector*. The World Bank Group, Note no. 268, February.

Birley S. and Muzyka D.F. (2000) *Mastering Entrepreneurship*. Harlow: Pearson.

Davies H. (2002) The Howard Davies Review of Enterprise and the Economy in Education. Norwich: HMSO.

Deakins D. and Freel M. (2003) *Entrepreneurship and Small Firms*, 3rd edn. Maidenhead: McGraw-Hill Education.

Drucker P.F. (1985/1994) *Innovation and Entrepreneurship: Practice and Principles*, 2nd edn. (revised). Oxford: Butterworth-Heinemann.

Government Action Plan for Small Business: Making the UK the best place in the world to start and grow a business (2004). DTI Small Business Service, HMSO.

Handy C. (1999) *The New Alchemists*. London: Hutchinson.

Household Survey of Entrepreneurship (2003) The Small Business Service, HMSO.

Kirby D.A. (2003) *Entrepreneurship*. Maidenhead: McGraw-Hill Education.

Morgan G. (1997) *Images of Organization*. London: Sage.

Roure J. (1997) Ten myths about entrepreneurship. In: S. Birley and D.F. Muzyka (2000), *Mastering Entrepreneurship*. Harlow: Financial Times Prentice Hall.

Schumpeter J. (1934) *The Theory of Economic Development*. Cambridge MA: Harvard University Press.

Small Business Service (2004) A Government Action Plan for Small Business: Making the UK the best place in the world to start and grow a business. DTI Jan 2004. www.sbs.gov.uk

Small Business Service (2005) *Small and Medium-sized Enterprises: Statistics for the UK*, 2004, September.

Wickham P.A. (2004) *Strategic Entrepreneurship*, 3rd edn. Harlow: Pearson Education.

## Useful websites

http://www.bdo.co.uk/
http://www.businesslink.gov.uk
http://www.chamberonline.co.uk
http://www.dfes.gov.uk
http://www.dti.gov.uk
http://www.englandsrdas.com
http://www.nfea.com
http://www.pybt.org.uk
http://www.sbs.gov.uk
http://www.sfedi.co.uk
http://www.socialenterprise.org.uk

## Key words

| | |
|---|---|
| catalyst for economic development | economic, cultural or social motive |
| continuum of enterprise | enterprise capability |
| creative destruction | enterprise culture |

entrepreneurship
government intervention
high-growth firms
incremental innovation
innovation
intrapreneurs

learn by doing
multifaceted activity
narrow and broad definitions
not-for-profit sectors
private business enterprises
public sector organizations

## CHAPTER 2

# What entrepreneurs are like, and what they do

By the end of this chapter the reader will be able to:

- evaluate the concepts and theories of what entrepreneurs are like and what they do;
- recognize how personal circumstances can affect an individual's motivation to become an entrepreneur;
- analyse how entrepreneurial behaviour is distinguishable from managerial behaviour;
- understand how entrepreneurial capacity can be developed;
- evaluate the value of building entrepreneurial capacity in organizations and in the economy.

## Introduction

In this chapter we will consider the characteristics, traits, skills and actions of entrepreneurs – what they are like, where their talents lie, and how they act. Of course, there has been a lot of academic research over the years into these elusive individuals, trying to find a personality type that fits the entrepreneur, and looking at how their behaviour differs from that of owners and managers in a more general sense.

We begin by discussing aspects of the entrepreneurial personality, exploring whether a common personality type does exist and the utility of trying to categorize entrepreneurs in this way. One presumes that if only this genetic prototype could be found then it would be easy to pick out the winners, invest in them and train those with some of the characteristics to become clones, thus transforming our economies and our communities. The fact that it has not yet been possible to do this suggests, perhaps, that, in reality, things are a little more complicated.

As individualism is implicit in the nature of entrepreneurs, perhaps it would be a mistake to try to categorize them so simplistically. These 'special' people are not a homogeneous group. The question must be posed as to whether there are in fact a number of 'types' of entrepreneur, and, if there are, then maybe some might be likely to be more successful in some contexts than in others given that in the last chapter it was suggested that enterprising people can be found in all walks of life.

Although it is recognized that some people are exceptionally creative and contribute significantly to the economy through their entrepreneurial talent, it does not mean that people who do not conform to this stereotype are never creative, that they are unlikely to have good ideas, or will probably never be successful in business. We move on to consider issues of nature versus nurture, considering whether the definition of who is and is not entrepreneurial means that some individuals can never be enterprising. We suggest that it is not an either/or situation at all, and that many people have the potential to be enterprising hidden somewhere within them.

Given our suggestion that most people have the potential to behave in more enterprising ways, we conclude by exploring how we might nurture and develop entrepreneurial capacity. In Chapter 1 we suggested that innovative organizations rely on enterprising individuals. By implication, it would seem to be advantageous if such organizations could encourage individuals to acquire entrepreneurial skills, and/or improve them. If this is possible, then, in reflecting on their own attitudes and skills, individuals might choose to adapt their behaviour, which in turn might have a positive impact not only on the organizations in which they work, but on their own lives, and the communities in which they live.

## What entrepreneurs are like

The stereotypical image of the entrepreneur is of the flamboyant extrovert, a spontaneous individual who acts intuitively, inspiring and motivating others to help them realize their ambitions and bring their business ideas to fruition. It is easy to see entrepreneurs as somehow different from the rest of the community, as 'special', because of the charisma that their success seems to bestow upon them. They are often held up as role models, people to admire, and others are encouraged to aspire to be more like them. But it must be questioned whether this image is a true reflection of the truly innovative and creative entrepreneur or whether it is the stuff of myth and legend. Other people appear to display the same **traits and characteristics** as entrepreneurs but have failed in business. Indeed many successful entrepreneurs fail before going on to spectacular success. Moreover, it is interesting to consider whether or not there is there a non-entrepreneurial personality profile.

Hindsight is an exact science, and when we see a successful individual it is, perhaps, only natural to home in on their exuberant personality, their drive and enthusiasm, their persistence against all odds, and to believe that these traits led to their success. But maybe there are other, equally successful, entrepreneurs who go about their business more quietly, being less extrovert, more humble individuals. Collins (2001) would certainly draw our attention to the truly great company leaders who triumph through 'a paradoxical mixture of personal humility and professional will', often after life-changing experiences.

Carter and Jones Evans (2000: 134) summarize the historical development of thinking about the psychology of the entrepreneur. They explain that research first considered whether it was possible to define a personality profile of the entrepreneur, and that this led to attempts to define what an entrepreneur really is and what they actually do. As thinking evolved, it became apparent that entrepreneurs act at different stages in business development and the focus of research then shifted to looking at how different personality traits correlated with organizational performance at these stages. Despite the research, trait theory proved an unreliable predictor, and so interest moved to the motivations of entrepreneurs and why some people choose entrepreneurship while others do not.

Despite the difficulties, some commonalities exist, and these may be of use in understanding how individual enterprise can be nurtured, and how this might be harnessed by organizations who wish to pursue more innovative strategies.

## The 'entrepreneurial personality'

McLelland (1961) identified a 'need for achievement' as a key driving force in the personality of entrepreneurs. They are able to see and act on opportunities, they are assertive; and they demonstrate commitment to others.

They also have a high locus of control and believe that they can influence events rather than passively accepting what fate bestows upon them. Consequently they behave in a proactive way, taking initiative. The downside of this is that because they feel that they are able to achieve success and to a significant degree influence their own destiny, they may actually view their chances of success too optimistically. There is a fine balance between obtaining the maximum impact from the resources available and trying to achieve the impossible. This probably explains the high risk of failure.

Meredith, Nelson, and Neck (1982) agree, suggesting that entrepreneurs exhibit five core traits:

- self-confidence
- risk-taking activity
- flexibility
- need for achievement
- strong desire to be independent.

Bolton and Thomson (2003) in discussing the action factors that distinguish entrepreneurs, refer to their creativity and innovation, their determination in the face of adversity, their networking abilities, and their ability to manage risk. Handy (1999) summarizes entrepreneurial characteristics under the headings of dedication, doggedness and difference, comparing them to Francis Galton's belief (in the mid-nineteenth century) that three things were necessary for great achievement: 'ability, zeal and a capacity for hard work'.

Critics of the **personality trait approach** might say that it is too static as entrepreneurship is such a dynamic concept. There are a significant number of traits that appear to have relevance, but research has failed to find any conclusive answers as to whether they are all necessary; whether some are more important to entrepreneurial success; or whether the relative importance of different traits might change according to contextual circumstances (e.g. whether the business is newly established or mature; whether it consists of an entrepreneurial team or whether the entrepreneur has social support or not).

Critics also offer the view that rather than being fixed, some entrepreneurial characteristics might be learned, and that the environment in which we live can shape our perspective on life and so the entrepreneurial characteristics of individuals are changed according to the situation.

Questions might also be asked about the purpose in being able to identify a particular entrepreneurial personality given that it is unlikely, at least for some time to come, that entrepreneurs will be bred genetically with the required traits.

## Enterprise in Action 2.1

### When is support not support?

Speaking at an Investment Fair, Jon Moulton, a leading venture capitalist, criticized the nature of support given to start-ups, saying that 'the negative side of support is that support can support that which should not be supported'. He told his audience that, from a venture capitalist's point of view, fewer than one in three of the businesses present would secure investment. Having invested in 50 early-stage technology companies personally, he ought to have more idea than most about the types of business that are likely to succeed.

He criticized the targets culture, as linking public funding to volume targets was, in his opinion, relatively unlikely to create good companies. He feels that the country needs fewer, better and bigger companies to be put together rather than chasing citation counts and spin-outs.

Every year the agencies have to meet targets set by the DTI, which include the number of new businesses and jobs created. A spokesperson for the Regional Development Agencies explained that while the targets weren't perfect, they were obliged to meet them, and that it is important that funding decisions about small companies are made in a rigorous way. Despite the criticism, 90 000 people found secure employment with RDA support.

*Adapted from*: Richard Tyler, 'Start-ups have too much help', *The Daily Telegraph*, 22 November 2004

**Question:** What should be the criteria for deciding what types of businesses should be supported?

Perhaps the utility in this approach lies more in identifying the non-entrepreneurial personality, to avoid wasting resources on them and to enable resources to be targeted where the potential for impact is greatest. Following this line of thinking, deciding to exclude certain personality types in this way might ignore considerable latent entrepreneurial potential in individuals. We have already seen that entrepreneurs are not a homogeneous group; they come from very different backgrounds and have very different capabilities. Some entrepreneurial characteristics are apparent in very young people. Steve Perez (see the case study at the end of this chapter) was using Bunsen burners at school to provide snacks for his friends, but in some people the talent does not emerge until much later in life. Other people are always entrepreneurial, moving from one business idea to another whereas others have just one entrepreneurial moment. There are many examples of experienced managers running large departments, who would not describe themselves as having entrepreneurial characteristics, who do set up a business, perhaps following redundancy, and then manage it in much the same way as before.

If it were simply an issue of personality, then entrepreneurship would have to be defined very narrowly. The trait approach seems to be too simplistic to explain all aspects of entrepreneurial behaviour in its broader definition, and so it becomes necessary to consider what other factors might have impact.

---

## Enterprise in Action 2.2

### Heading for the City Rich List?

Damon Buffini, 43, is a managing partner of Permira, a London-based private equity firm that buys companies such as Homebase with cash and borrowed funds, improves the effectiveness of their business model, and sells them on at a profit. He also runs a restaurant business with his wife and sister.

He was brought up in a two-up, two-down house in Leicester, and was educated at a boys' grammar school in the city. His father was a black American serviceman who was never part of the family. One of his former teachers said that this made him stand out, but did not hold him back. He was popular, and an excellent athlete and scholar, always willing to question theories and debate issues. When told how well her son was doing, his mother would always ask how he could do better.

The grammar school took their football team to play Fitzwilliam College, Cambridge, so that the boys could see what they might aspire to. Damon did end up studying law at Cambridge, graduating in 1984. A fellow student described his contemporaries as the first generation of Thatcher's children – they talked about the usual student things but also about business and what they aspired to in life.

Buffini became a management consultant at LEK, getting a £1000 signing bonus and a 70-hour-a-week workload. In 1986 he used an LEK scholarship to study at Harvard, where he was exposed to American-style capitalism. On returning home, he took a job at Schroder Ventures, and rose as a clients' man. When Schroder's parent company chose to sell off its private equity operation, a management group led by Buffini bought it, and the rest, as they say, is history. His net worth is around £18 m, and when future bonuses come on stream his peers believe that he will cross the £40 m threshold necessary to make the City Rich List. Despite his success, he shuns publicity. How long he can maintain his low profile remains to be seen.

*Adapted from*: Peter Koenig, 'Young, gifted and black', *Sunday Times*, 10 July 2005

**Questions:** Which of the typical personality traits of an entrepreneur do you think Buffini exhibits? Are there any other factors in his profile that you feel may have driven him towards an entrepreneurial career?

---

## Nurture rather than nature

As well as the genetic cocktail, it is a fact that the family provides children with role models and certain perspectives on life through the socialization process in their formative years. Young children are naturally inquisitive, but the education system often seems to knock this out of some individuals whereas others flourish within it or in spite of it.

Schools, as institutions, are the first organizations that children are exposed to after the family. During adolescence, an individual's sense of identity is shaped into the way they view the world and the expectations they have of the role they will play in it. There are a variety of influences in this process. Some of these are fairly obvious, for example, the contributions of peers and the education system. Sometimes there are less obvious influences, such as critical incidents (positive or negative) that happen and fundamentally shift the individual's perspective on life.

It is worth also considering whether social development has a role to play in the making of entrepreneurs, and whether it comes down to **nurture rather than nature**. The predisposition of an individual to be entrepreneurial, in terms of their personality, appears to be significant, but is unlikely to be all-important if looked at in isolation from other factors and experiences. It is likely that the issue is more complex, depending upon the balance and relationship between these internal factors and external circumstances.

## Early life experiences

Kets de Vries (1977) writes about the **dark side of entrepreneurship**, suggesting that entrepreneurs have often had a harsh experience of early life, many being part of fatherless families. He argues that childhood experiences and family backgrounds characterized by deprivation and hardship lead to low self-esteem, insecurity, and a repressed desire for control that ultimately leads to rebellion. This makes it difficult for these individuals to 'fit in', and so they are often categorized as deviants, social misfits, and nonconformists. He suggests that entrepreneurial success is often followed by personal crises. There are examples that support this, but many entrepreneurs come from happy and stable backgrounds and so contradict the theory. But in highlighting that there can be negative attributes and experiences in the background of the entrepreneur, perhaps de Vries helps to explain them as human beings, with anxieties and failures just like the rest of the community.

Schumpeter talks about negative experiences in terms of social marginality. For many people self-employment is the only way that they can achieve social distinction. If people feel marginalized, they may not be able to see any route to success within 'the system'. Similarly, where people feel trapped in their employment situation they may feel less anxious about setting up on their own, and more willing to take a risk given that they may feel they have little to lose. Life circumstances can influence the entrepreneur's thinking and **motivations**. Setting up and managing an entrepreneurial venture is a complex task. While many people realize that running their own business is a career option, few actually do it. To understand entrepreneurs, therefore, it is necessary to understand what factors motivate them to actually take that step.

## Motivations of entrepreneurs

It is often assumed that profit is the motivator for entrepreneurs, but this would be a dangerous assumption. We have seen that entrepreneurs have a need for achievement, and while one entrepreneur might measure success in terms of profit, another might measure it in terms of fulfilling their ambitions. Achievement means different things to different people. Indeed, for many entrepreneurs, becoming rich may not be the end in itself but rather the means by which the entrepreneur can demonstrate that they have achieved success by establishing a sustainable organization. For many, their motivations are a complex set of interrelated values and drivers, as illustrated in Enterprise in Action 2.3.

### Enterprise in Action 2.3

#### Stephen Beetham – reviving Liverpool

Stephen Beetham was born into a religious sect on the south coast. His father left the sect when Stephen was 7, and Stephen's parents were divorced. He ran away at the age of 16 to join his dad in Liverpool. Once you left the sect you were cut off and told you were a failure. Stephen says he has been told that maybe this is what gave him his drive to succeed.

He started his career as a gardener/handyman in the family firm. He then moved on to property development, renovating a house in Wavertree, Liverpool, and selling it at a profit. It wasn't to be the last time that he made money in the property market. Beetham Organization now has fixed asset investments in 32 different companies, and Stephen (now 30) is ranked seventh on the Sunday Times Young Rich List.

He has come a long way from the day when he was told he 'must be mad' when he wanted to convert a former polytechnic library into luxury flats in the heart of Liverpool's business quarter, but the Walton House development was a success. He had done his homework. There hadn't been much interest in 'City Living' in the 1990s, but the trend was well anticipated.

His next project was a bit more ambitious – he needed £8 m to renovate Wilberforce House, an old Sixties-type building that had formerly housed the council's planning department. Eighty-five banks refused to back him on the basis that the scheme was in Liverpool, before the Anglo-Irish Bank and its strong connections with the city's Irish contingent said yes. 'Beetham Plaza' is now one of the most sought after addresses in Liverpool, and is home to a restaurant owned by celebrity chef, Paul Heathcote.

His street credibility was improving somewhat by now, although he was still only in his mid-twenties. He then paid what was thought to be a very high price for the site of the former St Paul's Eye Hospital in Old Hall Street. The £60 m development now known as 'Beetham Tower' has changed Liverpool's skyline. It includes a residential tower, which Beetham owns, a 4-star Radisson Hotel and an office block. The latter two are jointly owned in a 50:50 partnership with the family that once owned the Ethel Austin store chain. The going price for a top-floor penthouse is around £1.2 m. Planning permission has also been approved for a second 40-storey tower nearby. His faith in Liverpool has made a huge difference to the face of the city, and has also made him a millionaire several times over.

Stephen is now developing his brand elsewhere. The company is building a £150 m tower in Manchester city centre and something similar in Birmingham. However, its most ambitious proposal to date is a £500 m, 68-storey residential tower planned for Central London, at the site of the former Sainsbury's headquarters near Blackfriars Bridge.

Sue Marriott, various public sources

**Question:** What do you feel might have motivated Stephen Beetham in his drive for entrepreneurial success?

Some people are always entrepreneurial, but some give this up after a certain period of time; others choose to be so later in life after pursuing other options. Having the motivation does not necessarily mean that action will follow. Some are **sequential entrepreneurs** – they only run one business at a time but they may well run many in succession (e.g. James Dyson, who had a ball–wheelbarrow business before moving on to cyclone vacuum cleaners) whereas others have one venture and then never repeat the experience. Some are **portfolio entrepreneurs** who run several businesses simultaneously, e.g. Richard Branson.

It is possible to categorize portfolio entrepreneurs into three types:

1. defensive serial entrepreneurs who move on because of forced exits from previous enterprises (not necessarily failures);
2. opportunist serial entrepreneurs who see opportunities for gain even if an enterprise is only on a short-term basis; and
3. group-creating serial entrepreneurs – where creating a number of businesses (either from scratch or by acquisition) is fundamental to the strategy they are pursuing. They can do this by organic growth or by making deals – acquisitions and mergers.

Irrespective of what type of entrepreneur they eventually become, in taking that first step an individual will be making a significant and possibly life-changing decision. They will consider what they would hope to achieve, what the likelihood is that they can achieve it, what risks they will need to take, and how comfortable they are with the level of risk that they perceive exists. It sounds like a simple cost–benefit calculation, but of course it is not. There are often many variables to consider, and likely outcomes can be difficult to predict. The '**tipping point**' for each individual is different, as what can seem like two identical situations might result in different choices.

## Pause and Reflect 2.1

### Terence Conran

When Terence Conran was 12, convalescing from a burst appendix, he made dolls' house furniture which he sold in the local shop. Never having much patience with schools and courses, he briefly worked with an architect designing furniture and textiles, before making his own furniture in the basement of Ballet Rambert. Needing to make more money, he and a friend set up a soup kitchen, fitted out with his own furniture. He saw a need for a 'place where people like us could eat cheaply'.

In 1964, owing to being disillusioned with retailers who refused to buy his furniture or to sell it with any confidence or imagination, he set up Habitat. Its success led to him achieving millionaire status, building an international chain of Habitat and Conran stores over the next 20 years.

He then began collecting other people's shops and chains – Mothercare, Richards, Heals, and BHS. Habitat/Mothercare embarked on a joint publishing venture with Octopus Books under the name Conran Octopus. The company produced books about interior design, cookery, gardening, crafts and decorative arts. Habitat/Mothercare merged with British Home Stores to create a new parent company, Storehouse plc, of which Terence became chairman and chief executive. He believed that he could apply his design flair to revive these ailing brands and to some degree it worked but his natural leanings were as a creator rather than a manager. After installing a chief executive and a chairman at Storehouse to replace his dual role he went back to the world he was familiar with. It seems that his natural inclination was for entrepreneurial activity, finding the more routine aspects of his role at Storehouse less inspiring.

He has turned Butlers Wharf into a mixed development of eateries, residences, businesses and the arts, and established a charitable foundation which set up the Boilerhouse Project, a gallery and resource for students, designers and the public to stimulate design awareness and discussion, at the Victoria and Albert Museum. In 1987 this became the Design Museum at Butlers Wharf.

He still has a range of stores throughout the world including London, Tokyo and New York; and is renowned for his restaurants, 12 in London alone. In 2000, in a joint venture with Wyndham International, he established the Great Eastern Hotel. Conran Restaurants is responsible for the management and running of the four restaurants and three bars within the hotel.

Throughout his life he has been able to mix creative design and business flair, enthused by his interest in people and how they live, his instincts and ambitions still as strong as they were 40 years ago.

*Adapted from*: Handy C. (1999) *The New Alchemists*, Hutchinson: London; and various public sources

**Question:** Using the categorization suggested by Wright *et al.*, discuss which type of entrepreneur you feel that Terence Conran is. In doing this, consider whether you would come to different conclusions regarding the various stages in his entrepreneurial career.

Although the decision to become an entrepreneur is an individual and personal one, it is possible to see some commonalities in the '**push and pull**' factors that influence the personal decision to choose self-employment, which are summarized in Table 2.1.

**Table 2.1**
Push and pull factors

| Push factors | Pull factors |
| --- | --- |
| Limitations on financial rewards | Working for oneself |
| Job insecurity | Financial rewards |
| Job competition | Work-life balance |
| Career limitations | Sense of achievement |
| Lack of opportunity for innovation | Freedom to innovate |
| Lack of recognition and being a misfit | Gaining social standing |
| Dissatisfaction with bosses | Flexibility |

Again, the interrelationship between personality traits and life circumstances is evident. If trait theory is valid, we would be able to identify potential entrepreneurs, but as we pointed out in our introduction we still find this notoriously difficult to do. If the behavioural approach is valid, we might be able to help people to learn to be more entrepreneurial. Timmons (1994) tries to form a view as to which traits are innate and which can be learned, drawing our attention to the fact that some of these traits are actually management skills. This begs the question of what actually distinguishes entrepreneurs from others, especially as many of these traits appear to be shared by any successful manager. One suggestion could be that being able to deal well with failure is an important attribute. So if behaviours are important, perhaps we should explore what it is that entrepreneurs actually do. If we can identify what it is that entrepreneurs do differently from 'regular' managers, then it might help us in understanding how to develop both individual and organizational entrepreneurial capacity.

## What entrepreneurs do

## Entrepreneurs as managers

Wickham (2004: 8–10) says that 'we recognize entrepreneurs, in the first instance, by what they do, the tasks they undertake'. He suggests that entrepreneurs are simply managers who manage in an entrepreneurial way. They actively pursue opportunity and drive change to create new value, take the strategic view, and learn as they go. In summarizing the tasks they perform, he suggests that entrepreneurs:

- own organizations (although ownership issues can be blurred by outside investment, managers with shares in businesses and community enterprise);
- found new organizations (but they can also turn around or develop existing ones);
- bring innovations to market (whether these are new products or services, or new processes);
- identify market opportunities (actively seeking them out);
- apply expertise;
- provide leadership;
- accept risk.

It is often difficult to differentiate the **actions of entrepreneurs** from those of managers in general. After all, any responsible manager will scan the environment with an eye to opportunities for growth; all of them apply expertise and provide leadership. Some own shares in the organizations that employ them. Moreover, simply bringing an idea to market is not enough as the process of entrepreneurship is only complete if customers have been identified and won over to create a sustainable new organization. Many of these activities could be described as managerial. So what is it that makes someone an entrepreneur as opposed to a good manager?

## Spotlight 2.1

### Owen Promotions

Michael Owen is best known for his football skills, but accounts filed at Companies House reveal that his firm, Owen Promotions, had £1.3 million in the bank at the end of the 2004 season. In the past, he has signed lucrative endorsements for companies such as Persil and Burton, and he has also agreed on a £15 m deal with Umbro, the sports-kit maker. The company is the main receptacle for his 'show-business earnings' and produces his official calendar.

Owen is just one of many famous footballers to use their 'celebrity' to advantage in the commercial world. David and Victoria Beckham exploit their fame both individually and collectively. It isn't a new phenomenon – Gary Lineker is well known for promoting Walker's crisps.

Success on the field obviously helps in creating opportunity in the business world. A good performance in the World Cup in Germany in 2006 will no doubt be a platform for further earnings potential.

*Source*: various public sources

**Question:** Is Michael Owen a good manager or an entrepreneur?

Often it is about scale as, for example, an organization may have systems for monitoring trends in the environment and changing customer preferences and a planning cycle that forces a management team to consider the implications for the company, but an entrepreneur will be actively doing this, actually seeking out opportunities. They champion their projects, trying to engage the enthusiasm and commitment of others, stimulating and motivating people to become involved. They act as ambassadors for the cause at every opportunity, continually convincing a broad range of stakeholders (investors and customers in particular) of the value of the venture, and then maintaining their support so that the organization can prosper and grow.

## The entrepreneur–administrator continuum

Stevenson (2000) says that 'entrepreneurship is an approach to management that we define as *the pursuit of opportunity without regard to resources currently controlled*'.

Stevenson explains that at one extreme is the 'promoter', who feels confident of his or her ability to seize an opportunity regardless of the resources under current control. At the opposite extreme is the 'trustee', who emphasizes the efficient utilization of existing resources. While the promoter and the trustee define the end points of this spectrum, there is a range of managerial behaviour that lies between them. **Entrepreneurial management** is not an extreme example, but rather a range of behaviour that consistently falls at one end of the spectrum.

He considers six critical dimensions of business practice, discussing the difference between administrative and entrepreneurial management. These are:

- strategic orientation
- commitment to opportunity
- commitment of resources
- control of resources
- management structure
- reward philosophy.

Different contexts might pull an organization towards the entrepreneurial or administrative end of the spectrum. The approach Stevenson describes is applicable to both entrepreneurs and intrapreneurs, in small or large organizations. He concludes that it is a cohesive pattern of managerial behaviour. If we accept his argument that it is about patterns of behaviour that range from one end of a scale to the other, this implies choice. Individuals might choose to behave differently, developing more **entrepreneurial behaviour patterns**. They are unlikely to move to the other extreme of the spectrum, but if all managers moved a little in that direction, the cumulative impact could be substantial.

Enterprise in Action 2.4 addresses the issue of where on the continuum franchising might be placed. Franchises arise in a variety of sectors. The established company offers a brand, a reputation, sometimes management training and/or support. In return franchisees have to agree to prescribed procedures for running the business, invest some of their own money at the outset, and pay a percentage of profits to the parent company. They still bear the responsibility of running their own business, but are sometimes frustrated in the long run by the strings attached to the franchise agreement. It can, however, offer a sort of halfway house between running their own business and working for someone else. As with any business, it is important to research the proposition thoroughly and be very clear about the terms and conditions on offer.

## Enterprise in Action 2.4

### Entrepreneurship and franchising

Fred De Luca borrowed 1000 dollars from a family friend when he was 17 to open a sandwich store in Connecticut. He opened four more, with varying degrees of success, before deciding to franchise the operation that we now know as Subway. In some ways the ill fortunes of another famous franchise, McDonalds, offered opportunities for businesses like Subway that appeared to present a healthier eating option to customers.

Unlike many franchisers, Subway uses 'development agents' who buy the right to a geographical territory and have to find enough sites and franchisees to meet their contractual quotas. De Luca feels that this offers them more flexibility and opportunities for innovation than many franchise agreements do. Subway also takes a relatively high royalty from its franchises rather than demanding large initial investments. The practicalities of this mean that it is in the agents' and Subway's interests to open as many shops in an area as they can to maximize the likelihood of hitting targets. If demand falls, the franchisees take the first hit and, if they have to sell up, their stores can be resold to new franchisees for more upfront fees. While to some degree having a good presence in an area reinforces the brand and image and can help sales at some point, the volume becomes counterproductive in that they undercut each other's market.

The relatively low upfront costs tend to tempt people who are not particularly confident about taking the risks of a new venture. Many are also of limited means, or recent immigrants, who simply do not have access to much capital. Subway also allows UK franchisees more independence by allowing them to form purchasing consortiums to find the best price for supplies, and it doesn't take revenue from the sale of equipment to them.

*Adapted from*: Lucy Mangen, *The Guardian*, July 18 2005; and other public sources

**Question:** Using Stevenson's continuum, explain the comparative positions of De Luca, a development agent, and a franchisee.

## Entrepreneurial actions

Bolton and Thomson (2003: 213–219) suggest that there are 10 key **action factors** that characterize entrepreneurs. First and foremost, entrepreneurs make a significant difference. They are able to do this because they:

- are creative and innovative;
- spot and exploit opportunities;
- find the resources required to exploit opportunities;
- are good networkers;
- are determined in the face of adversity;
- handle risk;
- have control of business;
- put the customer first;
- create capital (which can be aesthetic or social as well as economic).

They show the connectivity between these factors within two process models. Entrepreneurs do not have to be equally good at all of these activities; for example, they do not have to be an inventor, but instead can successfully commercialize someone else's idea but still be an innovator.

### Enterprise in Action 2.5

**Success on a pallet**

John Scott, 34, has just won the Microsoft Young Director Award at the Institute of Directors. Scott Timber is Europe's fastest growing pallet manufacturer, with three sites in Scotland, one in Wales, and six in England. John has worked hard for his success, and explains that it requires dedication and commitment. It meant him having little by way of a social life and losing touch with most of his friends in the early years.

The sawmill belonged to his parents, but when his father died John took it over. He was only 18, and his first year in business coincided with an unusually harsh winter, which meant no one was interested in buying fences. It was a question of survival, and John knew he had to come up with something. He heard that BP Grangemouth urgently needed pallets, and so he rang their buyer – day after day – until eventually they agreed to come and have a look at the company. Scott Timber were only a small company, unknown to BP, and he needed to make an impression. He persuaded all his mates to come to the mill and pretend to be employees for the day. Whether the buyer cottoned on or not, John will never know, but they gave him an order for £125 000, which saved the firm. BP were so satisfied with the service they received that a year later they gave John half of their pallet business, increasing the company's turnover by 50 per cent. John certainly exploited the opportunity he'd spotted, and with a turnover of £47 m seems to have made it pay!

*Adapted from*: Findlay McCallum, 'Wood you believe it … John has his success on a pallet',
*Daily Express* (Scottish Edition), 4 August 2005

**Question:** How does John Scott compare with regard to Bolton and Thomson's 10 action factors?

Some argue that pure entrepreneurial activities are only intermittent – they end when the firm has been created and then only arise from time to time thereafter. This would mean that entrepreneurs as individuals would have to perform non-entrepreneurial activities between these times. Dynamic market conditions might heighten the need to be constantly alert to new opportunities, but there may be lengthy periods of quite routine activity. Some can handle this but others cannot and move on to other entrepreneurial tasks rather than engage in these routine activities.

Perhaps it could be said that entrepreneurs manage change, because they do not leave the world in the same state in which they found it. They bring people, money and resources together to build new organizations or to change existing ones. The value that they add is more about the difference that they make than the results of their activities. Managers tend to maintain the status quo, sustain an established organization and maintain its market position. This is important in itself as it is essential to the effective running of many organizations, but it is not primarily about driving change, which distinguishes the entrepreneur. Of course the effective entrepreneur also recognizes when it is appropriate not to embark on a venture, but this is a conscious choice, a decision taken, rather than a way of behaving.

To summarize, entrepreneurs have a personal vision, which they use to transform a disparate group of stakeholders into the people who will act to realize this vision in practice. Achieving this means communicating with stakeholders; developing the culture; building expertise; gaining credibility; and creating the environment in which success can happen. This all implies a steep learning curve because, at the outset, there is a need to learn about suppliers, customers and markets; as the organization grows entrepreneurs need to learn about delegation, teamwork, leadership, managing people, and managing cash flow and other resources. They need to develop a business model that supports their ambitions and establishes appropriate systems and processes. As crises occur, they need to solve problems. They need to make decisions, think laterally, and take risks. Some of this is down to innate ability, but they acquire the skills, knowledge and experience which will continually improve their effectiveness.

Given their vitality and their insight they are valuable assets to any organization. But they can become bored with the routines of business management and, if they choose to move on to new things, the organization must try to fill the gap, to harness and retain some of that entrepreneurial capability, and to build capacity, so that it can maintain its competitive edge.

## Pause and Reflect 2.2

### Andrew Ritchie: Time to get on his bike?

Andrew Ritchie, 58, has devoted the last 30 years of his life to building the best portable bicycle in the world. He has worked tremendously hard, never married, and never had a family. For years he had no income at all, thoroughly obsessed with his project.

Brompton Bicycle is one of only two volume manufacturers still making bikes in Britain. Over the life of the company Brompton has made almost 100 000 folding bikes, and aims to produce 14 000 in the coming year. It started off with a conversation his stockbroker father had with an Australian trying to raise money for Bickerton, a British company which made the first genuinely portable bike. He thought his son might be interested in the product and so engineered a meeting. Ritchie thought the design was in need of improvement, started sketching out further designs, and became besotted.

He persuaded 10 friends to part with £100 each so that he could build a prototype. It worked, but Ritchie wasn't satisfied. Prototypes 2 and 3 followed, with Ritchie doing all the work from the bedroom in his flat. He tried to license the design to a large manufacturer like Raleigh but no one was really interested. However, he did persuade 30 people to order bikes and pay in advance, which gave him a little working capital. Speculating to accumulate, he built 50 with the help of one employee who was doing the brazing, hoping to be able to sell the rest. It took him 18 months to build them, but they did all sell.

He then tried to get investment backing, but his timing was poor (the industry was in decline) and he didn't exactly have the type of personality that would impress the venture capitalists, so that didn't get very far. He did manage to persuade Julian Vereker (of Naim, a hi-fi maker) to guarantee an overdraft of £40 000, and his father and friends came to the rescue again, putting in roughly £50 000 in equity.

Production got under way in 1988, but one thing after another went wrong. Everything, that is, except sales, because whatever was made was sold right from the start. The company now exports 60 per cent of what it makes, the biggest sales going to Holland, unsurprisingly.

Ritchie says that in many ways he is glad that he was unsuccessful in securing investment because the fact that he had private backing allowed him to be a perfectionist. He feels that a large company might have wanted him to compromise. He still manufactures in London, too, although rent and rates are higher. Manufacturing abroad might be cheaper, but there would be uncertainties like rates of exchange and so on to consider. Ritchie offers bespoke bikes, reckoning that with different colour-combinations, handlebars, gears, lighting, etc. there are around 13 billion permutations that he could build tomorrow.

Brompton are hugely successful, but now Ritchie wants to reap the rewards of all his hard work. He wants to travel, play tennis, garden, and enjoy his life a little more.

*Adapted from*: Ben Laurence, 'The bicycle that turned into folding money', *The Observer*, 7 August 2005

**Question:** What would you advise Andrew Ritchie to do at Brompton to create more space in his personal life?

## Entrepreneurial capacity

As we outlined in Chapter 1, entrepreneurship depends on both individual and organizational enterprise. **Entrepreneurial capacity** will, therefore, be a function of both individual and organizational capacity. We have seen that entrepreneurs play an important role in driving organizations forward, but they cannot do this alone. Not only do they draw on the skills and experience of other individuals; they need to establish and embed behaviour patterns and processes that support continual innovation and enterprise. There are a number of dimensions of entrepreneurial capacity which merit consideration.

## Dimensions of entrepreneurial capacity

### Entrepreneurial management of information

Cognitive psychology looks at how people see the world; how they process information and how this affects the way they make decisions. We are all bombarded with information continually, and it would be impossible to consider all that is available to us every time we made a decision. We develop 'rules of thumb' based on our experiences to date and filter the information to help us to make sense of it. In this way our experiences can begin to colour the way we interpret events and situations. This does allow us to speed up the decision-making process, but it can also allow us to fall into habits that limit our understanding of the issues, and make it less likely that we will challenge our preconceptions.

Baron and Shane (2005: 56) refer to research that shows that the more experience people have in a given field, the more likely they are to identify opportunities in it. In exploring why this may be the case, they consider issues of memory, schemas and prototypes, and limitations on **capacity to process information**.

*Memory:* We do not only remember facts, but we remember processes (referred to as procedural memory). An entrepreneur's ability to recognize an opportunity is a **decision-making process**, but over time it becomes automatic, and so the entrepreneur cannot really describe the full complexity of the process that they go through.

***Schemas and prototypes:*** The information retained in the memory is only part of the story. New information also needs to be interpreted and then integrated into the information already stored in the memory. Schemas are cognitive frameworks that represent our knowledge and assumptions about the world, and prototypes are abstract idealized categorizations, such as the mental image we hold of what a gym is like. These can both help and hinder creativity and opportunity recognition as we described earlier.

***Limited capacity to process information:*** The memory may have unlimited capacity to store information but processing capability (working memory) is limited. To use a computer analogy the hard disk is vast but RAM is limited. This means that for most people their ability to create something new is limited, because there is a bottleneck in the process of making sense of new information in the context of our existing memory. Because of this the brain takes short cuts, especially in times of stress when large amounts of information have to be processed quickly; for example when important decisions have to be made on incomplete information or to short timescales, which can lead to mistakes. In taking short cuts, the likelihood of error increases. These situations are faced commonly by entrepreneurs, and it could be argued that as a consequence of this their decision-making is more susceptible to such error. Baron and Shane further argue that other biases may creep into the way entrepreneurs process information in making decisions, in that they may have a tendency to view desired outcomes more optimistically; that they more readily recognize information that confirms their current beliefs; and that they believe that fate is under their control to a greater extent than it actually is.

Despite many studies that have considered how cognitive approaches might affect our ability to spot opportunities and to assess the risk in exploiting them, there are no firm conclusions as to whether entrepreneurs process data differently from the general population in making decisions, although intuitively it seems probable that they are less likely to be fettered by habits of thinking given their ability to 'think outside the box'!

## Entrepreneurial decision-making

We have seen that entrepreneurs tend to be good networkers, and that they recognize the limitations of their own knowledge and exploit that of others (their staff, friends, advisers, etc). They accumulate as much detailed, relevant information as they can for themselves, often from their network, before forming a view and taking action.

Casson (2003: 34) believes that the judgement of entrepreneurs differs from that of other people, as they believe that without their intervention wrong decisions will be made or resources will be allocated less efficiently. The entrepreneur intervenes (in many ways) in order to exploit their superior judgement, to take advantage of the opportunity that exists for better coordination. This need to intervene might partly be due to a need for control, or partly be about self-belief; it may be a lack of trust in the ability of others which leads the entrepreneur to be unwilling to delegate, or it might be that an opportunity has been spotted to combine things in a different way which adds value.

It is our view that the way in which entrepreneurs make decisions might be a critical distinguishing factor. Their skill in decision-making might in part be because of their characteristics (for example, they are more willing to focus on a few key decisions and the implications, seek more innovative solutions or novel approaches, take a risk and go with gut feel) or it may be due to skills and experience (they learn from decisions they have made previously and adapt according to new contexts more readily than the average manager).

## Learning

Entrepreneurs tend to be action learners. They reflect on what they do, analyse what went well or less well, and adapt their behaviour to reflect their new understanding.

For an organization to build entrepreneurial capacity, it needs to encourage learning, and its application, at all levels. If it is accepted that personality is only part of the equation, this would suggest that experience and skills also have some part to play in entrepreneurship.

---

### Enterprise in Action 2.6

**By accident or design?**

Honda's successful entry into the American market in the early 1960s is well documented. Not only did they capture a substantial proportion of the large motorcycle market, but they partly created a new market for small motorcycles. Stunned by Honda's success, the British government hired the Boston Consulting Group (BCG) to explain what had happened and to advise the British motorcycle manufacturers how they could fight back. BCG concluded that Honda had had a highly competitive cost position through their competencies in large-scale manufacturing, which they used as a springboard to penetrate the American market, giving careful attention to growth and market share.

Honda's story was a little different, suggesting a more experimental approach, learning as they went along. Their managers said that, in reality, they had just wanted to see if they could sell something in the American market. They needed a currency allocation from the Ministry of Finance, who were sceptical; after 5 months the Ministry eventually gave the go-ahead but would only allow them to commit a fraction of the investment they wanted to make.

They knew their products were good, but not significantly better than those of the European manufacturers, and they had more confidence in the 250 cc and 305 cc machines. They debated how they should approach the market, and decided (without any compelling criteria for the rationale) to take four products in equal proportions: the 50 cc Supercub, and the 125 cc, 250 cc and 305 cc machines (although the dollar value of the bigger bikes was greater).

Having to start small, they chose more familiar territory, starting off in Los Angeles where there was a large second- and third-generation Japanese community, a climate that suited motorbikes, and a growing population. They were very short of money, and the three managers shared a small apartment, two of them sleeping on the floor. They made mistakes, as the motorcycle business was seasonal and the season had just ended. Learning from their experience of distributorships in Japan, they went direct to retailers, advertised in the trade magazine for dealers and by Spring they had 40 signed up.

Then their reputation was dealt a severe blow – their machines were leaking oil and the clutches were failing. In the USA, motorcycles are driven faster and further than they are in Japan. They had to send the motorcycles to the testing lab in Japan, an expense they could ill afford on the tight budget allowed them. It took a month to sort the problem out.

So far, they had not paid much attention to the smaller bikes as they seemed out of place in the US market where everything was bigger and more luxurious. They were using them themselves, however, and they were attracting a lot of attention. One day, a buyer from Sears paid them a call. With the larger bikes breaking down, despite their anxiety that pushing the smaller bikes might damage their reputation, they really had no choice but to let the 50 cc bikes move.

In reality, the strategy seems to have been more emergent than planned, and firmly grounded in a willingness to learn, quickly!

*Adapted from*: Backing into a brilliant strategy. In: H. Mintzberg, B. Ahlstrand and
J. Lampel (2005), *Strategy Bites Back*, Harlow: Pearson Education Ltd

**Question:** What lessons can be learned from Honda's experience?

## Developing entrepreneurial capacity

If the characteristics and behaviour that are considered crucial in staff of enterprising organizations are identified, it is possible to recruit, develop, and retain the people with those characteristics, and those who display those behaviours may be willing to learn how to behave in a more enterprising way.

Casson (2003: 31) looks at how scarce certain qualities are, and to what extent these skills can be procured through a delegate. If the intention is to buy the skill in (whether through employing someone or outsourcing), it is necessary to be able to screen for that skill, and so it is necessary to establish whether such screening is actually possible. The alternative to buying the skill in is to develop the skills internally, in which case it is important to know whether their enhancement or development is possible. If neither option is possible, it might be essential for the entrepreneur to have the skill.

If the entrepreneur does choose to delegate some tasks, he or she will then need to have delegation skills, and probably organizational skills too. If the entrepreneur does not have these skills, the question is whether they can be enhanced by training, to enable the entrepreneur to delegate effectively and ensure that tasks are undertaken effectively. But then the danger is that in spending time delegating and organizing, the entrepreneur is distracted and might lose innovation capability as a consequence. For a one-person company, delegation skills are not essential but as the company grows at some point they do become essential, and the choice does have to be made.

So the task of building entrepreneurial capacity becomes complicated, and has implications for the way in which the organization operates.

## Process

First it is necessary to identify which skills or qualities are essential. In the example given in Table 2.2, Casson's qualities have been used as a starting point, but you might prefer to develop your own. The framework offered in Table 2.2 is not meant to be definitive, and the assessment is somewhat subjective, but it does offer a starting point in assessing current capacity, and making plans for developing it within an organization.

Having identified the qualities that are deemed essential, the next step is to assess the extent to which these are held within the organization.

Where there are gaps in skills that are deemed essential, it is necessary to fill them, either through buying them in or developing them internally, for example through training. With existing staff, the behaviour they exhibit in their working lives might seem to evidence some skills (indicated by a tick in the 'Observable over time' column) although it might be difficult to screen for these in recruiting someone (indicated by a tick in the 'Difficult to screen for' column).

Where a quality is essential, rare, difficult to screen for, and cannot be enhanced through training, it is necessary to find someone unique, possibly that elusive individual we have been referring to as the entrepreneur. But the good news is that, according to Casson, many of the qualities are screenable and are capable of development. This suggests that it is possible to build entrepreneurial capacity.

**Table 2.2**
Assessment of current entrepreneurial capacity (adapted from Casson, 2003)

| Quality | Essential | Rare | Difficult to screen for | Observable over time | Capable of development |
|---|---|---|---|---|---|
| Foresight | ✓ | ✓ | ✓ | ✓ | ✓ |
| Imagination | ✓ | ✓ | ✓ | | |
| Communication | ✓ | | | ✓ | ✓ |
| Self-knowledge | ✓ | | ✓ | ✓ | ✓ |
| Autonomy | ✓ | ✓ | ✓ | ✓ | ✓ |
| Search skills | ✓ | | ✓ | ✓ | ✓ |
| Analytical ability | ✓ | ✓ | | ✓ | ✓ |
| Networking skills | ✓ | | | ✓ | ✓ |
| Manage risk | ✓ | | | ✓ | ✓ |
| Delegation | | ✓ | ✓ | ✓ | ✓ |
| Organizational skills | | ✓ | ✓ | ✓ | ✓ |
| Industry knowledge/expertise | ✓ | | | ✓ | ✓ |

However, if a skill is essential, scarce and difficult to screen for, then even if it were capable of enhancement it would mean that it would be necessary for people to identify the need to develop this for themselves, and to alert the organization to any support that they need in doing this. This suggests that some form of individual **reflection** would need to be built into any process that the organization adopts. It also implies that the organization would have to rely on the individual's ability to reflect on their own capabilities and on their willingness to take responsibility for their own development.

Ideally, the process of reflection should extend to peers and colleagues, as individuals are not always able to identify their own strengths and weaknesses objectively. For example, it can become apparent to others that someone is less able to analyse issues in depth than another individual (in student assignments this becomes immediately apparent!). Giving feedback to that individual might help them to recognize that they have a developmental need and to take up an opportunity to enhance their skills.

We suggest that this ability to reflect is a crucial part of the entrepreneur's learning processes, and again may be a distinguishing feature of success. We explore this further in Chapter 4.

## Summary

- We might draw the conclusion that there is not any such thing as a typical entrepreneur, that it is impossible to put these people in boxes and label them, and that each one is unique. However, some characteristics seem more common, and predispose individuals to entrepreneurial behaviour.
- There is a complex interrelationship between genetics and environment that makes it difficult to predict where entrepreneurship will flourish.
- The decision to become an entrepreneur is a personal one, but is affected by life experiences and circumstances, and the favourability of the environment.
- Some people have one entrepreneurial moment and others have many in succession. It is not necessary to behave in an entrepreneurial way throughout life; it is possible to opt in and out.
- Entrepreneurship is a style of management, and entrepreneurial behaviour occurs to varying degrees along a spectrum.
- Many entrepreneurial skills and attributes can be developed, making it possible to develop entrepreneurial capacity within organizations.

## Chapter questions

1. Are entrepreneurs born or can they be made? Justify your view by making reference to examples of success and/or failure of entrepreneurs.
2. What are the key personality traits and characteristics of entrepreneurs? Explain which of these you feel can be acquired through learning, giving examples.
3. Your organization is to offer a prize for 'Entrepreneur of the Year'. What criteria would you use to select the winner, and why?
4. Imagine you are leaving your full-time managerial position to set up a business of your own. How might your successes and failures as a manager help you in becoming a successful entrepreneur?
5. If you were employed by the Regional Development Agency to encourage entrepreneurship in your region, how would you choose which start-up businesses to offer support to?

## Case study

### Steve Perez

Steve Perez grew up helping out in his father's restaurant, peeling potatoes, washing dishes, collecting glasses and stocktaking. His enterprising nature was evident from his schooldays, when he made good use of the Bunsen burners in the school labs by cooking steak sandwiches, which he sold to his classmates!

Steve was 19 when his father died, and the family were left with very little when the business had to be sold. It took Steve some time to recover and get his own career back on track, eventually settling into a career with Tetley's. He hoped to become an area manager, but when he was told that his chances were poor as he didn't have a degree, frustration set in and he left without having another job to go to. He had noticed the popularity of beers like Grolsch, Budweiser, and Becks. He had a £600 van, and decided to buy these beers and sell them into the local pubs and off-licences. Steve built the turnover to £10 million before cross-border shopping began in the early 1990s. There was a lot of 'cheap booze' on the market, and Steve had cash-flow problems. He told the bank and they called in the receivers, who asked for the keys of his car, and Steve walked home.

He barely held on to his home, having used it as security on some of his business loans. Not one to give up, he did a deal with some friendly suppliers, who were willing to give him some credit. He had a little warehouse, and four people who had worked for him in the previous company who were willing to work without wages until he could afford to pay them.

Alcopops had had a bad press, and there was a lot of bankrupt stock on the market. He made a bit of money buying and selling it, but this didn't have long-term prospects. The ready-to-drink (RTD) products were very pricey, so Steve decided to develop a product of his own that would compete on quality with the brand leaders, and shake up the market a bit. He noticed that people were mixing Vodka with Red Bull, went to the flavour companies and told them he wanted something like that. There was a need for a serious adult brand.

GBL launched VK (Vodka Kick) in 1999 with a few posters and no marketing budget. Steve and his staff delivered the product themselves, trying to build some distribution and to get some people drinking VK. Customers liked it, and before long there were problems in producing it in sufficient quantities.

Simplicity was the key – a short, catchy name, unrelated to the alcohol content, and innovative packaging and design. 'You need something simple. On a Friday night in a packed bar, when you're shouting at the barman, you don't want something with more than two syllables.'

GBL has gone from strength to strength. The export market has grown significantly, and the company's continuing success has made expansion into larger premises possible. Steve said 'We never really expected all this. We came up with the right product at the right time. Success in business is made up of one-third skill, one-third hard work, and one-third luck.'

Sue Marriott (various public sources)

### Questions:

1. With reference to appropriate concepts and theory, evaluate the extent to which Steve's success derives from his personality, his skills, or his luck.
2. What could he do next?

## References and further reading

Baron R.A. and Shane S.A. (2005) Entrepreneurship: *A Process Perspective.* Mason OH: Thomson South-Western.

Birley S. and Muzyka D.F. (2000) *Mastering Entrepreneurship.* Harlow: Pearson.

Bolton B. and Thompson J. (2003) *The Entrepreneur In Focus: Achieve Your Potential.* London: Thomson.

Carter S. and Jones-Evans D. (2000) *Enterprise and Small Business: Principles, Practice and Policy.* Harlow: Pearson.

Casson M. (2003) *The Entrepreneur – An Economic Theory,* 2nd edn. Cheltenham UK: Edward Elgar Publishing Inc.

Collins J. (2001) Level 5 leadership – the triumph of humility and fierce resolve. *Harvard Business Review,* January, pp. 67–76.

Handy C. (1999) *The New Alchemists.* Hutchinson: London.

Hisrich R.D. and Peters M.P. (2002) *Entrepreneurship,* International edn. New York: McGraw-Hill.

Kets de Vries M. (1977) The entrepreneurial personality: a person at the crossroads. *Journal of Management Studies* 14: 34–57.

Kirby D.A. (2003) *Entrepreneurship.* Maidenhead: McGraw-Hill Education.

McLelland D.C. (1961) *The Achieving Society.* New Jersey: Van Nostrand.

Meredith G.G., Nelson R.E. and Neck P.A. (1982) *The Practice of Entrepreneurship.* Geneva: International Labour Office.

Stevenson H. (1997) The six dimensions of entrepreneurship. In: S. Birley and D.F. Muzyka (2000), *Mastering Entrepreneurship.* Harlow: Financial Times Prentice Hall.

Timmons J.A. (1994) *New Venture Creation: Entrepreneurship for the 21st Century,* 4th edn. Illinois: Irwin.

Wickham P.A. (2004) *Strategic Entrepreneurship,* 3rd edn. Harlow: Pearson Education.

## Key words

action factors
actions of entrepreneurs
capacity to process information
dark side of entrepreneurship
decision-making process
entrepreneurial behaviour patterns
entrepreneurial capacity
entrepreneurial management
motivations

nurture rather than nature
personality trait approach
portfolio entrepreneurs
push and pull factors
reflection
sequential entrepreneurs
tipping point
traits and characteristics

# Innovation and its management

By the end of this chapter the reader will be able to:

- identify the nature of innovation and appreciate its role in entrepreneurial activity;
- evaluate the stakeholder benefits that result from the opportunities identified and exploited;
- understand the categories and dimensions of innovation and the features of the innovation process;
- understand innovation and the market breakpoints that often provide the spur to new developments;
- compare the alternative innovation stances;
- understand the critical success factors in innovation and the reasons for failure.

## Introduction

Innovation is the process by which the opportunities that have been identified through individual and organizational creativity are exploited. We have emphasized earlier that innovation and entrepreneurship must co-exist for individuals and organizations to be considered to be enterprising. Innovation is an essential element in enterprise by creating new business activity, in generating growth and ensuring survival for an existing business.

It seems quite natural for organizations to want to do things better and differently in order to gain a competitive edge over competitors and, in most organizations (albeit to different degrees) there is the ambition to seek out and exploit new opportunities with the aim of improving overall performance throughout the business. However, it must be remembered that innovation does not occur spontaneously. Organizational innovation is driven by creative and enterprising individuals.

In this chapter, therefore, we begin by discussing the nature and role of innovation, its impact in different types of organizations and the benefits it creates for a wide range of stakeholders. For example, the recipients of the organization's offering, its customers, consumers, clients, etc., expect to receive periodic improvements in the benefits they obtain. The organization must address this expectation through a comprehensive range of developments throughout the functions of the business. While the organization might have good intentions and aim to develop many new, successful ideas in practice, there are many challenges to overcome before a new idea becomes commercially successful and so we address some reasons for the failure of innovation.

Innovation is best coordinated through an effectively managed process and we discuss how this can be used to achieve efficient control and continual improvement through learning good practice from the organization's collective experiences.

Innovation takes many forms and we particularly distinguish between the major-step-change innovations that generate considerable improvement in the added value for the various stakeholders of the organization by doing things differently, and the smaller-scale incremental developments that are concerned with doing better what is already being done.

Finally, we consider the alternative competitive stances that organizations might adopt and the implementation strategies that might be used to realize their objectives.

## The nature and role of market-based innovation

It is appropriate to begin the discussion with some comments on definitions of innovation and creativity.

## Innovation and creativity

Many definitions of **innovation** have been offered, and some examples are given in Figure 3.1.

From reading through many definitions it is clear that choosing an appropriate definition of innovation seems to depend on the perspective being taken. Given the approach of this textbook to take a broad view of enterprise we favour an inclusive definition of innovation, embracing the exploitation of ideas in profit and non-profit organizations.

**Creativity** also has many different definitions depending on the context. For our purposes we consider it to be the generation of ideas, usually as a result of individual or small-team endeavour which will add value for organizations and/or their stakeholders. The ideas may not even be new but could simply be applied to a new situation.

Within the heading of innovations we take a market-based perspective of innovation that underpins entrepreneurship:

■ Invention is not essential. The popular misconception is that innovation is the same as invention but the common view of writers in the field is that innovation does not necessarily involve invention. Indeed, Bolton and Thompson (2003), in the 'envision' stage of their entrepreneur process model note that the inventor need not be the opportunity spotter, nor the project champion who takes the idea forward to commercialization.

**Figure 3.1**
Some definitions of
innovation.

Innovation is the successful exploitation of new ideas (Innovation Unit, Department of Trade and Industry UK, 2004)

Innovation is the specific tool of entrepreneurs, the means by which they exploit change as an opportunity for a different business or service. It is capable of being presented as a discipline, capable of being learned, capable of being practised (Drucker, 1985)

Companies achieve competitive advantage through acts of innovation. They approach innovation in its broadest sense including both new technologies and new ways of doing things (Porter, 1990)

Turning opportunity into ideas and putting these into widely used practice (Tidd, Bessant and Pavitt, 2005: 66)

■ It is not just about having ideas. Many people have ideas but do not have the desire, the vision and/or the know-how to be able to commercialize them.

■ Every function of the organization can contribute to innovation by adding value for stakeholders.

■ Technology and non-technological developments are included.

■ Both step change and incremental improvements are valuable in improving organizational performance.

Wickham (2004) points out that it is the opportunity that is ultimately most important, not the innovation itself.

While our emphasis is on the entrepreneur or the innovator that profitably exploits the ideas, it is difficult to conceive of innovation without some creative input, whether that is in inventing a new product or in seeing new and better ways of doing things. By profitable exploitation, we do not only mean making money. In the public sector it can mean designing a new initiative, or finding a more economical way of delivering a service.

The UK, for example, has long recognized that it has a successful record of scientific and technological invention but is lagging behind in exploitation, innovation and setting up new businesses (DTI, 2003). According to the Global Entrepreneurship Monitor (GEM) Report 2000, the UK is lagging behind its competitors in certain respects. In particular, the level of new business start-ups is significantly behind countries such as the USA, Australia and Canada, and the entrepreneurial culture – particularly the tendency to identify and exploit business opportunities – is not well developed.

The UK government has sought to foster better links between research establishments, including universities, and industry in the hope of bringing more innovation to market (Innovation Report Online Update, DTI, UK, Feb 2005). They have also sought to forge partnerships between the public and the private sector, with the avowed intention of bringing greater commercial awareness to the delivery of public services, which could be described as innovation in process. In practice there has always been evidence of considerable creativity in the public sector, but this has been accelerated by best-value delivery and outsourcing programmes so common in the 1980s.

## Adding value through innovation

Before discussing the various categories of innovation and processes in detail it is useful to consider how customers and organizations might benefit from innovation.

### Customer benefits from innovation

If opportunities are successfully exploited, the recipients (consumers, customers, clients, etc.) of the organization's products, services, processes and ideas should receive additional value that will ultimately provide greater satisfaction than before, through the combination of tangible and intangible benefits that they receive from the new offering.

Innovation might increase the **tangible benefits** of the product or service that appeal to the recipients' senses, in the form of better value; perhaps a product with a larger range of functions, better durability, or better design, is easier to use or is lower priced than the competition for a similar specification.

The **intangible benefits** take the form of a better designed or functioning product or service, efficient customer service, a better experience, and a feeling of greater satisfaction or enjoyment from the purchasing and usage process. The value of intangible benefits becomes obvious as products that appear to be physically the same may be perceived differently by customers if they carry a well known brand or are supplied by a company with a positive reputation. The customers may be prepared to pay a premium price or remain loyal to the supplier if they perceive that the brand offers extra intangible value. For example:

- a shirt made from the same material to the same specification in the same factory might be sold at a higher price if it carries a fashion label;
- customers are prepared to pay a higher price for a car with a VW badge rather than a Skoda badge, despite much of the engineering being to the same specification;
- Fairtrade products are differentiated from competitor products on the basis of using ethical business practices. It is difficult for individual consumers to assess the actual tangible benefits to farmers and so the appeal may be a 'feel good' factor for consumers who believe in the principles and trust the Fairtrade brand to deliver them.

Increasingly, other aspects of the purchasing and usage process are assessed and valued by customers, including the disposal of the item after it is no longer useful. For them there are many other improved benefits that an organization can offer: for example, by providing an effective service for customers that solves problems, removes 'hassle' from their lives, and offers greater convenience and accessibility, a 'fun' experience or simply the pleasure of being served by caring, interested and helpful staff. While on the face of it offering high levels of service may not seem as innovative as a technological product innovation it still requires creative management and delivery and the impact is equally important and often more difficult to achieve consistently in practice. For example, the success of many high-tech products is just as dependent on creative branding, distribution or advertising as it is upon the features of the product, as shown in Enterprise in Action 3.1.

---

## Enterprise in Action 3.1

### Steve Jobs creating a lifestyle

Apple Computers has always been the underdog in an industry dominated by giants but the genius of Steve Jobs, its founder and chief executive, is that he has managed to make what is essentially a rather boring technical product a lifestyle choice, for teens to technology geeks to business executives.

This has been achieved by not just including leading-edge technology in its Macs, Powerbooks and iPods, but by creating desirable products through design, innovative retail strategies and grassroots market appeal. Jobs has been particularly effective in leveraging limited marketing budgets to gain maximum publicity, often through partnerships, such as those with Volkswagen and Pepsi.

In 2004 Apple took steps with the introduction of the $99 iPod Shuffle and $499 Mac mini to extend its appeal to an audience that has not so far been able to afford its products.

Apple's weakness, as with many entrepreneurial organizations, is closely linked to the personality of its entrepreneurial CEO. Jobs is passionate, often not politically correct and has not always selected the best team of executives to make the best of Apple's ideas.

*Adapted from*: A. Cuneo, Marketer of the year Apple, AdAge.com and Apple unveils low-cost 'Mac mini', BBC Online, 11 January 2003

**Question:** How can an entrepreneur with limited resources create intangible benefits for customers?

---

Providing these benefits requires the organization to configure its business model in a way that delivers them more effectively and efficiently than can the competitors. This requires establishing strong links across a range of functions. For example, it does not only require financial resources for R&D, but it needs appropriately skilled staff to be recruited and trained, it needs marketing to analyse changing customer needs, and it needs operations to deliver efficiently.

### Organization benefits from innovation

Success for most organizations is determined by the degree of customer satisfaction that is delivered, but clearly this must not be 'at any cost' and so central to innovation is the concept of exchange and providing customer benefits in a way that the supplier organization can sustain.

In a private sector business the benefit for the owners of the organization might be in the form of increased wealth, which comes from the development of more profitable products and more efficient use of assets. For public or not-for-profit organizations the benefit will be in the form of being more effective (securing more impact for the same investment) or more efficient deployment of resources (lowering the cost of delivery without lowering quality or reducing outputs). For example, in an NHS Trust, innovation in systems might lead to more patients being treated per hospital bed.

In healthcare, innovations are frequently at the public–private sector interface, where innovations are often the result of cooperation between individuals from public and private sector organizations. Martina Rieder in Enterprise in Action 3.2 has designed and patented a new skin contact adhesive and a high-tech gel that soaks up excess moisture. It has the potential to ensure that ileostomy and urostomy bags remain secure and dry for longer, thus reducing costs, and increasing customer comfort.

---

## Enterprise in Action 3.2

### The UK's most enterprising student improves patient dignity

Martina Rieder, a student at the University of Sussex, was on a summer placement with Welland Medical Limited, who specialize in ileostomy and urostomy bags (used to remove waste from a patient's body after small-intestine and bladder surgery respectively). The 8-week placement was part of the Shell Technology Enterprise Programme (STEP) and she received an award as the UK's most enterprising student for her work.

She knew nothing about the use of the bags when she started but careful research, coupled with empathy for the wearers and a determination to improve the patients' comfort and dignity gave her the idea for a new patient-friendly product – a gel seal to stop leakages between the bag and the stoma (the artificial opening in the body), which is now being patented.

The problem was that the bags had to be connected through the stoma. There have always been problems with leakage of urine, which causes the patients considerable skin discomfort, and frequent problems with the failure of bags and seals, making it necessary to change them very frequently.

Staff and patients were impressed by Martina, who took time to listen and then develop a solution. For her part, Martina was shocked that no one had done anything before to overcome these patient problems.

*Adapted from:* J. Elliott, 'Giving bladder op patients their dignity back',
BBC News Online, 15 October 2004

**Question:** What are the success factors that an innovator should focus on?

Other stakeholders, such as the community at large, can benefit from an organization's innovation. For example, there would be community benefits from an organization developing a novel energy-saving policy. While the policy might also help to improve the organization's image and reputation among its consumers it may not necessarily reduce energy costs or otherwise improve product performance.

## The alternative categories of innovation

Accepting the broader view of innovation that covers the dimensions of invention – technological and non-technological, and step change and incremental innovation, we now turn to the alternative categorizations of innovation that have been proposed.

The starting point is the four categories (the 4 Ps of innovation) identified by Utterback (1994), which describe the space in which the innovation takes place.

*Product innovation:* changes in the products and services the organization offers; for example, M&S sell a small portion of pre-prepared Brussels sprouts in a microwaveable bag.

*Process innovation:* changes in the way products and services are created and delivered; for example, online banking and betting.

*Position innovation:* changes in the context in which products and services are introduced. For example, it was originally thought that older people would want to buy cars specially designed for easy access, economy, and high levels of safety, and with equipment to cope with increasing disability. In practice an increasing number of older people appear to be buying high-performance sports cars to relive their youth!

*Paradigm innovation:* Changes in the underlying mental models which frame what the organization does, as shown in Spotlight 3.1.

## Spotlight 3.1

### Paradigm shift for SMP

SMP are an SME supplier of hot and cold pressed track components for rail systems and in the 1980s 95 per cent of turnover derived from their principal customer British Coal. By 1990 the coal mine closure programme was accelerating and SMP were losing sales rapidly. They realized they could not survive as a supplier to the UK coal industry and would have to diversify.

In 1990 they reformulated their strategy and company structure. First, they redefined their business from coal mining to 'anywhere there is a tunnel' and, second, from the UK to export markets. From a zero base in 1990 exports grew to the point where they contributed 60 per cent of the revenue in 2005.

The reasons for the success of SMP were:

■ clear top-management vision of the company they wished to build;
■ the tenacity and resilience of the entrepreneurial CEO in driving the company in this new direction;
■ identifying two niche target markets, railways and construction, wherein they could compete;
■ being small and lacking experience they used alliances with partners to grow the business;
■ they focused on quality processes throughout the organization.

*Source*: Isobel Doole, Sheffield Hallam University

**Question:** What are the barriers likely to be for a paradigm innovation?

An alternative characterization of new products was proposed by Booz, Allen and Hamilton (1982) who suggested that the key criteria were newness of the product to the company and newness of the product to the marketplace. Based upon research in the 1980s in the USA they concluded that the prevalence of products in the categories was as shown in Figure 3.2.

■ New-to-the-world products that create a totally new market; 10 per cent
■ New product lines that enable the company to compete in a new product category; 20 per cent
■ Additions to existing product lines; 26 per cent
■ Improvements and revisions to existing products; 26 per cent
■ Repositionings of existing products to appeal to a new customer segment; 7 per cent
■ Cost reductions to provide similar performance at lower cost; 11 per cent

*Source*: Booz, Allen and Hamilton (1982)

**Figure 3.2**
Categories of new products.

## Technology and step changes

Technology is not an essential element of innovation but it often plays a key role in facilitating change. Tidd, Bessant and Pavitt (2005) explain that the eighteenth-century economist Joseph Schumpeter suggested that entrepreneurs use technological innovation to get strategic advantage and for a while this allows them to make a lot of money (monopoly profits). This step change or discontinuous innovation, according to Schumpeter, involves creative destruction. Step change innovation can be thought of as doing things differently. It usually follows a period of market stability and the innovation will cause substantial disruption. There is likely to be considerably greater uncertainty and unpredictability in the technical success, customer acceptance and competitor response. However, other entrepreneurs will imitate this and, as a result, other innovations (incremental innovations) will emerge, resulting in many new ideas that chip away at the 'monopoly profits' until equilibrium is reached and the process starts all over again.

## Technological discontinuities

Foster (1986) illustrated the 'S' curve of the technology life cycle, as shown in Figure 3.3. This plots investment in product development and performance improvement perceived by the customer.

Investment in product, service and process development results in a stream of small performance improvements that add customer value. However, at the top of the 'S' curve, when the mature phase of the life cycle has been reached, even for quite large research and development investment made there is little further improvement in performance. For example, analogue TVs reached this point and even substantial additional investment could not achieve further small improvements in customer satisfaction. As digital TVs have become affordable, so the demand for the old products has declined quickly. This pattern follows a similar breakpoint and progression from black and white to colour televisions. You might speculate what the next breakpoint could

**Figure 3.3**
R&D effort and
discontinuity.

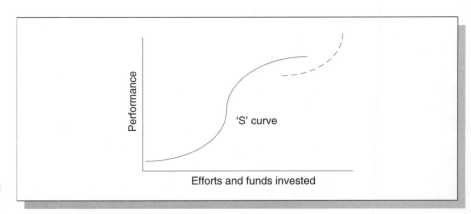

be; for example, it might be a totally new level of interactivity or 3D imagery.

## The vicious circle of technology evolution

Technology evolution drives change within an industry sector but also provides the means for entrepreneurs to respond to change and build competitive advantage, as shown in Figure 3.4. Entrepreneurs are able to adapt and apply 'pure' science and technological inventions to create new commercial solutions in the form of new products, services and processes.

The entrepreneurial organizations that successfully embrace a new technology and find a practical application, for example by creating a new product, service or a new route to market will gain a new source of competitive advantage. This usually results in new standards being set for the industry sector and leads to competitors having also to meet these standards if they wish to compete in the market in the future. All competitors in the sector then embrace the new technology. Consequently, the innovator firms have to find a new innovation or technological advance that allows them to get ahead of the competition again.

This cycle of technological development in the sector leads to creative new ideas, not just in the products and services of the 'for profits' sector. For example, it is just as important for a charity to use the latest communications methods to compete in fund-raising, as shown in Pause and Reflect 3.1.

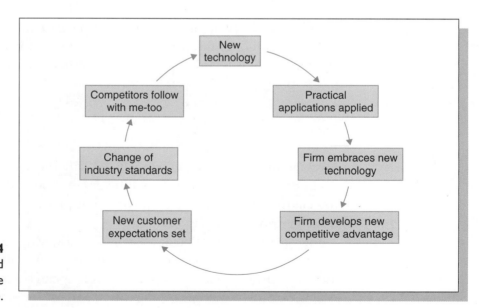

**Figure 3.4**
Technology and
competitive
advantage.

## Pause and Reflect 3.1

### Charity innovation at Oxfam

The constant challenge for charities is to overcome donor fatigue, and the dilemma is which route to customers will deliver the most benefit. Oxfam is challenging the traditional ways of operating charities. For example, e-mail will soon overtake traditional mail in terms of communications expenditure. Now Oxfam is using the latest information and communications technology to target different groups for different purposes. Students tend to make good activists, young adults have money to donate and older people are willing to work as volunteers.

Oxfam's new approach is obtaining very high response rates. For example its campaign to persuade Nestle to drop its calls for debt repayment from Ethiopia involved asking people to e-mail the CEO of Nestle. Seventy to eighty per cent of the people contacted e-mailed the CEO and the debt was cancelled.

By tracking website navigation Oxfam is able to obtain information about the interests, commitment and willingness of people to donate and it has changed its targets for communication as a result. It has been better able to integrate its communications to maximize its impact in collecting donations. Now Oxfam has launched video e-mails using newsreel type footage to complement TV ads and news items. It has described the response to its appeal for donations for Sudan as phenomenal.

*Adapted from:* 'Treating them differently', *Marketing Direct*, February 2005

**Question:** Are there any restrictions to innovation in the not-for-profit sector?

# Incremental and architectural innovation

So far our discussion has focused on step change innovation, driven by technology but, as we said earlier, innovation is more broadly based.

## Step change innovation

**Step change innovation** occurs not just because of technology changes but as a result of groundbreaking, creative ideas throughout the organization, and this is addressed in greater detail later in this chapter and in Chapter 9.

## Incremental innovation

**Incremental innovation** covers all the small-scale improvements that occur on a daily basis throughout the organization. Toyota, for example, has claimed that its quality improvement programmes generated over 60 000 improvements in one year.

Incremental innovation also involves considering all the technological alternatives, and in necessity invention, shown in Pause and Reflect 3.2 and Enterprise in Action 3.4, old technology can be applied to solve current problems, sometimes being integrated with new technology too.

## Pause and Reflect 3.2

### Grassroots innovation

There are many necessity inventors around the world who are developing low-technology solutions to solve day-to-day problems. In Gujarat, India, Mansukhbhai Jagani has developed a field cultivator, which was developed by replacing the rear wheel of an Enfield Bullett motorcycle. Whereas a tractor costs $6000, the modification costs $450. He has also developed a seed and fertilizer dispenser and a bicycle-mounted sprayer.

Arvindbhai Patel developed a natural water cooler, invented when his wife applied a water-soaked cloth to his forehead when he had a fever. It consists of a 10-foot copper pipe wrapped in a wet cloth that carries water to a container. The water is chilled in the process. Another inventor added a lever to the pulley used for drawing water from wells. It stops the bucket from falling back when the pulley operator stops to catch a breath.

The problem for individual inventors of this type is a lack of funds to develop the ideas into marketable products. To solve this, in the 1980s Anil Gupta set up the Honey Bee Network to create a database of grassroots technology innovations and traditional knowledge, which now has 51 000 ideas. The Grassroots innovation Augmentation Network was set up by Gupta in 1997 to identify promising ideas, do market research, and prepare business plans to attract the necessary financial support.

*Adapted from*: S. Sinha, 'Successes in rural inventions', BBC News Online, 8 July 2005

**Question:** What do you consider to be the main challenges for low-technology inventors?

## Architectural innovation

Tushman and Anderson (2004: 6) explain that **architectural innovation** are the changes in the subsystems and linking mechanisms that are necessary to obtain the best benefit from minor technological changes. Honda adjusted its business model to market small motorcycles by selling through bicycle shops in the USA rather than motorcycle dealerships. In the 1990s IBM failed to respond to the implications of disk drive technology moving from use in mainframe computers to PCs. Competitors were faster at seeing the opportunity, made the architectural change to their businesses and took a high market share, with the result that IBM suffered considerable losses.

Tushman and Anderson (2004: 92) suggest that the best firms are 'ambidextrous' and can effectively manage incremental innovation, architectural innovation and technological discontinuities. They are continually learning and acquiring detailed knowledge of specific technologies, markets, customers or competitors, reflecting on the combined areas of knowledge, re-evaluating the new knowledge against the background of the current situation, and reformulating the organization's mix of activities to exploit the new opportunities.

Innovation can therefore be understood as a knowledge-based process. For small-scale incremental innovations the level of uncertainty, for example, in the expected technical success and customer acceptance of the new offer is likely to be low. Step change innovations involve greater uncertainty but if the organization has experience, expertise, a track record of innovation and adopts a learning approach, it is likely to be able to predict the outcome of projects with a higher degree of certainty.

## Innovation throughout the life cycle

As we have suggested earlier in this chapter, customers expect continual improvements in the overall product or service offer throughout its lifetime in order to maintain their interest and loyalty to the organization.

### Life cycle

The fundamental principle of the **product life cycle** is that most brands, ideas, products, services, processes and technology follow a life cycle similar to that shown in Figure 3.5. The life cycle follows the stages of introduction, growth, maturity and finally, decline, as new brands, products, services, processes or technology replace existing offerings.

The life cycle concept suggests that businesses should be constantly innovating to ensure that new introductions are ready when replacements are needed, to further ensure a constant and growing revenue stream. It might be that products and services need to be revitalized to

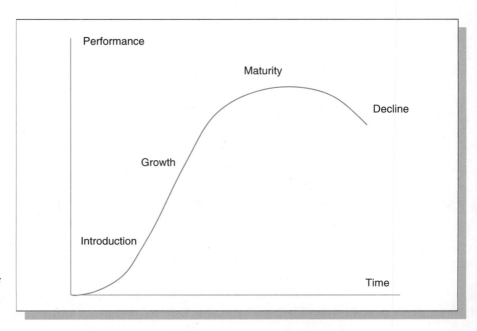

**Figure 3.5**
The life cycle of products, technology.

extend their life or replaced when they have become obsolete. For some sectors, such as high technology, it is possible for experts to accurately predict when a product will have reached the decline phase of its life and will be replaced by a new product, because they know that new scientific or technological inventions are already in the pipeline. You might consider how long you think it will be before your mobile phone, TV, and audio and video recording equipment will need to be replaced as new, better designed, more functional, possibly cheaper replacements become available. You may not be able to guess which supplier will be the innovator or what the technology base will be, but you just know that a replacement will be available in the next two to three years.

Fashions and fads appear in not-for-profit sectors too. For example, in many countries the main political parties appear to be increasingly adopting the middle ground. The policies of rival parties are becoming increasingly indistinguishable, offering voters little real choice. Accordingly, innovative new parties formed by entrepreneurial politicians do have the opportunity to make an initial impact on bored voters. However, many of these are short-lived 'fads' often linked to the short-lived popularity of one issue or a particular personality.

For mature markets it is often difficult to predict when a product will start to decline. Coca-Cola, Kellogg's Corn Flakes and Heinz baked beans seem likely to continue in the mature phase of the life cycle for some years yet and replacements are not yet obvious. It is perhaps unlikely but not impossible that consumer taste or dietary advice will change so much that a replacement will be needed. Consumption patterns of various foods have changed dramatically as new diets, such as Atkins and GI, gain and lose favour.

## The innovation response to different life cycle situations

The strategic response to different life cycle situations is through innovation in different aspects of the organization's operation and marketing. Clearly the introduction stage of a product life cycle involves a 'break through' innovation and a product, service or process that is entirely new to the market. Small-scale innovations that create incremental improvements to the product, service or process maintain the organization's competitive position through the growth phase and into the mature phases of the life cycle. These innovations might include 'new improved' versions, brand and line extensions, or lower-cost versions that maintain the customer's interest and loyalty.

When a market reaches maturity and is on the point of decline, either more significant innovations are required to revive the product or to create an entirely new offer to the market. Sometimes architectural innovations enable organizations to break into an adjacent market or target a new customer segment; for example, supplying home users rather than business users of office equipment may not require different technology but may require product or business model adaptations.

It is important to re-emphasize at this point that it is not always product and service innovations that are essential in a new offering. As we shall see later, a new offer can emerge following the adoption of a new method of communication, ordering and payment system, pricing strategy or distribution channel. To maintain growth and to extend the life cycle it is necessary to introduce a stream of small-scale innovations in every function of the business that will help to improve efficiency, lower cost and add customer value through improved features and benefits. The stage of the life cycle that a product has reached may be different in different markets and this requires adaptations, as Enterprise in Action 3.3 shows.

---

## Enterprise in Action 3.3

### Turning back the technology

As in many other less developed countries the electricity supply in Vietnam is unreliable and the lights often go out. For patients on life-support machines on an intensive-care ward in a Vietnamese hospital, however, the consequences can be much more serious.

Roger Eltringham, a consultant anaesthetist at Gloucester Royal Hospital in the UK, developed a ventilator in his spare time to supply oxygen that copes with electricity failure. It is already saving lives in Africa, parts of Asia and Eastern Europe. When working in the developing world he realized that the sophisticated machinery used in the developed world required back-up and could not cope with the local conditions, so he set about developing a new product to solve the problem.

Eltringham's machine costs £15 000 compared with £40 000 for a traditional machine and 50 machines have already been sold. It can be used without electricity, has a 14-hour oxygen supply rather than 1 hour 40 minutes in the more sophisticated products and has lower running costs than the conventional machines have.

The only problem is that some hospitals want the most sophisticated machines so they can be regarded as being 'leading edge'. They have to be persuaded that a less sophisticated machine is more suited to their situation.

*Adapted from:* J. Elliott, 'My machine is saving lives globally', BBC News Online, 28 May 2005

**Question:** Where does the stimulus for innovations come from in developing countries?

## Industry breakpoints

The step changes in life cycles that result from the 'new to the world' introductions are referred to by Strebel (1996) as *industry breakpoints* after which the industry 'will never be the same again'. Strebel identified two types of breakpoints that have the effect of significantly increasing either customer value for money or organizational performance through cost reduction:

> *Divergent* breakpoints – associated with sharply increasing the variety of competitive offerings resulting in increased value for the customer; and
>
> *Convergent* breakpoints – the result of improvements in the systems and processes used for the delivery of the offerings, leading to lower delivered costs.

Industry breakpoints occur because of either a technological innovation, based upon invention, or a marketing or operational breakthrough, that may only partially be influenced by technology developments. For example, online travel agents made it easier for travellers to use their own ingenuity to save money on travel and create exciting holiday packages, through carrying out their own research.

## Marketing and operational breakpoints

Over the last few years many industry breakpoints have been the result of technological or scientific research, which it might be concluded are the main drivers of change. However, industry breakpoints are also created through entrepreneurial creativity by using a mix of existing and new business models, supporting technology and new designs, marketing and business processes. One of the most significant breakthroughs in the mobile phone sector came as a result of innovations in payment methods, as we discuss in the case study at the end of the chapter. eBay and Betfair have used the Internet to develop new ways of auctioning products and gambling.

## The categories of innovation and commercialization challenges

It is easy for entrepreneurial organizations to fall into the trap of assuming that the benefits of new innovative products and services, which are so obvious to the innovator, will also be obvious to customers. However, customers are rarely as involved or as interested in the new product or service introduction as is the innovator. They may be still relatively happy with the existing product and see no real reason to change and would not be prepared to go out of their way to do so. Rarely do customers form a queue at the door to buy unproven products or services! Innovations change the pattern of customer buying and usage and, even when the benefits, improvements and additional customer value appear to be obvious, the supplier must still market and sell the product effectively. Equally, organizations can fall into the trap of believing that the organization is flexible and can easily accommodate new developments without disruption of operational efficiency. Alternatively, some believe that an innovation is superior and command a premium price, and that these factors will offset inefficiencies in its operation.

Robertson (1967) identified three categories of innovations according to the disruption they cause to customers' buying and usage patterns and thus the amount of customer education and promotion that might be needed. The suggestion is that the more disruption, even if the result is greater benefit to customers, the more education and persuasion is needed. The problem is that providing high levels of customer education can be very expensive and sometimes beyond the means of some smaller organizations that have limited resources and limited capability in many business functions.

## Continuous innovations

Continuous innovations to the product require little change to the purchase and consumption behaviour in customers. For example, the introduction of fluoride in water, additives in food, and new chemicals in fertilizers or the use of CFC-free refrigerants in refrigerators would appear to have no significant effect on the purchase process or use of the product at least so far as the consumer is concerned.

Consumers are becoming more knowledgeable and demanding however, and, with pressure groups raising questions, they are more likely to question certain types of continuous innovations. The introduction of genetically modified (GM) foods has raised fears in consumers' minds and made them reluctant to purchase the products without greater proof of their safety.

## Dynamically continuous innovations

Dynamically continuous innovations have a more disruptive effect on the way that the products and services are used. For example, the introduction of the DVD recorder required some changes in routine to ensure that it is used effectively but it operates in a very similar way to previous recording formats. If the innovation is dynamically continuous it can be difficult to explain to customers the advantages compared to existing products or services, especially if the price is much higher.

Discontinuous innovations have a highly disruptive effect upon usage and purchasing patterns and these innovations require a high level of marketing to explain the benefits and to educate consumers about how the product should be used. Microwave ovens had a significant effect on customer lifestyles but it was necessary to explain to customers that the invention was safe; that there were convenience benefits; and that a change in cooking methodology was possible. MP3 players for music downloaded from the Internet have a more disruptive effect on purchasing and usage behaviour of customers as they require different customer skills and knowledge.

The more disruptive the innovation is to customers' normal purchasing, consumption, and disposal patterns the greater the investment that is needed to educate these customers in respect of why they need the innovation, how they will benefit from it and how they should use it (and not use it). In the early days of microwave ovens, for example, suppliers omitted to tell consumers that they were unsuitable for drying cats after they had been out in the rain, with disastrous consequences!

## Creative destruction and the internal organizational challenges

As well as posing new challenges for marketing, discontinuous innovations and, slightly less so, dynamically continuous innovations, cause disruption to the internal operations of an organization. If the innovation is disruptive it might require a radical change in the firm's management processes such as manufacturing, distribution and marketing. It might even need a complete re-invention of the firm's business model and practices. One example of this is the introduction of digital photography, as shown in Enterprise in Action 3.4, which has not only had a huge effect on the major film and camera manufacturers but also on smaller organizations, including for example, those involved in film processing.

---

### Enterprise in Action 3.4

**Disruption in the photography industry caused by discontinuous innovation**

A digital camera can fall into both discontinuous and dynamically continuous categories. If a digital camera is used to take pictures and the memory card is then taken to a photographic shop for processing it has little effect on use and purchasing and could be categorized as a dynamically continuous innovation. If a digital camera is used by the customer in conjunction with a computer or special printer for processing, this is considered discontinuous.

As well as changing customer purchasing and usage behaviour the companies involved have suffered considerable change to their operations over a very short time period. Kodak, for example, had to shed 25 000 jobs in two years as digital sales replaced film-based sales. In the second quarter of 2005 it made a loss of \$146 m following a loss of \$136 m for the year before. To show the rate of change, its digital sales rose in the second quarter by 43 per cent.

While there is probably little that could be done to avoid this problem, film processing companies seem largely to have failed to seize the opportunity to retain business following the industry breakpoint caused by the introduction of digital cameras. They either took their customers for granted and assumed that they would continue to bring in memory cards for processing or believed that all customers would print their own photographs and so their business would have no future. They failed to explain to their customers that their services extended to digital photography and that there were benefits in having digital images professionally printed.

*Adapted from*: 'Kodak to slash 10,000 extra jobs', BBC News Online, 20 July 2005

**Question:** What can the entrepreneurial organization do to avoid the risks of disruption to its established business?

---

### Disruptive technology

Christensen (1997) introduced the concept of **disruptive technology**. In the 'S' curve the performance of a new technology is usually inferior to that of the old technology. Often, because the new technology appears to be creating a new market, it is not taken sufficiently seriously by the existing players in the established market. For example, the first mobile phones were cumbersome and performed much worse than fixed line phones. By the time the fixed line players started to become interested in the new market, the new entrepreneurial mobile phone suppliers were already strong competitors.

Christensen suggests that contrary to popular belief large firms are aware of new disruptive technologies but their customers are resistant to change and continue pressing for improvements in existing products and would react adversely to being offered a product that was based on a radical technological change.

## Creative destruction

As a result of these discontinuities industries are characterized by **creative destruction**, or waves of new firm creation and failures, often referred to as 'shake outs'. Less entrepreneurial organizations find it difficult to switch resources to new opportunities and, instead, continue to invest heavily in existing products, and become committed to and dependent on them, even when they are in decline. Baron and Shane (2005) point out that firms are reluctant to cannibalize sales and this would explain for example, why Barnes and Noble were slow to move into online book sales, losing out to Amazon. Because such firms have considerable assets tied to a particular process they may be reluctant to change to a new technology or process and unwilling to aggressively seek a replacement that might require huge investment in new development and marketing to support it.

Tushman and Anderson (2004: 39), contrary to the opinion that revolutions usually arise outwith an industry, suggest that at the point of discontinuity the leaders in an industry will only become the losers as a result of creative destruction if the innovation is competence destroying, wiping out their considerable investments in soon-to-be obsolete skills and technology and eliminating the barriers to entry. Baron and Shane (2005) explain that the newcomer should spot and prepare to exploit those opportunities that result from breakpoints when they are at an advantage, and the established firms have no particular advantage. Dyson introduced new technology to create innovative household cleaning products, the low-cost airlines competed with major airlines, and online retailers such as Amazon challenged traditional retailing processes.

It is also important to reconfirm that at a breakpoint the bright idea, alone, does not lead automatically to commercial success. As we have seen, suppliers of a profitable existing product often defend the present, predictable revenue stream, rather than turn enthusiastically to a more risky, less predictable income stream from the replacement product. Even when they do introduce a new product, such organizations often introduce it without real commitment and fail to convince customers to change. By contrast a newcomer to the market is likely to be totally dependent on the sales of the new product and will be fully committed to its success. However, if the newcomer does not have the entrepreneurial, business and marketing skills and the necessary commercial relationships the introduction may not succeed.

An example of a competence destroying innovation is given by Drucker (2001), who comments that none of the giants of the electronic industry, such as GE (USA), Siemens and Philips (Europe) and Toshiba (Japan), who rushed into computers in the 1950s, were successful. By contrast there are plenty of large firms that are innovative, such as Johnson & Johnson in healthcare and 3M in a variety of sectors. He comments that it is not about size but about attitude; it does not come naturally but must be worked at.

## The innovation process

Over many years a number of researchers have studied innovation performance and concluded that the most successful organizations have developed innovation processes in order to address a number of challenges:

- the need for market and technological scanning to obtain early information about new opportunities and developments;
- the high cost and the need to manage finance and other resource issues;
- the uncertainty and unpredictability of the outcomes in trying to do things differently or better;
- the need to coordinate the contributions of various departments (such as research and development, operations, marketing and finance);
- the need to get the time of the launch of the new product right;
- the need to plan to allow staff the time away from their day-to-day responsibilities and the scope to carry out developments.

The value of developing a process of innovation is that if it can be defined it can be used to overcome the commercial challenges by anticipating the potential problems, and managing and controlling the various contributions to the process. Moreover, by reflecting on the successes and failures, learning from the experience thereof and continually improving them, the success rates of the new developments will increase. In practice various models of the innovation process have been developed over the years and it is to this that we now turn.

# Technology push, market pull

An early concept in the evolution of the process drew a distinction between technology push and market pull as the different drivers of innovation.

## Technology push

Often, high-technology science- and engineering-based firms pursue scientific exploration unhampered by the consideration of specific customer and market requirements. For example, small bioscience companies carry out chemistry research in the expectation of eventually producing a chemical compound that might ultimately become a commercially exploitable drug. In the early stages of development the therapeutic outcomes and actual customer benefits cannot be precisely predicted.

## Market pull

In some organizations the innovation is focused solely on meeting carefully defined customer needs. For example, a company supplying supermarkets with own-label products relies on the supermarket to forecast consumer demand. It will carry out only the development work that is necessary to satisfy the needs of the supermarket, defined in terms of a precise product specification and maximum price it is prepared to pay.

These stances might be considered to be at the opposite ends of a continuum. Most organizations adopt a stance in between these extremes and include elements of technology push and market pull. For example, in the past, pharmaceutical companies adopted the technology push stance but in more recent times they have increasingly focused on specific therapeutic areas in order to exploit a reputation for excellence in one area of therapy gained over time, for example, in cancer or anti-ulcer treatments.

Part of the reason for this is that with increasing competition a deeper understanding of patient need and response is required and more support activity may need to be provided. For example, an innovative pharmaceutical product designed to combat obesity might perform satisfactorily only if patients are prepared to change their lifestyle. The success of the product for the company is therefore dependent on providing support programmes that will help to achieve this.

Equally, suppliers of own-label products to supermarkets can increase the value of their offering by proposing technological innovations which might create a superior product to the branded product that is supposedly being 'copied'.

It can be argued that while the positions at the extremes of the continuum can provide a sustainable position for an organization they are potentially risky too. For example, unhampered exploration may never lead to a saleable product offer and meeting market needs may never allow the organization to create a competitive edge and charge premium prices.

# The innovation models

Booz, Allen and Hamilton (1982) produced the best known model of **new product development** (illustrated in Figure 3.6) and this provides the basis for the evolution of the innovation process. There are a number of key features of this model:

- It involves a systematic, linear process involving a number of stages, with decision points at each stage.
- For each stage (e.g. idea generation, setting criteria for screening, etc.), it is necessary to develop a set of operating principles, and apply the appropriate tools and techniques for choosing the option to pursue.

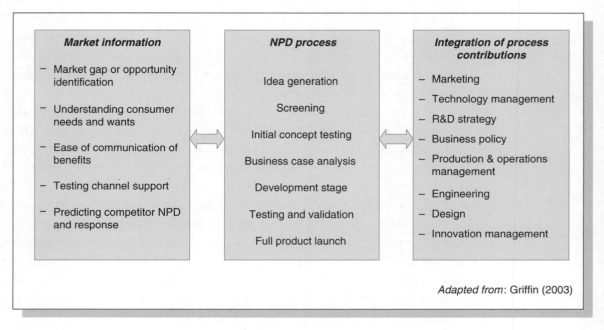

**Figure 3.6**
New product development process.

■ It is desirable to undertake the lower-cost activities such as carrying out the concept and business analysis that involve staff time only and not additional resources, very early in the process, in order to eliminate likely failures as quickly as possible, so incurring low levels of unproductive expense. Failures late in the innovation process can be very expensive.

■ Delay the most expensive activities, such as prototyping a product until there is a strong likelihood of commercialization.

■ The model separates technology push and market pull in order to ensure that the customer demand is defined separately from the technological analysis.

■ It is necessary to break up the overall process into a series of clearly defined tasks so that the activities, roles and responsibilities in the process can be managed and controlled.

There are, however, a number of problems that arise when implementing these basic models including:

■ the problem of separation of activities along functional lines within the organization, as this often leads to conflict between, for example, research and development, marketing, operations and finance. A balance has to be struck between the benefits of functional specialization against cross-function synergy in solving problems;

■ in more bureaucratic organizations the delays caused by the linear approach and the need for decisions at various stages – this can extend the time it takes to get the innovation to market with the danger that the launch might be delayed, so allowing competitors first-mover advantage;

■ the process possibly being too cumbersome for incremental changes that are better managed and controlled with a 'light touch';

■ the process overly focusing on internal activities and not adequately including external contributions from partners to the development process.

Rothwell (1992: 102) has identified the newer developments of the process which enhance the basic model by addressing some of these weaknesses. These models include:

■ parallel activity, which addresses the problem of an extended time to market. For example, the screening of the alternative designs of the final product appearance, the concept testing and the business case analysis can progress in parallel with the preparation of the launch plan where an organization must launch a new product into the market at a specific time;

■ integration of the functional responsibilities and activities – this is facilitated by setting up cross-function project teams to take joint responsibility for progressing the innovation;

■ recognition of the role and specialist contributions of outside organizations, such as suppliers, customers and advisers (specialist design, research, marketing consultancies, etc.), and the collaborations with partners, who can contribute complementary skills and expertise;

■ use of systems, particularly IT based, to facilitate the integration of the contributions, networking and information sharing and to support internal product and service concept evaluation.

## The management of innovation

Having discussed the features and evolution of the innovation process models, we now turn to the management of the process within an organization. The starting point is to develop an innovation strategy as a subset of the business strategy and, particularly, for the organization to adopt an appropriate innovation stance.

## Developing an appropriate innovation stance

Developing an appropriate attitude and stance to innovation ensures that a consistent approach to decision-making is adopted by the managers and staff in the organization. The organization's approach must achieve an appropriate balance between:

■ market context, customer demand, innovation opportunities and competition within the sector;

■ the organization's growth ambitions;

■ the organization's available resources;

■ the organization's own creativity and entrepreneurial capability.

The alternative stances are:

*Pioneers* spot market gaps, track market and technology changes and aim to be the first to introduce new products and services, and make process improvements.

*Second-in organizations* watch the pioneers and follow their lead, learning from any mistakes they make in order to improve on the first products and process improvements that are introduced to the market.

*Imitators* copy the products and service innovations with me-too products that are lower priced and usually offer customers value for money. This category includes supermarket own-label products.

*Defensive organizations* tend to watch but largely ignore the innovations going on and pursue their own path, usually in sectors that are changing little. They become involved in innovations only when it is absolutely necessary.

## Pause and Reflect 3.3

### Stepping up environmental innovation

Examples of innovation appear in all areas of activity and there are many individual contributions that can be applauded for their ingenuity and determination. Jonathan Douglas, a Sheffield Hallam University student on a STEP programme, sponsored by Shell, worked for Sheffield-based Recovery Insulation, a manufacturer and distributor of environmentally friendly recycled textile insulation material.

His job was to assist with the workshops that are the company's Schools and Homes Education Project, which runs in the region under the banner Plugging in the Sun. By discussing approaches to learning with teachers the company has been able to improve its education work, refining and developing existing products and designing new concepts, such as a solar powered barbecue, a hovercraft and a remote control plane. With innovation the benefits often go to the innovator and the organization too. In this case Jonathan was the regional winner of the STEP award and goes forward to the finals. He has been offered part-time work by the company after the project has finished, looking into new alternative energy driven concepts, including the solar powered barbecue.

*Source*: Enterprise Centre, Sheffield Hallam University

**Question:** What drives an individual to be innovative?

While larger firms would be expected to have a clearly defined stance on innovation and a well-funded innovation strategy with medium- to long-term timescales, it might be supposed that this is not necessary for start-up and early-stage firms. However, in practice it is critical. Smaller organizations must adopt a consistent stance as innovation is geared to survival and growth and must be focused on commercial success. Innovation in smaller firms is constrained by limited resources and, for example, time to market can be critical, so the R&D work should be rarely open-ended. Moreover, the failure of a critical new product, service or process, or spending more on innovation than the organization can afford can result in bankruptcy. However, as shown in Pause and Reflect 3.3, it is often the motivation of individuals that leads to success.

# The key innovation process steps

The key steps of the **innovation process** are:

- using the information available to signal the opportunities for the organization;
- considering the alternative strategic options and choosing a way forward that will encourage and support innovation;
- developing an implementation plan to efficiently manage the process.

Later in this book we deal in detail with these steps including the different contexts, and the practical application of the concepts of innovation. Here we focus on the process management issues.

## Searching for the trigger signals

As we will discuss later, deep reflection of the key information indicators is likely to be of greater benefit than superficial analysis of large quantities of information in producing the trigger signals that initiate the innovation process. Equally it is worthwhile considering many ideas at an early stage rather than prematurely deciding on one or two ideas to take forward. It is also useful to envisage an innovation 'funnel', which is wide at one end to accept many early ideas and narrow at the other as the ideas that are close to commercialization emerge, having successfully completed the various stages of the innovation process.

## Selecting from the strategic options

By the very nature of innovation there are many different directions that the organization could take. In making decisions about which options to pursue it is necessary to determine a set of criteria against which the decisions should be made.

## Assessing the strategic options in innovation

In developing a strategy for innovation it is essential that it fits with the corporate strategy of the organization and some of the key issues to ensure the acceptability, feasibility or suitability (Johnson, Scholes and Whittington, 2005) of the innovation strategy. The organization will decide which of these elements the innovation must fit. For example, a finance-driven organization may only be concerned with risk and return, whereas a production-oriented organization may only encourage innovations that result in new products it can produce.

### Fit with business strategy

Overall the innovation strategy should reflect the vision and objectives of the organization, support the development of the generic strategy (focus, differentiation and cost) and reinforce the competitive stance and market approach discussed. The competitive stance of some firms is closely associated with innovation. Enterprise in Action 1.4 showed that Gripple have the objective of 20–25 per cent of turnover coming from products that have been launched in the previous three years.

The innovation strategy should not only enable customer value (e.g. benefits and problem solution) and organization value (e.g. return on investment) to be extracted from the existing resources and capabilities, but it should facilitate the creation of assets and resources that will be useful in the future. For example, building a reputation for solving the customers' own problems can be used to generate new business.

### Portfolio management

Having set the parameters for innovation by ensuring its fit with the business, and marketing and operations strategy, a strategic approach must be taken to manage the range of innovation activities. A portfolio of activities might include:

- work on breakthrough innovations that will cause a step change in the market and the organization's performance;
- incremental innovations of products and services to keep them 'fresh' in customers' minds;
- a continuing programme of process improvement;
- some limited curiosity research undertaken by individual members of staff to explore entirely new ideas.

It is vital that staff time and financial resources devoted to these activities is balanced with other responsibilities and that the benefit to stakeholders is periodically assessed.

Without a portfolio management strategy there is a danger of:

- poor screening of ideas, so taking on too many new projects and spreading the available resources too thinly to complete a project in a reasonable timescale;

■ failure to kill off failing projects early enough, particularly the boss's 'pet projects', thus limiting the time and resources available for more promising projects;

■ lack of focus and strategic direction resulting in wasted marketing and operations costs;

■ failure to monitor, evaluate and learn good practice in managing the innovation process and the failure to improve the success rate of new projects.

## Implementation

The implementation stage of the innovation strategy is concerned with managing and supporting the innovation process. A number of studies highlight the following essential elements of effective innovation process implementation. For example, Griffin (1998) suggests that the best companies:

■ had better success rates with 80 per cent vs 53 per cent for the rest of firms studied, so concluding that practice and repeating the process improves success rates;

■ reduced the time to market for new products by 30 per cent in five years;

■ had higher revenue contributions from new products – 50 per cent vs 25 per cent for the rest;

■ used a version of the innovation process;

■ had a specific strategy;

■ had multifunctional teams;

■ were using more market research to become more customer-driven and engineering tools to automate design and prototyping.

## The lessons of success in the innovation process

Despite employing well-qualified staff and operating a highly resourced research and development department, some of the largest, well-established organizations find it difficult to develop an effective innovation process that routinely commercializes new innovations. By contrast others appear to repeatedly and successfully introduce new developments. It is useful for entrepreneurial organizations to learn these lessons of success and avoid making the same mistakes as the failures. In looking at the critical success factors in innovation, identified in a number of innovation studies, Tidd, Bessant and Pavitt (2005: 87) suggest that, while there is considerable variation in innovation across different sectors, the following conclusions can be reached.

- Innovation needs to be regarded and managed as a process rather than as a single event or series of events.
- The outcomes of the process can be improved by good management.
- Success routines can be learned over time through the experience of repeating the process steps and will result, for example, in launching new products faster and more reliably.
- Effective integration of the contributions to the process is an essential ingredient.

In support of these steps the following are essential.

- A system of data-gathering supported by analysis – this will provide the trigger to a new product development project.
- The project should have a strategic fit with the firm's capabilities, resources and strategies, as discussed earlier.
- Continual monitoring and management of the project.
- Decisions are needed periodically to decide when the project should be continued, be terminated or be accelerated through the allocation of substantial additional funds.
- The new product launch programme must be a success and thorough and detailed planning is needed to ensure this.
- Periodic reviews of the innovation process, activities and management should be carried out in order to maximize the organization's learning.
- The whole innovation management process must be systematic and not ad hoc.

The following dangers apply.

- An organization that over-focuses on leading-edge technological R&D may fail to place sufficient emphasis on meeting customers' more functional, technically less demanding needs. This can be particularly the case for smaller firms that are managed by staff with a strong technical background, who find R&D challenges more interesting than the commercialization challenge of meeting customer needs in a competitive environment.
- Some firms are dismissive of ideas and innovations generated outside the firm and adopt a 'not invented here' approach.

- In some organizations innovation is the responsibility of one particular department. In this case they may miss out on the innovative capacity of the organization as a whole.
- The concept of 'the boss knows best' often results in the ideas of senior managers being progressed, even when they are not appropriate, and other staff being unwilling to contribute ideas as they will be considered worthless or unimportant by comparison.
- Some organizations devote the majority of resources to breakthrough rather than incremental innovation. Some firms expect the innovators, like magicians, to produce a rabbit out of the hat to get the firm out of trouble or suddenly improve its fortunes. If this breakthrough fails to materialize there is no fall-back position.
- Taking a narrow view of the strategic objectives of innovation might mean that spin-off opportunities and opportunities that result from mistakes are not exploited.
- Some firms fail to recognize the benefit of collaborative innovation and networking between different organizations.

## Reasons for failure in innovation

Many large organizations believe that it is controlling and getting the most out of the resources that they own that is the best route to success, effectively maximizing their return on investment. The danger, of course, is that too much effort can be spent on trying to obtain a return from the existing assets, which may now be obsolete (doing better what we do now – even though it might not be what the market wants), and too little effort spent on pursuing opportunities to generate returns in the future which might involve doing things differently.

As Figure 3.7 shows, doing things differently might be in direct conflict with many of the objectives of the organization – to control resources by using tried and tested methods. The result is a risk-averse approach, in which innovation is limited by the organization's management approach and rigid processes, and by the limited ambitions of the managers, who may be concerned at the effect an innovation failure might have on their future careers. While recognizing the importance of innovation, large organizations live off past successes and use their huge resources to insulate themselves from immediate market pressures, often by acquiring competitors or fast-growing entrepreneurial companies. Many public sector organizations use the excuse of

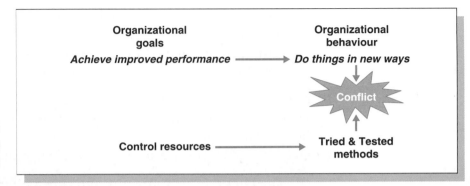

**Figure 3.7**
Innovation and
organizational
conflict.

'political pressures' to justify their failure to develop creative solutions to problems and fall back on simply fulfilling their responsibilities for delivering routine services in the same old way. In both cases, however, the risk of doing something and it not working can be greater than the risk of doing nothing. Smaller organizations often realize that they have to innovate merely to survive, so the risk of doing nothing is far greater than the risk of getting an innovation wrong.

## The challenges in managing innovation

Whether the organization is large or small there are a number of practical challenges in generating new products, services and processes and in **managing innovation** generally, including:

- picking the winners from the many ideas that might be suggested;
- developing appropriate organizations, structures or teams capable of effectively exploiting new ideas;
- developing stimulating climates in the organization to encourage innovation and avoid a 'blame' culture;
- accessing finance and deciding how much to spend;
- deciding when to terminate projects;
- meeting timescales during the process and being first to market;
- handling the interface between the business functions and departments and handling the conflict that sometimes arises;
- working out how to cope with uncertain technologies and unpredictable outcomes;
- deciding when to employ external technological and business expertise and learning how to manage it;
- communicating internally and externally the strategies and support available and the successes achieved;

- ensuring that top management are committed to and lead innovation as a corporate-wide task;
- giving individuals more responsibility for new product development.

In entrepreneurial organizations gaining commitment is usually not a problem but persuading the entrepreneur to 'let go' and involve others can be more difficult.

In larger organizations Drucker (2001: 138) comments on:

- the importance of structure and cites a number of firms, such as Johnson & Johnson and 3M, who set up new business units to exploit innovation. This is illustrated in Spotlight 3.2;
- the importance of having a high focus for the innovative business unit to enable support and fast decision-making from the top executives;
- keeping the new venture away from the burdens that it is not able to carry.

and explains that organizations should avoid:

- mixing entrepreneurship and management;
- innovations that cause the organization to diversify its activities too much; and
- buying in entrepreneurial companies, because this usually does not work.

---

## Spotlight 3.2

### The different structures for innovation

One dilemma for large organizations is how to structure to maximize their innovation activity. There are a number of different approaches in the food and drink manufacturing sector, as listed below.

- The Brand marketing manager is responsible for new product development in Kraft, Unilever, Bestfoods and Procter & Gamble.
- An innovation team reports to the marketing director, in McVities, Diageo and Nestle.
- An innovation team reports to the board in Coca-Cola Great Britain.
- Some global companies, such as Unilever, hand responsibility to one country. For example, the UK handles Lynx deodorants, while France handles the shampoo sector, including Sunsilk.
- Skunkworks: Some firms follow the Drucker view and set up totally separate units, such as Unilever Ventures, physically outside the other offices in order to maximize independence and creativity.

*Adapted from*: Murphy C., 'Innovation masterminds', *Marketing*, 15 May 2003

**Question:** What are the arguments for and against having a totally separate innovation business?

The successful innovators recognize the critical importance of effective marketing and operations management, including:

- gaining deep insights into user needs, expectations and attitudes, recognizing multiple levels of customers such as wholesalers, retailers and consumers and different roles and expectations in the purchasing and usage decisions of the technical specifier, quality controller, user, financial controller, order approver;
- carrying out more thorough development and design work in order to meet these needs and expectations;
- the ability to effectively launch new products, services or processes, to provide effective after-sales servicing and to generate repeat purchasing through effective marketing communication, pricing and distribution;
- protecting the newly launched product or service using patents and/or other aggressive marketing behaviour;
- focusing on targeting and capitalizing upon high margin markets.

Successful innovators also recognize the importance of building alliances and collaborations with outside partners, which can work well if carried out in a planned and structured way. Collaborations can be problematic, however, if there are unclear objectives, lack of shared understanding of complementary expertise and roles, a failure to monitor performance and suspicion about the other party's motives. Collaborations are risky but can be more rewarding if the organizations involved contribute complementary expertise.

Ultimately, success in innovation is the result of having staff with the generic and specific skills and abilities of innovation, and managers, who are capable of getting the best out of the available resources and the entrepreneurial abilities to ensure that the ideas are exploited. The skills that are needed for managing innovation have been identified by Tidd, Bessant and Pavitt (2005) and are listed in Figure 3.8.

## Summary

- Innovations can be valuable in all areas of activity and success is dependent on matching the innovation to the context in which it is exploited.
- Innovation is a corporate-wide activity involving all the functions of the business and includes technological and non-technological ideas that offer customers significant benefits.

- Recognizing the environmental triggers of change
- Aligning the innovation with the business strategy
- Acquiring the knowledge assets to fill gaps in the organization's resources
- Generating knowledge in-house
- Choosing the most suitable company response to the opportunity
- Executing the company projects that will deliver a solution
- Implementing the necessary changes in the company to ensure the success of the project
- Learning through evaluation and reflection in order to make improvements to the innovation process
- Developing the organization by embedding the structures, processes and underlying culture

*Adapted from*: Tidd J., Bessant J. and Pavitt K. (2005: 84) *Managing Innovation*, 3rd edn. John Wiley.

**Figure 3.8**
Core abilities in
managing innovation.

■ New innovations can cause significant disruption for the customer purchasing and usage patterns and for the organization's operations and this must be recognized in the innovation strategy.

■ Effective and efficient management of innovation is improved by following a process and 'practising' innovation.

■ Organizations must decide what innovation stance to adopt and ensure that it fits with their situation and objectives.

■ Critical to an organization's approach to innovation is a culture in which there is:

a fundamental and sustained commitment to innovation
a willingness to accept risks
an ability and willingness to commit resources
a degree of flexibility
top management commitment.

## Chapter questions

1. Explain the concepts of technical discontinuities and industry breakpoints. Using examples from one sector explain how the opportunities that result from them can be exploited by an entrepreneurial organization.

2. Choose an organization that you consider to be very innovative. How has it achieved success so far and how can this be maintained in the future?

3. With a track record of successful entrepreneurship you have taken over responsibility for an organization that has a poor

record of innovation. Explain the issues you would expect to have to resolve and the key actions that you would take to achieve a more innovative culture within the company.

4. As a speaker at a conference of managers of small- and medium-sized organizations from both public and private sectors, you have been asked to give a talk entitled 'Innovation in the small organization'. Prepare the slides for your talk and include notes that refer to the important concepts you wish the delegates to remember and examples to illustrate the points you make.

5. As a newly appointed town centre manager in a run-down region of the country explain the steps you would take to begin the process of regeneration.

## Case study

### Mobile breakthroughs

The mobile-phone industry provides an excellent example of innovation and illustrates many of its concepts. The industry has given the opportunity for many entrepreneurial organizations to achieve spectacular growth over the period since the introduction of the first mobile phone. It is a little more than a decade ago that phones became truly mobile. Old films show the early mobile phone as a contraption the size of a brick used only by the most powerful business executives. In the early days phones were simply used for talking and it seemed that it was only business executives that needed to be constantly in touch. A key development was having a phone in the car.

Today the mobile phone is a multifunction essential gadget that is capable of delivering almost every communication need or a universal must-have accessory, and which is a target for many thieves.

In the early days of mobile phones Jorma Ollila was the chief executive of a small diversified Finnish conglomerate. He had a vision to make Nokia the world's leading maker of mobile phones. Nokia was one of the fastest growing companies of the decade and in 2003 shipped 160 million handsets, more than twice that shipped by Motorola, the next largest competitor. Nokia, like other hardware and software manufacturers, used the latest technology to develop and manufacture miniaturized multifunction products.

As the products became fashion items for young adults and teenagers, design was critical and Nokia lost market share substantially in 2004 after it failed to develop a clam shell design, which swept the market. Technology and design breakthroughs continue as the 3G phones enable Internet access and the transfer of photographs, audio and video clips. The functionality of these phones is being enhanced as the communications technology is being combined with better photographic and screen technology and integration with mobile audio devices, such as the iPod.

Having swept through the developed countries, market development in emerging markets such as India and China is now key. But, as the market matures, the barriers to entry are falling and in these emerging markets entrepreneurs are developing competitive products offering high value for specific customer segments.

The breakthroughs in the industry have not been restricted to new technology and design. The growth of service providers, such as Vodafone, has been phenomenal too. Vodafone's growth has been driven by effective marketing and recruitment of customers, using a myriad of different contracts and partnerships with mobile-phone suppliers that enabled them to give away phones within the service contract as the bait to hook high-call revenue. Competition between service providers increased as new entrants offered 'free minutes'.

A significant breakthrough was achieved by 'Pay-as-you-go', which challenged some industry assumptions. In a similar way to other utilities, the customers of fixed-line suppliers had contracts, paid a monthly rental charge for the line and then paid for calls on top. Prepayment for mobile phones enabled customers to have more control over their expenditure and so led to the mobile phone becoming a children's and teenagers' 'must-have'.

Perhaps one of the most surprising breakthroughs, because its success was not predicted, has been texting. It was never imagined that this technology would be embraced so enthusiastically by teenagers, who often even prefer to text rather than talk to their friend standing next to them. For some customers the criteria for choosing a mobile phone is not the design or multifunctionality but the speed at which they are able to text.

At the same time as these major breakthroughs there has been a continual stream of small-scale innovations in every aspect of the sector.

*Source*: Robin Lowe from various public sources

### Questions

1. Use the concepts discussed in the chapter to explain the nature of innovation in the mobile-phone sector. Among other concepts, you might include, for example, some explanation of technological discontinuity and non-technological breakpoints, life cycles, alliances and innovation stances.
2. Why in general have the entrepreneurial organizations, such as Vodafone and Nokia, been more successful in the mobile market than the former state-owned telecommunications businesses?
3. What do you expect to be the next breakpoint in the sector? Justify your answer from your reflections on customer demands, competition and environmental changes, such as technological developments.

## References and further reading

Baron R.A. and Shane S.A. (2005) *Entrepreneurship: A Process Perspective.* Mason OH: Thomson South-Western.

Bolton B. and Thompson J. (2003) *The Entrepreneur in Focus: Achieve your Potential.* London: Thomson.

Booz E.G., Allen J.L. and Hamilton C.L. (1982) *New Product Management for the 1980s.* New York: Booz Allen Hamilton Inc.

Christensen C.M. (1997) *The Innovator's Dilemma: When New Technologies Cause Great Firms to Fail.* Boston MA: Harvard Business School Press.

Cooper R. (2001) *Winning at New Products.* London: Kogan Page.

Drucker P. (2001) *The Essential Drucker.* Oxford: Butterworth-Heinemann.

Foster R. (1986) *Innovation: The Attacker's Advantage.* New York: Summit Books.

DTI (2003) Economic Paper No. 7, Competing in the Global Economy: the innovation challenge, November, sourced at http://www.dti.gov.uk/economics/economics_paper7.pdf

DTI (2003) Innovation Report: Competing in the Global Economy: the innovation challenge, 17 December, sourced at http://www.dti.gov.uk/innovationreport/

Griffin A. (1998) Overview of PDMA survey on best practices. In: *Visions*, Product Development Management Association. www.pdma.org

Griffin A. (2003) Marketing's role in new product development and product decisions. In: D. Hoffman *et al.*, *Marketing Best Practice*. Mason OH: Thomson South-Western.

Innovation Report – Competing in the Global Economy: the Innovation Challenge, Online Update, Feb 2005. http://www.innovation.gov.uk/

Johnson G., Scholes K. and Whittington, R. (2005) *Exploring Corporate Strategy*, 7th edn. London: Financial Times Prentice Hall.

Porter M. (1990) *The Competitive Advantage of Nations*. London: Macmillan.

Robertson R.S. (1967) The process of innovation and the diffusion of innovation. *Journal of Marketing* **3**(1): 14–19.

Rothwell R. (1992) Successful industrial innovation: critical success factors for the 1990s. *R&D Management* **22**(3): 221–239.

Strebel P. (1996) Breakpoint: how to stay in the game. *Financial Times*, Mastering Management, part 17, pp. 13–14.

Tidd J., Bessant J. and Pavitt K. (2005) *Managing Innovation*, 3rd edn. Chichester: Wiley.

Tushman M.L. and Anderson P. (2004) *Managing Strategic Innovation and Change*, 2nd edn. New York: Oxford University Press.

Utterback J. (1994) *Mastering the Dynamics of Innovation*. Boston MA: Harvard Business School Press, p. 256.

Wickham P.A. (2004) *Strategic Entrepreneurship*, 3rd edn. London: FT/Prentice Hall.

## Key words

adding value

architectural innovation

creative destruction

creativity

disruptive technology

incremental innovation

industry breakpoints

innovation

innovation process

intangible benefits

managing innovation

new product development

organization benefits

paradigm innovation

position innovation

process innovation

product innovation

product life cycle

step change innovation

tangible benefits

technological discontinuities

## CHAPTER 4

# Learning, decision-making and leadership

By the end of this chapter the reader will be able to:

- explain how thought processes affect individual learning and decision-making;
- understand how organizations can harness individual learning capabilities for competitive advantage;
- understand how entrepreneurial organizations manage the tensions and ambiguity in maintaining core business whilst investing in innovation;
- identify the characteristics of successful learning organizations;
- evaluate the role that the development of a robust learning capability has in the successful identification and implementation of entrepreneurial strategies.

## Introduction

Although the literature has produced a considerable body of theory and practice relating to the subject of learning organizations, a lot less attention has been paid to understanding the role of learning in the process of entrepreneurship, particularly in small organizations. It seems that the capacity for entrepreneurs to learn from their experiences is a fundamental behaviour that is crucial to their ability to succeed. They learn from all aspects of their experiences, such as their networks, the problems they face and resolve, and (critically) from their mistakes. The focus for their learning is the decisions they make.

Throughout this book we discuss the fact that most successful organizations have developed the capability to make incremental changes to their products, services and processes, but relatively few manage to make the really crucial step-changes that transform the way markets operate. We have suggested that the ability to make breakthrough innovations (in products or in processes) in part or in whole may be attributable to the way organizations (as collectives of individuals) learn from events that surround them and the choices they make. Transformational learning is a rare phenomenon. It is unusual to find people eagerly challenging long held beliefs and assumptions and behaving in radically different ways. Commonly, what happens is that a few adjustments to behaviour are made, almost in a tokenistic way, and much goes on the way it always did. While the inertia, power and market influence of large bureaucratic organizations mean they can 'muddle through' in this way, entrepreneurial organizations cannot survive without innovation and critical decisions.

To understand why it is that entrepreneurial organizations seem to be able to sift the signals from the environment, synthesize the conflicting messages, make a decision and take action more quickly than their competitors, it is necessary to explore a number of issues.

First, we will consider how individuals differ in their approaches to learning, how their individual creativity can be developed, and how the habits of thinking can affect the way in which decisions are made. Specifically we consider whether entrepreneurs apply their learning differently from other managers when making choices.

We then move on to look at organizations and how they can remain competitive whilst encouraging innovation. To innovate, an organization needs to be outward looking by focusing on changes in its market and in the environment in order to anticipate and plan for the future. But it also has to focus on maintaining profitability, managing products out that are no longer needed, and unlearning business practices that are no longer appropriate, developing internal capability and capacity to succeed when the future is uncertain. This suggests some degree of 'navel-gazing'. One of the difficulties presented by investing in innovation is the tension between resourcing this development activity and maintaining the core business. The effective management of these tensions is critical for entrepreneurial organizations.

This leads on to the role of leadership in entrepreneurial organizations. After taking all the decisions and carrying out the tasks during the start-up phase, the entrepreneur faces the challenges of delegating tasks and decision-making to the management team. Moreover, the implementation of entrepreneurial strategies requires the entrepreneur and other strategic leaders to provide an environment in which the abilities of the creative thinkers in the organization are able to flourish. The team must also be 'managed' in a way that maximizes their contribution to the effectiveness of the organization.

Isolated innovations may not transform the culture of the organization, but sustaining innovation over time depends upon the ability to develop and sustain learning capability. We discuss the values necessary to maintain the commitment to learning and innovation and why it is that some organizations can harness the knowledge and creativity of their employees, gaining their commitment, and exploiting this to secure competitive advantage whereas others fail to develop an effective learning organization.

Finally, we explore the links between organizational learning and the successful implementation of entrepreneurial strategies in the longer term by considering how important learning capability is to entrepreneurial success, and how organizations can permanently embed learning in their strategic thinking.

## The nature of individual learning and enterprise

The starting point in considering the relationship between learning and enterprise, entrepreneurship and innovation is to define what the differences are in the **skills, knowledge and attitudes** that are needed to be considered enterprising compared with the everyday skills, knowledge, and attitudes that all managers have.

Entrepreneurship and innovation are, ultimately, about enterprising people behaving in enterprising ways and so if this difference can be defined, it might be possible to help more people to learn how to become more enterprising. For this reason we return to education. Earlier we alluded to the fact that the UK government are pursuing policies that are designed to encourage enterprise in schools. The Office for Standards in Education (Ofsted) suggests that enterprise is 'the ability to handle uncertainty and respond positively to change, to create and implement new ideas and new ways of doing things, to make reasonable risk/reward assessments and act upon them in a variety of contexts, both personal and work'.

This definition suggests that enterprise might be something that is skills-based. It is certainly something to do with action and doing things. We have suggested that the way entrepreneurs and intrapreneurs process information and use it in making decisions, and the way they reflect on their knowledge and actions may be crucial in distinguishing them from managers in general. In this chapter we will look at learning in both an individual and an organizational context, and the role it plays in the successful implementation of entrepreneurial strategies.

## Skills, knowledge and attitudes

Bolton and Thompson (2003: 74) argue that entrepreneurship is a function not only of temperament or talent but of technique. Talents are natural abilities, things that people are born with, and temperament reflects their needs and drives. Using the analogy of a crystal, Bolton and Thompson argue that talent and temperament make the entrepreneur what he or she is. Temperament has to be managed if the most is to be made of talent. If we identify people with the right talents and temperament, we can improve their techniques to add value; returning to the crystal analogy, the craftsman's techniques transform a rough diamond into a very valuable one. With entrepreneurs Bolton and Thompson suggest that even with exceptional talent, inappropriate temperament can be their downfall. Conversely, the right temperament can compensate for lesser talent. Technique can be the vital link between the two. Bolton and Thompson liken this to a sports coach, who can not only impart the techniques that develop talent, but helps the athlete to manage temperament. However, they remind us that talent and temperament should be enhanced by technique rather than diminished; they see a danger in concentrating on technique at the expense of spontaneity and creativity. Too great a focus on technique can lead to the entrepreneur relying less on instinct; it is important to accept that mistakes will occur and that they can be learning experiences.

In our view, people may be born with a certain temperament but they do not have to behave in accordance with it on every occasion. They can, as Bolton and Thompson suggest, learn to manage their temperament. This 'managed temperament' is what we refer to as **attitude**.

We also believe that, although entrepreneurs do exhibit certain talents, there are many individuals who have talents that lie dormant, unexplored and unrecognized. Talent is part of the story, but life opportunity and experience dictate whether it is ever uncovered. Talent has to be recognized if it is to be put to use. If an individual's education or life experience does not afford them an opportunity to uncover and practise that talent, it will wither on the vine. If Beethoven had never encountered a piano, would his musical talent have been recognized? As such, we believe that knowledge and experience should not be overlooked. **Knowledge** encompasses not only the natural talents that an entrepreneur has, but the experience and understanding that they have acquired. This combination gives them a unique resource to draw on at any particular moment in time.

The third element is **skills**. We have considered the talents, experience, temperament and preferred behaviour of entrepreneurs, but if they cannot employ these successfully to achieve a desired outcome then all is in vain. If they perceive an opportunity through their knowledge and understanding of an industry, have the desire to turn that into a commercial proposition, but have no negotiating skills or are unable to assemble resources, it is unlikely that they will be able to exploit it successfully. At the point of entrepreneurial choice, it is the combination of their knowledge, attitude and skills that determines the action actually taken.

## Intuition and luck

Coulter (2003: 91) emphasizes the value of **intuition** on generating ideas, where we subconsciously make decisions based on our accumulated knowledge and experiences. It is often referred to as gut feeling and can be a powerful source of ideas, when used appropriately. The most successful entrepreneurs also often comment that they were lucky in having the right idea at the right time. The truth is that structured idea generation combined with intuition is probably the successful approach to idea generation and, undoubtedly, leads to lucky breaks too.

In practice, it is the balance between these and intuition that defines entrepreneurial and innovative capability. The question is how much of this can be learned, and how effectively the skills can be transferred to different contexts (see Enterprise in Action 4.1).

## Enterprise in Action 4.1

### Learning to do a deal

Alicia Rossman is 18, and has been earning cash by mowing lawns for the last three years with an old push mower. Unable to afford a new mower, she walked into the corporate offices of a dealership and asked them to give her a riding lawnmower for free, producing a business card and offering to mention the company in her fliers. The general manager was a little taken aback, but she presented her case well, she 'could talk the talk'. If she can get insurance they are going to reward her initiative by giving her one.

Rossman said that she would never have had the nerve to do it if it hadn't been for an after-school business programme that she had been involved in. She and a group of friends had set up and run a bookmark business. They had to form a company, seek out funding, develop and produce a product and sell it, liquidating their assets six weeks later with the profits going to charity. Representatives from local businesses acted as mentors to the various groups of students. They made magnetic bookmarks for 18 cents and sold them for $2.00. Expecting to sell 500, they actually ended up making a profit of more than $1300 dollars on over 1100 sales.

She said that she had learned that 'it's not hard to approach the owner of a business. All you need is the courage to talk to them, and if they say no, then oh, well. But if they say yes it's a good thing you asked'.

*Adapted from*: Scott Brooks, 'Junior business leaders achieve success',
*The Union Leader* (Manchester NH), 30 May 2005

**Questions:** Which aspects of Alicia's skills, knowledge, and attitude were critical? Is this true of all entrepreneurial actions?

## The alternative education approaches

Enterprise in Action 4.1 highlights the relationship between learned skills, attitudes, and knowledge. It also draws our attention to how important the education system can be in fostering talent.

The education system that most of us have grown up with teaches logical, deductive thinking, and those who flourish within it become very well practised at the art. By contrast, few are really exposed to **lateral thinking**, a term that was introduced by Edward De Bono. It describes an alternative approach to problems, coming at them from a different angle. In De Bono's opinion, schools need to do a better job at teaching thinking skills (see Spotlight 4.1).

### Spotlight 4.1

**More enterprising approaches to education?**

De Bono wants to teach people to think creatively. He argues that the brain is not inherently logical; it is more like a machine that recognizes patterns and moves from one pattern to the next rather unpredictably. He also suggests that every creative idea is logical in hindsight, and uses science as an example. Scientific papers are written in a very logical way, but the substance of them was born from experimentation and based on hunches, imagination and often accidents and luck.

He argues that education has been too much concerned with reactive thinking. It has been about information and right or wrong answers, and so analysis, critical thinking and logical deduction have been emphasized at the expense of perceptual skills. Many people in education and business have relied on analysis not only to solve problems, but to generate ideas, but this does not fit with the way the brain works. The mind can only see what it is prepared to see, and to a large degree this is shaped by what has gone before. When there is a scientific breakthrough we often realize that much of the data we needed to make that breakthrough had been available for a long time, but we had been blind to it because we were trapped in the habits of our old way of thinking. These paradigm shifts are vital to creativity and innovation, and yet we seem willing to leave them to chance.

Critical thinking is insufficient to bring about true creative thinking also, because it can focus on one element that we feel is not quite right and ignore the rest. This also can lead us to believe that if we cannot see faults we cannot improve. De Bono reminds us that the opposite of 'why' is 'po' – looking forward to what might be, which is only partly based on what currently is. We need to be able to perceive better alternatives, different futures. Education then ceases to be a question of 'Have I got this right?' but a process of exploration – 'I can think about this'.

He feels that thinking can be improved by attention and practice just as other skills can. The brain naturally seeks to form patterns and to use them, not to cut across them, and so creativity is not a natural process. We can use a number of techniques to help us to challenge our preferred patterns of thinking – for example, his six thinking hats approach, which puts different contexts around an issue, asking people to adopt a different mindset in each case. Once we accept that truth is not objective but subjective, based on perception and emotion, we can challenge our prejudices, our habits of thinking, and become more prepared to see new concepts. He suggests that it might be useful to 'learn backwards', working from the known to the unknown rather than the other way around.

*Adapted from*: De Bono E. (1991) *I am Right. You are Wrong*. Penguin: London

**Question:** What aspects of this approach are relevant for entrepreneurs?

The government is concerned to encourage **enterprise in education**, and concurs with the findings of the Davies Review of Enterprise in the Economy and Education (Feb 2002) that effort to build a deeper and wider enterprise culture must begin in schools. Although extra funding has been made available, and some excellent initiatives are being piloted, one has to wonder whether these 'add-ons' are sufficient, or whether a more radical rethink of the way we educate our young people is required if we are serious about stimulating enterprise.

One initiative which appears to be having some impact on the way children learn has been piloted in Sheffield (see Enterprise in Action 4.2). This appears to be successful in developing a more autonomous approach to learning.

## Enterprise in Action 4.2

### The 4 Rs

Mosborough Primary School in Sheffield has been participating in a project called 'Building Learning Power' which is based on the work of Professor Guy Claxton. The project is based on the premise that children will become better learners if they develop the following:

*Resilience*:  knowing how to stick with things and work through difficulties. This includes being able to become absorbed in learning, to manage distractions, to notice patterns and details in experience, and to persevere in the face of difficulties.

*Resourcefulness*:  being able to learn in different ways, and to use internal and external resources. This includes being able to ask questions, see connections between things, using your imagination, call up reasoning skills to think methodically and examine arguments, and draw on the full range of resources in the wider world.

*Reflectiveness*:  being ready and willing to plan, take stock, and draw on your experiences as a learner in order to get the best out of yourself. This includes thinking about where you are going and how you are going to get there, being flexible, distilling the essential features of what you are learning, and knowing how you learn.

*Reciprocity*:  being ready and willing to learn alone or with other people. This means knowing when it is best to learn on your own or with others, knowing how to collaborate, understanding how to listen to others, and constructively imitating other people's methods and values.

Sue Marriott: various public sources

**Question:** When is the right time to build enterprise skills?

## Lateral leaders

Michalski (2005) characterizes lateral and vertical leaders, the **lateral leader** having some similarities with the people we are describing as entrepreneurs. He describes them as inspiring others, leading from alongside, encouraging constructive dissent, rewarding risk-taking, sharing prestige, being focused on the creativity and innovation of the team in reaching goals, and looking for ideas from anywhere. He says that 'Today's president, CEO or managing director needs to be a disruptive influence, having the imagination, vision and courage to lead the organization to new territory'.

## The link with professional development

Much of this has resonance with the principles of **reflective practice**, required by many professional bodies as part of their commitment to encouraging continuing professional and personal development. They see the need to continue to challenge the tried and tested methods, rules and regulations to see if these are still as relevant today as they were when they were first established, probably many years ago. Professional development should focus on encouraging their members, both organizations and individuals, not just to do things more efficiently, but more effectively.

## Personal reflection

The principles of reflective practice are to encourage individuals to think about their thinking, and to bring their assumptions out into the open so that they (and possibly their peers) can scrutinize and where appropriate, challenge these assumptions. Unfortunately the worst part of ignorance is that people do not realize that they suffer from it; they often are unaware of the consequences of their actions and do not realize the impact that their patterns of behaviour are having unless this is brought to their attention. We have already talked about how the brain filters information, and how people can become trapped into habits of thinking. Reflective practice encourages individuals to explore and test the validity of their perceptions.

## The process of reflection

Many people engage in reflection, but much of it happens unconsciously. It is a very personal process, looking at experiences, analysing what went well or not so well, and taking the learning from this forward to improve the process next time around. It encourages individuals to recognize the role they played in events, and consider how the outcome of events may have been changed by alterations in their own actions, attitudes or behaviour.

*Formalizing the process:* This is a process of consciously reviewing not only what actually happened, but why it happened, and of exploring the feelings that emerged and why those feelings were engendered; the similarities to or differences from other experiences (in similar or in different contexts); what the consequences of choosing different behaviours might have been; what the implications are for future action; and (importantly) how a better outcome could be secured next time around.

*Alone or with peers:* Sometimes it is appropriate to go through the process alone, but often individuals can be over- or under-critical or focus on the wrong issues. Often it helps to have someone to help to probe the issues, to challenge preconceptions about self, behaviour, and actions, and to pose the 'what if?' questions.

*Taking time:* One of the important aspects of reflection is that it introduces a slight time lag. This might not seem to be a good thing in business, but perhaps this interval in which time is taken (albeit briefly) to challenge assumptions before hastening to action, is just the interlude needed for creativity to flourish. A pause for reflection can prevent us from premature action. There is a difference between this 'pause for thought' and inertia, which would lead to stagnation as opposed to innovation.

*Experimentation:* Reflection can be part of action-centred learning, with the idea of breaking down a complex activity into a series of tasks and then reflecting on each separately. A key part of this is experimentation, in which there is a deliberate attempt to try something different in order to get a better result. Experimentation involves reflecting on the situation and deciding what could be tried differently, however small, doing it and then learning from the experience as Enterprise in Action 4.3 shows.

## Enterprise in Action 4.3

### Learning through experimentation

The salesman for an entrepreneurial business visited the buyer of its major customer, a national retail pharmacy chain, every month and had a good and successful relationship. Every three months, however, there was a formal meeting, which he had to attend with his boss, the owner of the entrepreneurial organization, the buyer, and the purchasing director. The salesman dreaded these meetings because the purchasing director would berate him for an hour detailing everything that was wrong with the company, its products, the way they did business and, particularly, how he failed as a salesman. It was all part of the game to put the supplier at a disadvantage in price negotiations as the director knew how valuable the business was. For the salesman it was very embarrassing as his boss expected him to be able to manage the customer better. He faced the problem of how to get the relationship with the director on the same footing as he had with the buyer.

Attending an interpersonal skills training course, the salesman discussed this with the trainer, who explained that it is easier to verbally attack someone who is sitting at the opposite side of a table than someone who is sitting alongside. The salesman and his boss had always sat on one side of the table, while the buyer and the purchasing director sat on the other side.

When they were shown into the room for the next meeting the salesman and his boss sat on opposite sides of the table, so that the purchasing director had to sit next to the salesman and would be less able to verbally attack at such close range. At this meeting the problems were discussed and resolved in a more businesslike way. While not expecting this approach to work every time the salesman had learned the value of experimentation.

*Source*: Robin Lowe

**Question:** Do you carry out experiments of this nature and learn from them?

In terms of survival and growth of the business, given the importance of the customer, the relationship with the purchasing director could be critical. This experiment and seemingly insignificant innovation could have been a critical event for the organization.

## Making choices

In making choices, at first there are many options and it is not unusual to feel unsure as to which is the most appropriate action to take. The desire to find new ideas leads to a state of tension when they do not spring forward immediately. Often, ideas surface in periods of reflection, as with Archimedes and his Eureka moment in the bath, when the subconscious mind can synthesize information. The process is one where previous experience is not rendered irrelevant, but is only allowed to inform rather than shape current thinking. It is only human to want to fill the void with something certain, some knowledge that enables action to be taken, relieves the tension, and restores a more comfortable state of mind. This temptation needs to be resisted in order to give ideas the time to surface.

## Overcoming the fear of failure

Entrepreneurs learn from their experience and this, of necessity, requires them to take action. There is a danger in lengthy procrastination; perfect information will never be available. Entrepreneurs recognize when they have 'good enough' information; they rely on their own judgement and are willing to be accountable for it. They accept that this might mean that they will sometimes fail, but they do not let that fear stop them. If many ideas are brought forward, it is inevitable that some will fail. However, it is also more likely that one will be transformational! They see failure as a point for reflection and learning.

# Critical incidents

**Critical incidents** are another opportunity for learning that entrepreneurs often quote as being fundamental on their route to success. Some event may occur, either in their business or personal life, that causes them to take stock and reflect. This need not be a major life event, but it is a critical one as it changes perspectives. For Dee Dawson (see Enterprise in Action 9.3) the critical event was the loss of her husband's lucrative business; Richard Branson reputedly decided that airlines might be a useful business proposition when his flight to the Virgin Islands was cancelled and he made a small profit by hiring a plane and selling tickets to the other passengers. This introduces a different perspective to their thinking which sometimes is the catalyst to new ideas, which can then be exploited commercially.

## Leadership and learning capability

If we accept that creativity and innovation are unique resources that must be exploited effectively to develop entrepreneurial success, we must consider the extent to which leaders and managers encourage the cooperation and collaboration that are essential to support creative capability in organizations.

In practice some entrepreneurs find it difficult to delegate and wish to take every decision themselves. These entrepreneurs equate leadership with managing detail, and often pride themselves as being 'hands-on', with apparent disregard for the fact that this can demotivate the people that work alongside them. Such involvement may well be necessary in a start-up situation but may become a liability as the organization grows. It becomes very difficult to be involved in the minutiae of everyday operations in fast-moving competitive markets. As the organization becomes more complex, decision-making becomes paralysed unless the entrepreneur accepts that there is a need for delegation. Richard Branson is an example of how important delegation can be in large entrepreneurial organizations. It would be impossible for him to be involved in all of his many businesses, and although he retains strict control over the Virgin brand itself, the businesses are allowed the autonomy they need to flourish.

Those who front organizations typically pursue their own vision and their own interpretations of the opportunities in the environment but, also, to a greater or lesser extent, they are able to create a climate in which the skills and ideas of those who work for the organization can flourish, maybe even generating the very capabilities which could be the source of competitive advantage.

## Vision as a driving force for learning

Senge (1990) describes the circumstances in which vision can be a driving force for learning within organizations. He argues that vision is a state that is desired because of its intrinsic worth rather than its relative worth, and that it should not be confused with competition. It is a multi-faceted concept, includes personal desires and reflects personal values. But many people feel uncomfortable discussing their visions because 'real life' is often far removed from the vision they hold dear. Senge sees this gap as the source of creative energy and calls it **creative tension** – if individuals hold true to their vision, they move reality towards it. However, some people do the opposite. Because they are uncomfortable with the emotional tension, they resolve it by diluting the vision. They convince themselves that it was rather idealistic anyway and that the current situation is not so bad after all. Within organizations this can lead to compromising goals and aspirations; rather than be the one who points out things are not going well, it is easier to pretend that things are fine and redefine the standard by which success is judged. Given that mobilizing people in support of a clear vision is one thing that characterizes entrepreneurs, then again they have a head start in innovation and in using vision positively to enhance the learning capability of the organization. Shared visions emerge from personal visions and they can be the source of commitment, energizing and enthusing whole companies. After this energization, these individuals will want to move things on, and will become frustrated if they cannot do so.

## Innovative climate

Individual learning has intrinsic value, but sustainable innovation in organizations depends on them being able to exploit the knowledge, imagination, and creativity of the people who work within them, and to do so effectively over time. Some organizations seem to be able to stifle enterprise extremely effectively. Effective leaders of innovative organizations create an **environment in which individual learning can flourish**, and systems and processes embed learning as an integral part of the strategic thinking process.

## Alternative leadership styles

We have already seen that 'typical' entrepreneurs like to retain control, and find it difficult to delegate, which may suggest a tendency towards an autocratic style of **leadership**. On the other hand, they are good networkers, and communicators, and they sweat their assets (which includes their staff) and this may suggest that they would recognize the benefits of a more consultative leadership style.

The idea of leadership implies that there is a combination of skills and personal qualities that allow some people to draw exemplary performance out of their employees better than others can in similar situations. But there are two parties to this relationship, the leaders and the led. There are no leaders without followers. As a consequence, the needs of those who are led also need to be taken into consideration. If an organization has deliberately employed innovative and enterprising people, it would seem incongruent to expect them to be content to follow orders unquestioningly, for example. This has implications for leadership styles.

Collins (2001) conducted a five-year study of companies that were able to sustain great performance. The outcome of that research was that he now questions the general assumption that transforming companies from good to great requires larger-than-life leaders, such as Iacocca at Chrysler and Welch at General Electric.

In the past, charisma and vision may have been sufficient. In some small organizations this may still be the case. But in the more successful entrepreneurial organizations, the required style of leadership is different.

Organizations are driven more by the needs of customers, and there is a need for managers and employees to cooperate to meet these increasingly sophisticated demands. Teamwork becomes crucial, and the contributions of people at all levels in the organization must be recognized, and rewarded.

Managers function more as performance and career 'coaches' than as judges of performance, and leadership does not take place in a hierarchical framework, but in a more 'collegiate' framework. The philosophy underlying leadership is that the future of the organization is *jointly* determined, and that 'empowerment' of individuals is very important.

Collins (2001) found, contrary to his expectations, that the companies which did move from good to great performance and sustained it for 15 years or more invariably had what he describes as a Level-5 leader in charge (see Pause and Reflect 4.1). This was true irrespective of whether the company was in crisis or steady state, or of which sector it operated in. In addition, the absence of Level-5 leadership also showed up consistently across the companies included for comparison.

## Pause and Reflect 4.1

### Learning to lead?

- Level 5 – builds enduring greatness through a paradoxical combination of personal humility plus professional will.
- Level 4 – effective leader; catalyses commitment to and vigorous pursuit of a clear and compelling vision.
- Level 3 – competent manager; organizes people and resources towards the effective and efficient pursuit of predetermined objectives.
- Level 2 – contributing team member; works effectively with others to achieve group objectives.
- Level 1 – highly capable individual; makes productive contribution through talent, knowledge, skills and good work-habits.

Level-5 leaders tend to apportion credit for success to factors outside of themselves; they are humble in assessing their achievements. When things go less well, they accept the responsibility themselves. They seem to subjugate their own needs to that of the business, and concern themselves with protecting its longevity beyond their tenure. Some people are more focused on what they get out of leading a successful company – fame, power, adulation, etc. – rather than on what they contribute.

*Adapted from*: Collins J. (2001) 'Level 5 leadership: the triumph of humility and fierce resolve', *Harvard Business Review*, January

**Question:** Identify a successful entrepreneur, and consider their leadership abilities through reference to Collins' categorization. Do you think it is possible to learn to be a Level-5 leader?

The irony is that the charisma and personal ambition that is needed to make a good Level-4 leader (and a good entrepreneur!) is somewhat at odds with the personal humility needed to achieve Level 5. It might be appropriate to consider the relatively small number of entrepreneurs who continue to head up successful organizations over long periods of time, and how far this is due to their reluctance or inability to be a Level-5 leader. Many move on after the initial challenge of start-up, turnaround, or period of rapid growth.

Although leadership style was a distinguishing feature of these very successful companies, it was not the only one. There was a symbiotic relationship between leadership and other factors which, in combination, made the difference. These other factors included a focus on getting the right people on board, a faith that despite current realities all would come good in the end, consistent effort, focus, discipline, and a paradoxical relationship with technology (i.e. an aversion to jumping on the latest bandwagon, but a pioneering attitude towards technology that was closely related to the achievement of the core objectives). This implies that the critical factor in sustaining an innovative edge is achieving a fit between the entrepreneurial personality and the business model to exploit opportunities consistently over time. We will return to this discussion in later chapters, in considering the implementation of entrepreneurial strategies.

## Entrepreneurial organizational learning

Having discussed some dimensions of individual learning, we now turn to organizational learning. We suggest that the link between individual learning and organizational learning is more critical in entrepreneurial organizations, because, usually, the entrepreneur or entrepreneurial team has such a strong role in influencing how the organization operates, and particularly how knowledge is acquired and applied, how decisions are made, and how ambiguity is managed. To understand how individual learning can be harnessed and exploited for competitive advantage within the entrepreneurial organization, we first need to understand what a learning organization is.

## The learning organization

It is useful to begin with larger organizations in considering the **learning organization**. Senge (1990: 2) describes learning organizations as 'organizations where people continually expand their capacity to create the results they truly desire, where new and expansive patterns of thinking are nurtured, where collective aspiration is set free, and where people are continually learning how to learn together'. But organizations can only learn if individuals learn. He argues (1990: 4) that 'learning organizations are possible because, deep down, we are all learners. No-one has to teach an infant how to learn'.

Huber (1991) suggests that effective learning organizations are skilled in five main activities:

1. **congenital learning** – which is based on prior experience, either internally or inherited; e.g. a new CEO would have their own way of viewing the world.
2. **experiential learning** – choices that we make colour our perceptions of how events will turn out – things that worked, or

did not work in the past influence our thinking in the present (although Senge [1990] reminds us that the nature of employment is such that we rarely stay with an organization long enough to see the consequences of our strategic decisions, and so we may be deluding ourselves to talk of learning from direct experience).

3.  **vicarious learning** – learning through someone else's experience. Organizations may do this through networks or others within an industry; this type of learning is particularly useful when a company has little relevant experience.

4.  **grafting** – where organizations learn by grafting knowledge from the relationships they have established, e.g. supply chain partners. The greater the level of trust and interaction, the greater the opportunities for the partners to learn from and with each other. However, the effectiveness of the process depends largely on consensus in terms of what is acceptable to share and how it is to be used.

5.  **searching** – scanning the internal and external environment for information that enables an organization to identify trends – opportunities and threats, and adapt accordingly.

But, even if organizations acquire information in all of these ways, the important thing is how it is used. Learning in itself is not enough unless it leads to inappropriate behaviour being changed, and changed 'for the better'. There is a tendency for people to learn anyway despite organizational priorities – the fundamental question is do they learn what the organization wants them to learn? Appropriate mechanisms for learning may exist, but the content of that learning may be inappropriate. An away day may be an appropriate mechanism to communicate and consult on strategy but after the event the participants often come away muttering that everything was so vague and riddled with platitudes that nothing was actually communicated, or that so much was open to interpretation that it meant nothing, thereby rationalizing their decision to go back to work and carry on exactly as before.

There is a difference between the learning organization *per se*, and **developing organizational learning capability**. Learning organizations need to use their capability to develop and sustain competitive advantage – this can only be done if knowledge exists, is recognized as valuable to an organization, and can be transferred to appropriate and relevant contexts, and if the organization can do all this better than its competitors. Arguably, this is the core competence that distinguishes entrepreneurial organizations.

# Decision-making in entrepreneurial organizations

Decision-making is central to the operation of the organization. Decisions are influenced by knowledge, context, management style and culture. It is therefore pertinent to explore the role that decision-making takes in entrepreneurial organizations.

It would seem to be common sense that organizations that encourage learning and anticipate trends would be better placed to minimize emergent threats and exploit weaknesses. Neither would it be surprising that such organizations, in anticipating the future, may have (even subconsciously) begun to consider how they might best meet those challenges. However, any company that involves itself in strategic planning would be familiar with the concepts of environmental scanning and analysis, generating options and evaluating these, making choices and implementing the changes decided upon. It is useful to see how this apparently objective process differs in entrepreneurial organizations.

## Three approaches to decision-making

To do this, we will first look at three **approaches to decision-making** suggested by Mintzberg and Westley (2001).

*Thinking first* According to Mintzberg and Westley (2001) there are limitations to 'thinking first' as a way of making decisions. 'Thinking first' is defined as a rational process of define, diagnose, design and decide. But, they say, in practice this rational approach is less common than might be expected, and that in reality the process is less clear cut, messier, and involves much that is beyond conscious thought. They suggest that there are two other approaches to making choices: 'seeing first' and 'doing first'.

*Seeing first* involves insight and the courage to recognize it. 'Deep knowledge, usually developed over years, is followed by incubation, during which the unconscious mind mulls over the issue. Then with luck (as with Archimedes in the bathtub), there is that flash of illumination'.

*Doing first* is the realm of the pragmatist, who just gets on with it and learn as they go. The pragmatist experiments, where possible, so that he or she can learn. Although individuals may have a preferred approach to making decisions, all three approaches can be present to some degree, and each has its strengths and weaknesses. Mintzberg and Westley conclude that there are advantages in combining the three approaches. We might speculate that an entrepreneurial organization would have an advantage here, in that the entrepreneur's vision and often the predilection towards action-learning balances out the traditional decision-making processes common in many organizations.

For example, large bureaucratic organizations (administratively managed) use rigid strategic planning and monitoring and control systems to reinforce rationality, justification, resource control and so on. This is counterproductive to innovation, for example budgets are allocated as far as 12–18 months ahead, so there is no flexibility in resource decisions should an unexpected opportunity or threat arise after the annual planning round is completed.

## Dealing with ambiguity in decision-making

Much research has already been conducted into the difficulties that many organizations face when trying to combine incremental development in an existing business while searching for breakthrough innovations. Innovation requires change, and change can be disruptive. We have suggested that both step change and incremental innovation are based on continuous learning, but also that this might well entail a reorientation or even a complete reinvention of the organization's business model and processes.

O'Reilly and Tushman (2004: 75) suggest that successful innovation while maintaining the performance of the core business requires organizations to be 'ambidextrous'. They argue that 'the companies who are successful at both exploiting the present and exploring the future ... separate their new, exploratory units from their traditional exploitative ones, allowing for different processes, structures and cultures; at the same time, they maintain tight links at the senior executive level'. They suggest that this allows for cross-fertilization while preventing cross-contamination, as expertise and knowledge can be shared but energy is not diverted from the core business and the incremental improvements that are essential to competitiveness.

Drucker (2001: 139) also suggests that, because entrepreneurial organizations need their systems and processes to reinforce the culture of innovation, in order to be successful 'the new' has to be kept separate from 'the old': 'The new project is an infant and will remain one for the foreseeable future, and infants belong in the nursery. The "adults", that is, the executives in charge of existing businesses or products, will have neither time nor understanding for the infant project. They cannot afford to be bothered'. This is not to infer that 'the new' is less important, quite the contrary. It needs to be high up the corporate agenda, and to be able to pull on the resources it needs to be effective. But unless it has a special locus, and it is a clearly defined responsibility, it runs the risk of being neglected.

---

### Enterprise in Action 4.4

#### Skunkworks

In the 1970s it was common for innovation to be handled in research and development departments, and as a consequence new product development ran the risk of being product rather than customer focused. The 1980s saw a trend for marketing departments to take responsibility, the danger in this being that the focus can then become too related to building the brand and gaining shelf space which might lead to a disproportionate emphasis on short-term product adaptations.

Cross-functional teams have been tried as a way of securing the collaboration needed and balancing functional interests, but the danger in this approach is that the logistics involved may lead to excessive bureaucracy which slows the process down.

Some companies set up 'skunkworks' as totally discrete units from the 'parent' company to maximize creativity. Unilever set up Unilever Ventures as a way of encouraging employees, scientists and entrepreneurs to work together on product innovation by giving one-off payments or the opportunity to work with brand teams, etc. GlaxoSmithKline set up the futures group, its first product being Plenty, a juice drink. They launched it under a new brand, The Ealing Juice Company, but had given considerable thought to whether they should do this or launch under the GSK brand.

*Adapted from:* Murphy C., 'Innovation masterminds', *Marketing*, 15 May 2003

**Questions:** What are the advantages and disadvantages of using the 'skunkworks' model for new product development? What implications does this have for building creative capacity in organizations?

---

De Geus (1988) sees strategy as an art that can be managed by accelerating the learning process. He argues that the mind cannot see things that it has not experienced before and quotes a story of British explorers who take a tribal chief to see the technological wonders of Singapore. The chief reportedly saw only one thing of relevance – a market vendor pushing a cart laden with bananas. This had resonance with him – his tribe carried bananas on their backs. He had missed all the other signals. Perhaps companies do the same – only taking heed of things that have some degree of resonance with their own experience. De Geus argues that decision-taking is learning, but that the natural learning process is slow. We need to somehow speed it up. The learning process involves receiving signals, embedding them in our existing ways of seeing things (our theories of how the world is), drawing conclusions and then acting upon them. Anticipating future scenarios and their potential impact is only part of the story. If we move from the realm of the possible to the realm of the problem, and ask the question 'When this happens, what would we do?', we complete the cycle.

In this way he says that we create memories of the future as well as those we hold of the past – we have had a little practice in a range of potential scenarios. It is difficult to live with the ambiguities of the future, and such ambiguity can be uncomfortable, because it feels fraught with risk. If we take this approach, some scenarios will feel more familiar when they emerge; we can relate to them, at least in part. We can build capacity for anticipating options, and we also link the signals we see to potential action, allowing us to 'see' opportunity beyond the blinkers of our own experience. If techniques like this have impact in companies, then perhaps it does become possible to 'manage' innovation in the sense that it can be developed and facilitated.

## Pause and Reflect 4.2

### Knowledge transfer

As universities prepare their strategies for income generation in anticipation of the introduction of top-up fees, they are once again paying attention to technology transfer and business-education links. The Lambert report into the links between higher education and commerce has set challenges for the sector, and survival for many will depend on the generation of 'third stream' income from commercialization, reflecting, to some degree, the US model.

In the late 1990s, Cambridge University provided the model. Lambert highlights both the achievements and the failures. The University asserted its intellectual leadership in the sector, and the region benefited from the creation of 5000 jobs per year, GDP rising by 6.3 per cent per year compared with the national average of 3.4 per cent. However, critics say that this was achieved despite the University. Although the knowledge was valuable as a resource, the University's governance left much to be desired. Confusing policy on intellectual property and its failure to adopt a businesslike approach were said to dampen progress and were far from the entrepreneurial approach required. In addition, the local economy overheated creating problems in transport, services, housing and so on.

The high-tech cluster that developed around the University has struggled since the dot-com bubble burst but, paradoxically, the University has used the downturn to improve its links with industry. There is now a well respected technology transfer office, and the University is active in working alongside local partnerships such as the Greater Cambridgeshire Partnership. It is also collaborating with the Massachusetts Institute of Technology (MIT), backed by £65 m of taxpayers' money, to explore ways in which better links with industry can be developed. One idea that has resulted from this is Knowledge Integration Communities (KICs). Groups are set up with the aim of developing a specific technology transfer product, drawing on students, graduates, academics, other universities, companies, suppliers, government agencies, etc.

The problem in the past has been that although research goes well, development does less well. The ideas are generated, but commercial success is elusive. Cambridge University now has a reasonable support infrastructure (venture capitalists, legal expertise, etc.) but it has taken 30 years of development to get to that point.

*Adapted from*: Kelly J., 'Spin out doctors', *The Guardian*, 2 March 2004

**Question:** How can the links between universities and businesses facilitate the transfer of knowledge, to the commercial benefit of both?

## Learning capability and entrepreneurial strategy

When we talk about strategic management we almost intuitively link the concept with that of gaining and maintaining competitive advantage. Students of strategic management and strategic marketing management will be familiar with the views of Michael Porter and Hamel and Prahalad. Porter (1985) argues that the key to success lies in effective positioning within the industry, and how well the company can defend itself against competitive forces or manipulate them to improve its competitive advantage.

Hamel and Prahalad (1994) argue the resource-based view, in which the organization is able to develop a distinctive competence, which allows it to outperform its competitors. This approach suggests greater proactivity, being more to do with exploiting capability to succeed in a variety of environments, rather than ensuring alignment between the organization's strategic capability and the environment in which the firm operates.

## Single- and double-loop learning

Argyris and Schon (1978) introduced the concept of single- and double-loop learning. The underlying principles are that in the former, we learn within our existing frames of reference, whereas in the latter we challenge the underlying assumptions that we make. Similarly Senge (1990) talks of adaptive and generative learning. In the positioning view, we might need to reconsider the bases of competition in an industry, as the no-frills airlines have done. In the resource based view we might need to recognize how our competences can be stretched to meet the needs of new markets or sectors that we have not explored before.

Doole and Lowe (2005) suggest that these approaches are only partial explanations of how success is sustained. Certain skills will be needed, and in sustaining competitive advantage over time there must be a dynamic learning process within the organization, through which it decides how best to maintain its competitive advantage. If the speed of learning lags behind the pace of change in a market the inference is that this learning deficiency would be likely to lead to an eroding position in the market and strategic drift. They argue (2005: 33) that: 'A firm's long term strategy tends to be incrementally built as a firm undergoes the process of reflecting on its experiences and responding to the challenges faced. If firms are to build this capability two types of learning activity are important, the learning necessary to *signal* critical developments and trends, and the learning necessary to *reflect, re-evaluate and respond*'.

## Signal and 3R learning

**Signal learning** involves the environmental scanning process – having systems in place to monitor trends and to include the information in strategic decision-making. The organization gains knowledge about the environment in which it operates and can adjust its strategies accordingly to maintain its position. It would be dangerous to assume that all organizations do this well, or even do this at all. Although some organizations do not have formal systems in place, they are learning in an ad hoc way. The danger is that as people leave the organization vital knowledge and experience can be lost.

For entrepreneurial organizations in the early days this gives them a competitive edge as the entrepreneur is the fixed centre of the business. However, as the organization grows, signal learning is in itself insufficient, as success increasingly depends on effective learning throughout the organization (see Spotlight 4.2).

Doole and Lowe (2005: 36) go on to argue that **3R learning** (reflect, re-evaluate and respond) occurs in anticipation of, or in response to, critical events occurring in a firm's markets. It is this second type of learning that organizations who successfully reinvent themselves undergo in reflecting on the demise of traditional markets, e.g. Dell, Ryanair, and Skoda. An example of such reflection is given in Enterprise in Action 4.5.

---

### Spotlight 4.2

**Translating learning into commercial success – a personal reflection**

'I come from a small family – my father, my mother, my grandmother, my elder sister, and my baby (my dog) Lyca who is such a big part of our family. We have always been in business, and being the only daughter who was interested in taking an active part, I started working quite early in my life.

I had to learn to manage our shipping crew consultancy business at 16. My father travelled out on business often and so my aunt would look after things in his absence. However, one day my father was out of town and my aunt was not available. At this time there came an urgent requirement for senior crew on our client's ships. It was quite hilarious to see the expression on the faces of Senior Captains coming in to be interviewed by a chit of a 16-year-old. At the end of the day I did get a pat on the back for a situation well handled. It was quite amusing but I think it helped me to build up a lot of confidence early on, to be able to tackle any work situation and to interact with anybody.

Over the years, along with my education, I learned a lot about computer programming and helped computerize the office functions. Due to that background in technical computer education it becomes much easier for me to now understand the digital economy as I can also visualize what is actually happening in the "back-end."

About five years ago we entered into the IT-enabled services business with a foray into transcription services for firms/individuals in the USA in 1997. Transcription started with a boom in India, but because most organizations did not know what they were getting into at the start, many shut down again equally quickly. However we had, quite rightly, invested in good training and so our company was one of the few that survived through a bad patch when many USA companies were pulling back from India due to complaints of poor quality.

Now we are quite a big company hiring almost 400 people in-house and partnering with and providing work to numerous vendors within India. The first five years of setting up the business was very hard work – dealing with manpower shortage, training, bad infrastructure in India in terms of Internet and power facilities, less work due to the USA market not having too much trust in Indian companies etc. Luckily we had not lost any of the work we already had; it was only the expansion that was taking time, so we coped.

Things drastically changed in about 2003 when through a lot of Internet marketing and personal visits, we acquired a very big contract for transcription and also full-text data conversion services for a library in a university in the USA. Then expansion was very rapid and now we are a very successful transcription, data conversion and other IT-enabled service providing organization in India. We plan to grow in the IT-enabled area offering other specialized services like high quality CAD/CAM conversions for architects, digitization of road maps and industrial design, back office accounting and more.

At this time we have more lower level staff than management. However we do need to structure the company better to run it more professionally. It is always better that someone from the family learns some management techniques before getting any other professionals. I had decided to do a management course outside India about three years ago, but at that time it was just not possible to leave the business on its own. The Internet has really made e-management a reality and now I only have to monitor the business online. After working for three years towards making time to do my MBA, I have managed to make e-management work for me and so have the time and the opportunity to do an MBA. Already I feel that this MBA is contributing to my knowledge in this area and I hope to also make a dent in the UK market for providing IT-enabled services from India after my MBA is completed.'

*Source*: Bijali (Nikki) Pradhan

**Question:** How have the combination of signal and 3R learning, and experiential and formal learning contributed to Nikki and the family firm building competitive advantage?

---

## Enterprise in Action 4.5

### Surviving in the digital era

John Pluthero, speaking at the Royal Television Society's Cambridge convention, warned the television industry of the challenges posed by changing viewer behaviour.

The days of mass audiences are coming to an end as technological change threatens the broadcasters' business models. Personal recorders mean that viewers can fast-forward through ads, and 3G mobile phones can operate as mini televisions. Broadband Internet access means that content can be easily downloaded, having the potential to make the television obsolete. Pluthero pointed out that he had quite happily watched the exciting finish to the Ashes series from the South of France using Channel 4's broadband service, and he predicts that over half the country will have such access by 2010.

If we follow the thinking of this scenario, we can see a shift in power between the supplier and customer in relation to content – viewers will decide what to watch and when. This audience fragmentation could have devastating impact on advertising revenue.

Will the television industry be less complacent than the record companies were? Pluthero worries that the broadcasters 'will be a bit Marks & Spencer-ish about changes, and keep making St Michael jumpers while their customers get old and drop dead'. He says he despairs at TV's idea of interactivity being to ask viewers to text in votes. While at Freeserve in 1999, they commissioned the world's first interactive soap opera online, where viewers could choose what happened next in the story line or what outfit a character wore to a party.

Product placement may be one way to replace lost revenue, but Pluthero would like to see broadcasters create more content in tandem with advertisers.

*Adapted from:* Robinson J., 'TV's nice and cosy, but could soon die', *The Observer*,
18 September 2005

**Question:** What learning processes would you recommend to organizations in this sector to ensure that they are able to respond quickly enough to change?

This takes the learning process one step further as it challenges the implicit assumptions that are made about markets, likely responses from competitors, customer needs, etc. In challenging traditional ways of thinking, reflective practice is developed – the new concepts are considered and, where appropriate, built into strategic thinking.

## 3R learning and innovation

From time to time many organizations experience periods of rapid, and sometimes discontinuous, change. During such times the learning curve is very steep, and only those organizations that can learn rapidly and effectively are able to maintain their competitive advantage. However, this means that the organization also has to be flexible enough to reconfigure its business model to exploit the emerging opportunities, or avoid the potential crises. Individual learning is necessary but insufficient as the knowledge has to be shared so that strategic thinking is re-evaluated, and so that it can be transferred to different contexts.

Doole and Lowe (2005: 38) subsequently conclude that '3R learning is a central component of building a culture of innovation and creativity in an organization' and (2005: 39) that 'a company that is committed to 3R learning can enhance its innovative capability in the following ways:

■ It is more likely to have developed the internal competence to build and market a technological breakthrough.

- It has the knowledge and the ability to understand and anticipate latent needs in potential customers and so has the ability to spot opportunities created by emerging market demand.
- An organization committed to 3R learning is likely to have a greater innovation capability than its competitors and be much more prepared to learn from its failures as well as its successes'.

Wang and Ahmed (2003) suggest that companies may be able to develop this type of learning activity by:

- questioning existing products, services, processes and systems and examining how they strategically contribute to the future marketplace;
- learning how to discard things they have done previously in order to create the capacity to make step changes or even quantum leaps. This is what is referred to as organizational un-learning;
- creating new knowledge through radical changes. The development of an innovative capacity is developed through a continuous process of knowledge creation and not necessarily the simple accumulation and retention of existing knowledge.

## Enterprise in Action 4.6

### Rethinking lending

If you are self-employed or work freelance, borrowing money can be a problem as you may not seem sufficiently creditworthy. Zopa (Zone of Possible Agreement) has been set up to get around this problem by allowing borrowers and lenders to bypass the high street banks in what is described as a 'lending and borrowing exchange'.

Zopa is an online membership organization which matches people who want to borrow with people who want to lend, and makes its money by charging borrowers 1 per cent of their loan as a fee.

James Alexander, and his colleagues David Nicholson and Richard Duvall, have experience in the industry, having been involved in the launch of Egg and Smile, both online services. They secured investment from two private equity firms, and now have 26 000 members. Loans range from £2000 to £5000.

Returns for lenders are around 7.6 per cent. Some see it as lending to family members or a community. Others are pure entrepreneurial investors who understand risk and portfolio diversification, lending to Zopa alongside other investments. They have no protection against default, although any borrowers who fail to pay will be pursued through the usual channels and get a black mark on their credit rating. Zopa says there are 20 countries showing an interest in franchises, the most important one being the USA, although there are regulatory difficulties to overcome there.

Borrowers can find rates of 5.9 per cent, and see Zopa as a cost-effective way of borrowing over shorter periods. But with a slowdown in consumer spending and high levels of debt, attracting creditworthy borrowers may be a challenge. Zopa have relied on word-of-mouth and online marketing so far; however, one investor said that it was 'one of those things that could catch on but probably won't'.

*Adapted from:* Paul Davies, 'Lending exchange that bypasses high street banks attracts interest', *The Financial Times*, 22 August 2005

**Questions:** Do you think Zopa will successfully challenge the taken-for-granted assumptions in the way this industry competes? Why?

## The learning spiral

Doole and Lowe (2005: 41) describe the learning process as a **learning spiral**. Knowledge is acquired through signal learning, but is then reflected upon. This enhanced understanding would lead to a strategic decision being made which would realign the firm with the changes in the environment. The lessons learned from doing this would then be fed back into the decision-making process. In doing this, the organization would incorporate a re-evaluation of its strategic thinking as to how it can respond as it strategically realigns to further build its competitive advantage. The learning generated from this success would enhance further strategy development and lead to a step change in the level of aspirations, enabling a more creative and innovative strategy and a more complex network of relationships to be developed ... and so the process continues.

Learning becomes central in sustaining entrepreneurial success. Traditional strategy formulation does involve environmental scanning and analysis, and some anticipation of future scenarios, but there is a difference in scale within entrepreneurial organizations which develop this as a core competence, giving them sustainable competitive advantage. The more entrepreneurial organizations embed the learning process into their strategic decision-making processes, and reflect it consistently in their business model. We return to this in Part III.

## Summary

- Building learning capability is crucial to sustainable entrepreneurial success.

- Effective organizational learning depends upon effective individual learning, and both depend on reflective practice.
- In organizations, effective learning processes incorporate reflection, re-evaluation and response.
- In individuals, effective learning processes are characterized by resilience, resourcefulness, reflectiveness, and reciprocity.
- It is possible to develop the learning capability of both organizations and individuals, and consequently improve their innovative and entrepreneurial capacity.

## Chapter questions

1. What is your preferred learning style? What implications does this have for your personal capability to be an effective manager of an entrepreneurial organization?
2. Analyse the extent to which learning capability is a prerequisite for the development and implementation of effective entrepreneurial strategies.
3. To what extent do you agree with De Bono that schools need to teach thinking skills if we are to encourage the development of an enterprise culture?
4. Are entrepreneurial decisions made by the heart or the head? Analyse the role of intuition and gut-feel in entrepreneurial decision-making.
5. Argue for and against the view that entrepreneurs are more capable leaders than 'ordinary' managers.

## Case study

### WellData Ltd

WellData is an IT support-based company incorporated in March 1999, representing the vision of its founder – Phill Clayton. Phill had more than 20 years' experience in the IT industry, working in project and associated management roles for major IT installations including many blue chip organizations.

Experiencing difficulties in recruiting staff and in team management issues, Phill concluded that there had to be a better way, and decided to set up WellData Ltd. A great deal of IT expertise and an innovative approach to IT issues had earned him much praise and stature within the industry, but he had little experience in running a business. Nevertheless he embarked on his journey, which proved to be both painful and exhilarating!

From its inception in March 1999 the business grew rapidly, based primarily on the results of a mailshot aimed at UK IT installations. The immense interest and subsequent take up of contracts led to frenzied recruitment activity in an effort to offer the support promised to clients. This saw the employment of 12 IT experts over a nine-month period, whose primary role was to support client systems both on-site and remotely. The organization's recruitment, financial structure and operational systems were put under severe strain – although this was never apparent to clients.

The events of 9/11 had a dramatic impact on the company, as clients sought stability and consolidation as opposed to innovation. A 'batten down the hatches' approach was prevalent, fuelled by the virtual collapse of staff movement owing to uncertainty and stability in the jobs market. Additionally, potential clients were not willing to commit to changes such as outsourced resources while the world recovered from the attacks.

WellData found this period very difficult, with falling client numbers and a newly appointed workforce of highly paid staff. This led inevitably to redundancy and a battle to convince existing clients to hang on. To further compound these issues the company bankers were unhappy about borrowing in view of the low asset value of such a service-based enterprise and general world uncertainty.

The company has weathered the storm, recruited staff again, and is now financially secure with a solid customer base. Phill has recognized the importance of strategy in matching internal resources to external opportunities and is now an extremely competent entrepreneur.

The general understanding of world events and their effects on business (large or small); a strong financial grasp; the importance of putting the right people in the right place at the right time; the creation of appropriate structures and systems; and the need for vision and planning have been valuable lessons. Phill now feels that he has the blueprint for success and understands his role is to provide direction and stewardship for this vessel through whatever storms may prevail – working on the business and not in it is the secret. Phill says 'I have just completed the most expensive MBA (Masters of Business Administration) known to man – but I've enjoyed it. What's next?'

*Source:* Jim Kent

### Questions

1. What were the critical incidents that provided learning opportunities for Phill in his first entrepreneurial venture?
2. Analyse the advantages and disadvantages of a theory-based approach to learning (such as an MBA) as against the experiential route that Phill adopted.
3. If he had completed an MBA, would that prior knowledge have helped in avoiding the downturn in his business? Why?

## References and further reading

Argyris C. and Schon D.A. (1978) *Organisational Learning: A Theory of Action Perspective.* Reading MA: Addison Wesley.

Argyris C. and Schon D.A. (1996) *Organizational Learning II: Theory, Method and Practice.* Reading MA: Addison Wesley.

Bolton B. and Thompson J. (2003) *The Entrepreneur in Focus: Achieve your Potential.* London: Thomson.

Collins J. (2001) Level 5 leadership – the triumph of humility and fierce resolve. *Harvard Business Review,* January, pp. 67–76.

Coulter M. (2003) *Entrepreneurship in Action,* 2nd edn. Upper Saddle River NJ: Prentice Hall.

De Bono E. (1991) *I am Right. You are Wrong.* London: Penguin.

De Geus A.P. (1988) Planning as learning. *Harvard Business Review,* March–April, pp. 70–74.

Doole I. and Lowe R. (2005) *Strategic Marketing Decisions in Global Markets.* London: Thomson.

Drucker P.F. (2001) *Innovation and Entrepreneurship: Practice and Principles.* Oxford: Butterworth-Heinemann.

Hamel G. and Prahalad C.K. (1994) *Competing for the Future.* Boston: Harvard Business School Press.

Huber G.B. (1991) Organizational learning: the contributing processes and the literatures. *Organizational Science* **2**: 88–115.

Michalski R. (2005) Forward thinking sideways. *CMA Management,* April, pp. 21–25.

Mintzberg H. and Westley F. (2001) Decision making: it's not what you think. *MIT Sloan Management Review,* Spring, pp. 89–93.

O'Reilly III C.A. and Tushman M.L. (2004) The ambidextrous organization. *Harvard Business Review,* April, pp. 74–81.

Porter M.E. (1985) *Competitive Advantage: Creating and Sustaining Superior Performance.* New York: The Free Press.

Senge P.M. (1990) *The Fifth Discipline: The Art and Practice of the Learning Organization.* New York: Century.

Wang C.L. and Ahmed P.K. (2003) Organizational learning: a critical review. *The Learning Organization* **10**(1): 8–17.

## Key words

approaches to decision-making

creative tension

critical incidents

developing organizational learning capability

enterprise in education

environment in which individual learning can flourish

intuition

lateral leader

lateral thinking

leadership

3R learning

learning organization

learning spiral

reflective practice

signal learning

skills, knowledge and attitudes

# Integrated personal development activity

Introduction

In Part I of this book we have introduced a variety of concepts relating to entrepreneurship and innovation. We have discussed the personality traits and characteristics that theorists have identified as typical of entrepreneurs, and also considered whether entrepreneurs can be distinguished by their actions. We have also suggested that entrepreneurs may approach learning and decision-making in a different way, and that the choices they make are a key aspect of their learning processes, even when they have made mistakes. We have argued that learning capability is a prerequisite of sustainable entrepreneurial success, and that reflective practice is a critical aspect in developing both individual and organizational learning capability.

Most people interact with organizations in some way or another at some point in their lives, whether they choose to engage in economic activity or not. Their career paths will differ – some will at some point become entrepreneurs, but most people will be employed by others, in a waged or voluntary capacity. In reading Part I of this book and in carrying out the tasks included within the four chapters, the reader will have developed a greater awareness of the personality traits, skills, and attitudes exhibited by 'typical' entrepreneurs in a range of contexts (for example, as an intrapreneur within an existing organization; as an economic entrepreneur; or in a social enterprise). They may, informally, have begun to consider where they sit on the entrepreneur–administrator continuum, and make decisions about whether that position is one that they are comfortable with considering their own personality, values, and ambitions at this moment in time. In beginning to consider their own skills and abilities in the context of their aspirations, and challenging some of the things that they may have taken for granted about themselves, readers are taking the first steps towards reflective practice. This integrated learning activity is designed to provide a framework for the reader to use in developing their skills as a reflective practitioner.

The task for the reader is to:

1. Consider their own aspirations, not only in terms of their career and academic ambitions, but in terms of their personal lives. For example, the reader may conclude that they have the skills and ability to succeed as an entrepreneur, and the required knowledge of the industry to capitalize on their ideas, but be unwilling to commit the time needed to establish the venture because they prefer to focus on the needs of their family.

2. Then, the reader is challenged to assess their own skills, knowledge and attitudes and compare them to those needed to successfully reach their chosen goals.

3. Finally, the reader must identify and then prioritize some key areas for development. These may relate to the acquisition of knowledge (for example, industry data or a new area of theory); skills (for example, negotiation or delegation skills); or attitudes (for example, determination in overcoming obstacles or being prepared to make a contribution in discussions).

## Learning objectives

By the end of this section the reader will be able to:

- assess their own knowledge, attitudes and skills against those of a 'typical' entrepreneur;
- reflect on how their personal knowledge, skills and attitudes may impact upon their ability to achieve their personal, career or academic aspirations;
- develop an action plan to address areas that may limit their ability to achieve their potential.

## Getting started – a framework for reflection

### Step 1: Determining your aspirations and ambitions

To help you in carrying out this task we have made some suggestions for areas that you might like to consider.

What do you hope to achieve academically? What degree classification do you hope for? Do you want to continue in higher education now, or in the future? Do you want to achieve some professional or vocational qualification?

What personal ambitions do you have? For example, are you hoping to run a marathon? Become a volunteer for the Prince's Trust? Win a Business Planning Competition?

What career ambitions do you have? What type of job do you want to do? What sector do you want to work in? What type of business?

Do you feel that you would like to run a business of your own at some point in the future? When would you ideally like to do this? What are your reasons for timing it this way?

If you don't feel that self-employment is for you, would you prefer to work in an organization whose culture supports innovation, or not? Do you prefer more routine and predictability in your day-to-day activities, or do you find variety stimulating? Would you be more comfortable operating at the administrative or entrepreneurial end of the spectrum of managerial behaviour?

Then there are issues of context. Whether you choose employment or self-employment, would you be more comfortable working in a private, public, or voluntary sector context? Would you prefer to work in a small or large business? Do you hope to focus on a specific industry?

## Step 2: Assessing your own knowledge, skills and attitudes

Complete the questionnaire 'How enterprising are you?' on page 137.

Look at your responses to the questions. Where you have ticked the 'V' column you fit the entrepreneurial profile most closely. Where you have ticked the 'N' box, you would need to work on developing the particular skill, knowledge or attitude. Where you have ticked the 'S' box you might reflect on the circumstances or context in which you do/do not fit the profile and why.

This questionnaire is offered as indicative guidance only. If you refer back to the concepts introduced in Chapter 2, there may be other personality traits, characteristics or behaviours that you would like to add to the list. Similarly, in considering the various concepts that you have been introduced to in Part I of this book, you may conclude that some are less helpful or relevant than others, and choose not to apply them.

## Step 3: Reflection in the light of personal aspirations and ambitions

In Chapter 4 we defined our understanding of knowledge, skills and attitudes.

We described these as:

**Knowledge** – the experience and understanding that an individual has acquired, as well as facts and theoretical knowledge.

**Attitude** – managed temperament. You may have certain personality traits and have learned certain ways of behaving, but you have a choice as to whether you behave 'true-to-type' or modify your behaviour to secure different outcomes.

**Skills** – individuals may have appropriate knowledge and attitudes, but be unable to use these to their best advantage because they lack specific skills, for example negotiation or delegation skills.

Refer back to the self-assessment that you have completed in step 2, and analyse your own strengths and weaknesses in terms of your knowledge, skills and attitudes.

Consider the personal aspirations and ambitions that you identified in step 1. Think about an individual who has succeeded in achieving similar ambitions to those that you have. Consider what characteristics and attitudes they exhibit, and the knowledge and skills that they have. How do you compare to that profile? How ambitious are you, what personal motivations drive you? How much does it matter to you that you realize your goals?

It would be helpful to refer to the concepts introduced in Part I to help you in this process. Each individual will be different, but there are some general pointers given below to get you started.

You may not wish to become an entrepreneur, but do you consider yourself to be enterprising? Would you want to be more enterprising than you currently are? In what way? (It may help to refer to Stevenson's typology in Chapter 2).

If you aspire to lead others, or to be a manager, do you think you have the skills and characteristics to be able to manage creative people? (It may help to refer to the section on Leadership in Chapter 4).

What is your preferred approach to learning? Do you accept limitations or do you challenge assumptions? (It may help to refer to Chapter 4 – the section on Signal and 3R learning, or the 4 Rs framework piloted by Mosborough Primary school may be relevant).

## Step 4: The action plan

In order to be successful, what do you feel are the priorities for your personal development? There is no point in having 15 or 20 action points; try to focus on a small number of key areas that really matter to you personally.

You will need to think about how you might improve on your weaker areas, and how you can make the most of the things that you are good at.

It may be appropriate to work on your strengths and weaknesses alone, but it is important to recognize when other people can help you. For example, some people may have valuable knowledge that they can share with you, or they may be able to put you in touch with people who might offer you work experience.

You will need to consider timescales. How soon do you need to acquire the knowledge or skills, or modify your attitude? Is this feasible? If not, then does this mean that you have to rethink your objectives, or can you still achieve them by rethinking the way you go about your personal development?

You will need to set targets, and monitor your progress. This will mean defining exactly how you will know that you have been successful, and taking time to reflect on the process, either alone or with others.

Then you need to commit to taking action. We have suggested a format for action planning that you may wish to use, but it is important that it is meaningful to you, and so you may adapt it to suit your personal circumstances.

## How enterprising are you?

The personality traits and characteristics of entrepreneurs may be a contributory factor in entrepreneurial, or intrapreneurial, success. Certainly many investors look beyond the business idea and the business plan, assessing the likelihood of the individual having the drive, skills and confidence to run a business successfully. Equally, innovative companies look for employees who display ambition, have ideas, and are prepared to work hard to achieve their goals.

Where do you fit on the scale of entrepreneurial capability? Read the statements below, decide the degree to which each characteristic on the list most accurately describes you, and tick the relevant box.

V = very much like me; S = Somewhat like me; N = Not like me at all.

| A 'typical' entrepreneur: | V | S | N |
|---|---|---|---|
| **Is independent, self-confident, and takes the initiative**<br>Entrepreneurs are self-starters, they are prepared to put their money where their mouth is and have the courage to act on their convictions | | | |
| **Is decisive**<br>Entrepreneurs tend to take decisions quickly, and are willing to rely on instinct, appreciating that they will never have perfect information. | | | |
| **Needs to achieve**<br>Entrepreneurs are less likely to be motivated by money than by the desire to make a difference – to do what they know is right and to prove to others that they were! | | | |
| **Has vision, and can persuade others of its value**<br>Building on the need to achieve, entrepreneurs know exactly where they want to be and are able to communicate that vision effectively to others, persuading them to commit to the venture | | | |
| **Is dedicated, dogged and determined**<br>Entrepreneurs work hard, often longer hours than those who are employed. They will give all that it takes to make their idea work, often at the expense of family life and friendships | | | |
| **Can take criticism and rejection**<br>Entrepreneurs bounce back; they are not easily discouraged. | | | |
| **Is creative and innovative**<br>Entrepreneurs see opportunities where others see problems; they come up with ideas – not only for products or services but for better ways of doing things | | | |
| **Is prepared to take calculated risks**<br>Entrepreneurs are not foolhardy, but they have a greater tolerance for risk – both financial and personal. | | | |
| **Sees how the pieces fit together**<br>Entrepreneurs see the bigger picture – how all aspects of the venture combine to add value for the customer/end user | | | |
| **Networks successfully with others**<br>Entrepreneurs learn from others, and make contacts that they can draw on to help them achieve their objectives | | | |
| **Knows their personal strengths and weaknesses, and builds effective teams**<br>Many ventures fail because entrepreneurs find delegation difficult. The more successful ones recognize their weaknesses, and build teams of people around them whose skills are complementary to their own. | | | |
| **Find the resources to make things happen**<br>Entrepreneurs are not constrained by the resources they have, or don't have. They will actively seek out what is needed – and this includes people as well as money. | | | |
| **Like to have control**<br>Entrepreneurs like to know what is happening in their ventures. They need to know what customers want, where the money is being spent, where the business model is not functioning quite the way it should. | | | |
| **Come from a small business background**<br>Entrepreneurs who have a small business background have a better chance of success – perhaps because they have seen first-hand what it takes and are better prepared. | | | |
| **Have developed expertise from experience or education**<br>Entrepreneurs who have some knowledge of the sector they are entering into, either through experience or education, have a better chance of success | | | |

Action plan

| Area for development | How might I do this? | Who might help me? | When will I have achieved this? | How will I know that I have achieved this? |
|---|---|---|---|---|
| | | | | |
| | | | | |
| | | | | |
| | | | | |

# Contexts

Having introduced in Part I some of the fundamental concepts of enterprise, entrepreneurship and innovation and the learning processes that support these activities, in the second part of the book we turn to the contexts in which they occur, and the environmental factors that can inhibit enterprising behaviour. The first two chapters look at the environmental factors that support or hinder individual and organizational enterprise. The final two chapters specifically explore the social and multicultural contexts in which entrepreneurship and innovation thrive and the lessons that can be learned from them. They consider how learning can be transferred from one context to another in order to improve our knowledge and understanding of the concepts.

We start in Chapter 5 by discussing how the individual's decision to become an entrepreneur is affected by the environment. This includes the barriers that individuals perceive as inhibiting their choice, the personal and professional support available to them, their life circumstances and their tolerance for risk.

In Chapter 6 we consider the enterprise environment that determines how an organization competes in its sector and discuss the nature of the macro environment and micro environment, focusing on how organizations connect with customers. We also discuss how entrepreneurial organizations and innovators from all sectors respond to the rapidly changing environment.

In Chapter 7 we move on to exploring the different contexts in which innovation and entrepreneurship are exhibited, recognizing that the motives of entrepreneurs are not always profit-related. Enterprising people flourish in the public and not-for-profit sectors also, making equally significant contributions in terms of the performance of the organizations they work within, and in the broader community. The literature in this area is less well established, but it is a growing field of study, and an increasing number of creative people are making a difference in social and community enterprises, public–private partnerships, quangos, local and central government and other public sector agencies.

In Chapter 8 we conclude this section by taking an international perspective. Entrepreneurship and innovation seem to thrive more readily in some cultures than others and the nature and role of entrepreneurship varies according to the different stages of development of a country. Moreover, the pattern of internationalization of entrepreneurial organizations is influenced by the different cultural contexts in which an organization operates.

The integrated personal development activity will enable the reader to explore an issue/concept in two different contexts, reflecting on what can be learned from comparing and contrasting different approaches/concepts, and how that can develop their understanding and skills.

# The personal enterprise environment

By the end of this chapter the reader will be able to:

- identify the personal factors that influence entrepreneurial activity in a range of different contexts;
- understand how self-perceptions can influence the decision to engage in entrepreneurial activity;
- identify the categories of personal risk involved in pursuing an entrepreneurial career;
- analyse how culture can affect the rates of entrepreneurship;
- analyse how access to personal, public and private sector support can facilitate entrepreneurial activity.

## Introduction

We have seen that entrepreneurs are a heterogeneous group of individuals, and that the ventures they engage in are equally diverse. We have discussed the different degrees to which people exhibit entrepreneurial characteristics and the extent to which they exhibit entrepreneurial behaviour. We have suggested that encouraging enterprising behaviour is possible, that people can learn to be more enterprising, and that if they did so there would be a positive impact on both social and economic well-being. In this chapter we move on to consider the various barriers that individuals might encounter in engaging in entrepreneurial activity, and how they may be supported in overcoming these. In doing so we will consider a number of personal contexts (female entrepreneurship, ethnic minority entrepreneurship, and family businesses). We will identify some of the perceived barriers and difficulties that these groups face, and explore the issues that are pertinent to their specific circumstances. We will also consider timing, perceived risk, and culture, and how these factors can influence the individual's decision to engage in entrepreneurial activity. Ultimately this choice is a personal one, and is very significant in the lives of the people concerned. The right type of support at the critical moment can be significant. For this reason we conclude by considering the nature of the support available (both public and private sector) and the extent to which it helps in overcoming the barriers to enterprise.

## Female entrepreneurship

Although women entrepreneurs have become a significant economic force in the UK, and rates of activity are catching up with those of men, the literature on **female entrepreneurship** is still relatively underdeveloped. When we look at studies into entrepreneurship there still appears to be a male bias in terms of the sample chosen and the examples given. Even when studies are conducted specifically on female entrepreneurs there is often a tendency to interpret the data in terms of male models, constructs and standards.

## Typologies

Goffee and Scase (1985) classified women entrepreneurs into four types, based upon two factors: their attachment to entrepreneurial ideals and their willingness to accept conventional gender roles.

### Conventionals

This group are committed to both entrepreneurial ideals and conventional gender roles. In the main, they are working-class women with fragmented work histories forced into self-employment by economic necessity.

## Innovators

Innovators are committed to entrepreneurial ideals but not to conventional gender roles. They tend to be professional women who choose self-employment as a solution to restricted career prospects.

## Domestic entrepreneurs

This group have little attachment to entrepreneurial ideals but are strongly committed to conventional gender roles. They tend to fit their business duties around their family responsibilities.

## Radical entrepreneurs

This group hold little attachment to either factor. They are frequently involved in collective ventures, political in nature, and aim to promote women's interests.

Carter and Cannon (1992) identified five types of women entrepreneurs:

1. **Drifters:** usually young, choosing self-employment as a route out of unemployment.
2. **Young achievers:** usually well-educated, and with aspirations and limited business experience but enhanced knowledge through training.
3. **Achievers:** similar to the above in terms of attitudes and values but generally older and with relevant work experience.
4. **Returners:** choosing self-employment as a way back to work after a career break.
5. **Traditionalists:** typically older women (over 45) who had worked in family-owned and managed businesses.

Typologies like these offer some insight into the motivations and aspirations of female entrepreneurs but are limited in their utility as women entrepreneurs are just as diverse a group of people as are entrepreneurs in general. Additionally, societal norms in respect of gender issues have altered significantly over the last 20 years and so studies become quickly outdated.

## Hidden entrepreneurial activity

The most recent statistics from the Global Entrepreneurship Monitor (GEM) report on Female Entrepreneurship (2004) give us some up-to-date facts and figures, but it is worth remembering that much female entrepreneurial activity lies hidden. For example many businesses that are registered as male-owned, in reality are co-managed by a spouse, partner, or other family member whose contribution is significant and yet not formally acknowledged.

## Facts and figures

According to the 2004 Global Entrepreneurship Monitor (GEM):

- on average, men are 50 per cent more active in entrepreneurship than women. This varies from country to country, the gap being widest in France, Greece, Hong Kong and Spain. It is statistically insignificant in Ecuador, Finland, Hungary, Japan, South Africa and the United States;
- many more women than men are involved in entrepreneurial activity because of the lack of alternative job opportunities;
- women tend to be more affected by their local environmental conditions than are men;
- women who are employed and know other entrepreneurs are most likely to set up their own businesses;
- in low and middle-income countries, the peak years for women to become engaged in entrepreneurial activity are between the ages of 25 and 34. In high-income countries it is 35 to 44;
- in high-income countries, women with post-secondary education are more likely to start a business;
- businesses started by women tend to:
    use less capital than those started by men, and (as with men) these women tend to provide most of this themselves (65 per cent of it approximately)
    be smaller, and less expensive to operate
    have slower growth in the early stages (possibly by design)
    be in established markets and operate with known technology.

In the UK around 130 000 women decided to set up their own business in 2003, a rise of 10 000 year on year. The government wants to increase the percentage of small firms owned by women from its current level of 14 per cent to 20 per cent within two years (SBS, 2003).

# Perceived barriers

## Lack of credibility

Historically there has been a tendency in society to believe that women are less serious about business than are men. This may be because of social stereotyping, and making the assumption that women will prioritize family over business. It may also, in part, be the result of there being more social pressure on women to balance the needs of their family and their business.

## Lack of experience and knowledge

The fact that some women choose to take time out to cover domestic responsibilities such as caring for young children does disadvantage them. During their career break they do not gain recent experience, usually lose opportunities to build up capital, and are not making contacts in the sectors in which they will potentially be able to operate in business.

As there is a tendency to choose business areas which pose least obstacles, this lack of up-to-date experience, capital and contacts does affect the choice of sector that a woman might move into. It may lead them to choose stereotypically female sectors (such as those related to caring, health and children) not really as a positive choice, but because it makes sense given the practicalities of the situation.

## Access to funds for start up

We have already seen that businesses started by women tend to require less capital than those started by men. It is difficult to ascertain whether this is because the finance is more difficult to raise as the business case is not so strong, or whether women entrepreneurs choose not to approach banks or choose not to run the risk of borrowing money.

If finance is more difficult to raise for women entrepreneurs, it could be the result of 'traditional' attitudes prevailing among the support infrastructure organizations such as banks and business support agencies. Although gender-based discrimination may be one cause, it might also be a perfectly rational phenomenon based on the fact that women presenting to banks do indeed have less experience of the sector and less experience of management, which would make them a higher risk. If the latter is the case, then we should now be beginning to see a shift in the pattern, given the changing sociocultural trends – for example, the fact that greater numbers of women have chosen to continue to work after having families.

---

### Enterprise in Action 5.1

#### Pick of the bunch

When Karen Anne Jones walked away from her violent partner she had only the clothes she was wearing, her three-year-old son, his pram and a bag of dirty washing. She had been working in a flower shop for six years, but felt undervalued, her self-esteem at rock bottom.

She worked for a couple of other florists and learned some new techniques, but she had always felt that she might like to own her own business. Her home had been repossessed, though, and this meant she had a low credit rating and was unable to obtain bank funding.

Then someone recommended the Prince's Trust. She showed them her business plan and in January 1998 she was awarded a £3500 loan and £1500 grant, and set up Pick of the Bunch.

Every bit of her money was invested in stock, and she knew that if she didn't sell flowers she'd be finished within a month. She took £800 the first week; then it was Valentine's Day, and Mother's day a month later. Everyone helped – her dad was making the deliveries, and her mum was making the tea and keeping the place tidy. People were queuing outside the shop, and her reputation grew.

Now she deals with seven of the nine funeral directors in Darwen and Blackburn, wedding venues, churches, schools and lots of industrial businesses in the area. She has two full-time and two part-time employees. The shop is small, so she never has enough room, but Karen still feels that there's potential for growth in the business.

She keeps in touch with her mentor from the Prince's Trust, who had not only offered business advice, but given encouragement when she was low on motivation.

Each setback she encountered in the early days of the business made her stronger and more determined to succeed. Her tip is to stay positive, go forward and don't look back. She says 'If you don't jump in with both feet then you'd stand on the edge forever. I'm glad I did!'

*Adapted from*: http://www.princes-trust.org.uk, accessed 1 October 2005

**Question:** Analyse how critical the different types of support were in helping Karen to overcome the barriers she faced in setting up her business.

---

## Different perspectives

Schaper and Volery (2004: 398) suggest that women have **motivations** different from those men have for starting a business (women often stating that personal goals are as important as business goals). If this is the case, it may also be true that, having different aspirations in business, women may choose different **criteria for measuring success**, such as self-fulfilment, or goal attainment. Certainly in the UK the government tends to judge business success in external quantitative terms such as profit, turnover, or numbers of employees rather than qualitative internal criteria that may more accurately reflect the way women entrepreneurs are measuring their own success.

According to the GEM (2004) survey women entrepreneurs prefer to operate smaller businesses, which they believe may reflect their preferences in terms of management style. Women tend to forge strong personal ties in managing people, whereas men do not. The survey suggests that women prefer to operate egalitarian coalitions, whereas men operate hierarchical ones. This makes for different 'natural' structures for monitoring and control of the business, women relying less on incentives and monitoring systems. Larger businesses need more formal management structures, which men are more comfortable with.

## Self-belief

GEM (2004) suggests that having strong positive **perceptions** about their own abilities and the local economic environment is particularly crucial for women in making the decision to engage in entrepreneurial activity. Issues like subjective perceptions about one's own skills, the likelihood of failure, and the existence of opportunities are all crucial to the decision to start a new business. In middle- and high-income countries, most women believe they do not have the skills required to run their own business, whereas the opposite is true in low-income countries. Of course, the perceived level of ability may differ from reality, but it is a critical issue.

## Pause and Reflect 5.1

### No room at the top in retail

Of 66 publicly listed retail companies, only three have female chief executives. Female chief executives of plcs, such as Kate Swann at WH Smith, are still the exception. Even in women's fashion, where you would expect women to have knowledge, skills and expertise, although the customer base is predominantly female, the boardroom is still predominantly male. Stuart Rose at Marks & Spencer does not have a single female voice on his board despite being the largest womenswear business in the country.

In some sectors, such as pharmaceuticals, there might be an argument for there being an absence of female talent to promote from, but that is hardly supportable in retail, where the shop floor workers are predominantly women and there is plenty of talent in middle management.

Jacqueline Gold (of Ann Summers and Knickerbox) has been chosen as the 'Number One Inspirational Businesswoman' by Barclays Bank and Handbag.com. She believes that women who succeed in retail tend to be ones who have had a good idea and set up their own business. She thinks role models are crucially important, and hopes that her own story can inspire others to have belief in their own ability to succeed. If she can do it, without any formal business training, they can too.

She remembers hearing a speech from a man who headed up a make-up company talking about understanding women and their needs, and yet not having any women on his board. 'They were selling *make-up* and it was all men!' she says. Although she takes a 'run by women for women stance', she does not support positive action, insisting that she employs people who are right for the job. 'Women are so underestimated. A lot of men are intimidated by successful women. Maybe that's why women are suppressed in the hierarchy.'

*Adapted from:* 'Never top of the shop' by Sarah Ryle, *The Observer*, 7 August 2005

**Question:** What are the advantages and disadvantages of using positive action initiatives to encourage under-represented groups to participate in entrepreneurial activity?

## Policy issues

Some initiatives have been specifically targeted at women, and there are arguments both for and against such segmentation. On the one hand it allows confidence to be built up, and for some cultures women would not join any network that included both sexes. It is argued that women network differently from men, and so all-female networks might be an appropriate response. On the other hand, the business world requires that women interact and compete with men, and so it could be argued that reinforcing female patterns of interaction does nothing to help them achieve success.

In a speech to the World Bank on Women's Enterprise (2005) Martin Wyn Griffith (CEO) argued that 'A pound invested in developing women's enterprise provides a greater return on investment than a pound invested in developing male owned enterprise' because:

- women are more likely to be innovative than men in their approach to business development and new ideas;
- women are, on average, more qualified than men. Around a quarter of self-employed women (24 per cent) have a degree or equivalent, compared with the lower level of 18 per cent of self-employed men. Research shows that more highly qualified entrepreneurs grow their business at a faster rate; and
- women are more likely to move from unemployment to self-employment; around one in five women come into self-employment from unemployment compared to around one in

15 for men. So, on entering self-employment from unemployment, women make a more immediate contribution to GDP in that we see less economic displacement.

According to the GEM (2004) report on Women's Entrepreneurship, schemes that provide role models, and networking opportunities, have had significant results in promoting female entrepreneurship.

In the UK, the Small Business Service are working in conjunction with 'Prowess' (a membership network of quality business support providers) to promote entrepreneurship as a viable option for women. The campaign includes:

- encouraging more role models to come forward;
- setting up a new enterprise panel of successful female entrepreneurs to look at the options for a Women's Business Council to champion female entrepreneurship;
- launching a regional tour with leading businesswomen from across the country to accelerate the Women's Enterprise Plan in each region;
- initiating an action plan to help women gain access to finance.

Government intervention is, however, fraught with difficulty because of the complexity of the interrelationships. For example, if the government chose to provide free or subsidized childcare to support working parents, it could have a negative effect on female entrepreneurship because a current 'push' factor is the ability to work more flexibly around the needs of children.

Rates of participation will continue to improve, possibly catching up with rates for men, as women's participation in the economy in general expands. The need for intervention to address issues of representation is declining as a consequence.

Increased participation may offer an opportunity in policy terms to consider a different perspective on how to create, manage and grow new ventures, based around more participative, democratic and consultative approaches to business management. This is not to suggest that such approaches are always the most appropriate to use, but there may be lessons of good practice that would be useful more generally in business.

## Ethnic minority entrepreneurship

There are, of course, many ethnic minority groups in the UK, all with their own entrepreneurial characteristics. Policy has tended to focus upon supporting **ethnic minority entrepreneurs** to integrate into the mainstream, often being focused on neighbourhood renewal for disadvantaged communities, although we should beware of 'stereotyping' these groups, as it is important to recognize the diversity of successful ethnic minority entrepreneurs across all sectors.

# Facts and figures

People in employment from Pakistani and Chinese groups are more likely to be self-employed than those in other ethnic groups in Great Britain. In 2002/03, around one quarter (23 per cent) of Pakistanis in employment were self-employed, as were around one fifth (18 per cent) of Chinese people. This compared with fewer than one in ten black people (http://www.statistics.gov.uk).

Ethnic groups are more likely to be thinking about starting a business than the country as a whole. It is unfortunate that this may be because of discrimination as 38 per cent of non-white business owners say they have experienced discrimination of which 90 per cent was racially motivated (SBS 2003).

# Push and pull factors

Basu and Goswami (1999) identified a range of **push and pull factors** influencing ethnic minority entrepreneurship, which are summarized in Table 5.1.

**Table 5.1**
Push and pull factors influencing ethnic minority entrepreneurship

| Pull factors | Push factors |
| --- | --- |
| Independence | Lack of salaried employment |
| Financial improvement | Underpaid work |
| Higher social status | Discrimination in labour market |
| Greater personal control | Redundancy |
| Best use of expertise | |
| Previous experience | |
| Identification of growth market potential | |
| Niche market | |

*Source:* Basu and Goswami (1999) South American entrepreneurship in Great Britain; factors influencing growth. *International Journal of Entrepreneurial Behaviour and Research* 5(5).

These factors might also apply to other groups, notably women. The conclusion that could be drawn from this is that ultimately it is a combination of personal and environmental circumstances that influences the decision to engage in entrepreneurial activity at any specific point in time.

## Dislocation and hardship

Ethnic immigrants have played a significant **role in economic development** in the UK. Deakins and Freel (2003) explain how these ethnic groups have demonstrated a willingness to accept new practices and have brought in skills that have facilitated economic development. They say that this continues in the modern economy, for example in the case of Asian entrepreneurs who were the first to challenge our cultural norms by opening retail outlets on Sundays.

Perhaps the very experience of surviving in a difficult and sometimes hostile environment requires certain qualities which might be relevant to entrepreneurship such as resilience and determination.

Schaper and Volery (2004) describe the experience of the ethnic Chinese experience of entrepreneurship in the Pacific Rim. They say that organizations owned by ethnic Chinese families make up 70 per cent of the private business sector in Singapore, Malaysia, Thailand, Indonesia and the Philippines and are rising influences in Australia, New Zealand and Vietnam. Most Chinese ethnics left the mainland with very little, and had to face discrimination and prejudice.

Sharing language, culture and ethnicity gave them a sense of communality upon which a base of mutual trust developed. In an area where formal business agreements were difficult to enforce, family offered the most security. Networking and trust are well known characteristics of Chinese culture. The emphasis on tradition and Confucian roots served the Chinese family well against a host of economic policies implemented by the host governments. Greater collectivism, centralized control and clear vertical order helped them to achieve massive growth. The strong work ethic and thriftiness helped them to accumulate wealth quickly.

## Geographical concentration

The **location** of ethnic minority businesses tends to reflect ethnic settlement patterns in a country. In the UK, these businesses are often located in the inner city where physical dilapidation, the depressed economy, and low spending power can constrain business performance. These are often the very same aspects that have led other businesses to leave the market. For example, it is very difficult for a business to achieve growth if it operates in a sector that is characterized by low entry costs and high levels of competition, and relies on the co-ethnic market in a depressed area. Holistic support strategies are needed, to include improving access to broader markets and finance to exploit these, and developing a broader range of contacts through networking initiatives that include mainstream businesses.

## Enterprise in Action 5.2

### Andrew Ramroop

Andrew Ramroop came to London from Trinidad in 1970, and was totally overwhelmed by the crowds of people, but having left with such enthusiasm he felt he could not go back however much he disliked the city. Against the odds, he learned to flourish in a new country, thousands of miles from his home. By 1988 he had become the first black business owner on Savile Row.

In the early days he encountered prejudice, being turned down for many jobs on Savile Row, as he did not present the required front-of-shop image. In 1974, he started work for Maurice Sedwell on Savile Row, after studying at the London College of Fashion.

In the early days, Mr Ramroop was confined to making alterations, but little by little Mr Sedwell encouraged him to come to the forefront of the business. The big break came when a client personally asked for Mr Ramroop to oversee the entire fitting. His reputation grew by personal recommendation and at one point he was dressing half-a-dozen cabinet ministers. Famously, he also designed the cashmere jacket worn by Princess Diana in her Panorama interview.

During those years, Mr Sedwell sold Mr Ramroop shares in the business, until he had accumulated 45 per cent. In 1988, when Mr Ramroop wanted to leave to set up his own business, he sold him a further 45 per cent in the business and persuaded him to stay.

Eight years after taking over the business, Mr Ramroop expanded the premises from 500 to 3000 square feet. But he had problems borrowing money from banks to invest in the business, even though he had made profits every year. Even the bank, which Maurice Sedwell had banked with since 1938, wouldn't help. In the end, his clients lent him the money, which he has since repaid.

'They had the confidence in what I did, and had the confidence in me that I could do the business', Mr Ramroop said. He believes that his ethnic background provided him with the extra spur to do well, and claims further that 'what has been perceived as a disadvantage is an advantage. I have been forced to try harder than someone else'.

*Adapted from*: news.bbc.co.uk, 'Workplace success', by Emma Clark, accessed
1 October 2005

**Question:** Would Mr Ramroop have been so successful if he had not faced setbacks owing to the prejudices of others?

## Policy issues

The Small Business Service acknowledge that there are many entrepreneurial people in Black and Minority Ethnic (BME) businesses and that we can learn a great deal from their experiences. However, in looking at the range of initiatives that target this sector the focus tends to be on tackling barriers for underrepresented BME groups.

The Ethnic Minority Business Forum (EMBF) was set up in July 2000 to advise ministers on appropriate support for ethnic minority businesses, and to consult with such businesses in order to accurately represent their views. The forum itself, and the communities it consults with, have expressed concern about the fact that ethnic minority businesses are less likely to use Business Link's support services than other businesses. They suggest that diversity training for BL advisers may help.

Although we have not addressed **generational issues** in ethnic minority enterprise, younger people have different aspirations from their parents. Policy will need to be more flexible, and more closely targeted at the specific needs of individual ethnic minority entrepreneurs and their businesses.

## Family businesses

While a **family business** shares many of the problems that any business would, there are some unique aspects that are brought into sharp focus by the complexity of personal family relationships. While the individual circumstances of each and every family enterprise will be unique, these businesses often do face similar challenges.

## Definitions

If we chose to adopt the broadest view, a family firm could be defined as any organization in which more than one member of a family is involved, or any organization that defines itself as a family business.

Westhead and Storey (1997) argue that a family firm should meet at least three of the following four criteria:

- has undergone an intergenerational transition;
- has more than 50 per cent of the shares held by the family;
- has more than 50 per cent of family members involved in day-to-day management;
- speaks of itself as a family firm.

Barclays Bank in their 2002 report on family businesses say that for a firm to be defined as a true family business, the family should hold a majority of the company's shares, and in the case of a public company, an individual family group must hold at least 25 per cent of the voting shares.

BDO Stoy Hayward similarly highlight ownership, management participation, and longevity in their definition:

- a single family holds more than 50 per cent of the voting shares;
- supplies a significant proportion of the company's senior management, and is effectively controlling the business;
- more than one generation is involved in the business; and most importantly;
- the family regards the business as a family business.

## Incidence

According to the BDO Stoy Hayward Centre for Family Businesses (http://www.bdo.co.uk/) up to 76 per cent of UK businesses are family-owned. Only 30 per cent of family businesses survive to the second generation and 15 per cent to the third, which highlights **succession planning** as one of the key issues for family businesses. Grant Thornton conduct an annual report on Family Businesses across Europe, and they also consistently highlight planning and succession issues as crucial.

## Insularity

Family businesses can become quite insular in their approach, and bringing 'outsiders' into a firm is useful in that it offers an opportunity to introduce some fresh ideas and challenge some taken-for-granted assumptions. But doing this introduces some problems also. For example, should shares be made available to non-family members? This has implications for the way reward and remuneration packages are constructed.

Taking 'outsiders' for the top jobs in a family business can put them in an impossible position. Expectations are often unrealistically high; they are unlikely to be able to produce the sort of magic that will be the key to an instant turnaround of fortunes if a business has been stagnating for a number of years, for example. It is also quite easy to unwittingly upset family sensitivities, although the fact that they are not aware of such sensitivities can be advantageous as their thinking is not constrained by the politics and they can often do what is not possible for family members.

## Conflicting priorities

Personal relationships within families can impact upon the effectiveness of the business. For example, should the MD of a small firm put their personal feelings aside when faced with the choice of promoting their offspring over a non-family employee? The rational approach would be to choose the most able candidate, but irrespective of which candidate succeeds, interpersonal tensions arise. The son or daughter of the MD would face scrutiny of their performance, having to prove their capability, if they were chosen, and if they were not chosen the inevitable injuries to pride would (however temporarily) affect the relationship with the parent.

Issues like this are commonplace; they are not isolated occurrences. The ongoing psychological stress might also affect the ability of the owner to manage effectively.

## Communication

Communication is often informal in families, but, as with any business, relying on informal communication can leave some people feeling that they are excluded or that they do not have an equal opportunity to express their views. Some members of the family, for example, might not actually work in the business but feel that they have a stake in it. In such circumstances there is an issue in relation to the level of influence that is appropriate in making decisions about the future of the organization.

Another common problem is the 'Sunday lunch decision-making' syndrome, where the family decides on what should be done outside the office (at the family Sunday lunch). The outsider, not having been invited to this informal gathering, is informed of what is going to happen on Monday morning! The opposite can also be true, when family disagreements take place 'on the shop floor' in front of staff, and sometimes (even worse) in front of customers.

### Early experience of enterprise

The SBS 2003 Household Survey states that having an entrepreneur as a parent significantly increases the likelihood of an individual setting up their own business. Thirty-four per cent of 'doers' have a parent who is or has been an entrepreneur compared with about a quarter (26 per cent) of the general population. However, doers do not seem to have been influenced by any other relationship. They are not significantly more likely to have siblings or friends who have been or are entrepreneurs.

This might partly be genetic, but **early exposure to small business** seems to socialize children to be enterprising. Role models are very important as influencers and, in addition, the offspring of business owners often have ample opportunity to practise their skills by working in the family firm in the evenings, at weekends and during holidays. Perhaps, having seen business management at first hand, children are also able to absorb learning informally.

## Succession

We would like to think that families are harmonious entities but this is not always true. There can be intergenerational differences in values, aspirations, and opinions as to how the business should be managed. For example, Lachlan Murdoch (who has long been regarded as his father's successor) recently resigned from the News Corp media empire, reportedly following a number of arguments with his father. His sister, Elisabeth, stepped down from Sky five years ago to set up her own television production company. Rupert Murdoch has made no secret of his wish for one of his children to take over the reins, but now only his younger son, James, remains in the family business. Similarly, the Pathak family were drawn into lengthy and acrimonious legal arguments when Anila Shastri and Chitralekha Mehta claimed that they were owed a share of the business empire founded by their father more than 40 years ago. Mrs Pathak said she and her husband, who died in 1997, never intended their daughters to own shares in the company. When the daughters married they became the full responsibility of their husbands. However, the daughters argued that they were the victims of a Hindu culture in which male inheritance is still customary and women are treated unequally.

Although the founders of the business might want to pass on the baton to the next generation, it does not necessarily follow that such an inheritance would be welcome. On the other hand the desire to inherit might be strong, but there are doubts in the current management about the successor's competence to run the organization effectively.

Sometimes, the need to plan for succession is not recognized, or is not recognized in time. Planning for succession needs to begin well in advance (see example in Enterprise in Action 5.3). For example, if the plan is to sell the business, the timing of that sale might be crucial in terms of the general state of the market or the performance of the business.

---

## Enterprise in Action 5.3

### Glenmorangie

Glenmorangie is not just any old whisky. It is a single malt made at the Tain distillery in Ross-shire, where, so the legend goes, the 16 'men of Tain' still hold the secrets of the distillation process that gives the whisky its characteristic flavour.

The MacDonald clan founded Glenmorangie in 1893, and hold just over 50 per cent of the voting shares and a third of the value of the company. The decision to sell had not been a sudden one. Although he had four daughters, two of whom work for the firm, David was the last of the family who wanted an executive role with Glenmorangie. He had retired as chairman a decade ago, and, at the age of 71, had to decide how the family wealth should be passed on.

Paul Neep had been chief executive for the last seven years. Under his stewardship Glenmorangie had been marketed as an upmarket brand for the discerning whisky drinker, and shares were approaching all-time-high levels. City investors tend not to like family shareholdings. It made sense to sell.

When the sale is complete, the 25 or so family members will be worth around £100 m. Although David MacDonald could have been portrayed as betraying Scotland's whisky heritage, he has been treated with understanding. An employee said 'If I had the chance of £100 m in the bank, I'd sell too'.

*Adapted from*: Frank Kane, 'A neat scotch – at £300m', *The Observer*, 12 September 2004

**Questions:** Why is it important to plan for succession in a family firm? How might this differ from succession arrangements in a non-family firm?

---

BDO Stoy Hayward highlight a range of practical options for the founder, each of which bring their own advantages and disadvantages. They suggest that the founder can choose to:

- appoint a family member;
- appoint a caretaker manager;
- appoint a professional manager;
- liquidate the business;

■ sell, in whole or in part;
■ do nothing.

They point out that this decision will be influenced by:

■ the availability of suitable family or non-family successors;
■ the family's requirements from the business (for example whether funds need to be brought out of the business to support the founder in their retirement);
■ the personal and corporate tax implications of the various options;
■ the health and size of the business;
■ the business environment at the time of succession.

The Small Business Service commissioned research into the Business Support and Policy implications of SME Ownership and Succession, which was published by the UCE Knowledge Management Centre in April 2002. This research concluded that the businesses most vulnerable to succession failure were where they:

■ had lifestyle and personal, rather than strategic, goals;
■ were performing poorly;
■ were dependent upon the owner for day-to-day management;
■ had no natural family or internal successor; or
■ were ignoring the need to make arrangements for succession.

Part of the problem in planning succession is the former leader themselves. After spending so much of their life in a business, some entrepreneurs find it hard to accept that it is time to let go. Others are looking forward to taking the money and enjoying life. In Figure 5.1 some stereotypical alternatives are identified, each having different consequences for the businesses they leave (or fail to leave) behind!

**Figure 5.1**
What does the former leader do?

> **The monarch** – they don't go easily. It takes a revolt or they die!
> **The general** – they retire for a short time but then return to save the business.
> **The ambassador** – these people go gracefully, often serve as mentors to others, and still act as ambassadors for the business.
> **The reborn entrepreneur** – they start again somewhere else.
> **The hedonist** – they take great holidays or play golf, finally indulging themselves.
>
> *Adapted from*: Sommerfield and Spence, *Family Business Review* 2(4), Winter, 1989

## Support needs

Barclays (2002) found that when family businesses were asked what additional help they would like from the government, tax relief on succession was mentioned most frequently – one in four family business owners want support in this area. Provision of loans, grants and subsidies, better advice and reduced business rates were also highlighted.

## Young entrepreneurs and grey entrepreneurs

## Young entrepreneurs

Although there are many examples of successful **young entrepreneurs**, there are specific barriers that might hinder them in setting up in business, for example:

- lack of credibility;
- lack of experience and knowledge;
- lack of a network of contacts;
- lack of access to funds for start up.

The Prince's Trust is a UK charity that helps young people to realize their potential. In 2004 it helped 12 793 young entrepreneurs through its start up programme (www.princes-trust.org.uk). It offers a range of support including business advice, and small grants and loans to young people between the ages of 18 and 30 who are unemployed or work less than 16 hours per week (see Enterprise in Action 5.1).

---

### Enterprise in Action 5.4

**Arctic Monkeys**

Alex Turner decided to defer his entry to university to see if he and his former schoolmates could make a living from their band. They had started to take their hobby seriously when two of them were given their first 'proper' guitars at Christmas. Their first gig was at The Grapes in Sheffield, but it had been a year before they actually went on stage, wanting to get things right first. Lyrics had been a bit of a problem in the early days until Alex admitted he had been writing lyrics since he had been at school. He had kept quiet about it, expecting to have the mickey taken. But nobody is laughing at him now. Arctic Monkeys have signed a recording contract with Domino, and have taken the industry by storm.

They didn't contrive things – their agent advised them to take a different approach to promotion, telling them to have confidence; if they were good enough, the industry would find them. They decided to give away demos at the gigs they played, and also put their music on the web. When they played the Boardwalk in Sheffield, the entire crowd were singing along to When the Sun Goes Down, which was a song that hadn't even been released.

Alex sings in a distinctive South Yorkshire accent about real life, things like fights outside nightclubs and odes to girls that got away. The band doesn't just play, they perform.

Zane Lowe played the band's Bet You Look Good On The Dance Floor on his Radio 1 show back in November 2004 and they pick new fans up everywhere they go. The one single that they did release was a limited edition, and is now quite a collector's piece available through eBay! Recently, having oversold a concert, they put on a second gig and offered extra tickets to the first people who returned their originals. Again there is a good market on eBay. Word of mouth has spread in a way that the industry simply cannot keep up with. It looks like their agent knew what he was talking about.

Sue Marriott and various public sources

**Question:** How might Arctic Monkeys' enterprising approach be compromised as their fame spreads?

## Grey entrepreneurs

In the year to September 2003, Office for National Statistics (ONS) figures show that the largest increase in self-employment came from **older entrepreneurs**. For full-time male entrepreneurs the group with the largest increase (86 000) were those aged 35–49, and a further 30 000 were aged 50–64. For part-time entrepreneurs these figures were 21 000 in the 50–64 age bracket and 9000 for age 65 and over. A similar pattern exists for women. Numbers of full-time self-employed women increased by 16 000 in the 35–49 age group and by 17 000 for those aged 50–59. Part-time women entrepreneur numbers grew by 18 000 in the 35–49 age group.

These people have often had considerable experience in their careers. Their motivations vary. Some are frustrated by the lack of opportunity and recognition within their employment; others are creative and innovative and leave employment or take early retirement to exploit opportunities. They have the advantage of specialist expertise, industry knowledge and contacts that they have developed over time. Many also have considerable knowledge and experience of business management. They are at a stage in their lives where they may be more confident about their ability to manage their personal circumstances, sometimes having paid off mortgages and been relieved of familial responsibilities.

Environmental trends may also be part of the reason why there is a growth in 'grey entrepreneurship'. For example, some pension schemes have failed to provide the level of income that had been expected, leading to a need to generate additional income. Also, the flexibility of self-employment might offer a tempting lifestyle where early retirement or redundancy has been offered.

## Self-perceptions

### Readiness for self-employment

Confidence is all-important in taking the first steps into self-employment. As shown in Figure 5.2, over time individuals gain experience and knowledge. We gain background knowledge of the way the world of work operates through our experiences at school, from the media, from our families and eventually from our own experience. Exposure to the world of work is a gradual process, and as well as developing knowledge and understanding individuals acquire skills, gaining confidence in their ability to identify problems and find solutions to them. As responsibility develops, problems become more complex until a level of expertise is achieved which instils a degree of confidence that most situations can be managed. At this point an individual might feel ready to take on the challenge of running a business of their own. Of course, eventually age takes its toll and the demands of a steep learning curve can appear too great a demand on both time and energy.

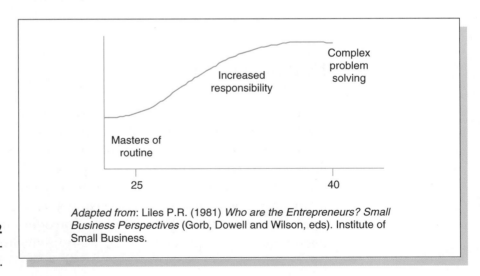

*Adapted from*: Liles P.R. (1981) *Who are the Entrepreneurs? Small Business Perspectives* (Gorb, Dowell and Wilson, eds). Institute of Small Business.

**Figure 5.2**
Readiness for self-employment.

### Enterprise in Action 5.5

**A nose for business**

Laurice Rahme was born in Paris. Her parents were in the restaurant business, but Laurice wasn't convinced that she wanted to do likewise. She was a rebellious teenager, but luckily fell in with a good group of friends. They were experts in antiques and took Laurice with them to flea markets and taught her the tricks of the trade. She started a small shop eventually, but when the area was renovated she was priced out of the market.

She sought help from one of her customers, who suggested she might be able to indulge her wish to travel by taking a job with Lancome in the Middle East. She said at 21 she was eager to do this, although very few other French women shared her adventurous spirit at the time (1970s). In 1976 she received a phone call from Lancome in New York, asking her to open the first Lancome Institut de Beaute in America. She again seized the opportunity and moved to Manhattan. She loved her time in America, and had to think long and hard about her future when the time came to go back to her old job.

On a flight to Paris she met someone who persuaded her to take a position at Annick Goutal, the fragrance designers, and after a year of negotiations she took the job. She became a partner with a 22 per cent stake, making about $0.5 m when she sold her stake back to them six years later. In the meantime she learned a lot about running a successful business.

Her next venture, at Creed Perfumes, experienced problems arising from discounting in America, and she decided that the time was right to leave and manufacture her own perfume, Bond No. 9, so that she could have total control. Sales are now $6 m a year. She says that entrepreneurs should start small, go slowly, and have as little debt as possible.

*Adapted from*: Julie Earle Levine, 'Sweet scent of success', *The Sunday Times*, 16 January 2005

**Question:** What are the advantages and disadvantages of this step-by-step approach to developing entrepreneurial success?

## Self-perceived effective capacity

However, actual competence and capability are different from **self-perceived efficacy**. A range of internal and external factors might affect an individual's perceptions of their own capability, and the likelihood of success. Circumstances can appear to limit choice, and sometimes the risks appear greater than at other times. The window of opportunity opens and closes as the context changes. Figure 5.3 shows a typical pattern, although it should be recognized that this does not suggest that it is representative of every individual's circumstances.

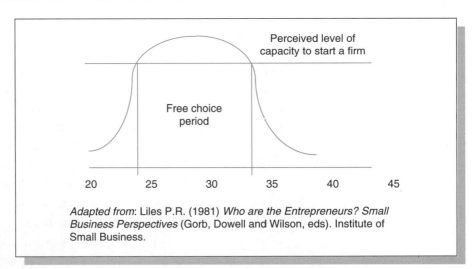

**Figure 5.3**
Self-perceived
effective capacity.

Whether or not an individual feels free to make the decision to engage in entrepreneurial activity will depend upon:

- the distractions and obligations they have (such as running the local under-11 football team, being a local magistrate);
- their family commitments and the level of security they need to provide (for example the mortgage, two children, partner, ageing parents);
- the salary and benefits they perceive themselves to need (such as the company car, private health insurance);
- the status they seek, and its source (for example, is being a senior manager important to you, would self-employment enhance or diminish your self-esteem, and does that matter?);
- the desired level of responsibility (for example, for some entrepreneurs responsibility increases as they establish their own business, but for others it is a lessening of responsibility);
- loss of their power base (for example, for a managing director of a company that employs 500 people, becoming a one-person operation means some diminution of power and authority, and might also mean the loss of someone to do the photocopying and make the tea!).

## Risks associated with entrepreneurship

During the free-choice period, an individual might seriously consider starting a new business. At this point they will consider the risks as they see them. Liles (1981) suggests that there are four types of **risk**:

- **Psychic risk.** Often the business is the personification of the entrepreneur, and if the business fails it has devastating consequences for their psychological well-being.
- **Financial risk.** The entrepreneur may have invested money (perhaps all of their savings) in the venture. Often banks and other funders demand collateral, and this may mean the risk of losing the house and/or personal bankruptcy.
- **Career risk.** If the business fails, the entrepreneur may need to seek paid employment in the future. They will need to consider how perceptions of business failure might affect their career prospects. Also, the focus on general management might mean that they are less able to keep up with the latest developments in their areas of specialism, and the loss of relevant knowledge and expertise might again disadvantage them if they have to return to paid employment.
- **Family risk.** Family life and relationships can suffer because of the demands of the business on the entrepreneur's time, energy and emotions.

In addition to these, there are also risks associated with:

- **Personal history.** The entrepreneur will need to consider their own capabilities and assess whether they are being realistic about their own skills, knowledge, attitudes and experience.
- **The environment.** Consideration needs to be given as to whether the entrepreneur has sufficient insight when analysing trends in the environment.
- **Commercialization.** There are risks associated with the commercialization process. Although market research might reduce these risks, the only way to really know what the demand is, is to go to market. The risk is equally great for predicting too little demand as well as too much.
- **External support.** While drawing on the experience of others, and while services such as grants and soft loans, can be invaluable, there is also the danger that the entrepreneur might rely too much thereon, so becoming dependent and losing autonomy.

The final decision comes down to the individual, and some of these areas of risk will be more pertinent to some individuals than to others. In Pause and Reflect 5.2, issues of readiness for self-employment, self-perceptions and attitudes towards risk could all play a part in Lee's decision. One of the distinguishing features of entrepreneurs is their willingness to take on risks and manage them.

## Pause and Reflect 5.2

### Inspired by gardens

On leaving university, with a degree in Business and Hospitality Management, Lee took up a well-paid job in recruitment, and he and his girlfriend (a teacher) bought their first home. At first the job was fulfilling; Lee gained confidence through interviewing candidates and dealing with employers. But in time much of this became routine, and the long hours and target-driven culture became less appealing.

His real passion was gardening, and he was spending most of his spare time turning the piece of land attached to his house into a 'proper garden'. Friends and family were quick to exploit his talents, and Lee seriously wondered whether he could turn his hobby into a business.

He had seen an advertisement for a BBC competition designed to give aspiring gardeners an opportunity to turn their dreams into reality. Not really expecting to succeed, Lee applied. Much to his surprise, after an arduous selection process (deliberately designed to test the perseverance and commitment of the applicants) he was chosen from 4000 hopefuls to be one of eight 'apprentice gardeners' on a BBC 2 documentary. He gave up his job, and moved to RHS Wisley for six months to take up what he described as 'a life changing opportunity'.

Having had a unique experience, Lee now has to decide whether self-employment is for him. He has had the courage to give up paid employment, and has relied on the financial and personal support of his girlfriend while being involved in the making of the programme.

Lee has had six months of high-quality tuition at Wisley, and has gained considerable horticultural experience. He was part of a silver medal winning team at Tatton Flower Show, has made extensive and invaluable contacts in the industry, and has been inspired by some of the gardening world's most famous characters.

*Source*: Sue Marriott

**Questions:** Should Lee have taken the plunge? How might his aspirations, and his perception of the risks involved, have altered in the light of his experience at Wisley?

## Culture

Geert Hofstede (1980) has proposed a framework for differentiating between cultures in four dimensions (see Figure 5.4):

1. level of power distance
2. individualism
3. masculinity
4. uncertainty avoidance.

The predominant **culture** in a country or society would have an impact on the entrepreneurial climate. For example, in America the cultural climate is dominated by masculine values, looking for material gain, a competitive spirit and dogged determination. These values are the ones that we commonly read about in the literature as typifying entrepreneurs. We

**Figure 5.4**
Cultural dimensions.

> **Level of power distance:** the extent to which a society accepts that there will be an unequal distribution of power. Even the less powerful accept the situation.
>
> **Uncertainty avoidance:** the extent to which a society feels threatened by ambiguity. For example, they might establish formal rules, frown on deviant ideas, etc. These societies also seem to be characterized by anxiety and aggressiveness, and a strong work ethic.
>
> **Individualism–collectivism:** an individualist society would be one in which people are expected to take care of themselves and their immediate families only; the social framework is very loosely knit. A collective society is the opposite – clan-like – where people expect their 'in-group' to take care of them, and they owe reciprocal loyalty.
>
> **Masculinity–femininity:** the extent to which dominant values in society are 'masculine' in orientation, i.e. assertiveness, acquisition of money and things, not caring for others or the quality of life.

might question how far this perception of successful entrepreneurialism is typical, or, indeed, helpful. In Finland, for example, quality of life issues assume higher importance and the welfare of community would take precedence over material gain. We might expect to see a different pattern of entrepreneurial behaviour in such a climate. We have talked about how we are all culturally conditioned, how we see the world in the way that we have learned to see it. Hofstede questions whether the theories developed in one culture (specifically the American one as that is where many management thinkers originate) apply in others, for example Japan and India. There is, similarly, some utility in exploring different cultural contexts for entrepreneurial activity to test whether the concepts do remain valid. We explore this further in Chapter 8.

## Degree of fit

It is likely that the entrepreneur will, consciously or unconsciously, assess the degree of fit between their individual values and those in the community at large. In considering whether entrepreneurship is the right career path, this cultural aspect would have an effect on perceptions of the likelihood of success. It might also affect the choice of sector and the nature of the business. An individual with masculine values, high power distance and high individuality might be more successful in the private sector whereas an individual who has feminine values, low individuality, and low power distance might prefer to operate in the public or not-for-profit sector, or become a social entrepreneur, for example.

## The support infrastructure

Although running a business can be a rewarding and exhilarating experience, it also demands considerable investment. This investment is not only financial, although that burden can be significant, but means commitment of time and energy. This can have serious implications for the personal life of the entrepreneur, and those close to them.

## Personal support networks

Self-employment is often described as a lonely experience. It is not easy to carry the burden of running a business, and support networks might help in alleviating this.

A supportive family is a real asset, but family relationships can also be a business liability. If tensions surface because the family feel neglected, or because the needs of the business are constantly being prioritized over family needs (for example, lack of holidays, working through weekends, bringing business anxieties home, not being at school open evenings or sports days and so on), the entrepreneur can come under intense pressure.

However, there is a difference between **personal support networks** and general business networking. The quantity and the quality of the external linkages between an organization and its environment are crucial to its success. Entrepreneurs rely on networks for information and access to resources.

## The know-how and know-who of social networks

The phrase 'it is not what you know but who you know' is in common usage, and there is some truth in the sentiment. Networks are sources of skills, information, contacts and ideas, and are, arguably, more important in the growth stage than in the start up stage. Non-supportive networks such as families that are inexperienced or opposed to entrepreneurship may make risk judgement difficult or may distract attention or sap motivation at key moments.

How networks are used is a critical issue. We have already discussed how women use networks differently from men. They are involved in smaller, more personal networks, and establish stronger individual relationships. The entrepreneur can be supported, or hindered, by his or her social networks.

Businesses can sometimes compete more effectively through collaboration, and an example of this is given in Enterprise in Action 5.6. In this example, a local Business Link was piloting a network broker scheme, the objectives of this being to facilitate collaborative ventures between a number of businesses targeting a specific customer group. Through presenting an integrated service to the customer, the network of businesses achieved more sales than they could have done acting independently.

## Enterprise in Action 5.6

### The Wedding Network

During a discussion with a local stationer who was exploring routes to market for her products, her personal business adviser from Business Link pointed out that there must be many other local firms providing 'wedding related' services. Thinking together, they identified around a dozen commonly required elements for a wedding (flowers, cars, gowns and so on). The Business Link was piloting a network brokerage service, and the adviser drew on support from this pilot scheme to set up The Wedding Network. He brought together a number of small businesses who could offer the complementary services that a customer would want when arranging a wedding, and facilitated the management of the network business in the early stages of the evolution of the network.

The group considered the adviser's presence to be critical to the effective management of the network, and as they began to win contracts the businesses developed trust through their shared experiences. This common understanding included the network broker however, and although it was expected that the broker would exit the group as it matured, it became increasingly difficult for the broker to withdraw. When the free time from Business Link expired, the network chose to pay for the service to continue.

*Source*: Chris Wroe, Sheffield Hallam University

**Question:** Argue for and against the view that this story exemplifies how, with the best of intentions, public sector support can inadvertently create dependency.

## Supporting enterprising people

If we accept that we need more enterprise in the economy, it makes sense to consider how we might support people in their attempts to be more enterprising, whether that lies in the setting up of their own business, being enterprising in employment, or developing an innovative corporate environment to stimulate innovation and growth. We will briefly consider two contexts in which support can be provided. First, **public sector and private sector support** in stimulating an enterprise culture, and, secondly, stimulating creativity in the employed workforce.

# Public sector support

In general terms, governments are aware of the importance of entrepreneurship and innovation in the economy, and seek to support it through a range of measures. Opinions vary as to how best to support enterprise, and the actual measures taken vary between nations and over time within countries, regions, and local communities. We cannot offer a comprehensive evaluation of such initiatives here, but seek to highlight a few issues and pose some questions to stimulate debate.

## Does government intervention make a difference?

It is a point of debate whether there is a case for public intervention in enterprise at all. In the UK there has been an interest in the creation of an enterprise culture for at least the past 25 years, but there is little research evidence that any of the various policies have had a significant impact on attitudes. It is difficult to prove causality in any event, as initiatives brought in by government are just one part of many changes that have occurred in the structure of the economy and attitudes in society in general, such as the decline of the manufacturing base and changing expectations of employment.

There are also qualitative considerations such as the nature of jobs created and how long they are likely to last, and whether there is a legacy in terms of improved workforce skills when we assess impact.

The investment of business itself in both time and money will always dwarf the investment that a government can make, and so it can always be argued that the achievements should be credited to the businesses themselves. Given the difficulty in proving causality, some argue that the public sector should concentrate upon offering direction and coordination rather than intervening directly.

The various agencies involved in supporting businesses (Chambers of Commerce, Enterprise Agencies, the Training and Enterprise Councils, Business Links, and now the Small Business Service) can all point to individual success stories, but the question arises as to whether these agencies actually make a significant difference when we cannot know what would have happened anyway had no intervention taken place.

## Social costs

As well as the perceived benefits of investing in enterprise there are costs. In any investment, there are opportunity costs. If we spend money on enterprise initiatives to support specific sectors or businesses, we cannot also spend it in other areas, for example education. One argument might be that if we are serious about generating an enterprise culture, it may be more appropriate to consider how to foster creativity and innovation in schools. If we invest in the young, they will be more enterprising throughout their lives. This may be more productive in the longer term than targeted business support.

Economic conditions obviously affect enterprise; for instance, more businesses fail in a recession. When failure rates are high, governments could be criticized for investing public funds in start ups, for example. If the business should fail, bankruptcy has a high social and personal cost. In supporting high-risk ventures, it could be argued that the potential social cost is greater, and that this should be weighed in the balance where public money is involved.

## The nature of support

If we accept that government intervention is desirable, the next question to be addressed is what type of support generates the most **impact**? Over time there has been a wide range of initiatives (in fact a term in common usage is 'initiative fatigue') designed primarily to encourage business start up and growth. The last 25 years have seen the arrival and departure of initiatives such as the creation of enterprise zones (waiving rates in some areas to encourage enterprise); subsidized workspace; technology transfer schemes; a variety of grant schemes to promote innovation; support for export and internationalization; the Enterprise Allowance Scheme to support unemployed people in starting a business; training programmes to support business planning for new-start businesses; one-to-one counselling and advice; subsidized consultancy services; and a range of information services. Some generic services are free in the initial stages, others are partially funded.

Although most business support initiatives in the UK are delivered through the Business Link network, it should be remembered that they are but one part of a complex array of support for businesses. Significant proportions of businesses never avail themselves of this support and rely instead on their own networks, trade associations, professional service providers such as their accountants, and funding providers. Some are suspicious of government agencies, thinking that information could be passed on to the Inland Revenue and so on. It is also argued that the investment in targeted initiatives is misplaced, and that generic support, e.g. fiscal measures, is more effective in supporting businesses competitiveness.

## What type of firm to support?

In investing public funds, accountability issues inevitably arise, and governments (and the people that elect them) understandably want to get the best return from their investment. Some people argue that support should only be given to those businesses that have the greatest capacity to grow. Supporting, for example, a mobile hairdresser would probably displace other mobile hairdressers, as there is a limit to how many times people in an area will have their hair done and demand cannot stretch indefinitely. This displacement means there is little net gain overall in terms of impact.

On the other hand, supporting a high-tech business means that there is real potential for wealth creation. But the issue is more complex than this. These businesses do have the potential to make a significant individual contribution to economic growth, but there are very few of them. They may also create wealth, but not necessarily employment.

Using public money to change the industrial make-up of an area is a laudable aim, and is common in areas badly affected by economic decline. But it could be argued that this is displacement of a different kind. Entrepreneurs are very good at getting more for less, and there is a danger that, where sectors offer significant potential for profit, the entrepreneur might have resourced the opportunity anyway.

## Picking winners

Some suggest that rather than supporting certain types of business, public investment should focus on individual entrepreneurs. Many entrepreneurs start in low-tech, sometimes low growth potential sectors, but eventually become very successful. For example, would people like Gates, Dell, and Branson have been spotted as winners and given support? The other pertinent question, of course, is did they actually need it? Of course there may have been other people with entrepreneurial potential who 'fell by the wayside' but who may not have done had support been available.

## Employer support

Many potential entrepreneurs take the plunge after working as employees in other organizations. Employer attitudes to encouraging (or not!) staff to leave employment to start their own business could be a crucial factor for some individuals. Although it would not seem to make sense for employers to encourage staff to set up on their own (especially as the knowledge and experience of such employees might mean that they would choose to compete in a similar industry), it might help in developing innovation within their own organization. It might also give the employees sufficient job satisfaction to persuade them of the benefits of staying.

Tried and tested methods include secondments to provide business or entrepreneurial management for charities, government, etc. or opportunities to pursue new ideas within the organization.

## Categorizing entrepreneurs

The support needs of entrepreneurs are, as we can see, many and varied. Some rely entirely on personal support, and never engage with public sector provision at all. But at any one point in time, the support needs of a specific individual will depend on a combination of some or all of the factors we have discussed in this chapter. In an attempt to simplify this complexity, it may be useful to consider whether we can categorize entrepreneurs in the way they think about entrepreneurship, and their attitudes towards it as a career path.

In Figure 5.5 potential entrepreneurs are categorized on the basis of the extent to which the right support infrastructure influences their decision to become an entrepreneur. Some people will take this step irrespective of support; others would only do it if the support were guaranteed. This does not help in determining the nature of that support, which will also vary depending on the individual's needs, aspirations and attitudes.

---

Entrepreneurship is:

- **The only route** – the individual will do it, whatever the personal circumstances, context and support
- **The best route** – the individual feels it is their preferred career path, and will do it when their personal circumstances and the context is favourable
- **An acceptable route** – the individual could be persuaded if the context, infrastructure and support are in place
- **A possible route** – the infrastructure and support available are an integral part of the decision, and may be instrumental in determining whether it is right for that individual

**Figure 5.5**
Attitudes towards entrepreneurship.

## Spotlight 5.1

### High Growth Start Up in South Yorkshire

The High Growth Start Up (HGSU) Initiative was launched in South Yorkshire in October 2002 as one way of increasing levels of business start ups in the region where numbers have historically been lower than in any other sub-region in Yorkshire and Humber. Since its launch, HGSU has created 404 businesses and 1309 jobs in industries that have been earmarked as having better potential for growth than others. High-growth industries include areas such as advanced engineering, digital industry, food and drink, chemicals and bioscience.

Denis Healy, Head of Enterprise at Business Link South Yorkshire, explained: 'The High Growth Start Up programme in South Yorkshire is like nothing else in the country. It has been designed with the entrepreneur at its heart. The specific needs of people with the real drive and ambition to create a high-growth business are catered for in ways that have never been available before. All the targets for the first phase of the programme have been exceeded, with more jobs being created, more businesses starting up, and more turnover being generated. It has been a great success story for the region.'

Despite its success, funding for HGSU, which is managed and delivered by Business Link South Yorkshire, was due to run out in March 2005, but Yorkshire Forward agreed to invest a further £3 million with a further £3 million coming from the Objective One European Regional Development Fund. The extra finance will see the initiative run until March 2009.

*Source*: Adapted from a Yorkshire Forward press release, 13 January 2005

**Question:** Assess the advantages and disadvantages of supporting high-growth start ups. To what extent would these businesses be set up irrespective of whether they received public sector support?

## Summary

- The decision to engage in entrepreneurial activity is influenced by a range of environmental and personal circumstances.
- These interrelationships are complex, and two individuals in similar situations may well make different choices.
- Although all entrepreneurs face similar barriers to enterprise, there are factors that are context specific, and this demands a degree of flexibility in helping people to overcome them.
- Self-perception, and an individual's readiness for self-employment, will vary over time and this will impact on their willingness to act on their entrepreneurial inclinations.
- Culture colours people's perceptions of appropriate models of entrepreneurship and this may affect their willingness to take the risk of starting their own business.
- Support networks can play a vital role in encouraging enterprise.
- Personal support is just as vital as external support.
- Public sector support needs to be flexible if it is to respond to the needs of different categories of entrepreneur.

## Chapter questions

1. 'The key to success in entrepreneurship is motivation'. Discuss this proposition with reference to (a) entrepreneurs from ethnic minorities, (b) entrepreneurs that are female and (c) entrepreneurs under the age of 25.
2. Is it valid to claim that women are more consultative owner–managers than men?
3. What factors might account for the more positive attitudes to enterprise by younger people in the UK?
4. Analyse your attitudes towards risk and consider how this might influence your career preferences.
5. If you were to consider setting up in business, what social and business networks would you need to develop, and why?

## Case study

### Babylicious

Sally Preston's parents hoped she would become a doctor, but she knew she couldn't get the grades she needed to do that. After doing work experience with a dietitian, she took a degree in food sciences instead. She then joined Marks & Spencer, spending 11 years working her way up to be a senior food technologist there. But she had never really felt she belonged in the corporate world, so at the age of 33 she left to start her own food consultancy.

In the back of her mind she also had an idea to set up a frozen baby-food company. Having two small children of her own she could see a gap in the market, and wondered why no one else had exploited it.

But before she could do so herself, life dealt her a rough deal. Her marriage fell apart, and she had to take the children with her into rented accommodation. Then she was diagnosed with skin cancer. She was resilient, however, and overcame the obstacles, having the malignant mole removed, and buying back the family home with the help of her parents.

Two years later, the business idea resurfaced on her list of priorities. She had big ambitions from the start, always intending to sell through the big retailers. She started out with recipes that her own children liked. She did a deal with a factory in Leicester that could make them for her in ice-cube portions so that parents could use as much or as little as they liked. The next step was to create a brand – mortgaging her house she raised £55 000 to hire a design company and Babylicious was born. However, when she tried to register the brand someone had beaten her to it – by 11 days. It transpired that the name had been lodged, in bad faith, by a woman Sally knew, but it took nine months to get the court to rule in her favour, and in the meantime the threat of litigation meant she had to change the packaging, the corporate stationery, the website, the marketing materials, etc. It cost her £30 000.

Within weeks Waitrose agreed to stock the products – but they wanted her to deliver them herself so she had to go out to buy a freezer van. She then needed to convince other retailers, and persuade them that they should install freezers in the baby section of their stores rather than stock Babylicious alongside traditional frozen foods.

However, after all the setbacks, she had finally turned the corner. By 2003 she had several industry awards behind her, and some welcome publicity when it was made known that Victoria Beckham was feeding her son Romeo with the product. Earlier this year she raised £1 m from selling 25 per cent of her equity to private investors, and her products are now stocked by Asda, Tesco and Sainsbury. Sales this year are expected to be around £9 m.

Sally says 'This is such an obvious business opportunity that if I hadn't done it I would have been forever frustrated that somebody else had. I wanted to prove I could do it. I wanted to be in control of my life. When it is my son's school sports day, I know I can be there. I don't have to ask anybody's permission.'

> *Adapted from:* 'Baby meals give mum time to chill', Sally Preston – How I made it. *The Sunday Times*, 14 November 2004

**Questions:**

1. Identify the barriers that Sally Preston encountered in getting Babylicious up and running and analyse how her personal skills and characteristics helped her to overcome them.
2. To what extent was Sally pushed or pulled into entrepreneurship?

## References and further reading

Basu A. and Goswami A. (1999) South Asian entrepreneurship in Great Britain; factors influencing growth. *International Journal of Entrepreneurial Behaviour and Research* **5**(5).

Carter S. and Cannon T. (1992) *Women as Entrepreneurs*. London: Academic Press.

Deakins D. and Freel M. (2003) *Entrepreneurship and Small Firms*, 3rd edn. Maidenhead: McGraw-Hill.

Dr Stuart Fraser, Centre for Small and Medium Sized Enterprises, Warwick Business School, University of Warwick: *Finance for Small and Medium-sized Enterprises: A report on the 2004 UK Survey of SME Finances* http://www.wbs.ac.uk/downloads/research/wbs-sme-exec.pdf accessed 14/8/2005

GEM (2004) Report on Women's Entrepreneurship.

Gibb A.A. and Ritchie J. (1981) Understanding the process of starting small business. *International Small Business Journal* **1**: 26–46.

Goffee R. and Scase R. (1985) *Women in Charge: The Experience of Female Entrepreneurs*. London: Allen and Unwin.

Goffee R. and Scase R. (1987) Patterns of business proprietorship amongst women in Britain. In: *Entrepreneurship in Britain*, pp. 60–82. London: Croom Helm.

Hofstede G. (1980) Motivation, leadership and organization: do American theories apply abroad? *Organizational Dynamics*, Summer, pp. 42–63.

Liles P.R. (1981) *Who are the Entrepreneurs? Small Business Perspectives* (P. Gorb, P. Dowell, P. Wilson, eds). Institute of Small Business.

Schaper M. and Volery T. (2004) *Entrepreneurship and Small Business: A Pacific Rim Perspective*. Milton: John Wiley & Sons Australia Ltd.

Westhead P. and Storey D. (1997) Training Provision and development of Small and Medium-sized Enterprises, Research report No. 26. London: HMSO.

Zimmerer T.W. and Scarborough N.M. (2005) *Essentials Of Entrepreneurship And Small Business Management*, 4th edn. New Jersey: Pearson Education Ltd.

## Useful websites

Barclays 'A Family Affair' 2002 http://www.familybizz.net/res_europe.asp accessed 15/8/2005

Office for National Statistics: *Changes in self-employment in the UK 2002–2003*, last accessed 15/8/2005 at http://www.statistics.gov.uk/articles/labour_market_trends/self_employment_1203.pdf

Small Business Service (2003) Household Survey of Entrepreneurship (DTI, July 2004) accessed 15/8/2005 at http://www.sbs.gov.uk/SBS_Gov_files/researchandstats/householdsurveysummary.pdf

## Key words

| | |
|---|---|
| criteria for measuring success | perceptions |
| culture | personal support networks |
| early exposure to small business | public sector and private sector |
| ethnic minority entrepreneurs |    support |
| family business | push and pull factors |
| female entrepreneurship | risk |
| generational issues | role in economic development |
| impact | self-perceived efficacy |
| location | succession planning |
| motivations | young entrepreneurs |
| older entrepreneurs | |

# The enterprise environment and the entrepreneurial response

By the end of this chapter the reader will be able to:

- explore the nature of the macro environmental context for entrepreneurial activity and the challenges organizations face during a downturn in demand;
- understand the changing nature of the micro environment, customer attitudes and purchasing behaviour and competitor activity;
- compare the responses of entrepreneurial organizations with those of more predictable organizations;
- identify the changes in approach of entrepreneurial organizations in highly competitive, dynamic and fast-changing markets;
- understand the alternative market approaches of organizations from different sectors.

## Introduction

In this chapter we consider the nature of the various environments in which entrepreneurial organizations operate and their responses to the changing environmental situations that they encounter. In doing this we begin by considering the changes that take place in the environment that both offer opportunities and pose threats for entrepreneurial organizations.

We consider the nature of the changes taking place in the business environment on a national and international basis (the macro environmental factors) and attempt to understand how they might create and constrain business opportunities. We also consider how incremental changes, critical events and decisions are exploited as the source of opportunity.

Of more immediate impact for most entrepreneurial organizations are the changes in the market dynamics of the specific business sector in which the organization operates (the micro environmental factors). Changes in the market dynamics, including changing customer needs, competition and market structures create business opportunities and also pose very specific threats.

The specific characteristics of entrepreneurial organizations mean that they are likely to respond to environmental changes and specific situations differently from organizations that adopt a more administrative and bureaucratic style of management. This is because entrepreneurial organizations have both limitations and advantages in their scope for pursuing different strategies, owing to their size, market knowledge and capability, and financial and human resources. These factors affect their approach to the market and to business decision-making.

Successful organizations are good at spotting how the changes that take place (or could take place) might enable them to create future competitive advantage by creating value for customers and the organization. We therefore consider the alternative approaches to the market that are adopted by firms and focus particularly on the marketing approaches and competitive stances adopted by entrepreneurial firms.

## The entrepreneurial environment

The starting point for any entrepreneurial organization exploiting an opportunity and developing a strategy that will ensure survival and growth is to have an understanding of the market environment in order to identify the threats and opportunities that might affect the current and future prospects for the organization.

## The business environment

The business environment is usually analysed in terms of **macro factors**, constituting the global trends that affect all organizations, and the **micro**

**factors** that affect organizations in one area of the business environment, for example, a particular market sector or a geographical area. It is not our intention to discuss the process of environmental analysis in detail here because entrepreneurs rarely have sufficient time and resources to undertake a complete analysis. They do identify and respond to the factors that are most relevant and likely to have the greatest impact on their business. However, there is a potential danger existing, in that they focus continually on the same environmental factors and trends and do not notice unexpected changes in a related area.

Moreover, because of the particular characteristics of entrepreneurial organizations it is appropriate to consider some specific aspects of the interaction of entrepreneurial firms with their environment. Different organizations are affected by the environment in different ways. For a fashion boutique in a small town, macro factors, such as the growing national or world economy, might influence its development but will not necessarily be critical to success. Stocking the right products for the current fashion trend, having a good location in the right area where plenty of customers with high disposable income might shop or the decision of a larger and more powerful competitor to open nearby will be even more important. By contrast an international investment fund manager might be more significantly affected by a changing economic situation and currency fluctuations.

The macro environmental analysis is normally carried out using a systematic and comprehensive process and is explored in detail in many business textbooks. Macro environmental analysis is usually carried out under a series of headings, typically including Political, Legal, Economic, Social and Cultural, and Technological factors.

Micro environmental analysis of the specific sector or local geographic environment usually involves an analysis of customer needs and expectations, the nature and power of the competition and the structure of the market, including the supply chain and routes to market (e.g. distributors, wholesalers, retailers and direct selling through e-commerce).

All organizations, therefore, operate within a macro and micro environment that is constantly changing. They have no control over the changes that take place but it is these changes that create opportunities and threats and every organization must decide how, if at all, it should respond to the changes that it notices.

In Figure 6.1 are shown three key environments that influence the development of an organization:

1. the macro environment;
2. the micro environment; and
3. the organization's immediate environment.

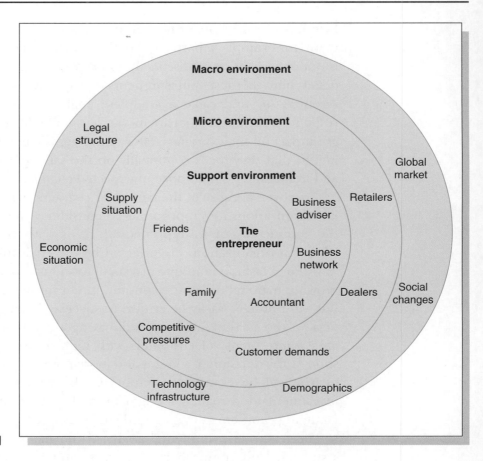

**Figure 6.1**

Before discussing the entrepreneurial responses to the macro and micro environment it is useful to refer to the previous chapter, which discussed the entrepreneur's environment. Personal circumstances and experiences may colour perceptions, and consequently impact upon the entrepreneur's predisposition to recognizing threats and opportunities.

# The entrepreneurial organizational environment

It is the organization working within its own immediate environment of **stakeholders** that enables it to respond to the macro and micro environmental changes taking place. Stakeholders are those individuals and groups that have an interest in what the organization does. The organizational environment is made up of some stakeholders the organization can choose, for example, accountants, lawyers, business advisers, funders, suppliers, and distributors, but also some stakeholders they cannot choose, for example, the government departments that apply controls and taxation.

For entrepreneurial organizations the organizational environment is often almost inseparable from the entrepreneur's personal environment. It includes not just their commercial stakeholders and business support network but their personal support network, such as family and friends, that will offer advice and support, and may even provide practical assistance in times of crisis.

While the organization can choose some of these stakeholders in its immediate organizational environment it cannot control them and so contribute to the uncertain environment in which it operates.

## The nature of macro environmental changes and the entrepreneurial strategic response

Changes in the environment require a timely organizational response. Before considering this interaction, however, it is useful to reflect on the characteristics of entrepreneurial organizations. Such organizations usually differ from more administratively managed organizations in the size of the business, the nature, style and culture of the management, the availability and limitations of their resources, their different market approaches, their different relationships with their customers and other stakeholders, and changes in the ways in which they interact with the market and compete. Typically they are more adaptable, flexible and responsive to the changes that affect them.

## Changes in the macro environment

Macro factors are the major trends and changes that affect all organizations within a nation, a region or the world and essentially include the major political, legal, economic, social, cultural, 'green' environments and technological factors. These factors include such issues as the increasing globalization of communications, the evolution of regional trading blocks, such as the expansion of the EU, the likelihood of a change of government in key countries, the ageing population in developed countries, the increasing concern about climate change, the changing attitudes of consumers in their purchasing and usage behaviour, and the prospects for the national and global economy that might affect demand and consumption.

The importance of analysing these changes is that organizations must develop an appropriate response to the factors that are likely to have the greatest impact on them. In Enterprise in Action 6.1 the impact of technological development on the gaming industry is discussed.

## Enterprise in Action 6.1

**Internet gaming – another way to make money?**

One of the most significant Internet success stories has been online betting. As with many industry breakpoints it has been entrepreneurial organizations that have been the main beneficiaries after developing new business models that offer an alternative to the old betting businesses and exploit new gaming fashions. By 2005 17 firms had floated on the stock market, valuing the founders' shares at £5.3 billion. Some have likened the gaming boom to the dot-com bubble of the late 1990s, but it has been claimed that there is a significant difference. Gaming businesses have stable income streams, even in times of recession and are very profitable.

The areas of interest and business models vary. The Internet version of conventional bookmakers must operate within a strict regulatory framework. However, other areas that are considered to be skills-based (known as cash skill gaming) are less heavily regulated. Betfair (see Enterprise in Action 10.4) along with a number of other smaller players is a betting exchange that matches those laying odds with those placing the bets. Party gaming, floated in 2005 for £5 billion, has exploited the online poker boom.

The cash skill gaming sector, which can range from chess to virtual billiards, grew by 40 per cent in 2005, and is expected to continue to grow, fuelled by new game fashions. For example, backgammon is particularly popular in Scandinavia, Greece, Turkey and the Middle East.

*Adapted from*: Goodman M. and Box D., 'Gaming winners', *The Sunday Times*, 7 August 2005

**Question:** What indicators can you identify that suggest that this is a short-term or sustainable business opportunity?

# The nature of the strategic response of entrepreneurial organizations to macro environmental changes

In discussing the nature of the response of entrepreneurial organizations to changes in the macro environment that will ensure survival and growth it is useful to consider the changes in the macro environment in four categories:

1.   incremental changes
2.   critical decisions
3.   critical incidents
4.   globalization trends.

## Incremental change

Certain changes are predictable and have been apparent for many years, for example, the ageing population, increasing obesity in developed countries and the increasing worldwide familiarity with and usage of communications technology. The most astute organizations have anticipated and prepared for the **incremental changes** that are most likely to affect them by modifying the way in which they manage their business and, where appropriate, by developing new products, services and processes.

Perhaps the most difficult challenge is timing the launch of new products and services and making management changes within the organization to obtain the maximum performance benefits. It can be expensive and wasteful to make management changes if they are not needed immediately or to launch new products and services if the market is not ready for them, so the entrepreneurial management skill is to get the timing right for the response to the changing macro factors. In different market sectors, firms such as Bodyshop, Subway and easyJet have grown spectacularly on the crest of a wave of incremental environment changes – more environmentally friendly beauty products, healthier fast food and lower-cost airline travel.

While it might appear from newspaper headlines that the successful firms have got the timing right and introduced products just as demand was about to take off, in practice many firms have grown at a slow pace until they got a lucky break as a result, for example, of a change of mood in customers or a change in the nature of the competition. Ryanair and easyJet are highly successful low-cost airline operators, but they were preceded and followed by a number of similar organizations that failed to make a significant impact on the market. The Subway fast food sandwich chain grew very slowly until customers became far more concerned with healthy eating than had hitherto been the case. In Enterprise in Action 6.2 (see below), it is shown how Saga followed a long-term trend by gradually adding further services to its initial offering.

## Enterprise in Action 6.2

### Saga – making a fortune with holidays for the over-50s

In 1951 Sidney De Haan offered off-peak holidays to retired people whom he identified as having the time to travel at any time of the year. The idea was to fill unused rooms in his hotel in Folkestone, UK. His first all-inclusive holiday cost £6.50. As the demand developed he introduced the first chartered train, pioneered the first passport-free trip to France and soon bought the first Saga cruise ship. Sidney was succeeded as chief executive by his son Roger and, with the continuing success of the holidays side of the business, the family-owned firm was able to offer more services targeting the over-50s including travel, publishing, insurance, home shopping, financial services and radio stations in selected regions of the UK. Times have changed and Saga has adapted, in 2005 launching discount cruising and a new range of cruises based on adventure and exploration, still for the over-50s. It has 7.6 million customers on its database and employs 3500 staff worldwide.

In 2004 Roger De Haan decided to retire to spend more time developing Folkestone Harbour, which he had recently bought. No other members of the family were interested in taking charge in his place so Saga was put up for sale. Against competition from outside bidders it was sold for £1.35 billion to a management buy-out (discussed in Chapter 11). It was estimated that Roger De Haan would take about £700 million with a further £300 million going to family trusts.

*Adapted from*: Goodman M. and O'Connell D., 'Saga family stands to make £1bn from sale', The Times Online, October 03, 2004 and www.saga.co.uk

**Question:** What are the success factors in exploiting an opportunity based on incremental change?

## Critical decisions

The second group of macro environmental changes are those that depend on a **critical decision**, which might be expected at a certain point in time. It may be difficult to predict the implications of key decisions as they may only become apparent after some time, perhaps one or two years later. Often critical decisions involve new legislation, for example, the introduction of the euro or environmental legislation, such as that relating to the disposal of refrigerators and freezers in the EU. Many firms appear to wait until the legislation has come into force before fully deciding how they should react. More enterprising organizations are able to work out what the implications are likely to be, decide on their response and so gain first-mover advantage in the market.

While it may appear obvious what specific opportunity these critical decisions create it is often surprising that they are not followed up immediately and a latent demand is often left unsatisfied. The real challenge for entrepreneurial organizations in responding to new legislation is not simply recognizing what the implications of a change in legislation might be, but deciding what the business opportunity will be as a result. Entrepreneurial organizations often do not pursue what might be the obvious opportunity but instead go for a different but related product, service or process that enables them to create a unique and highly profitable niche. Following new legislation relating to the need for organizations to remove a certain type of asbestos from their buildings one entrepreneurial organization set up a business to carry out surveys of buildings for major companies which identified the asbestos that needed to be removed.

## Critical events

Certain macro environmental factors are almost impossible to predict. Wars, environmental disasters, health concerns, such as Hurricane Katrina, computer viruses and 9/11 are largely unexpected and can have a devastating, often long-term effect on global, regional or national organizations. The effect can be varied and unpredictable depending upon the nature of the event. Events such as these can have an immediate and potentially catastrophic impact on organizations that were already vulnerable. For example, Sabena, the Belgian national airline, was financially weak and collapsed following 9/11 owing to the declining passenger numbers.

Even if **critical events** are anticipated it is unlikely that organizations can predict when they are likely to occur. Organizations rarely have spare resources and are unlikely to be able to afford sufficient resources to plan to cope with unexpected events. The only defence that an entrepreneurial organization has over larger, more powerful and better-resourced competitors is to respond very rapidly, by taking bold decisions quickly, ensuring their management and staff are flexible and can be mobilized to deal with the event.

Terrorism and various health scares, such as bird flu, have a very dramatic effect on international travel and tourism. While the problems of the biggest airlines hit the newspaper headlines after 9/11, smaller organizations that rely on tourism were most vulnerable. To survive in the market following 9/11 smaller entrepreneurial organizations had to respond quickly and effectively to the micro environmental changes (declining customer demand) by using their core attributes of adaptability, flexibility and responsiveness. The low-cost airlines, easyJet and Ryanair, responded to a severe downturn in bookings within days after the 9/11 incident by giving away free or low-priced tickets to customers to get them flying again. This was a survival strategy, as they had little scope or reason to make drastic cost cuts and would not have been able to continue in their business if they had not quickly got large numbers of customers flying and generated revenue immediately.

By contrast, the long-established airlines responded by immediately cutting staff, while trying to maintain high prices. It took some weeks for them to respond effectively to the post-9/11 situation by which time the 'no-frills' airlines had gone a long way to establishing the concept of low-cost travel in people's minds and were making inroads into the business market too.

Even disasters can provide opportunities. Fairweather (2005) reported that three weeks after hurricane Katrina hit the US coast, property developers were back and very active in New Orleans and, despite expect-ations to the contrary, the cost of houses had increased 30 per cent as people who wanted to move back into the devastated city to revive their businesses competed over a reduced housing stock. People with money were now also prepared to move into areas previously occupied by poorer people, who had left the city to look for work and were unlikely to return. The new prospective owners believed that the drug-pushers and crim-inal gangs had also left. The areas where houses needed to be demol-ished also offered property development opportunities.

Critical events do not always have to be disasters as Enterprise in Action 6.3 shows; on reflection, the Australians may have considered the scenario discussed a disaster!

## Enterprise in Action 6.3

### Fortune favours the brave

Cricket originated in England but for long periods the national team has not performed well against the other countries and, particularly, against its old enemy the Australians, the current world champions. As a result the market in the UK for cricket equipment was mature and unexciting.

It was against this background that Woodworm was set up in 2002 by Joe Sillett, its managing director and David Brawn and Michael Hiard, two investment bankers, to market cricket bats and other cricket equipment based on outsourced manufacture by six suppliers.

The company's original intention was to shake up the market dominated by the existing big players, Gunn and Moore, Gray Nicholls and Slazenger in much the same way that Callaway attacked the golf market some years ago. Their key products were two bats, the Wand and the Torch, which sold for prices ranging from £25 to £225 each. They are made from willow shipped from England to India, where the bats are made. In the 12 months to March 2004 the company made a loss of £123 000 on sales of £260 000.

The master stroke of Woodworm was to arrange a sponsorship deal with Kevin Pietersen and Andrew Flintoff, reportedly worth £250 000 a year. In the summer of 2005 England per-formed heroically against the Australians in the series of test matches, catching the imagin-ation of the British sports enthusiasts. Flintoff was the star performer of the series and Pietersen was the man of the match in the last critical game. Sales of bats rocketed from 200 a year to 15 000, giving the business a 10 per cent share of the UK market and increasing annual sales to more than £1 m in 2005. Woodworm were able to bring forward the business plan break-even point by 12 months. After the launch of a new bat in October 2005 sales in the following year were predicted to double or treble, bringing in a very healthy profit.

*Adapted from*: Hope C., 'Flintoff helps cricket bat firm into the record books', *Daily Telegraph*, 31 August 2005

**Questions:** What should Woodworm do to maintain its growth? What potential risks might it face from the environment?

## Globalization

Perhaps the most significant macro factor over the last few decades has been the increasing trend to **globalization**. Doole and Lowe (2004) identify a number of drivers of globalization that result in more organizations competing on a global scale and explain how globalization has had significant implications for many organizations by, for example, providing new market opportunities, new sources of supply of lower-cost components, manufactured items and services.

Many small- and medium-sized entrepreneurial organizations now find that they are supplying a global niche market, as shown in Enterprise in Action 6.4.

---

### Enterprise in Action 6.4

**For Sunseeker 'The World is Not Enough'**

When Robert Braithwaite built his first sports boat in the 1960s he never dreamed of how his company would turn out, despite his enormous ambition. After leaving school with no particular plans he went to work for his father's engine servicing company. In 1968, however, he founded his boat-building company, Sunseeker, with a team of seven. The first few years were 'horrible', as the team worked hard but got nowhere. However, they kept trying, even when it seemed impossible to succeed. Braithwaite decided to focus on powerboats rather than sailing boats and invested in innovation, technology and design.

By 2002 Sunseeker was rather different. It had 1200 employees, a turnover of £135 m and sold boats at up to £5 m each to millionaires, world rulers and sports stars, and Braithwaite had won an Entrepreneur of the Year Award. Ninety-nine per cent of the boats were exported. Braithwaite also recognized the importance of building the brand and his ambition was to make Sunseeker the 'Hoover' of the luxury powerboat industry. This strategy reached the heights of success of global awareness with a Sunseeker boat, appearing in the opening sequence of the film The World is Not Enough with the new James Bond aboard, churning up the Thames in front of familiar London sites as he pursued an attractive female assassin.

*Adapted from*: Clark E., 'Sunseeker scoops entrepreneur award',
BBC News Online, 8 October 2002

**Question:** What do you consider to be the critical factors for an entrepreneur in developing a global niche business?

---

### Competitive threats

The trend towards greater globalization also creates the threat of greater global competition. The consequence of this for entrepreneurial organizations is that while the smallest organizations have opportunities in foreign markets they must also compete with foreign competition in their domestic market. Even the local café must compete with US-owned Subway, KFC, McDonalds, Starbucks, South African-owned Nandos and so on, by developing a more professionally marketed, differentiated customer offering.

As the larger international players have sought to dominate the global market, so they have acquired many medium-sized competitors that have under-used resources, fill a gap in their product range, have strength in particular markets or simply offer a competitive threat. To survive in an increasingly global market, therefore, it is necessary for smaller- and medium-sized firms to identify a market niche by developing a product and service offer that is valued by customers, and then focus on further building competitive advantage, and reinforcing their own distinct niche by building barriers to entry of competitors attacking them.

From a strong domestic niche base, such firms then systematically enter new markets overseas and become global niche players. This traditional route to developing as a global niche player has been followed by firms such as McDonalds, Bodyshop and eBay, which are at different stages of globalization. A number of international charities, such as Oxfam and Save the Children have followed similar routes.

### Global communications

Perhaps the most significant driver of globalization is communications, such as the Internet. The Internet provides a low-cost approach to new-country market entry that has enabled even very local, specialized businesses to respond to the new opportunity and supply global customers. The Internet has enabled organizations more effectively to obtain feedback from customers around the world directly rather than through export agents and distributors. This is vital to improve their product and service development and delivery capability.

Global sourcing of manufacturing and services, until recently the preserve of larger firms, has also now become feasible for smaller organizations too, enabling them to improve the effectiveness of their contributions to the product and service value chain through managing worldwide supply chains more efficiently. It is the Internet that has facilitated the instant transfer of substantial amounts of data, essential for B2B and institutional purchasing, and enabled real-time transactions to take place. For smaller organizations that lack human and financial resources, this has enabled them to substitute virtual for physical presence and to build relationships with customers and suppliers around the world.

## Surviving an economic downturn

It is vital for organizations to develop a strategy to deal with those macro factors that will have most impact on them. Clearly the main focus is on those trends that offer opportunities. However, entrepreneurial organizations must be aware of threats too, and, for example, one of the key criteria for the success of an entrepreneurial organization is its ability to survive and grow during periods when the environment is suffering an **economic downturn** and a temporary or permanent decline in demand.

Many markets are cyclical in nature and demand ebbs and flows on a periodic basis. The cycle may be short and seasonal, for example, buying for holidays, Christmas or at the start of the new school year. Alternatively it might be affected by the economic cycle. A gloomy economic outlook will affect consumer demand, as people fear reduced earnings or even redundancy and so save more of their income rather than spend it on products and services. Businesses respond by becoming less willing to invest in new equipment and product developments. By contrast some businesses are based around what consumers consider to be essential purchases and this leads to more predictable cash flow. However, the nature of what is deemed essential is changing. Consumers may consider beauty products and a holiday essential and may cut down in other areas of their budget to fund them. Alternatively they may trade down, buying a cheaper holiday flight or beauty product, rather than do without.

Smaller organizations with very limited financial resources in reserve would probably always be expected to suffer more than larger, more well established and better financed, more powerful competitors. However, this is not always the case.

The reasons why entrepreneurial organizations might succeed better than their larger or better established rivals could be because of the following.

■ The organization's product or service is regarded by customers as a necessity and also so innovative that there is no current competition, so demand is maintained and growth in sales continues during periods when other firms might be offering more mundane products and services.

■ The entrepreneurial organization is able accurately to predict problems and take early action to anticipate their effects perhaps by cutting costs, production or service delivery capacity. More complacent organizations are often slow to react and, when they are forced to do so, often have to take more drastic action than they would otherwise have to. This can often reduce their ability to grow quickly when the economy picks up and the market becomes more buoyant.

■ The organization knows how to find new market opportunities to compensate for the loss of revenue in existing product and service areas that are vulnerable in periods of economic downturn.

## The nature of micro environmental changes and the entrepreneurial strategic response

As we have discussed, certain macro environmental factors such as changes in technology or consumer demographics can have a significant effect on certain market sectors and business opportunities. For example, Enterprise in Action 6.2 shows how the ageing population has helped Saga holidays to become a very successful business.

However, even here the key business development drivers for the firm came from within the micro environment and focused on the key market sector factors, customers, competition and market structure. Saga were able to define a clear niche within a competitive travel market by differentiating their product offer with tailored service and promoting it with empathy for their ageing customers.

The main micro environmental changes are key to business survival and success and involve changes in **customer attitudes and purchasing behaviour**, changes in the existing and new, often unexpected competition and changes in the structure of the market, which has occurred, for example, when some organizations have cut out distributors and retailers and dealt directly with customers.

## Changing customer behaviour

An in-depth understanding of customer needs and good anticipation of future expectations is essential for success. It is important that entrepreneurial organizations and, particularly, start-ups take time to address the following fundamental questions even if they do not undertake full-scale market research.

■ Who buys?
■ What do customers buy?
■ Why do customers buy?

◼ Where do customers buy?
◼ When do customers buy?
◼ How do customers buy?

## Who buys?

It is necessary to combine an understanding of customer attitudes, values and beliefs that affect buying and usage behaviour with an understanding of the dynamics of the sector. It is then necessary to understand the changes in customer buying patterns that are likely to occur in the future that present both threats and opportunities to new and existing suppliers. For example, products and services targeted at the next generation will need different features and will probably need to be promoted in a different way, compared to the current generation; you might think about what the differences might be.

It is also important to separate myth from reality; for example, there is a common view that older people are technophobes and therefore are unlikely to respond to e-business. In practice, many have been using computers for the last 20 years, and often have the time and knowledge to search for product information, buy online, download music for their iPod and so on.

B2B and institutional purchasing is different from consumer purchasing as there are likely to be a number of managers involved in a purchase decision; all need to be convinced although one or two are usually more influential in decision-making than the others, but all need to be persuaded. Clearly e-commerce is increasing, as are online purchasing hubs where real-time deals are done and auctions are becoming more common in B2B purchasing.

## What do customers buy?

Customers buy benefits including the tangible and intangible benefits that we discussed in Chapter 3, so more than an efficiently functioning product or service is needed. The latter needs to be designed well, and have a recognizable brand name from an organization with a good reputation. Customers expect better value from their chosen product and supplier than is offered by the competition. And good service is just as important for patients and visitors to a hospital. They subconsciously make comparisons with the service they receive from the local supermarket. If they are unable to find a place to park their car or find the reception, nursing or medical staff rude or obstructive they are likely to complain.

## Why do customers buy?

The motivations for buying are various and dependent on the situation. Smaller organizations and especially start-ups have to address the question posed by customers of 'Why should I buy from you?' An important consideration for customers is the perceived risk (Settle and Alreck, 1989) of buying a product and this is increased if the supplier is unknown or untried.

## Where do customers buy?

The entrepreneurial organization can create its own distribution channel, for example, using e-business, or it can use a number of third-party intermediaries. Of course, third parties have different objectives from the entrepreneurial organization and may not always promote the products enthusiastically. The key question is whether the entrepreneurial organization makes it easy for customers to deal with them. That is not to say that all products should be available everywhere, but rather that the information search, selection and purchasing process is 'customer friendly'.

## When do customers buy?

It is useful to consider a number of aspects to this, starting with the obvious questions of frequency of purchasing, the intervals between purchases, and when the product or service might be promoted during the interval, so that it is in the customer's mind when they are ready to buy. Some suggest (e.g. Shimp, 2003), that there is little point in promoting a product if the customer is not ready to purchase.

Typically, there are different levels of customers in terms of their willingness to try new products and services. They tend to follow the diffusion curve shown in Figure 6.2. The innovators will enthusiastically try new products and not be too concerned if the performance is not perfect. The early adopters willingly try the new product if there are no obvious adverse comments from the innovators. The main problem often arises after a promising start if the early majority fail to be convinced, or are offered an alternative product that they perceive to be more attractive.

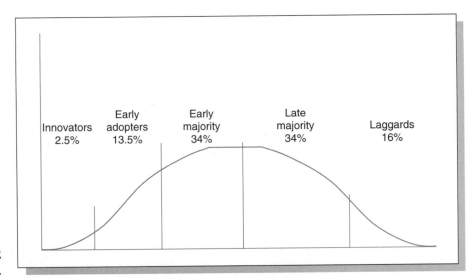

**Figure 6.2**
The diffusion curve.

## How do customers buy?

Clearly the whole process that customers go through needs to be understood so that the organization can influence them at key points. The choices, motivations, pre- and post-purchase behaviour and decision-making process need to be fully understood, so that promotion can be used at the appropriate points.

## Competition and its changing nature

The changing nature of competition in the sector also poses both threats and opportunities. Opportunities arise as a competitor grows and loses interest in certain small-volume products and services in its portfolio. These could still provide a significant opportunity for a smaller organization. The consolidation of competition as two competitors merge also often leads to product range rationalization in the combined company and opportunities for a smaller firm to exploit discarded product and service opportunities. A large organization often pays little attention to peripheral areas of activity and this provides the opportunity for an entrepreneurial organization to satisfy the possibly small but still existing demand.

Larger competitors often fail to appreciate the importance of concentrating on the service aspects of their offer, leaving the way open for more entrepreneurial organizations to build the business by being more customer oriented and providing higher levels of personalized service.

Competitors do pose obvious threats too. Larger competitors watch for niches to be developed by a smaller firm and then enter the market, either by generating their own competing product offer or by taking over the entrepreneurial organization that created the niche in the first place. Supermarkets have routinely and aggressively expanded their activities at the expense of local shops. An alternative approach is to take over the entrepreneurial organization that has created the niche, enabling the large organization to acquire the skills of the entrepreneurial organization too. This can provide the opportunity for an entrepreneurial organization to sell out at the best time, often making the owners personal fortunes. When these organizations are taken over by large firms they often fail to create the right environment for the acquired entrepreneurial organization to flourish in.

The response of entrepreneurial organizations to competition is critical. The large organizations have the benefits of size that can provide economies of scale, power in the market to increase customer awareness and influence purchasing behaviour, and adequate resources to invest in new projects. They also have the power to maintain loss-making products in order to price a competitor out of the market. The entrepreneurial organizations have to counter this with unique products, exceptional service and word-of-mouth recommendations.

Entrepreneurial organizations can move fast in the market and the large competitors can take a long time to respond to new market innovations; however, when they do they compete aggressively, they can have a substantial impact, as they leverage the benefits of huge resources, strong brands and high awareness levels among customers.

The nature of competition is changing. Competitors in the sector that the entrepreneurial organization has 'grown up' with are usually well known and largely predictable. However, totally new competitors might attack a market sector, often because of deregulation of certain market sectors. This, for example, has enabled supermarkets to sell petrol, pharmaceuticals and financial services. With increased globalization it is also the new, unexpected competitors that suddenly decide to attack a new geographic market.

## Market restructuring

A number of sectors have undergone major **market restructuring** with changing supply chain roles, discussed in Chapter 10, and new distribution channel arrangements. This has occurred largely because of e-business, and has provided opportunities for new business creation, for example online travel agents, booksellers and share dealing. Many of the recent market restructurings have come about because of the new service possibilities created by the Internet coupled with changing customer expectations. They have enabled even the smallest specialist organizations to offer their products and services directly to national or global customers without the need to appoint intermediaries – agents, distributors and retailers. The removal of intermediaries in the supply chain has been referred to as disintermediation.

Other market restructuring has involved the creation of intermediaries. As many competitive offerings become available online, customers find it time consuming to assess these offers individually. New online businesses, such as expedia.com and confused.com, effectively acting as brokers, have been created to enable customers to assess the competitive offerings, for example, from travel firms and insurance companies, and choose the best deal. This has been termed reintermediation (Chaffey *et al.*, 2003).

Entrepreneurs challenge the existing market structure when there appears to be scope for offering customers a lower-price product or service. In Enterprise in Action 6.5 is shown an example of how this has been done in spectacle manufacturing and retailing.

---

## Enterprise in Action 6.5

### A spectacle business success

When James Murray Wells went to an optician in Harrow, UK, where he was at public school, to buy some reading glasses he was shocked to find that they cost £149.99, equivalent to half a month's rent. After carrying out research he decided that the opticians were making very high margins from the very high prices they were charging and so in his final year at the University of West of England he set up Glasses Direct as an online business.

He is able to sell at prices well below High Street chains, such as Boots and Vision Express, for example, £15 for the equivalent of Alice C1 glasses, sold by Boots for £99.

In doing his research Murray Wells found that the manufacturers and laboratories that supplied opticians were not prepared to talk to him and he was on the point of giving up. Finally, one laboratory gave him the information he needed to demonstrate the business model. They made his original prescription for a fraction of the price charged by the Harrow optician.

Murray Wells set up a business in a room at his parent's house and using an advertisement on the university notice board found two IT experts to set up the website. Initially a hobby to give him pocket money at university, the business has grown and now occupies four rooms in the house and eight staff work there. Murray Wells still faces pressure from the bigger players in the sector as his business grows further. One supplier has suddenly stopped supplying him, presumably because of pressure from his competitors.

*Adapted from*: Goodman M., 'Online optician is making high-street chains see red',
*Sunday Times*, 16 January 2005

**Question:** What are the strengths and weaknesses of Murray Wells' business likely to be as it grows?

## Sector changes

The conditions in the market change continually but at different rates in different sectors. Some sectors have many suppliers, others are dominated by a few key competitors, for example, the retail food sector in most developed countries, and yet others are dominated by global competitors. Again, some sectors are mature whereas others are fast-growing and changing, such as the IT and communications sectors. This can pose problems for an organization with limited resources for keeping up with technological advances.

Some sectors are driven by technology application (push) and others by new consumer demand (pull). Competitor and customer behaviour may be predictable but on the other hand may be entirely unpredictable.

As we have indicated, market changes in the macro environment and market sector dynamics not only provide opportunities but pose threats, as discussed earlier. Entrepreneurial organizations look at a complacent, mature market and, no matter how unpromising it appears, will identify an opportunity. Tesco and other supermarkets dominate food retailing in the UK, but as signs appear that customers are beginning to resent this, niche retailing opportunities will appear.

## The public sector environment

The **environment for public sector** organizations is influenced, in particular, by political considerations that provide significantly different challenges and require a different type of entrepreneurial response. Innovative ideas from many different sources may be seized upon by a political party and become part of its manifesto, so being implemented if it comes to power through government. At this strategic level, however, there is often limited scope for managers in the delivery organizations to innovate because major innovations are taken out of their hands by politicians. Their entrepreneurial activity is often confined to tactical actions.

In addition to the long-standing organizations, such as local authorities and the National Health Service in the UK, the government creates so-called quangos (unelected quasi-public sector organizations) that are given the role of delivering certain services. These include, for example, business support and training organizations. However, as these are political initiatives they are likely to be changed or even disbanded for policy reasons, such as reallocating the funds, no matter how successful an individual agency has been or how valued by stakeholders it is. Often innovation in these types of agencies is concerned with the creative use of projects to attract additional funding and the manipulation of income and cost streams to obtain the greatest benefit for the clients from the resources available.

Many public sector regeneration programmes, such as neighbourhood renewal, are targeted at deprived areas and are reliant on short-term funding. Entrepreneurs who are determined to make a difference in their local communities often have to spend considerable amounts of time and effort trying to secure small amounts of money from different sources, each of which might be looking for different outcomes in exchange for the money allocated. Changes in policy and funding arrangements are often made on a whim by politicians with little thought to the implications for the programmes, staff and clients involved. This is illustrated in Spotlight 6.1.

## Spotlight 6.1

### Learning partnerships and being enterprising to survive

Learning partnerships (LPs) have a remit set at national level (revised in 2002) by the Department for Education and Skills (DfES) of:

- promoting partner collaboration in support of lifelong learning; and
- maximizing the contribution of learning to local regeneration.

They were originally set up in early 1999 to promote a new culture of collaboration between providers across a range of sectors (schools, further education (FE), work-based learning and adult and community learning). These LPs were also expected to rationalize the numerous existing local partnership arrangements covering post-16 learning. They were set up in interesting times, as the DfES announced that they intended also to rationalize the various ways in which lifelong learning was funded, and that local Training and Enterprise Councils would be closed and replaced by a more centrally managed body, the Learning and Skills Council (LSC). The funding for FE colleges would also become the responsibility of the LSC.

The changing political priorities made it difficult for the managers of these fledgling organizations to establish a strategic role, and their task of promoting a culture of collaboration was a tremendous challenge when so many of the key agencies involved in the delivery of learning activity faced such major upheaval.

The links to local regeneration were no less complex as the government introduced local strategic partnerships (LSPs). These are single non-statutory, multi-agency bodies, which match local authority boundaries, and aim to bring together at a local level the different parts of the public, private, community and voluntary sectors. They are central to the delivery of the national strategy for Neighbourhood Renewal.

In April 2003 responsibility for LPs passed from the DfES to the LSC. Learning partnerships had always needed to work collaboratively with partners to secure resources (both funding and people) to deliver any services needed in their local areas, but now their core funding for staff was also threatened. Despite their clear strategic remit, learning partnership managers (LPMs) were living from hand to mouth, and in such circumstances could be forgiven for adopting a more short-term approach. Despite this precarious political and economic environment, learning partnerships did contribute increasingly to local strategies for regeneration and many became the 'learning arm' of the LSPs.

The degree to which LPs are valued in their localities varies, but commonly partners welcomed the facilitation role that the LPM offered, and the resources to submit joint funding applications. The crisis came, however, when LSC support was reduced or withdrawn, with the result that so many of the partner organizations were unable to offer financial support because of their own constrained circumstances, and the pressure on them to do more with less.

Learning partnership managers have had to act entrepreneurially, working with partners to establish a shared strategic vision for lifelong learning and to find the resources needed to make a difference in the communities they represent. The vagaries of the political and economic context in which they work has made innovative responses difficult – the pressure to hit targets has made experimentation a little too risky in some circumstances. Their networking abilities and negotiation skills are pushed to the limit, as they have no power to direct partners but are tasked with responsibility. Some LPs have folded despite the commitment of their managers; in some cases their energy has been dissipated by the constant battle to survive and they have left for pastures new. Some have persuaded partner bodies to offer some core funding and continued their work; others have set up their own consultancies.

The sector appears to be characterized by churn, in both an individual and an organizational sense. Enterprising people move from organization to organization within the sector, committed to the principles and espoused values, but needing to constantly reinvent their careers in order to continue to make a contribution. Similarly, organizations are set up and then close down as political priorities change.

*Source*: Sue Marriott, adapted from various public sources including www.lifelonglearning.co.uk/llp

**Questions:** Do the politically inspired environmental changes and the need for survival drive creativity or hinder it? Can forced partnerships really develop sustainable innovation in delivering services?

## Other not-for-profit environments

With increased competitiveness, the environment is becoming more challenging for smaller organizations in all sectors. In Pause and Reflect 6.1 it is shown how the environment is becoming increasingly tough for small charities, no matter how worthwhile their cause, as the larger charities become more sophisticated in their management and marketing and become more aggressive in their fund-raising as they compete to increase public awareness and donations.

## Pause and Reflect 6.1

### Tough environment for charities

Small charities are facing a dilemma of how to compete in an environment where the larger charities are dominant. The Charity Aid Foundation (CAF) pointed out that Oxfam, the National Trust, RNLI and Cancer Research had been top ten fundraisers for 20 years. In 2004–05 the average amount of money donated to the top ten charities grew 2 per cent faster than the average for the top 500.

The organizer of the 2005 CAF awards ceremony, Daniel Phelan, noted that 'the projects for which the winners had been rewarded show perfectly that clever use of branding, collaborative projects between organizations working in specialist sectors, and smart management all pay dividends'. It is interesting to note, too, that the large charities had taken a collaborative approach to maximize the effect of their South-East Asian tsunami appeal.

The award winners demonstrate the broad range of work done by charities. The winner of the award for innovation and management excellence was Beatbullying, a small charity that, in collaboration with other charities, succeeded in standardizing anti-bullying policy in 21 local authorities. Other winners included the Cumbria Community Foundation, responsible for the Cumbria Flood Recovery Fund Appeal launched in response to a local flood disaster. The foundation, which raised nearly £700 000 in grant aid for flood victims, won the grant-making category.

And Mifumi-UK, which helps to run a grassroots campaign in Uganda to highlight the problem of domestic violence there, won the international aid and development category.

*Adapted from:* 'Small charities "face struggle" ', BBC News Online, 17 June 2005

**Question:** What are the main environmental factors that impact on the work of small charities and what do you consider to be the critical success factors for an entrepreneurial charity?

## Strategic response

It is useful to consider how entrepreneurial organizations respond to the changes in the micro environment. Inevitably, sectors are likely to be affected by certain factors much more than others and respond differently. In thinking about this it might be useful to refer to Table 6.1, which shows some of the trends in the characteristics of the next generation of customers, the changing nature of competition and the changing market structure, and the type of **strategic response** that entrepreneurial organizations might adopt. Of course the whole point of entrepreneurial organizations is that their response to market situations should be

**Table 6.1**
Strategic response to changing market characteristics

(A) Customer characteristics

| Changing customer characteristics | Strategic response from entrepreneurial organizations |
|---|---|
| More demanding<br>More willing to experiment<br>More sceptical of big company promotions<br>More fashion-conscious<br>Less brand loyal<br>Want more choice<br>More willing to complain<br>More comfortable with new technology | ▪ More customization and individualization of product offers<br>▪ Greater focus on design<br>▪ More personalized service<br>▪ More frequent innovations<br>▪ More focused customer communications rather than mass marketing<br>▪ More emphasis on explaining and delivering brand value |

(continued)

**Table 6.1**   (continued)

(B)  Competitors

| Changing competition characteristics | Strategic response from entrepreneurial organizations |
|---|---|
| More global competitors<br>Faster competition<br>Competition between supply chains<br>Unexpected competition<br>Better quality of competitor products<br>More standardized products<br>Global brand names | ■ Exploitation of global niche opportunities<br>■ Building closer relationships with customers<br>■ More willing to cooperate and form partnerships<br>■ Pursue opportunities to cut costs<br>■ Focused on products and process innovation and service enhancement<br>■ Exploit new ideas quickly, achieve success, sell out to competitors and start again |

(C)  Market structure

| Changing market structure | Strategic response from entrepreneurial organizations |
|---|---|
| Disintermediation<br>Importance of e-business<br>Unclear sector boundaries<br>International supply chains<br>Multiple level marketing<br>Multimode distribution channels | ■ Source components and services globally<br>■ Focus on value contributions<br>■ Integrate physical and online distribution<br>■ Exploit adjacent market opportunities<br>■ Work flexibly with distribution channel partners |

innovative, so you might consider how you would respond to some of these changes.

## Market approaches, competitive advantage and capability

Traditionally, many entrepreneurs have identified an opportunity, developed a product or service to exploit the opportunity and marketed it to customers.

Although they had limited resources they were able to grow incrementally and roll out the product into the local, national and, funds permitting, export markets too.

## The changing nature of competitive advantage

Today, however, most markets are much more competitive. Competitors can find out about a recently introduced, commercially successful new product or service, wherever it is in the world. Using the Internet, it takes minutes rather than weeks of research. This prompts competitors to attack the same market opportunity and a good idea can usually be copied and a new offering developed in months rather than years. Alternatively, and prompted by the challenge of the newcomer to the market, the competitor may introduce its own different ideas to exploit the same opportunity and put the newcomer out of business.

In many sectors product life cycles are shortening and so an organization will retain a technological lead for a shorter period. Consequently the payback period on the investment in research, development and marketing is shorter and so innovators have less time to generate a return and make a profit. Therefore, they must be faster into the market and widen the distribution channels to maximize sales.

Pressure is also applied to innovators as many of the more successful new product introductions are copied fast by lower-cost manufacturers from emerging markets. The latter are often now capable of achieving similar quality to the original and being able to offer more competitive prices. For example, it is well known that new fashion styles will be available in shops within hours of their first appearance on the catwalk. Further pressure is applied to innovators as research and development is increasingly outsourced by major companies to subcontractors in emerging markets.

Therefore, it can be concluded that an entrepreneurial organization's source of competitive advantage derives from the ability:

- ▪ to interpret environmental changes and changing market dynamics in order to identify opportunities; and
- ▪ to leverage its own capabilities and expertise in order to respond more quickly and effectively to the opportunities (and threats) arising than its competitors.

On the one hand, therefore, entrepreneurial organizations still need to pursue the approach of the 1980s, typified by Porter (1985), who suggested that understanding industry dynamics and competitive characteristics was critical to successful marketing and business performance. On the other hand it is vital for entrepreneurial organizations to pursue their opportunities in ways that exploit their own core competencies, the concept typified by Prahalad and Hamel (1994).

Universities develop leading-edge technological competence which can be the basis on which to build a business, as shown in Enterprise in Action 6.6. The challenge for the company will be to secure effective market diffusion of their technology, while working on further technological breakthroughs.

**Enterprise in Action 6.6**

**Cambridge Display Technology**

Cambridge Display Technology (CDT) was founded in 1992 and was based on research carried out in the Cavendish and Melville Laboratories at Cambridge University.

Jeremy Burroughes discovered that light-emitting diodes (LEDs) could be made using conjugated polymers. Over the next few years many patents were filed as CDT's 'PLED' technology was developed. PLEDs are based on organic chemicals that emit light when stimulated electrically and have application in the displays market and possibly in lighting too.

The technology allows brighter, higher-contrast, thinner displays that consume less power, while offering very wide viewing angles and video response a thousand times faster than current displays. CDT's technology is already used in Philips mobile telephones, MP3 players, a professional audio mixer and a TENS pain relief device. By 2007 CDT expect the technology to be used on large-screen televisions too.

In 2003 the company raised income exceeding £1.8 million from 32 licenses. The company was floated on the US Nasdaq exchange in December 2004 and raised $30 million from its initial public offering. The new funds are expected to be used for possible acquisitions and for ongoing research and developments.

*Adapted from*: information from Cambridge University at www.admin.cam.ac.uk and CDT at www.cdtltd.co.uk

**Questions:** What are the benefits and disadvantages of spinning out from the university? Are different skills, knowledge and people needed for the new environment?

Against this background entrepreneurs may have to place greater focus upon creating and extracting value for the customer and their own organization through their use of resources and capabilities. Given that it is customers that are the source of revenue and profit they will increasingly need to adopt appropriate approaches to the market.

## Approaches to the market

There are a number of alternative **approaches to the market** that entrepreneurial organizations might adopt. Hooley, Saunders and Piercy (2004) identify the following three approaches.

1.  *Product push marketing.* This approach focuses on persuading customers to buy the products and services that the firm is able to produce, deliver and improve easily. It is based on the organization's view of what the customers want but it is influenced mainly by what the organization can offer by using its tangible resources. Problems arise when the customers' demands are outwith that which the organization is capable of delivering.

2. ***Customer-led marketing.*** This is typified by those organizations that aim to satisfy customer needs. While this approach fits with the flexible, highly service oriented approach of entrepreneurial organizations there is a danger that the cost of flexibility and high service levels can exceed the revenue that is generated. Sometimes, too, customers are not good predictors of further trends.

3. ***Resource-based marketing.*** This is a balanced strategy between meeting the market requirements and building the organization's capabilities (assets, skills and competencies) to serve the market. It is discussed in more detail in Chapter 12.

Two other types of marketing are important to entrepreneurs.

1. ***Network marketing.*** This is an approach that is becoming increasingly significant as organizations, particularly those with limited resources, use connections through alliances or partnerships to exploit opportunities that they would not be able to pursue alone. Smaller firms that offer complementary products and services can work together to explore new potential markets.

2. ***Entrepreneurial marketing.*** In practice the marketing approach of entrepreneurial organizations is to focus on the opportunity or market gap, irrespective of whether or not this will make use of existing assets.

In practice the organization tends to pursue whichever marketing approach is appropriate for the market opportunity and is dependent on the market context and timing. However, entrepreneurial organizations are also driven by the personality of the owner or senior managers and so the marketing approach is often influenced by this. For example, some entrepreneurs have a sales orientation and are so convinced of the soundness of their idea that they adopt a product push approach, may be unwilling to participate in partnerships and may avoid network marketing. Others have a strong service orientation and would choose the customer-led strategy.

As we have seen already a particular dimension of entrepreneurial marketing is the capacity to be 'different from the rest.' Entrepreneurs do not tend to follow competitors in the way they approach the market and respond to changes. Very often they develop contrary strategies to those that seem to be the 'conventional wisdom'. Pause and Reflect 6.2 shows the different ways in which farmers near Bath, UK, have responded to the major changes in their sector by building on their assets and developing new competencies.

## Pause and Reflect 6.2

### Growing a new crop of ideas

Farming in Britain, as in many other countries, has faced tough times over the last few years with BSE and foot-and-mouth. There is also the bureaucratic maze of European Union regulations to negotiate. For example, farm subsidies are now based on acreage not production. Farmers are being urged to innovate and find new ways of making money and this has led many to reduce their farming activities.

Sometimes it is a unique situation that provides the idea. Pinston Mill Farm has an eleventh-century water mill and 15 years ago the Hopwood family, who owned it, opened it to the public and provided cream teas. This required a kitchen and lavatories to be installed and, while going to this expense, it seemed sensible to convert the barn into a function room. This proved to be a good investment as UK law has been changed recently to allow different types of premises to be licensed for weddings. The Hopwoods landscaped the farmyard and now have a three-year waiting list for weddings.

Hamswell is a sheep farm close to Bath and Bristol but well away from roads. It has streams, hills, a small lake and woodlands, ideal for a track for horses. The farm provides self-stabling for horse owners and access to the countryside. Although only 20 per cent of the total farm turnover, this business provides a much better return on capital than rearing 1000 lambs per year.

Park Farm, owned by Graham Padfield, has stayed closer to food production, starting to make organic cheese in 1993. Padfield says that cheesemaking is interesting but a 'labour of love', requiring significant capital outlay on buildings and equipment to control the temperature and humidity and a lot of hard work. Other family members work on the venture, which helps to keep the costs down.

*Adapted from*: Cameron J., 'Farming for new profits', *The Daily Telegraph*, 1 October 2005

**Question:** To what extent do you see these innovations as being a response to critical incidents or simply evolution of the farm as incremental change takes place?

## Market approaches in not-for-profit sectors

The market approaches of organizations in the not-for-profit sector are often more vulnerable to shifts in policy than is the case for private sector organizations, and so the political aspect of the macro environmental analysis often assumes greater importance. Although some voluntary sector and charitable organizations are quite large, and are able to raise sufficient revenue from donations/subscriptions to allow them some degree of autonomy, many are very small and living from hand to mouth in terms of funding. While this has led to them being extremely flexible and adaptive, it also leaves them vulnerable to shifts in policy. Many of these small organizations look to public funding for their survival, and the market for this funding is becoming increasingly competitive in the UK (e.g. Lottery, Neighbourhood Renewal, etc.). Changes in government policy in relation to the amount of money available through these sources and their priorities for granting funding can have a sudden and severe impact on the viability of these organizations.

It can also be a positive opportunity as the government is increasingly looking for ways to more efficiently deliver public sector contracts. It values the flexibility of the voluntary sector and is usually looking to include more voluntary and community sector (VCS) organizations in delivering public services. There are opportunities for more long term funding if the VCS organizations can secure such contracts but more robust finance and management systems are needed to ensure accounting standards are met, especially given that public funds are involved. However, in doing this a further question is posed: does this requirement endanger the flexibility of the organizational innovation and the cost advantage that government valued in the first place?

Over the years, this reliance on temporary and often meagre funding streams has led these organizations to develop their capability to do more with less. One of the strengths of this sector is vision and leadership, as even day-to-day operations can often depend on the ability of a single individual to communicate a sense of purpose and secure the commitment of staff (often limited in number) and volunteers to deliver the service.

Increasing pressure for efficiency and accountability in the delivery of public services has also driven innovation; for example, in the UK there have been creative approaches to improving the quality of school meals. However, it is always important to consider social and financial considerations. A development of the Meals on Wheels service, which provides meals for the elderly and infirm in their own homes, found that delivering ready-frozen meals that could be heated in the microwave cut costs because there were fewer deliveries necessary. However, while some customers liked this because getting their own meal ready-made, made them feel more independent, others were not enthusiastic because, to them, the most important thing was a chat with the delivery person.

## Market approaches through the Internet

The **Internet and e-business** activity that is associated with it is now part of the normal context in which the majority of well-established organizations operate. However, because for customers and clients in many sectors this is the only contact they have with the organization it is essential that it is effective. Timmers (1999) explains that private entrepreneurs have established new Internet-based business models, such as e-shops, e-auctions, virtual buying communities, collaboration platforms and electronic marketplaces (e-hubs). While it is not our intention to discuss the management of e-business activity it is useful to reflect on the opportunity for innovation to increase competitiveness.

## Websites

Websites and e-mail are perhaps the building bricks of the Internet and for entrepreneurial organizations a key question is what purpose the website serves and could serve in the future. Lindgren (2003) explains that there are four main categories, as given below.

1.  *An organization site.* This provides information for stakeholders about the organization: its beliefs, values, activities and internal organization. The question is how much of this information is useful, as the danger is that unnecessary information may make the site complicated and put off the customers.
2.  *Provision of service online.* Banks and logistics organizations use a website to inform customers of the current situation – for example, their account or where a parcel has got to. Many more applications of service delivery are being developed.
3.  *Provision of information online.* Media organizations provide news and information free, often with the objective of selling other services. The challenge is to provide a unique up-to-date information service that attracts customers routinely.
4.  *Facilitation of transactions online.* Many entrepreneurial organizations now use their website as a lower-cost method of transacting business but customers must have a reason to visit the site, either because of the attraction of the site or the unique value of the offering.

From your own experience you should think about the essentials of a good website. The starting point is probably that it is easily navigable, up-to-date, interesting or entertaining. More sophisticated e-business users are able to link the website to databases and so customize offers to better meet customer requirements, operate customer relationship management systems to provide improved customer service and use information to analyse customer trends.

Websites provide the opportunity for small organizations to develop a higher-profile market approach than their limited resources would allow them to do using traditional market approaches, but as well as developing effective, attractive sites for loyal customers, they have to ensure that potential customers find their website; so for example, ensuring that search engines list the website on the first page of search results is essential. Innovation in the use of the Internet by entrepreneurial organizations still focuses on its unique characteristics, identified as the 'Six Is' by Deighton (1996), namely:

1.  interactivity, and the opportunity for two-way communications;

2.  intelligence and the continual collection of data from customers and clients that can be analysed;
3.  individualization of offers, by using stored data to customize the products and services to customer needs;
4.  integration of many communications, systems and processes;
5.  industry restructuring, and the development and management of new supply chains and distribution channels;
6.  independence of location, which enables low-cost market entry.

## The failure of entrepreneurial organizations

Finally, although we discuss the high level of failure among entrepreneurial organizations at various points in this book it is worth commenting here that it is a significant feature of the business start-up. Because of the very dynamic nature of such organizations, their risk-taking, periods of downturn in the economy, crises in the environment, and other sector changes that reduce demand, many become vulnerable. This is usually because they:

■  fail to respond quickly enough to environmental changes that might seriously damage the organization's performance or even threaten its survival;
■  fail to anticipate future problems;
■  fail to adopt defensive strategies that are designed to deal with a decline in demand;
■  become complacent, believing that they do not need to act immediately but can ride out the storm;
■  fail to spread their risk and become dependent on one product, service or on one significant customer;
■  fail to keep resources in reserve; and
■  take a short-term view of the business, relying on short-term funding which creates additional pressures, such as paying high overdraft charges.

Of course, there are many people who believe that failure is not as bad as it seems. Inefficient and 'no-hope' organizations are removed, leaving the way for entrepreneurial organizations that are more in tune with the changing environment to progress and grow. Entrepreneurs learn valuable lessons through failure and most successful entrepreneurs had at least one failure. Consequently many believe that we should not worry too much about failure as churn (new business creation and failure) is healthy in a sector and economy.

## Summary

- The changing macro and micro environment creates opportunities and threats for entrepreneurial organizations and it is the nature and appropriateness of their response that is critical for success.
- All environments are becoming more competitive, including the public sector where there is greater competition for funding and political support and in the charity sector where there is greater competition for public awareness and donations.
- Smaller organizations in many sectors are able to compensate for their lack of resources with greater adaptability, flexibility and responsiveness to achieve the competitiveness necessary.
- Major changes in global competitiveness mean that, in the future, organizations must evaluate opportunities from a different perspective and change their supply chains to exploit new sources of components, manufacturing and services.
- Entrepreneurial organizations also need to review their approach to competing in markets, relying less on tangible assets, such as factories and equipment, and more on the knowledge, skills and reputation of the organization.

## Chapter questions

1. As the entrepreneurial owner of a small hotel in London that relies on tourists principally from outside the UK, you are keen to expand and diversify your business and you have the requisite funds. You are aware of the effect that the threat of terrorism could have on the numbers of visitors. What should you do and why?

2. Using examples to illustrate the points you make, explain the difference between how entrepreneurial organizations and more bureaucratic organizations respond to environmental changes.

3. Explain the key environmental challenges faced by a small not-for-profit organization and how they might respond.

4. A small engineering company based in the north of England has appointed a new chief executive officer (CEO), who has asked you, a personal business adviser, to offer some comments about the business. While the company is currently busy with lots of small general engineering jobs, mainly for a manufacturer of

catering equipment for restaurants and hotels, you are concerned that there could soon be a downturn in the economy. Suggest the key trends that should be watched and suggest what the CEO might do to prepare for a possible downturn in the business.

5. Explain the advantages and disadvantages of the alternative market approaches discussed, in responding to different types of environmental changes.

## Case study

### The Eden Project – showbiz meets science

Among Britain's lottery-funded millennium projects, there were a lot of high-profile flops, including the Dome at Greenwich, Sheffield's rock and pop museum and the Earth Centre in South Yorkshire. But the Eden Project in Cornwall, which opened in March 2001, proved to be a spectacular success. 645 000 visitors a year were expected, but it attracted 940 000 in its first six months alone and now has over 1.5 million visitors each year.

### The entrepreneur

Tim Smit, an Anglo-Dutch former pop producer, moved to Cornwall in the late 1980s to set up a recording studio. Next door to the studio was a large, neglected garden, which Smit restored as 'The Lost Gardens of Heligan'. Soon after opening in 1992 it became one of Cornwall's top tourist destinations. Smit's next brainchild was the Eden Project and his aim was to create a rainforest and other plant 'landscapes' underneath two giant 'biomes' built in a disused china clay pit. His track record gave the lottery's fund commission the confidence to award the project £37.5 m and helped him to attract the private investment that was necessary to match the lottery funding.

The early success of Eden was attributed to the fact that, unlike some of the other lottery-funded projects, it was a good idea looking for money, not money looking for an idea. Many projects of this type appeared to be the result of the determination of cities to get some of the lottery cash, irrespective of how viable the project was. The Eden Project was the vision of one entrepreneur, rather than the result of planning by committee. The most notorious failure – the Dome – was the product of bureaucratic compromise and inappropriate political intervention. After five years the Dome still has no real role.

### The vision

The Lost Gardens of Heligan had proved to Smit that the study of plants could mean good business in the right situation. Smit realized from his former background, however, that an element of showbiz was needed and his mission was to 'make science sexy'. Science appeals to both children and adults and seems to be good theme-park material. The message of the Project was also very serious – that man and plants have co-existed profitably together for centuries and must continue to do so – and this has enabled Eden to make a valuable contribution to education, research, awareness raising on important issues and campaigning. A new £15 million education centre was built in 2005. All the buildings have unique, instantly recognizable designs and are made, where possible, from locally available materials from sustainable sources.

## The regional contribution

Eden has a key role and fits in well in the region. There are a number of other garden attractions and so is a 'must' for adults interested in gardening and, given its location in a popular holiday area, it also attracts visitors looking for a day away from the beach. Many lottery-funded visitor attractions seemed to be isolated from other attractions and have no emotional attachment to the area, making it more unlikely that people would visit. Moreover, local people resent money that was intended for charitable purposes being spent on what they regard as pointless projects.

Eden employs over 440 people, 90 per cent of them being local. It has contributed significantly to the economy of Cornwall, one of the poorest counties in England. It claims to have appointed 200 local suppliers and to have put £150 million into the local economy in its first year. It also had a significant impact on the demand for accommodation, being partly responsible for the 96 per cent increase compared to the previous year.

## The potential for conflict

Despite the outstanding success of the Eden Project it does face continual challenges, dilemmas and potential conflicts. While it is not expected to pay off its original grants it does have to continually generate income to pay its way and justify further funding for new projects, some of which will not generate income. The fact that the number of visitors far exceeds the forecast, places considerable strain on the facilities and catering – areas where the staff try to avoid compromise and wish to maintain high standards.

Many of its show business activities are high profile and perhaps attract a different type of visitor. The Eden Project hosted the Africa Calling concert for 4000 people as part of the Make Poverty History Live 8 campaign in 2005. It was memorable in featuring black artists, answering the criticisms made regarding some of the other concerts put on. It is planning a repeat event in 2006. It also creates a giant skating rink as part of its winter event to generate additional income. It has been host to conferences and seminars attended by world experts discussing environmental concerns.

Events such as these create considerable disruption and heartache for the horticulturalists at Eden, whose work is devoted to creating the right conditions for the plants to be at their best. Neither the plants nor the staff take kindly to being trampled on or uprooted by the construction workers and electricians working on the next event, so the management team must try to balance the opposing interests and maintain the motivation of the staff who believed, when they joined, that they were working for a science establishment rather than one they feel is increasingly becoming dedicated to show business. Smit emphasizes that he is not a horticulturalist and that horticulture is not the primary aim of the Eden Project.

*Source*: adapted from various public sources including *The Economist*, 18 August 2001,
BBC News Online and www.edenproject.com

## Questions

1.  What do you consider to be the aims of the Eden Project and how does this fit with the macro and micro environmental factors?
2.  To what extent would you attribute the success of the Eden Project to the characteristics of entrepreneurship?
3.  How might the spirit of entrepreneurship associated with the Eden Project be capitalized upon (1) within Cornwall (2) by the Eden Project itself?

## References and further reading

Chaffey D., Mayer R., Johnston K. and Ellis-Chadwick F. (2003) *Internet Marketing: Strategy, Implementation and Practice*. Harlow: FT Prentice Hall.

Deighton J. (1996) The future of interactive marketing. *Harvard Business Review*, Nov–Dec, pp. 151–162.

Doole I. and Lowe R. (2004) *International Marketing Strategy: Analysis, Development & Implementation*, 4th edn. London: Thomson Learning.

Fairweather J. (2005) Carpetbaggers rush to take a profit on stricken city's property boom. *The Daily Telegraph*, 22 September 2005.

Hamel G. and Prahalad C.K. (1994) *Competing for the Future*. Boston: Harvard Business School Press.

Hooley G.J., Saunders J.A. and Piercy N.F. (2004) *Marketing Strategy and Competitive Positioning*, 3rd edn. Harlow: Prentice Hall.

Lindgren J. (2003) *E-marketing in Marketing Best Practices*. Mason OH: Thomson South-Western.

Porter M.E. (1985) *Competitive Advantage: Creating and Sustaining Superior Performance*. New York: The Free Press.

Settle R.B. and Alreck P. (1989) Reducing buyers' sense of risk. *Marketing Communications*, January, pp. 34–40.

Shimp T.A. (2003) *Advertising, Promotion, and Supplemental Aspects of Integrated Marketing Communications*, 6th edn. Mason OH: Thomson South-Western.

Timmers P. (1999) *Electronic Commerce Strategies and Models for Business-to-Business Trading*. Chichester: Wiley.

## Key words

| | |
|---|---|
| approaches to the market | incremental changes |
| critical decision | Internet and e-business |
| critical events | macro factors |
| customer attitudes and purchasing behaviour | market restructuring |
| economic downturn | micro factors |
| entrepreneurial marketing | network marketing |
| environment for public sector | resource-based marketing |
| globalization | stakeholders |
| | strategic response |

## CHAPTER 7

# The social, public and not-for-profit context

## Learning objectives

By the end of this chapter the reader will be able to:

- understand the policy context for the social and not-for-profit sectors, and the role of government in supporting their development;
- evaluate the impact of social and community enterprise in social and economic regeneration;
- assess the opportunities and threats facing voluntary and community organizations;
- identify the strengths of the not-for-profit organizations and the lessons that could be learned from the way they operate;
- understand the nature of innovation and enterprise in the public sector;
- analyse the similarities and differences between social and economic entrepreneurs.

## Introduction

When enterprise, innovation, strategy, and management are discussed in the literature the underlying assumption has tended to be that what is being discussed is the way these concepts apply to business, and, by business, the authors usually mean the private sector. In this book we have deliberately widened the scope to include the public and not-for-profit sectors and particularly highlighted examples of entrepreneurship and innovation in these areas.

Private sector businesses do not adequately deliver services for every situation and there are gaps. The traditional for-profit orientation of private sector businesses does not seem appropriate for some public sector services that have a social dimension to them that is less easily defined in 'product' terms. Traditionally these services have been delivered through public sector organizations. Increasingly, however, social entrepreneurship is being seen as a contributory factor in economic development and social regeneration. What is noticeable about the emergence of social entrepreneurship in the policy debate that surrounds it is the way in which it combines the language and the practice of business with social ideals and benefits. Consequently the definitions between what are private 'for-profit' and public 'not-for-profit' are less distinguishable and many organizations work at the interface between the two. A spectrum of organizational types can be envisaged with the traditional private and public sector organizations at the extreme but a range of entrepreneurial organizations in between.

In this chapter we explore entrepreneurship and innovation in the public and not-for-profit context. We begin at one end of the spectrum, and look at whether entrepreneurs are more likely to operate their businesses in socially responsible ways. We then move on to explore the scope and impact of social and community entrepreneurship, and innovation and enterprise in the voluntary and community sector. We conclude by comparing some key aspects of social and economic entrepreneurship, finally returning to the characteristics of entrepreneurs and discussing what it is that distinguishes social entrepreneurs from economic ones.

## Economic and social motives

In practice most organizations across the spectrum operate in a 'business-like' way and increasingly have a social conscience to some degree, and so it may be helpful to see the 'social' focus of businesses on a continuum, as shown in Figure 7.1. Organizations are placed on this continuum in accordance with the extent to which their motives are focused on profit or social benefit.

At one end there are purely profit oriented businesses in the private sector, followed by those that recognize the value of **corporate social**

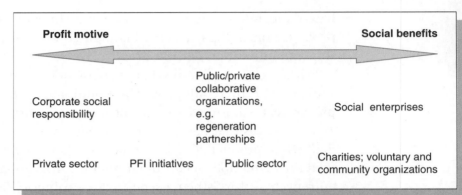

**Figure 7.1**
Economic or social
motives of
organizations.

**responsibility**, although their motives are primarily economic. The issue of whether this is a genuine ethical stance (which would suggest that the owners and managers would still adhere to it even if it made them less competitive) or whether it is enlightened self-interest (to enhance the organization's reputation and gain a marketing advantage) is not for discussion here.

At the other end are voluntary and community sector organizations, whose motives are primarily social, although they operate on a commercial basis, being accountable for delivering the results that their stakeholders expect in much the same way as private sector businesses are expected to deliver.

In between are a range of organizations. We see alliances between the public and private sectors in private finance initiatives (PFIs) for major publicly funded projects, and in a host of partnership bodies that enable collaboration between organizations from all sectors to drive social and economic regeneration in a locality. The public sector, and social and community enterprises, marry social benefit and economic profit. But there is no hint of 'dependency' in the language that these organizations use. There is a strong business orientation, and a strong association with individualist principles, incorporating both individual enterprise and organizational innovation.

Increasingly, over the last two decades, the UK government has been withdrawing from the direct delivery of public services and programmes. As quangos (unelected, publicly funded organizations) and the voluntary sector have become more important in the delivery of services they have come under increasing public scrutiny. Under pressure to do more with less, they have recognized the need to manage the resources they have to best advantage in achieving the impact they desire.

## Corporate social responsibility

# What is corporate social responsibility (CSR)?

Corporate social responsibility is the way an organization takes account of the economic, social and environmental impact that it has, maximizing the benefits and minimizing the negative consequences of its operations. It covers a wide range of issues including health and safety, employment rights, supply chain management, and environmental protection as well as the more controversial and obvious issues such as bribery and corruption. The business rhetoric about the need to maximize profits has often been used as an excuse to turn a blind eye to the ethical issues. In reality, businesses rarely follow optimum strategies and there are always trade-offs between profits and expenditure, and expenditure on ethical behaviour often comes second to profit generation. However, it is becoming increasingly important that businesses consider the legitimate expectations of all stakeholders.

## Drivers of CSR

In the Victorian era, Quaker families such as the Rowntrees and Cadburys were driven by charitable behaviour and philanthropy. Today the need for better corporate governance and the increasingly sophisticated demands of customers tend to be the more important. Charitable giving is no longer enough; increasingly, CSR is expected to be an integral part of the corporate business model. In the UK, Business in the Community now publish a Corporate Responsibility Index, and there are suggestions that organizations might be legally required to report on their CSR activities before too long. As with any change in environmental circumstances, organizations either behave defensively, reacting to circumstances as and when they need to, or they see them as opportunities to exploit.

## CSR as an innovative response

Entrepreneurial organizations have been quick to exploit the market opportunities that the increasing interest in business ethics has offered. The Co-operative Bank took an early position on ethical investment; Anita Roddick did likewise with Body Shop, and we now have a range of Fair Trade and Equitable Trade products on the shelves of super-markets. Drucker (2001: 51) argues that all organizations have to operate within a social setting. Healthy businesses cannot exist in sick societies, and so the business world has a vested interest in a healthy society. Sometimes social impacts are incidental to the main purpose of the organization, sometimes they are intended, but management is responsible for the social impacts of the business as well as economic ones. If the harmful impacts are not minimized, sooner or later the customers will object, and so ignoring social responsibilities will erode competitiveness in the long run. For example, organizations such as Nike and Gap have attracted adverse attention in the press for their sourcing policies which led to children being employed by their sub-contractors in Third World countries.

## Enterprise in Action 7.1

### Spotting when the goalposts have moved

Many people in developing countries are unable to access life-saving medicines. Before 2001, the pharmaceutical industry took the view that selling drugs to poor countries at a discount, or offering voluntary licenses to generic producers to manufacture cheap copies of their drugs was not in their business interests. Differential pricing and voluntary licensing might lead to smuggling; this could undermine their profits or lead to pressure to cut prices in their home markets; and they needed to preserve their margins to maintain investment in research and development. In any case, they were behaving in accordance with international patent regulations, so why should they do more?

Pressure to change came from lobbying by non-government agencies; a joint expression of concern from investors (ISIS Asset Management and the Universities Superannuation Scheme); and a threat from governments of developing countries to break the patent regulations and import generic copies of the drugs. This would threaten the international patent system, which is the foundation on which the major pharmaceutical businesses are built. Some companies have responded to this challenge and have improved access through a combination of differential pricing, voluntary licenses and donation programmes. The result is that some drugs are being made more widely available in some markets before patents would usually expire.

There had previously been a solid argument against this, but a little creative thinking has led to a compromise between business interests and a broader citizenship approach.

*Adapted from*: Barrington and Abbott (2005)

**Question:** How could an entrepreneurial organization have gained advantage from a more proactive approach to this situation?

Acting responsibly can add costs, but many argue that CSR policies become cost neutral in the long term. For example, investing in the development of renewable sources of raw materials may be costly initially, but offers a marketing opportunity, and helps to ensure a viable future. The elimination of undesirable impacts can be an opportunity in itself. Drucker (2001) quotes the example of Du Pont, who became aware of the toxic side effects of their industrial process, and as a result set up their Industrial Toxicity Laboratory. This laboratory developed tests for toxicity and processes to eliminate poisons, and it became a business in its own right selling this service to other organizations.

## Ethical standards of managers and entrepreneurs

The fact that these trends offered opportunities that were exploited by entrepreneurs does not necessarily reflect on their ethical standards, or their propensity to engage more actively with issues of corporate social responsibility. Bucar and Hirisch (2001) concluded that there was no significant difference between managers and entrepreneurs in Britain as regards their ethical standards and aspirations. Although ethical practice may have been a unique selling point in the past, it is now becoming expected of organizations. Being proactive in this regard may give the entrepreneur a competitive edge in some markets, but it would appear not to be a distinguishing feature of entrepreneurs in general. However, there are a growing number of entrepreneurs who are driven by social objectives, and it is to these that we turn next.

## Social and community enterprise

### What are social enterprises?

**Social enterprise** plays a significant role in the economy, and in urban regeneration. Businesses engaging in this dimension often provide services in areas where there is a market gap which the private sector does not see as viable.

In the introduction to Social Enterprise: A Strategy for Success (2002) Patricia Hewitt (in her role as Secretary of State for Trade and Industry) describes social enterprises as 'dynamic, progressive businesses that we can all learn from. They experiment and innovate, and have the advantage of being able to draw upon best practice in the voluntary sector, as well as the entrepreneurial flair that exists in the best of our companies'.

The strategy document goes on to explain how social enterprises provide a mechanism for bringing excluded groups into the labour market, raising skill levels and improving future employability. Many of them operate in areas of the country where economic activity and job creation are particularly needed, creating real opportunities for the people who work in them and for the communities that they serve – for example, some help to return difficult-to-employ people to the world of work, helping them to develop skills and build confidence. Many are concerned with environmental benefits, piloting recycling schemes or encouraging businesses to work on industrial estates where waste products from one organization can be used as a source of supply for others. Many are virtually indistinguishable from the average business, for example companies that offer IT support to other social enterprises.

The DTI describes social enterprises in the following way:

- businesses with primarily social objectives;
- surpluses principally reinvested for that purpose in the business or in the community, rather than being driven by the need to maximize profit for shareholders or owners;
- tackle a wide range of social and environmental issues;
- operate in all parts of the economy;
- include local community enterprises, social firms, mutual organizations such as cooperatives, and large organizations operating nationally or internationally;
- have no single legal model.

This description suggests that social enterprises are to be defined as **organizations that combine an income-generating or business-type activity with a social purpose** (with surplus reinvested in the 'cause'). However, there are also organizations that **generate social change and new approaches to social problems through implementing innovative ideas, which create social benefits**.

Although clearly having social objectives, both types of social enterprise are about generating new approaches through using business practices. Equally, both emphasize the role of individual social entrepreneurs.

## Pause and Reflect 7.1

### Hilary Cottam

Hilary Cottam is the head of the Design Council's red team (a think tank that explores new solutions to social and economic problems through design). In June 2005, she won the Design Museum's Designer of the Year award.

She does not see herself as a designer, but the judges said that her application of design to a wide range of issues, ranging from improved exam results for school students to lower reoffending rates among ex-offenders, made her an appropriate choice.

Before joining the Design Council she had set up two not-for-profit companies. School Works researched the design of schools in the UK, and the Do Tank did a similar job for prisons. Her vision for prisons involved study bedrooms rather than cells, and an Intranet system to facilitate the development of literacy and numeracy skills. Such a prison has not yet been built, but her ideas were incorporated into a building programme at Kingsdale Comprehensive in South London.

Hilary brings teams of professionals together to rethink the design of buildings and the delivery of public services, describing herself as 'part problem solver, part innovator, and part facilitator, but first and foremost as a social entrepreneur'.

*Adapted from: The Guardian, 10 June 2005*

**Questions:** Do you agree that Hilary Cottam is an innovator and entrepreneur? What would the policy and practical challenges be in building and operating a prison to her design?

## The nature of social and community enterprise

The Small Business Service Survey of social enterprises across the UK (2005) shows how diverse the sector is, and the contribution that it makes. Eighty-nine per cent of social enterprises are in urban areas (23 per cent are actually in London), but they operate in every region of the UK and they represent around 1 per cent of the UK's (employing) businesses. Social enterprises generate some £18 billion in annual turnover and employ over 775 000 people (two thirds of whom are employed full time). The survey found the following.

- The vast bulk of employment and turnover in social enterprises (82 per cent) derives from trading revenues, which account for £4.8 billion in total. Almost nine in ten (88 per cent) of those surveyed generate 50 per cent or more of their income from trading.
- The typical social enterprise employs 10 people. Almost half (49 per cent) employ fewer than 10 people, 38 per cent employ between 10 and 49, 11 per cent have 50–249 employees and 2 per cent employ more than 250. There are far fewer sole traders among social enterprises compared with the UK business population.
- Although around half of social enterprises receive grants, donations and subsidies (which account for 12 per cent of income), over 82 per cent of turnover derives from trading income.
- About a third of social enterprises derive their income from Health and Social Care; other important sources of trading income are social and personal services, real estate and renting, and adult education.

- Over 50 per cent of social enterprises are located in the 40 per cent most deprived areas and play a role in urban regeneration. Most social enterprises exist to help particular groups of people either through employment or by providing goods and services.
- The most common groups helped are those with disabilities, young people, the elderly and those on low incomes. Nearly a quarter of social enterprises had environmental objectives.
- The organizations surveyed were all 'companies limited by guarantee' or 'industrial and provident societies' as earlier research suggested that these types of business would cover the majority of social enterprises. Other kinds of social enterprise exist, but have not been included in this survey, and so the headline figures are an underestimate of the size and scope of the sector.

# Trends

## Ideology

In terms of ideology, it could be argued that there has been a continuation from Thatcherism (characterized during Prime Minister Margaret Thatcher's time in office by a very individualist approach and epitomized in Lord Young's drive to create an enterprise culture where people were self-reliant, and less dependent on state intervention) to New Labour's Third Way thinking. Individualism still underpins the rhetoric, but it is couched in terms of 'choice' and 'empowerment'. This seems to have softened the approach a little.

Experience over time has also proved that the private sector did not always have the answer to social and public issues. For example, the privatization of the railways and the creation of Railtrack led to concerns about shareholders taking money out of the organization rather than investing in the infrastructure at the same time that accidents were suspected of being caused by inadequate maintenance. Moreover, the performance of the various rail companies did not really improve once they were taken out of public ownership. Similarly, although private sector investment in infrastructure such as hospitals and schools has been welcomed through Private Finance Initiatives, there is now a debate about the longer-term implications of such investment as the rents are a significant overhead and the ethos of the 'landlord' is not always in accordance with those of the service provider.

Although enterprise remains a strong value, there is now a real attempt to bring the community back into the debates and to the policy arena. The dissatisfaction that is felt with many of our public services has also served to highlight the role of the voluntary and community sectors that have traditionally filled the gaps.

## Top-down and bottom-up

There is a tension sometimes between top-down government policy and programmes, and **local community action**. For example, in urban regeneration, there is a feeling that government policy is not really being that effective. This has led to the emergence of a range of support measures for grass-root initiatives (for example, the government has made money available through the Neighbourhood Renewal Fund for initiatives that support regeneration in deprived communities) and a general concern to support people taking responsibility for their economic and social well-being. There is also an acknowledgement of the need to create sustainable social provision both in economic terms and in the context of avoiding the creation of a 'dependency culture' where individual aspirations are low, people depend on the state for their livelihoods, and feel powerless to improve their situation in life.

---

### Enterprise in Action 7.2

#### Care for the community

Community Foster Care (CFC) was established in 1999 and was one of the first social enterprises to deal with foster care. Its approach was innovative, as it not only focused on the needs of the children but wanted to get carers from socially and economically disadvantaged areas into employment. By providing them with training, an income and qualifications, it builds self-esteem. It also helps the children, who can stay in their local area among their friends, attending the same school, and not having to admit that they are in care if they don't want to. The children need to feel that they belong, and being moved to rural areas with middle-class families with the stereotypical 2.4 children can be unsettling.

The application process is complex, and it certainly isn't easy money for the carers. Social services are referring children with increasingly challenging behaviour to fostering agencies. Most children placed by CFC have been sexually abused and, in turn, exhibit sexualized or violent behaviour. Not everyone can deal with this.

Half of the money CFC receives from local authorities goes to carers, the other half being reinvested in the business to pay for its link workers, the 24-hour support network, and training programmes. There has been scepticism from the local authorities, some not recognizing that a social enterprise could actually save it money. There have also been crises to overcome.

In 2000 a financial crisis at a social services department led to the withdrawal of a significant chunk of funding, and the Care Standards Act was expensive to implement. But CFC has survived, it is looking to expand into surrounding areas, and is considering a social franchise option to provide a toolkit for social service departments and other social enterprise set-ups.

*Adapted from*: Ben Flanagan, 'Revolutionising foster care',

*The Observer*, 24 October 2004

**Question:** What practical measures could be taken to help overcome cynicism regarding the effectiveness of social and community based enterprise within the public sector?

## Potential problems faced by social enterprises

### Local focus may limit the market

Although some social enterprises operate nationally and internationally, the majority do not. Given the fact that these businesses are often set up to serve a local geographic area, or to fulfil the requirements of a small niche where there has previously been market failure, this means that the market they serve can be limited. There is also the danger that such businesses may become trapped in a '**parallel economy**', unable to integrate with mainstream business and commerce. This may be particularly relevant where the social enterprise has been established specifically because there is a market gap deemed insufficiently profitable by the private sector.

### Lack of business skills may affect sustainability

Although committed to their cause, many of the businesses in the sector have **limited experience of operating commercially**. This may affect their ability to remain profitable in the longer term, or to transfer to the mainstream economy where it is appropriate for them to do so, and establishing capable management teams can be a challenge.

### Finding gap funding may distract organizations and lead to short-termism

Although trading forms a significant part of the income of many social and community enterprises, for some, the gap needs to be filled by competing with other agencies for public sector funds. These are often **short-term income streams** and place demands on the organization in terms of the nature of the outputs expected. Chasing funding can take up valuable resources (such as time) and sometimes distract the organization from its strategic objectives.

## The policy perspective

Although well-intentioned, government policy can place burdensome costs on these organizations. For example, consultation on policy and community involvement is a laudable objective, but the representatives of the sector have to give their time freely. Many literally cannot afford to become involved, despite it being in their long-term interests in terms of developing a profile with the public sector agencies and having a voice in the decision-making process.

The Department for Trade and Industry (DTI) has highlighted the role of social enterprises as models for maximizing public good through business solutions, as outlined in Social Enterprise: A Strategy for Success (2002). The aims of the strategy are:

- to create a more enabling environment for social enterprises by identifying and removing some of the barriers, constraints and challenges they may face such as supporting the development of a new legal structure;
- to make them better businesses, through the provision of business support and training as well as improving funding mechanisms;
- to develop a strong evidence base on social enterprises which will:
  establish the value of social enterprise
  inform policy development
  contribute to improving the delivery of services to the sector.

Because the sector is new and underfunded, and relatively little is known about the best practice that may exist, one of the critical tasks was to actually understand the nature and scope of the sector, and the DTI Small Business Service finally published a comprehensive survey of social enterprise in the UK in July 2005. Progress has been made in terms of development of the sector, and we highlight some of the current issues below.

## Procurement

The government believes there is more scope for public sector services to be delivered by social enterprises, and the issues are similar to those that face the voluntary and community sector, which we consider later in this chapter. In the government's view, by being close to their customers, and not needing to deliver dividends to shareholders, social enterprises can offer a more flexible and cost-effective service. However, it recognizes that there are two key issues that it needs to focus on if it is to enable such businesses to play a role in service delivery. There is a need to:

- promote understanding of social enterprises among those responsible for public procurement and those who audit and inspect their work in order to ensure that the sector is able to compete fairly with mainstream providers;
- develop expertise in the sector on public procurement practices.

## Legal structures

The government have introduced a new legal form to support the establishment of social and community enterprises, and appointed a regulator in April 2005, with the intention that organizations could begin to apply to become **community interest companies** (CICs) from the summer of 2005. Organizations can be public limited companies, or private companies limited by guarantee or shares, and they will be subject to an asset lock (which means they will be restricted in distributing profits and assets to their members to ensure that assets are used to benefit the community). They cannot also hold charitable status. However, if they need to raise investment, CICs limited by shares will have the option of issuing shares that pay a dividend to investors. The dividend payable on these shares will be subject to a cap, set by the Regulator (after consultation), in order to protect the asset lock.

## Business support and training

If social enterprises are to become better businesses, they will need appropriate advice and support. A key part of this will be in opening up mainstream support to the sector, and Business Links (agencies funded by the DTI to support business development in the UK) have been required to provide such support within their business plans since April 2003. Government support will focus on:

- training the trainers and business support providers;
- business training and support for social enterprises;
- building capacity and financial awareness to help social enterprises make stronger bids for financial support.

## Pause and Reflect 7.2

### Creation Recycling – Rotherham

Creation Recycling Ltd is an innovative social enterprise created as a result of a feasibility study undertaken by the Valley Community Partnership (an area of high deprivation in Rotherham) into options for kerbside recycling. One outcome of the study was that the Valley area, on its own, was seen as not being able to provide sufficient economies of scale for the project to be economically viable or sustainable; therefore three different community partnerships have lent their support to the project, which has seen Creation working across a wider area of benefit, i.e. 11 000 households or 10 per cent of the Rotherham Metropolitan Borough Council (RMBC).

Creation currently offers a weekly kerbside collection service of dry recyclables (glass, cans and textiles) to 11 000 households in the most disadvantaged and hard-to-reach communities in Rotherham, while future plans include a paper collection service and a kitchen waste service.

In addition to its collection service Creation also operates a materials handling and processing facility, which takes all the recyclable materials collected by RMBC in the remaining 90 per cent of the Borough.

Creation is currently financed for a two-year action research period, which will lead to self-sustainability by year 3. Funding comes from a variety of public sources. Year 1 funding had a high capital investment of approximately £250 k and revenue costs of £350 k but generated sales income of approximately £150 k. The current running costs for the initial kerbside collection and materials processing are estimated at £400 k per annum.

Creation employs a total of 15 staff (including 1 apprentice) and offers volunteer/training placements to a variety of people including young people, asylum seekers and people with learning difficulties. It offers a programme of education and awareness raising to local schools as part of a citizenship curriculum. Creation is currently applying for Investors in People.

Creation is delivering services on behalf of the local authority in disadvantaged areas, contributing to neighbourhood management and enabling the local authority to achieve stretched statutory targets. Through adoption of the proximity principle, Creation sources as much of its own requirements as possible, employs local people and involves the local community, thereby multiplying the economic impact of the project.

Creation Recycling Ltd has very strong environmental and social aims, which it is achieving, but the bottom line is – it is a business and aims to be a very successful one.

*Adapted from*: www.creationrecycling.co.uk/

**Question:** Evaluate the economic and social impact that Creation Recycling has generated in Rotherham.

## The voluntary and community sector

# The nature and role of the voluntary and community sector

Governments across the world have seen a shift in the relationship between the voluntary sector and the state over the last 25 years. In the UK, the Conservative governments of the 1980s and early 1990s introduced contracting out into the delivery of public service agenda. This meant that the utilities (gas, water, electricity provision) and rail services were privatized and local authorities were required to put many of their services out to compulsory competitive tender (CCT) in the interests of securing more economic delivery of services. Before this change, it had been presumed that public services should be delivered by the public sector but the Conservative government introduced the idea that the private sector could deliver public services more efficiently. Since 1997, the Labour government has extended this thinking, saying that services should be delivered by those who can do so most effectively within the resources available, and that this could be the public, private, or voluntary and community sector. This changing political perspective has led to recommendations (Treasury, 2002) designed to remove the barriers to the voluntary and community sector becoming engaged in the delivery of public services.

## Engaging in the delivery of public sector services

### Government desire to reform public services

Given the context of wanting to reform public services, improve choice for consumers, and deliver more efficiently and effectively, it is clear why government would want to open up delivery to a broader range of organizations. Although there are many entrepreneurial **voluntary and community organizations** (VCOs) that are keen to take this opportunity to expand their services, grow their businesses, and secure more long term sources of funding, there are also many for whom it is not appropriate. The consequences for these organizations also need to be considered.

### The decision to take on contracts for the delivery of public services

The VCO has to be clear about why it would make the decision to take on such contracts. The criteria on which it makes this choice would be similar to those of any entrepreneur looking at a strategic development opportunity, and it will ask questions such as:

- Is the service core to its mission?
- Can it add value to the particular service?
- Does it believe it can deliver the service better than competitors from either the public or private sector?
- Does it have niche experience or knowledge that means no one else is capable of providing the service?

The danger is that the opportunity could just be the path of least resistance in terms of income generation. Many organizations in the sector operate on very tight budgets, and securing external funding is crucial to their survival. There is a danger that they may follow the funding, fitting their activities to match the expectations of funders, in order to remain viable.

## Consistency with strategic purposes

VCOs have their purposes set out quite clearly in their governing documents and their trustees are bound to ensure that they fulfil these purposes. Funding opportunities should only be pursued if they are consistent with the organizations' purposes. There is a danger inherent in successfully securing contracts, in that these could skew the focus of a VCO and render the original mission marginal.

## Capacity issues

Equally, as with any business expansion, there might arise issues of capacity to deliver on a much larger scale, as this requires more complex systems and processes. This might mean restructuring the business model, and have implications for the culture of the organization. The VCO might find it difficult to make this step-change successfully. Once again we emphasize that the key to entrepreneurial success is not primarily about the idea pursued, but about being able to create an appropriate business model to exploit successfully the opportunity that the idea presents.

## Lessons from the not-for-profit sector

In relation to the voluntary sector in America, Drucker (2001: 39) makes some general points that apply in a broader context. From his analysis we can identify some lessons that can be learned from the way the not-for-profit sector operates, which we discuss below.

He argues that in two areas, **strategy** and the **effectiveness of the board** that runs the organization, these sectors are practising what the private sector only preach, and that in the most crucial area – the **motivation and productivity of knowledge workers** – they are pioneers, working out the policies and practices that business will have to learn tomorrow.

The reason for this is that the not-for-profit sector has increasingly recognized the importance of organization, leadership, accountability and performance. The bottom line is not defined in profits but in impact, which implies that the participating organizations focus clearly on their purpose. The implications of this are that the successful not-for-profit organizations are developing business models which are finely tuned towards the exploitation of the opportunity and the achievement of their strategic goals.

For example, charities such as Oxfam have to be concerned with income and expenditure, demonstrating to their stakeholders that they are spending money wisely in support of their primary mission. If they cannot demonstrate impact, their operations are called into question. The overarching importance of their mission focuses such organizations on action, which creates discipline, and prevents limited resources being spread too thinly on things that are less central to their purpose. It serves to focus them on a very small number of productive efforts.

Collins and Porras (1996) also recognize the importance of core values and core purpose, explaining how the companies that enjoy enduring success might change their strategies (the means by which they reach their goals) but never change the values and core principles that underpin their reason for being in business. Having a clear mission can also help in fostering innovation as it helps people see that, however much change flies in the face of tradition, it is necessary if they are to provide the best service for the communities that they serve.

This focus on accountability and performance means that the not-for-profit organizations have had to learn to define what 'results' mean for them. Once they have clearly defined what they mean by results, they need to be able to demonstrate the link between the activities they fund and the resulting impact. It could be argued that this is more similar to Japanese attitudes than to Western business practice. The Japanese organization would ask itself what it would have to make happen out in the marketplace to deserve a reward (profit). In Enterprise in Action 7.3 it is demonstrated how an organization has had to review its strategy and design a new business model, driven by changes in the external environment, but has remained clearly focused on its core values, and on doing what is right by the customer.

## Enterprise in Action 7.3

### Exploiting opportunity in the not-for-profit sector

A large catholic hospital chain in south-west America increased its revenues by 15 per cent despite sharp cuts in Medicare payments and hospital stays over an eight-year period. The nun who was the CEO recognized that they were in the business of providing health care rather than the business of running hospitals. When health-care delivery began moving out of hospitals for economic reasons the hospital chain promoted the trend rather than fighting against it. They founded ambulatory surgery centres, rehabilitation centres, X-ray and lab networks, and so on. They adopted the attitude that if the trend was in the patients' interests, they would have to promote it and then take responsibility for making it profitable. Paradoxically, their policy filled the chain's hospitals as well. This was because the freestanding facilities were very popular and provided a steady stream of referrals through to the hospitals.

*Adapted from:* Drucker (2001: 42)

**Question:** What lessons can the private sector learn from the way this business model was reconfigured?

Drucker (2001: 43) also highlights the way that the not-for-profit sector makes effective use of their boards, and says that there are lessons that entrepreneurial businesses can learn from this. Historically, not-for-profit sector board members have been closer to operations, taking a more active interest than in the private sector. The directors on not-for-profit boards also often invest more, particularly in personal terms, as they usually are very committed to the cause. They have often been volunteers themselves and so understand the business, and are very knowledgeable, which is not always the case for outside directors in the private sector who might only have a minority shareholding.

This has resonance with the way that entrepreneurs seek to manage their businesses, remaining actively involved, having a deep understanding of their business and their customers, and being reluctant to delegate the running of the business to others. As some of the not-for-profit organizations have grown, there has been a shift towards professional management as some of them have become far too big to be run by part-timers.

## Managing non-paid professionals in entrepreneurial not-for-profit organizations

Drucker (2001: 46) suggests that the not-for-profit sector has also learned how to secure the commitment and enthusiasm of the workforce. In the past, there tended to be a view that, as volunteers weren't paid, it was unreasonable to make too many demands of them. This view has changed, and the more likely approach today is to recognize that, precisely because they do not receive monetary rewards, volunteers must get greater satisfaction from their accomplishments. The reward is in terms of recognition, and knowing that their contribution makes a difference and is of value. This shift may have arisen out of the necessity of having to be more productive with the people already involved, as it can be difficult to find additional volunteers.

More and more volunteers are educated people in managerial or professional jobs, and are coming up to retirement. They are not used to being 'helpers', having held down responsible and demanding jobs. They are at a time in their lives where they are in a position to offer their services in a cause that they feel has value, but they do expect to be engaged in meaningful work. They may have been dissatisfied in their paid employment, or feel that it offers insufficient challenge or opportunity for achievement. They may feel that they are just a means to an end, that the organizations they work for have no real sense of mission or purpose, that everything is expedient to profit. If this is the case, they are not going to settle for the same as a volunteer; they need to see that their input of time and energy has worth and that it really does make a difference – and it has to be a difference that they value. To keep them, the organizations they commit their time to have to put their competence and knowledge to work. There is also a sense of mutual learning and teaching as the experience of the volunteers is put to good use in training newcomers, and learning new skills.

This has significance for the private sector as managing the knowledge worker for productivity is the next great challenge for management. Organizations increasingly need business brains rather than helpers. Stewart (1997) argues that intellectual capital matters. Those who are not knowledge workers are not rewarded as well as they were, and organizations that cannot manage knowledge workers may not be as successful as their competitors who can. The knowledge content of everyday goods and services is increasing rapidly, and there are few industries or companies that have not become more information intensive. Using such information intelligently in making decisions may, we suggest, distinguish the successful entrepreneurial organization. The move from non-profit volunteering to non-paid professionalism has meant that the voluntary and community sector has experience in managing knowledge workers. The organizations involved make high demands of their volunteers, with corresponding responsibility. However, the volunteers know what they are there for as there is a strong sense of mission, they are managed by objectives and self-control, there is accountability for results, and there is an opportunity for continual learning and teaching. These lessons are valuable for entrepreneurial organizations in all sectors.

## Tensions between social and economic imperatives in not-for-profit entrepreneurship

Although there are similarities between the social and economic imperatives, there are inherent tensions created by their overlap.

## Business approach and the political process

Traditionally, the voluntary and community sector has tried to secure social reform by lobbying governments and taking a political stance. Some of those who operate within the sector see their role being to challenge what they perceive to be injustices in the way society operates. The literature and policy on social enterprise tends to focus on it as a business process and creating change within the existing political system. This shift of focus from an ideological debate to practical discussion about business process consequence is argued to be a **depoliticization** of their role, and has created some tension in the sector.

Although there are undoubtedly benefits to be gained from the move towards greater involvement of the voluntary, community and social sectors in the delivery of public services, it could be argued that in giving these sectors a greater voice in decision-making, and in adopting a more collaborative approach to policy, their cooperation is being 'bought'. Decision-making becomes more complicated, and it is more difficult to achieve consensus as this requires greater compromise.

## Individual and community

In entrepreneurship, there is very much a focus on individualism. We have spoken previously about how the entrepreneur can seem to be a 'great person' and how businesses can become the personification of the entrepreneur. This is a little at odds with the values of the social enterprise, and even more so with those of the voluntary sector, who adopt a much more **collectivist approach**. This can lead to internal tensions. For example, if the person who heads the organization acts as a representative on policy forums, it can be seen as an attempt to develop a personal profile as opposed to raising the profile of the organization as a whole. Equally, if success is publicized, the person who 'fronts' the organization can be seen as becoming egotistical and failing to give sufficient credit to the team of people who are involved in achieving such social impact.

# Short-term deliverables and long-term sustainability

These trends are leading to an increasing focus on results, which might have the disadvantage of driving organizations in the sector to fit a project-based **short-term approach** when they need to look at longer-term sustainability and development to be really effective. Involvement in a series of initiatives, and securing funding from two or three sources, each demanding slightly different outputs, can lead to fragmented management, short-term focus, and a loss of strategic perspective. While the sector is seen as pioneering and capable of piloting new ideas, there also needs to be a focus on sustainability, and the critical resources and managerial and organizational competencies needed by a growing business. We have already discussed how focus on mission and values is a valuable element in the success of entrepreneurial voluntary and community sector organizations (VCOs), and so the funding regime that is predominant in the sector would seem to be at odds with the criteria needed for their long-term success.

In considering sustainability, it is also important to remember the diversity of the sector. There may also be a role for encouraging more innovation in the large established charities, for example, or in using their core competencies to bring about social change in different markets.

## Public sector

Successive governments in the UK have focused on the need for a strong enterprise policy for businesses. Since the early 1980s there has been a slow but gradual acknowledgement that entrepreneurship and innovation will not happen spontaneously in any type of organization but, perhaps, especially in the **public sector**. If innovation is valued, it needs to be fostered. This focus on developing individual initiative and enterprising businesses contributed to the growing interest in developing similar cultures in the public and voluntary sectors. The practical consequence of this has been the trend for contracting out of services that has been so prevalent in local government, for example, as mentioned earlier. Another example would be the creation of quasi-competition through the introduction of league tables to compare performance such as those used to measure the success of schools. However, the success of such measures is debatable as it could be argued that they can be self-defeating, as organizations focus on short-term tactics which enable them to massage the statistics to improve their immediate position rather than implement more substantial changes that may not be reflected in the league table position quite so soon.

## Bureaucracy and conservatism

In discussing the public sector, and the delivery of public sector services, the literature often speaks of bureaucracy and conservatism as obstacles to innovation. But as some of the giants of the private sector – such as 3 M – demonstrate, size does not have to be an impediment to enterprising behaviour and entrepreneurial strategies. Just because the sector is dominated by large agencies, for example the National Health Service, it does not mean that they cannot innovate, as highlighted in Enterprise in Action 7.4.

## Drivers of innovation

Innovation in the delivery of services has been driven by a number of factors, the principal ones being the drive for **efficiency and accountability**, and the desire to offer greater choice to consumers. The NHS Direct example (Enterprise in Action 7.4) illustrates how the need to operate more efficiently led to the development of a new business model in the National Health Service.

### Enterprise in Action 7.4

**NHS Direct**

NHS Direct radically changed the model of delivery of health care services and health care information in the UK. It was seen as a way of reducing pressure on GPs, ambulance services and hospital services by providing a 24-hour telephone advisory service staffed by nurses. These nurses were supported by diagnostic software which prompted them to ask particular questions of callers and suggest possible diagnoses and appropriate action. It was part of a package of services that also introduced 'walk-in' clinics, offering fast, convenient access, and an Internet-based health-care information service.

The service expanded rapidly, and drew concern that the recruitment of experienced nurses might adversely affect other services in the NHS. There were also concerns about how the nurses would keep their clinical knowledge up to date. Professionals questioned the motives behind the introduction of the service, accusing NHS Direct of being 'parasitic and destructive of the NHS', expressing concern that it might be a front to mask the shortage of doctors, and worrying that it undermined the central role of GPs in the provision of health care. There were also accusations that it shifted the business model from being needs-based to demand-led.

The anticipated reduction in demand upon GP and accident & emergency services has not occurred to the extent hoped for, although the implementation of NHS Direct is widely regarded as a success. It has a good safety record, functions as a gateway to a range of services, and helps to prioritize cases. It has played an important role in providing advice, especially as various health scares have arisen. The service is continuing to expand into new areas, e.g. dentistry, management of patient appointments, and emergency services cover.

*Adapted from*: Alex Murdock, *NHS Direct*. In: Johnson G., Scholes K. and Whittington R. (2002 and 2005)

**Questions:** What challenges do public sector organizations face in implementing such innovations in process? Is the current rate of expansion sustainable?

## Individual enterprise in public life

Some people in public life approach their careers with ambition and drive, and a clear vision of the difference they want to make. For example, Mo Mowlem's contribution to the peace process in Northern Ireland was unusual, and yet effective.

### Enterprise in Action 7.5

#### Mo Mowlem

Mo Mowlem worked as a university administrator and lecturer before pursuing a career in politics. Her enthusiastic, unpretentious attitude won her standing ovations and media awards, and earned her the respect of the public. She was popular with voters, partly because of her determination to carry on as Northern Ireland Secretary despite treatment for a brain tumour which caused hair loss. It is reported that she would often remove her wig in the middle of high-powered meetings, or kick off her shoes and put her feet up.

She took a political risk in 1998 by going inside the Maze prison when it became clear that the Peace Process would only succeed with the backing of the prisoners. The loyalist UDA/UFF prisoners had previously withdrawn their support for the process. She spent an hour with them and two hours later the paramilitaries' political representatives announced that they were being allowed to rejoin the talks. She told reporters at the time 'I didn't negotiate. I didn't do a deal. If you want progress, you ain't going to get it if you don't have talks'.

The failure of the Northern Ireland parties to agree on the implementation of the Good Friday Agreement and the release of IRA prisoners without the parallel surrender of arms led to calls for her dismissal, and in 1999 she was replaced as Northern Ireland Secretary by Peter Mandelson. She became cabinet 'enforcer' after turning down the job of Health Secretary. Her time in the cabinet was marred by rumours that someone in high places was briefing against her. She stood down as an MP in 2001. She was a vocal opponent of the war on Iraq.

Various public sources

**Question:** To what extent did Mo Mowlem's personal characteristics make a difference in Northern Ireland?

## Comparisons between social and economic entrepreneurship

At this point it may be helpful to look at some of the different aspects of entrepreneurship and **innovation** that we have discussed so far, and explore how social entrepreneurship compares with the more traditional economic role that the literature more commonly explores.

## Innovation

Although often criticized for being less accountable than government, the not-for-profit sector has arguably more flexibility to be innovative and to pilot new ways of doing things because it is closer to the beneficiaries of the service. Many social entrepreneurs have the opportunity to bring existing ideas together in new ways, which is consistent with Schumpeter's ideas of new combinations. Innovation may emerge in entrepreneurial approaches to:

- attracting funding and procuring resources;
- the design of innovative services and initiatives;
- a visionary attitude to identifying desired outputs and impact;
- motivating and engaging with 'difficult' clients;
- mobilizing the support of delivery agencies and partners.

## Risk-bearing

Social outcomes are in actuality difficult to quantify and hard to evaluate. However, social entrepreneurs do carry the risk of failure even if it is only to the extent that is so difficult to quantify success or to establish causality. Certainly in terms of personal risk, entrepreneurs with social motives may feel the failure more acutely in terms of failing the people who depended upon them. So although the nature of the risk may be different, they are still more willing to bear risks.

Unfortunately this difficulty in evaluating impact and demonstrating accountability also brings another risk. When coupled with a lack of professional management, there is a danger of mismanagement, or even fraud, arising. Of course this potential is not confined to social entrepreneurship alone!

# Spotting and acting on opportunities

Social entrepreneurs perhaps see **enactable contexts** rather than opportunities as such. The opportunities that they act upon are often connected with the identification of gaps in provision. Filling those gaps requires them to convince others of the need, secure commitment and resources to provide new services, or find different ways of using existing resources and services to provide a more comprehensive service. They consequently respond to identified needs by understanding or presenting an issue in a new way.

# Bridging between sectors, fields and resources

This is arguably a key strength of the public/community/voluntary sector that has long been expected to work in **partnership** with many agencies and groups to achieve results. Sometimes this is forced since, in order to secure funds, they are often required to work across boundaries and in alliances.

They need to mobilize resources (often bidding for funding) to achieve their objectives. Perhaps there is less emphasis on having the idea and more emphasis on communicating that idea and winning support for it in this sector.

# Leadership

The **social entrepreneur** and the leader of the Voluntary and Community Organization excel here. They are very expert in communicating their vision, exhibiting strong values/ideals, setting a mission and organizing people around it. Unlike purely economic entrepreneurs, a large part of their role lies in managing the politics of inter-agency working. This again brings us to the discussion about the role of entrepreneurs themselves, and the characteristics that distinguish them.

## Characteristics of social and economic entrepreneurs

Bolton and Thompson (2003: 66) identify a range of facets that characterize entrepreneurs. These are:

- focus
- advantage

- creativity
- ego
- team
- social.

They argue that which facets an entrepreneur possesses and the degree to which they are exhibited determine whether an individual's talents lie in business or in social entrepreneurship.

The focus, advantage, creativity, and ego facets are present to some degree in all entrepreneurs. The presence or absence of the team facet affects the growth potential of the firm, and the social facet affects the nature of the business.

Bolton and Thompson (2003: 148) offer an analysis of the building blocks of this social facet. They suggest that there are four building blocks, and that all need to be present. These are belief, values, mission and service to others.

As with the decision to engage in any form of entrepreneurship, the decision to become a social entrepreneur does not have to be one that

## Spotlight 7.1

**The building blocks of the social facet**

*Belief*

Beliefs are the guiding principles that individuals live by. They may believe in God, a particular political philosophy, or even themselves, but their belief provides them with a way of seeing the world, a mindset. Bolton and Thompson argue that the step from belief to values is the first dividing line between the business entrepreneur and the social entrepreneur, as they choose to embed their beliefs into their approach to business. They give the example of Souter, the Stagecoach boss, who is a devout Christian, but operates his business on economic lines. Some entrepreneurs have strong beliefs and yet partition their lives so that it does not affect their entrepreneurial behaviour. Applying one's beliefs in the world of business can seem difficult.

*Values*

We have spoken about values and ethics in business in discussing corporate social responsibility, and how adopting ethical practice might well be sound business practice. For socially minded entrepreneurs, values are an integral part of the way they operate. It is not about enlightened self-interest. They do not apply their values simply because it will give them an advantage. Socially minded entrepreneurs might have beliefs and values, but they do not make the next step – to mission, which is the next stage on the road to true social entrepreneurship.

*Mission*

Through mission, social entrepreneurs find a cause through which their beliefs and values can be channelled. Bolton and Thompson suggest that Anita Roddick made this step when she became a campaigner for social justice building on the success of Body Shop.

> ### Service to others
>
> The final step is doing something about it; taking action. Entrepreneurs act, they don't just talk about acting. Having seen the need the social entrepreneur behaves like any other entrepreneur and translates it into opportunity. The difference is in the focus – it is external, not internal. The motive is in helping others, not themselves.
>
> *Adapted from*: Bolton B. and Thompson J. (2003: 148–54)
>
> **Question:** To what extent do you agree with Bolton and Thompson's categorization? Use practical examples to illustrate your views.

lasts throughout life. Some people start out as social entrepreneurs and eventually move into the mainstream; others start out as traditional economic entrepreneurs and at some point in their lives find a cause that they feel is worth championing, whether for a short time or for the rest of their lives. Some combine the two, running commercial businesses that provide the profits to support social enterprises. Although the motive is social and focused on making a difference in other people's lives, their characteristics and actions have many similarities with those of entrepreneurs in general. The concepts are the same, but the context is different.

## Enterprise in Action 7.6

### One

Claire Goose (of Casualty and Waking the Dead TV programme fame) is helping her brother Duncan to promote One, his new not-for-profit bottled-water venture.

The idea came from a brainstorming session in a pub. Duncan gave up his job and lived off his savings to get the project off the ground. The water comes from the Radnor Hills in mid-Wales and all the profits go towards new water pumps in villages in Africa. They are called 'Playpumps' and replace traditional hand-pumps with roundabouts that children can play on. This frees up people's time, as the water is pumped straight from the ground into storage tanks.

The first bottle came off production on the day that Bob Geldof announced Live 8, and so it seemed appropriate to try to use the event to promote the concept. Claire spoke at the Edinburgh rally, and Duncan in London. Bottles of One water were given to all Live 8 performers and were also available in Edinburgh.

Although there are six years between the siblings in terms of age, Claire says 'We are very similar in personality. We will give anything a go. It's been an emotional roller coaster. A friend is the designer and everyone on the project has given their time for free. Everyone is doing it because they want to do it.'

*Adapted from: The Guardian*, 16 July 2005

**Question:** Analyse the extent to which (a) Claire and (b) Duncan exhibit the facets of an entrepreneur as described by Bolton and Thompson.

## Summary

- The UK government's 'modernization agenda' in the delivery of public services offers opportunities to entrepreneurial social enterprises and the voluntary and community sector.
- Social enterprise makes a significant contribution to urban regeneration and economic development.
- Although the potential exists to secure longer-term funding through contracts for delivering public sector services, voluntary and community sector organizations need to ensure that this supports their mission and objectives. Some will need support in developing appropriate strategic capability.
- Entrepreneurial organizations can learn lessons from the not-for-profit sector in terms of strategy and values, governance, and the management of knowledge workers.
- Innovation and enterprise is being driven by the push towards efficiency and accountability in the public sector.
- Social and economic entrepreneurs exhibit similar traits and characteristics despite the different contexts in which they operate.

## Chapter questions

1. Compare and contrast the characteristics and actions of social and economic entrepreneurs. Draw on practical examples to illustrate your analysis.
2. Are the economic needs of an entrepreneurial organization always opposed to those of the broader community?
3. If you were the manager of a voluntary sector organization what would you see as the advantages and disadvantages in securing a public sector contract?
4. How might an economic entrepreneur apply the lessons of best practice from the not-for-profit sector?
5. In creating an enterprise culture, to what extent should public sector support be focused on social enterprise as opposed to economic entrepreneurship?

## Case study

### Locanda dei Girasoli

Locanda dei Girasoli is a 100-seater pizzeria in Rome's working class Tuscolano district. It has a regular clientele, attracted by the better-than-average quality of the food. But what makes the experience unique is that its waiters have Down's Syndrome. Valerio, Claudio and Viviana (the waiters) love the human contact involved in the job. They serve customers with aplomb, help in the kitchen, and even turn a hand to baking a pizza as they have been taught all the necessary skills at school. Their confidence and cheerfulness is infectious, and regulars are now quite used to being greeted with an affectionate hug!

Sergio Paladini founded the project. He and his wife, Agostini, hoped that it would give their Down's son, Valerio, 'a purpose in life'. Although they had no experience of the industry, they and seven partners (including the three waiters) formed a cooperative to run the restaurant. They continued to work during the day and run the restaurant at night. They found it emotionally very difficult when, at first, some customers would walk out when they saw it was a Down's person who was serving. After four years, they decided to close because of repeated losses and sheer exhaustion.

The left-wing city hall saved them, finding new investors and staff in the form of committed cooperatives who could better support Sergio and Agostini. They are about to move into bigger premises and hope to employ up to 20 people with Down's.

Although at first the locals were put off by their prejudices, fewer people react badly these days. Sergio hopes that attitudes to disability are finally changing in Rome.

*Adapted from*: Bruce Johnston, Down's staff win over critics at pizzeria,
*The Daily Telegraph*, 14 July 2005

### Questions

1. Evaluate the impact that a restaurant such as this can have on the local community.
2. Should national and local governments rely on the commitment of social entrepreneurs to pioneer such initiatives, or should they share the responsibility? Justify your views.

## References and further reading

Barrington R. and Abbott C. (2005) What makes a multinational company a global citizen? Sustainable development challenges for companies operating internationally. In: J. Hancock (ed.), *Investing in Corporate Social Responsibility*. London: Kogan Page.

Bolton B. and Thompson J. (2003) *The Entrepreneur in Focus: Achieve your Potential*. London: Thomson.

Bucar B. and Hirisch R.D. (2001) Ethics of business managers vs entrepreneurs. *Journal of Developmental Entrepreneurship* **1**: 59–72.

Collins J.C. and Porras J.I. (1996) Building your company's vision. *Harvard Business Review*, Sept–Oct, pp. 65–77.

Drucker P.F. (2001) *The Essential Drucker*. Oxford: Butterworth-Heinemann.

DTI Social Enterprise Unit (2002) *Social Enterprise: A Strategy for Success.* London: DTI.

DTI Social Enterprise Unit (2003) *Social Enterprise: Delivering for All.* London: DTI.

Kirby D.A. (2003) *Entrepreneurship.* Maidenhead: McGraw-Hill Education.

Schaper M. and Volery T. (2004) *Entrepreneurship and Small Business: A Pacific Rim Perspective.* Milton: John Wiley & Sons Australia Ltd.

Stewart T.A. (1997) *Intellectual Capital: The New Wealth of Organizations.* London: Nicholas Brearley Publishing.

## Useful websites

http://www.ncvo-vol.org.uk
http://www.sbs.gov.uk/SBS_Gov_files/researchandstats/Social-Enterprise-Survey-2005.pdf

## Key words

collectivist approach
community interest companies
corporate social responsibility
depoliticization
effectiveness of the board
efficiency and accountability
enactable contexts
innovation
limited experience of operating commercially
local community action
motivation and productivity of knowledge workers

parallel economy
partnership
public sector
short-term approach
short-term income streams
social enterprise
social entrepreneur
strategy
voluntary and community organizations

## CHAPTER 8

# Multicultural entrepreneurship

Learning objectives

By the end of this chapter the reader will be able to:

- understand the nature, challenges and impact of entrepreneurship in market economies at different stages of development;
- compare the nature and strategies of entrepreneurship in different cultures;
- appreciate the size and impact of the informal economy;
- recognize the different patterns of international entrepreneurship and strategies adopted to develop international business;
- identify the different specific skills, attitudes and techniques prevalent in multicultural entrepreneurship.

## Introduction

So far in this part of the book we have discussed the various dimensions of entrepreneurship from the perspective of the generic skills, attitudes and techniques adopted by entrepreneurs in different sector contexts. In this chapter we discuss the dimension of different cultural and country perspectives on entrepreneurship. While many of the generic skills, attitudes and techniques that we have discussed so far are common across cultures and countries there are some differences too. There are considerable differences in the different international contexts for entrepreneurship, including for example, the nature of the markets, the competitive pressures and demands, expectations of customers and the support and resources available.

As we introduce the various topics to be discussed in this chapter it is also worth reflecting on the purpose of studying multicultural entrepreneurship within the aims of this book. Clearly it is useful to add to an understanding of how the different economic contexts that exist in different country situations impact upon, and are affected by, entrepreneurship within the economy. In conjunction with many other factors we will discuss how entrepreneurship contributes to the economic regeneration of economies and is therefore particularly important in emerging markets.

The attitudes to entrepreneurship and the support, encouragement and advice given to entrepreneurs are significantly affected by the cultural standards and values of the host country as well as its infrastructure, wealth and geography. The skills, attitudes and techniques of entrepreneurship in different cultures can therefore be given different emphasis. A discussion of the different value placed on them can lead the reader to review his or her own beliefs about the topic and possibly even resolve to embrace different skills and attitudes with new enthusiasm.

Learning about alternative entrepreneurial cultures can also be enhanced by gaining a greater understanding of the informal economy, which has such a significant impact on many developed economies.

Finally we will discuss the implications of international entrepreneurship and examine the various strategies that might be adopted by international entrepreneurs.

## The characteristics and impact of entrepreneurship in different cultures

In this first section we consider cross-country comparisons of entrepreneurial activity and the implications of some of the findings. Global Entrepreneurship Monitor (2004) (GEM) makes a distinction between the following two types of entrepreneurial activity.

1. *Opportunity entrepreneurship*, in which a perceived opportunity is exploited. **Opportunity entrepreneurs** make up on average 65 per cent of the total but are more prevalent in high-income economies; and

2.  *Necessity entrepreneurship*, in which the activity is undertaken because there are no other employment options or because the other employment options are unsatisfactory. Necessity entrepreneurs make up on average 35 per cent of the total, but as might be expected are more prevalent in low-income economies.

GEM makes cross-country comparisons using total entrepreneurial activity (TEA) as an index. TEA is defined as constituting *nascent entrepreneurs*, who are thinking about start-up or have paid wages or salaries for less than three months and *owner-managers*, who have been paying wages or salaries between 3 and 42 months.

## The prevalence of entrepreneurship in different countries

GEM divides the 34 countries studied into high-, medium- and low-income groups according to their per capita gross domestic product (GDP). It found that TEA averaged 9.3 per cent for adults between 18 and 64 and varied among the 34 countries studied from 1.5 per cent in the case of Japan to 40 per cent in the case of Peru. Generally, men are twice as likely to start a business as are women.

There can be many reasons for the differences in TEA and these are often cultural. Nueno (2000: 224) points out that, in Japan, leaving a large organization to start your own small business is not well accepted and previous business contacts are unlikely to be supportive of the new venture. The figure for the UK is 6.3 per cent and for the USA, 11.3 per cent.

To emphasize the scale of entrepreneurship in the USA, each year more than 600 000 new businesses are launched and this number has doubled in the last two decades. One year this figure reached 900 000. 10 million people are self-employed in the USA. Despite the high failure rate of businesses, according to the 2002 Census Bureau data, there was a 10 per cent increase in the number of businesses in the USA between 1997 and 2002; interestingly, the number of black-owned businesses grew by 45 per cent, Hispanic-owned businesses by 31 per cent, and the number of Asian-owned businesses by 24 per cent. However, minority-owned firms still make up only about 18 per cent of the country's businesses.

There are some significant differences as well as similarities between the countries. For example, low-income countries (low per-capita GDP) have the highest level of entrepreneurial activity for all age groups and most people who consider starting a business there have not completed secondary level education. In contrast the level of activity (around 28 per cent) is the same among those that have secondary education irrespective of the GDP. Usually people starting a new business already have a job (91 per cent in high-income countries, 81 per cent in middle-income countries and 77 per cent in low-income countries) and only 0.01 per cent of businesses start with finance from venture capitalists or business angels.

Despite some similarities across the countries, GEM concludes that the policies of individual governments to support entrepreneurship need to be tailored to each situation.

## Culture and attitudes to entrepreneurship, risk and failure

**Culture** plays an important role in influencing attitudes to entrepreneurship, risk and failure. Before considering the prevalent attitudes to entrepreneurship it is worth reflecting on the nature of culture, which Doole and Lowe (2004) explain has three essential components:

1. beliefs that reflect our knowledge and assessment of certain situations and activities;
2. values regarding what we consider to be appropriate behaviour; and
3. customs, which concern our behaviour in certain situations.

They also explain how culture is made up of a number of different components, including education, language, religion, social organizations, law and politics, the response to technology and material culture, and prevalent values and attitudes.

Against this background it is possible to see how the different cultures across the world influence the prevalence of entrepreneurship in various countries, because of different attitudes to self-employment rather than employment in large organizations, attitudes to risk, bankruptcy and starting again after a failure. Culture also affects the way in which business is organized and carried out, not just in terms of owning, financing, managing and growing the organization, but in terms of the nature of the relationships between those doing business together and those regulating how business is done. Culture also makes a significant contribution to how start-up organizations determine the vision, mission, objectives and what might be considered as success.

In order to illustrate some of these effects we now consider entrepreneurship in some of the regions of the world.

*Entrepreneurship culture in America:* Culture in the USA has always been characterized by the American dream that trying is everything, anything is possible, success is celebrated, bankruptcy is tolerated and entrepreneurs who fail are encouraged to try again. US entrepreneurship, as in many high-income countries, is driven by high levels of scientific and technological innovation and so many of the fastest-growing and most successful global US firms in recent years, such as Microsoft, Intel and Google, were high-technology start-ups.

*Entrepreneurship culture in Europe:* There are typically lower levels of entrepreneurial activity in Europe than in the USA and entrepreneurship in each region has a different focus although there are some similarities in the encouragement of technology-based businesses. For many years Germany has been proud of its core of entrepreneurial family businesses that are the heart of the economy, the *Mittelstand*. They have consistently achieved high growth and delivered excellent export performance to make Germany consistently one of the leading exporting countries. Much of the competitive advantage of these businesses has been based on their reputation for quality engineering and technology.

Many of the European Union countries have traditionally provided significant social benefits which afford a secure 'cushion' for individuals and act as a disincentive to become self-employed. Pause and Reflect 8.1 shows the possible political implications in Germany of the business environment ceasing to be supportive of its entrepreneurial powerhouse.

## Pause and Reflect 8.1

### The future of the *Mittelstand*

Fifteen years after the unification of Germany the country's two main problems were eastern Germany and unemployment, which was above 20 per cent in some parts and overall stood at 5.2 million. As a result customer confidence was weak and personal saving had reached 11 per cent of income, hitting retail spending.

The weak domestic demand hit the SMEs – the *Mittelstand* – hardest. Eighty per cent of employees work for these firms but many were cutting jobs and investing less. This reduced tax receipts and made it impossible for the government to kick-start the economy. This was in spite of a German export boom. The problem for the *Mittelstand* was that, at that moment, Germany appeared to be an entrepreneur's nightmare: it had a complex tax system, high levels of bureaucracy, restrictive labour laws, high social security, and health-care costs which made up 42 per cent of the wages bill.

But, in practice, technology-intensive firms were investing again, real wages had fallen and working hours were back up to 40 hours per week, as a result of welfare reforms undertaken by the government. Trades Unions were now prepared to negotiate flexible hours and lower wages to help hard-pressed SMEs. But continued high oil prices, an adverse euro exchange rate, global economic slowdown or a change of government to a party with fewer pro-business policies in the forthcoming election could slow recovery.

However, the biggest problem, German entrepreneurs admitted, could be that the Germans love to whinge instead of buying, investing and taking risks! The thing that would probably make the biggest difference would be raising the nation's morale, in particular if the home team did well when Germany hosted the football World Cup in summer 2006.

*Adapted from:* Weber T., 'Is Germany's economy recovering?' BBC News Online, 5 Sept 2005

**Question:** Which environmental factors are the most critical in supporting entrepreneurship in a developed country?

As well as reducing individual incentive to become entrepreneurs these high social costs cause high business costs and contribute to European firms being less competitive.

In the UK traditionally there has been a rather negative attitude to entrepreneurship with a low tolerance of risk-taking and little acceptance of failure. In the community there may also be a degree of envy of the most successful entrepreneurs and suspicion about the business methods that entrepreneurs adopt. Strenuous efforts have been made by the UK government to encourage enterprise generally and entrepreneurship specifically. Italy has had a strong tradition of family-owned businesses that has survived longer than in many developed countries but increasing competition and acquisitions coupled with the disintegration of the traditional family unit and lack of interest among succeeding generations poses challenges for the traditional family business.

A number of the central and eastern European states have been and still are going through a transitional period and Twaalfhoven and Muzyka (2000) explain that entrepreneurship is at different stages in different countries, with the more advanced being those that have gained accession to the European Union. Much of central and eastern Europe is still volatile because of the uncertainty of the politics and economics, and the unreliability of the infrastructure, resources and markets. It is important to recognize the impact of recent history on entrepreneurship, for example, the fact that in the former East Germany only 11 per cent of the population worked in firms with less than 50 employees compared with 50 per cent in the European Union (EU). This lack of entrepreneurial spirit and lack of business and management skills has contributed to Germany's recent poor performance, as Pause and Reflect 8.1 shows.

While foreign direct investment by highly efficient global manufacturers and service providers has a huge impact on economic regeneration the EU has recognized the need to increase the entrepreneurial and innovative capacity of indigenous organizations of the new EU states prior to their accession, as Enterprise in Action 8.1 shows.

---

### Enterprise in Action 8.1

**Helping CzechInvest to build the entrepreneurial supplier base**

Prior to the accession of the Czech Republic to the European Union a number of major multinational original equipment manufacturers (OEMs), particularly in the automotive, electronic and information technology sector, such as Philips and Volkswagen, invested in the country in order to benefit from low labour costs and a workforce with high technology and engineering skills, demonstrated by the success of the Skoda car in international markets.

CzechInvest, the inward investment support organization, had been very successful in attracting foreign multinationals but the problem for the Czech Republic was the weakness of its small business supply base, not in terms of technical skills, but in management skills, as a result of its recent history and the economy being managed centrally. The EU commission contracted with a partnership between CzechInvest, the UK Department of Trade and Industry and Sheffield Hallam University (UK) to provide programmes of training, consultancy and business advice for many small Czech entrepreneurial organizations, with support from the World Bank. By improving financial and human resource management, marketing, supply chain and operations management, the entrepreneurial organizations became better equipped to supply the OEMs and thus create a stronger supply base that would help to attract further investors against competition from other countries.

*Source*: Robin Lowe

**Question:** What enterprise skills would you expect to be most needed by an SME wishing to become an effective supplier to an OEM?

---

Entrepreneurship in Russia has also accelerated in recent years and provides a good example of entrepreneurs exploiting opportunities that are created through the chaos caused by economic and political change. It provides a specific example of the importance of entrepreneurs being in the right place at the right time and, in the case of Russia, having the right political connections to create huge businesses by exploiting valuable natural resources, such as oil. In these situations politics and business are tightly interlinked, especially so in high profile operations and hence it is particularly important to be able to deal with potential political enemies too. Roman Abramovich was elected as regional governor and his new businesses benefited from tax breaks but he was able to successfully manage the business, and his own wealth, through the changing political situation, whereas the founder of Yukos Oil, Mikhail Khordorkovsky, was not and was jailed for nine years on charges relating to fraud and tax. A typical strategy of entrepreneurs in this situation is to buy assets abroad, Chelsea football club in the case of Abramovich, to help legitimize the business and build the entrepreneur's public profile. In October 2005 Abramovich sold back his assets to the state, making a considerable profit in the process.

The business environment in Russia for entrepreneurship has generally been characterized by corruption and this is discussed later in Enterprise in Action 8.4.

## Asian entrepreneurship

Asian entrepreneurship appears to be dominated by the Chinese, who have a strong and very successful tradition of entrepreneurship, and overseas-based Chinese play a significant and often dominant role in the economy of many countries around the world as we briefly discussed in Chapter 5 and as is further emphasized in Figure 8.1.

Redding (2000: 231) explains, however, that the countries of the region vary in terms of political regime, stage of economic development (from the poverty of Cambodia to the super rich Hong Kong), and social and business culture. This has led to different types of entrepreneurship and organizational structures. In Japan successful entrepreneurship has led to the formation of the *keiretsu* – complex organizations such as Mitsui, Mitsubishi and Yusada, which are involved in many different activities, such as manufacturing, banking and international trading through the *Sogo Shosha*. South Korean entrepreneurs have created very disciplined family businesses, *chaebol*, that are tightly linked to

---

55 m overseas Chinese have contributed significantly to economic development.

They:

- Control $2 trillion in cash or liquid assets in the region
- Are the biggest direct investors in China ($26.5 billion in 1997, equivalent to 58 per cent of total foreign direct investment)
- Make up 9 out of 10 of the region's billionaires
- Own around two thirds of retail industry
- Are generally family businesses
- Make up 1 per cent of the population in the Philippines, control 40 per cent of the economy
- Make up 4 per cent in Indonesia and 10 per cent in Thailand but in both countries control half the economy
- In Malaysia make up one third of the population but control two thirds of the economy.

*Adapted from*: Ng (2000) and Nueno (2000)

**Figure 8.1**
Chinese family networks.

government policy of economic development. Examples include Samsung and LG, which have grown from being suppliers to multinationals, to eventually become global brands in their own right.

By contrast the ethnic Chinese have based their entrepreneurship on the development of small businesses that are not known globally. It appears that while the Japanese and South Korean entrepreneurial organizations have been able to organize and manage complex large organizations, the Chinese have achieved efficiency and scale of operations through an international network of family connections.

All three entrepreneurial approaches face future challenges and will have to adapt to change. For example, the Japanese *Sogo Shosha* (Doole and Lowe, 2004) are needed increasingly less as international trade increasingly moves from face-to-face negotiations to online transactions between the supplier and B2B customer without the need for an intermediary. The South Korean organizations have to adapt their ethnocentric roots to become truly global players. The Chinese have to overcome the problems of growing beyond a certain size by becoming better at managing complex organizations.

## Entrepreneurship in China

Perhaps the creation of global Chinese brands will stem from the previously state-owned enterprises that dominated the economy in China until the market reforms. They have impacted on the nature of entrepreneurship as the Chinese market has opened up. Nueno (2000) comments that following the economic reforms in 1978 the output from the state-owned enterprises (SOEs) has fallen rapidly, while the collectively and individually owned enterprises, often started by former SOE executives, have grown rapidly.

Entrepreneurship of this type is valued in China but the new companies experience recruitment problems because they do not make social provisions for their staff as do the SOEs and so find it more difficult to attract the most able staff. However, as in most parts of the world more aggressive competition and cost reduction is making it increasingly difficult for large organizations to fund social provision for their existing and retired staff.

The focus of entrepreneurship in China so far has been for the country to use its huge pool of low-cost labour to become the manufacturing workshop for the world, particularly in labour-intensive activity such as textiles and garment-making, but also in electrical goods and electronics.

Through the efforts of entrepreneurial chief executives, a number of the SOEs and newer businesses too, such as Lenovo and Hai'Er, are being transformed into truly global players with well-known brand names in a similar way to the South Korean companies mentioned earlier.

Increasingly China is encouraging foreign direct investment from multinational companies and foreign entrepreneurs, whose markets are typically international. Many 'blue chip' Western firms entered China quickly after the market reforms but struggled to adapt to the uncertainty of the Chinese legal and business environment and a different business culture. Many of the successful foreign entrepreneurs have built better connections based on a common culture and often through a Hong Kong office that acts as a bridge to Western customers and partners. An example of an entrepreneur gambling on how the authorities will relax controls in China is shown in Enterprise in Action 8.2.

---

## Enterprise in Action 8.2

### Racing in China

Taking risks is an inevitable part of entrepreneurship but Yun Pung Cheng, a Hong Kong toy maker, seems to be taking a bigger gamble than most. He has invested more than £33 million in setting up a complete racing and bloodstock breeding centre just outside Beijing, China, with a staff of 1000 including professional jockeys, 18 trainers recruited from around the world, and 1000 thoroughbreds racing on a perfectly maintained track. Only two things are missing – gambling and crowds of people.

China is considered to be the last frontier of horse racing. Despite China moving towards a free market and operating its 'one country, two systems' policy, which means that gambling is tolerated in Macao and Hong Kong, it has not allowed gambling in the rest of China since Chairman Mao took power in 1949.

Racing started in 2002 and crowds of 5000 were attracted to the first events. A 'guessing game' was used to get around the gambling ban but this did not last as the government clamped down following an investigation into illegal betting. Now the meetings are less frequent, there have been cuts in prize money, there is no 'guessing game' and the crowds have disappeared. The real gamble for Yun Pung Cheng is whether the government will change its mind.

*Adapted from:* Godfrey N., 'China's £33 m gamble under starter's orders: Vast untapped betting market the prize but few turning up'.

**Question:** Do you consider this to be a risk worth taking?

---

It is easy to forget that as well as the successful Chinese family firms there are very many necessity entrepreneurs, particularly in the poorer rural areas. They face the constant challenge of petty bureaucracy and corruption of local officials in attempting to comply with ever-changing regulations.

## The Chinese business culture

Having commented on the outstanding success of Chinese entrepreneurship (see Table 8.1), it would be useful to identify the reasons for this and the distinctive approach to business which Ng (2000: 200) believes can be only due to the distinctive Chinese business culture. The latter is based on Confucian principles and hard work, and there is a strong emphasis on traditional standards and values. It emphasizes collectivism and a focus on working for the benefit of the group rather than on individual achievements. There is considerable respect for authority and so there is centralized control and clear vertical order.

A significant underpinning principle that has led the Chinese to be so successful in internationalizing is that of *guanxi*, which means special relationships or favours. By using the extended family and other contacts it enables new business ventures to be started without the need to find sources of finance as the extended family will usually help to provide the initial capital. Often, too, the new-start business does not have to go to the trouble of immediately finding new suppliers or, in some cases, new customers. Once the new venture has been established it might be expected to return the favour for other family members who might require help with their businesses.

A major difference between Chinese and Western organizations is the approach to agreeing deals and contract negotiation. While Western organizations prepare a very detailed contract to protect themselves from anything that could conceivably go wrong, Chinese businesses rely on covenants, based on mutual friendship and trust, believing that if things go wrong it is better if both parties are committed to working together to take corrective action rather than the parties resorting to the contract to apportion blame.

## Indian entrepreneurship

As in China, the Indian economy has been transformed over the last few years. There is still abject poverty in some city and rural areas but there is a strong culture of entrepreneurship, evidenced by India having the second-highest TEA score in the GEM 2002 survey. The focus for the economic growth achieved has been in information technology (IT)-related activity, both in design, development and production of the hardware and software and in outsourced services, such as call centres and administrative activities. A number of Indian entrepreneurs have become very adept as spotting international business opportunities and have built up very effective businesses, for example, Lakshmi Mittal in steel, Azim Premji in IT and outsourcing and Mukesh Ambani in a range of sectors. Enterprise in Action 8.3 focuses on Ambani and the issue of greater partnership between the humanitarian and business world.

---

## Enterprise in Action 8.3

**Red Cross recruits Indian billionaire**

The Foundation for the International Federation of Red Cross and Red Crescent Societies was created in 1995 to more effectively manage its global fund-raising and humanitarian activities. In the past it depended on philanthropy but now recognizes that closer links with the business world may be beneficial too.

Billionaire Indian businessman Mukesh Ambani has been nominated as chairman. He is chairman and managing director of the Reliance Group, India's largest private enterprise with an annual turnover of US$ 15 billion. The group has operations in a range of business sectors, including petrochemicals, gas, textiles, telecoms, and financial services.

Ambani was persuaded to become a volunteer after being impressed by the work of the Red Cross in his home state of Gujarat in 2001, following an earthquake and the fact that it is a clear demonstration of corporate citizenship in practice.

*Adapted from*: 'Indian billionaire backs Red Cross Red Crescent Foundation',
27 May 2003, Press release International Federation of
Red Cross and Red Crescent Societies accessed at www.ifrc.org

**Question:** Who will gain most in an alliance between an entrepreneur from the private sector and the not-for-profit sector?

---

## Entrepreneurship in emerging markets

Much of the entrepreneurship in **less developed countries** is necessity entrepreneurship and is frequently based on a survivalist strategy. The opportunity identification and ideas of the majority of the self-employed entrepreneurs in these countries are influenced strongly by their own immediate circumstances, culture and traditional values, the locally available resources and the limitations of their own market knowledge. Without the opportunity to communicate with more distant potential customers they are unable to appreciate the requirements of a wider market, for example, in design, quality standards and values and so have little opportunity to tap into more lucrative business.

As we discuss later, many survivalist strategies can become firmly established in a parallel informal economy. For example, while it is indefensible that farmers in Afghanistan grow poppies for heroin production, it is also understandable. A buyer takes the crop directly from them and has the requisite manufacturing and distribution knowledge to get the product to the market via the criminal networks. Without a mechanism to help the farmers connect with the market for other crops, a supportive infrastructure and an effective supply chain network there is little chance of them being able to break the cycle of dependency on the heroin network that they are part of.

### Changing attitudes in developed countries

Although the levels of entrepreneurial activity do fluctuate from year to year the entrepreneurial culture overall does remain relatively constant. However, in practice the recent growth in self-employment in developed countries can also be partly explained by changes in the nature of work in established organizations, the greater degree of stress among staff caused by increased competition and inadequate management, and the consequent changing relationship between employer and employee. Privatizations, outsourcing of public and private sector and downsizing of some organizations has eroded the loyalty and trust between employer and employee in many companies and many disillusioned employees have concluded that they would be better off working for themselves. The life values of young people are also changing as they recognize that there is no possibility of a 'job for life' with a large organization. They no longer feel the need for security that a permanent job would give them – if it were possible to find one – and they are instead increasingly looking for independence and choice rather than predictability.

## The role of entrepreneurship in economic development

As we have seen in the previous section there is little doubt that private and public enterprise is essential for economic development. Larger countries, such as Russia and China were, until recently, command economies in which the state controlled the greater part of business activity and left little scope for enterprise. They are now moving to promote the private sector to create growth.

## Aid or business support

While few people would disagree that a global priority should be to tackle world poverty there is inevitably considerable disagreement about how it should be done. Many of the most vociferous protestors argue that privatization and capitalism should not be forced on poor African nations against these nations' will. In practice, however, there appears to be considerable anecdotal evidence that expanding the private sector is an important way of reducing these nations' dependence on aid and stimulating growth.

**International aid** can make up a huge percentage of an emerging country's budget; for example, in Uganda's case it accounts for nearly 50 per cent. While aid is vital to help with alleviating hunger, providing basic health care and addressing the most severe poverty it does little to enhance the dignity, independence and self-respect of the country's inhabitants. If people are able to earn even a small income they can begin to provide for their families.

While aid and the government's budget is essential to develop health, education and the country's infrastructure there is a limit to the employment that can be created in the public sector. Consequently it is the growth of the private sector and entrepreneurship that is needed to put money in people's pockets, increase domestic demand and generate tax revenues. The additional danger is that if there is no scope for entrepreneurship in the formal economy individuals will turn to the informal economy. In the latter type of economy, however, there is no protection for employees from the abuses thereof, such as child labour, prostitution and criminality.

## Political change and infrastructure development

For some governments the change to building and encouraging private sector growth may be contrary to their political principles. Bolderson (2005) comments that the previously Marxist Ethiopia has started rapidly to liberalize its economy and encourage foreign investment by giving tax breaks and enabling investors to avoid high import duties when bringing capital goods into the country. However, change is often difficult to adjust to as it often leads to foreign or part-foreign ownership. The Ethiopian government has still not released its grip on the telecommunications and freight industries; only the state is allowed to own land and the banking sector is not yet open to foreign ownership.

We have identified earlier the many push factors that motivate entrepreneurs to set up in business, and in emerging markets these are amplified by the prospect of escaping poverty or financial independence. However, the pull factors – the business support infrastructure – is often absent or even positively discouraging. For example, in Uganda the banks charge rates of up to 26 per cent on loans for repayment in five years (Bolderson, 2005).

## Low- and high-displacement companies

Having discussed the benefits of new business creation and the expansion of the private sector in general it is important to emphasize that certain firms benefit by the economic performance of a country more than others. Business growth generally creates wealth and employment, but for a new start growth results from creating new demand or gaining market share from the competitors. For certain types of business there is a fixed demand. In a developed country hairdressing or car repair is a good example of this. If the local demand is satisfied by the existing suppliers, a new-start hairdressing or car repair company can only succeed by taking business away from the existing companies, probably ultimately forcing one out of business. New companies in these sectors therefore have a **high displacement** effect on the existing businesses. Overall the local GDP does not expand as a result of a high-displacement start-up.

A **low displacement** start-up company sells a totally new product or service that is not currently provided locally and so creates a new demand or sells the product outside the local area, and so does not adversely affect any existing companies. Indeed it adds to the wealth of the local area and so increases the GDP.

## Export markets and cash crops

The ideal start-up company in terms of its effect on the GDP is one which exports, as the net effect is to increase the wealth of the local community and 'import' jobs. The competitive advantage of many emerging countries is their fertile land, a climate that is conducive to growing crops and low labour costs. The temptation is to sell the crops abroad to supermarkets (**cash crops**) in developed countries where there is huge demand and foreign currency can be obtained in exchange. There is considerable criticism of farmers growing cash crops in less-developed countries as they take the best farmland, where food crops for the local population could be grown and so alleviate hunger.

Another problem for small businesses that export mainly to global supermarket chains is that they are at the mercy of the ruthless supermarket-chain buyers, who have little concern for the implications of their actions for their growers (see Pause and Reflect 8.3).

## The multiplier effect

A significant further difference between the types of start-up companies is found in the overall effect of their supply chain on the local economy. Clearly some start-up companies, for example those in labour-intensive manufacturing and service delivery, will create more employment within themselves. In addition, some business activities also require many other companies to support their activities. For example the hairdresser and, possibly, the car repair company, do not depend on the supplies of other local companies and so have a low **multiplier effect**. One job in a start-up hairdresser will not create additional jobs in other local companies. Their supplies of beauty products and car components are likely to be imported or manufactured a considerable distance away.

A manufacturer of machinery – vehicles for example – might require many supporting local skills, such as metal fabrication, component manufacture, design, packaging and even catering services. One job in a start-up manufacturing organization can be multiplied a number of times in terms of the total additional jobs created in the local economy because of the jobs created in other local companies.

## Small-firm support or infrastructure development

We discussed earlier the dilemma of whether to provide aid or support to the development of the private sector in emerging markets. A further question is whether financial support should go to small firms directly or to the development of the wider business infrastructure. The World Bank approved more than $10 billion in the five years to 2003 for international aid agency programmes in emerging markets to provide targeted assistance for SMEs, with the purpose of accelerating growth and reducing poverty. Beck and Demirguc-Kunt (2004) highlight the arguments for and against the pro-SME policy. These arguments are as follows.

- SMEs enhance competition and entrepreneurship and so benefit efficiency, innovation and productive growth.
- SMEs are often claimed to be more productive than large firms but are let down by financial and other institutions.

Therefore infrastructure improvements of this kind made through direct government support boost economic growth and development.

■ Because SMEs are more labour-intensive, supporting the growth of the SME sector should help reduce poverty.

The arguments against SME support are listed below.

■ Large firms exploit economies of scale and more readily undertake research and development, pay higher wages and offer more stable employment.

■ The pro arguments above are challenged by research that suggests SMEs are neither more labour intensive nor better at creating jobs and weak financial and legal institutions constrain growth in all firms.

■ The optimum size of firm is dependent on the particular country context as, for example, the optimal firm size in countries open to international trade is larger than in those countries that are not open.

■ It is the business environment facing all firms that is critical, including low entry and exit barriers. Effective contract enforcement and access to finance is crucial for all firms.

The authors comment that previous research has demonstrated a strong relationship between the importance of SMEs and economic growth, but their own research suggests that a strong SME sector is not the reason for a high-growth economy but is a consequence of it. Their research appears to show that it is an effective business environment that causes growth and should be the focus of financial support rather than directly subsidizing SMEs. Therefore the state should focus on avoiding creating obstacles or, even better, remove barriers and thus speed up the growth of entrepreneurial activity.

## The infrastructure and availability of resources

It is the governments of the different countries and their attitudes to developing an effective business environment, their different approaches and different speeds of development of the financial infrastructure and business support that are critical. Of course, as most of the developing countries are recipients of financial aid it is the beliefs, standards, values of the donor countries and the policies of the international institutions, such as the World Bank that are funded by the developed nations that strongly influence the decisions many emerging countries take.

## Returning nationals

Many developing countries have suffered from wars and other forms of instability and this often prompts some of the most resourceful and entrepreneurial individuals to leave the country. This places the country at a significant initial disadvantage when finally there is peace and stability. Many return when peace comes, often with new and different knowledge, skills and attitudes. Along with the local entrepreneurs, they often form a network of new businesses and begin to create more reliable employment for local people.

## The challenges of entrepreneurship in emerging markets

In this section we first focus on the significant opportunities that exist for entrepreneurs – in large and small organizations – in emerging markets that recognize and are able to deliver appropriate solutions. We then discuss the informal economy. The informal economy exists in all countries but in many less-developed countries it constitutes over half the gross domestic income. Clearly if some of the informal economy can be converted into legitimate business activity that generates taxes for the government, the country and its people as a whole should benefit.

We have discussed in the previous section the macro factors that impact on the growth of entrepreneurship and the private sector in general in various countries, but here we discuss the constraints that pose specific challenges to starting up and growing a company. Social entrepreneurs have played a key role in addressing some of the barriers to growth of the smallest business activities but also have used their unique motivations and skills to find practical solutions to other social problems.

## The opportunity

The traditional view of the very poor in the world appears to be that they are economically inactive and this fits with the strategies of most

**Table 8.1**

The global pyramid of wealth

|  | **Global population (m)** | **Purchasing power** |
|---|---|---|
| The wealthy | 800 | $50 000 |
| The emerging middle class | 1500 | $1500–15 000 |
| Low income markets | 4000 | <$1500 |
| *Adapted from*: Prahalad C.K. and Hart S.L. (2002) The fortune at the bottom of the pyramid. *Strategy and Business* 26(54): 67. | | |

multinational enterprises that focus on the customers wealthy enough to purchase their goods and services. However, Prahalad and Hart (2002) have suggested that there is a **pyramid of wealth** (see Table 8.1) and those with the lowest incomes still have the potential to create a significant demand for goods and services that are designed to meet their particular needs and situation. In less-developed countries around the world and in the poorest neighbourhoods of more well-developed countries, entrepreneurs have devised creative solutions, often using a combination of the latest technology and practical approaches. These innovative solutions have flowed from large organizations, individual entrepreneurs and social entrepreneurs.

Hart and London (2005) have identified examples of innovative solutions that not only satisfy a demand but in so doing create a viable business model or network for self-help and support, or to facilitate business transactions more efficiently. They emphasize that the key for multinationals is to work with partners that they would never have considered before. These new approaches to doing business in the first stage enable the small businesses to survive and become more economically viable, but then in the second stage link with larger and more wealthy markets. We have provided examples too in various parts of the book.

## The informal economy

An area of economic activity that is largely overlooked in the business and management texts is the **informal economy**. The latter includes illegal criminal activity that ranges from trade in stolen goods, drug dealing and manufacturing, prostitution, to smuggling and fraud, as well as legal activities that are 'underground' because of tax evasion or avoidance. The size of the informal economy in a number of countries has been estimated, as shown in Spotlight 8.1. Because of its impact, particularly on the developing economies, and importance in crime, its nature and size should be of concern to all governments. An increasing amount of research is being done although the methodology for estimating the size of the informal economy is still debated (Schneider, 2002) as it is unlikely to be very accurate given the fact that those involved in the informal economy are unlikely to want to provide details of their activities. However inaccurate the estimates are, it is clear that the informal economy is significant and is driven by continual criminal entrepreneurship and innovation.

There is also some difficulty in estimating the size of the informal economy partly because of the lack of an agreed definition, but Lippert and Walker (1997: 5) explain the alternative types of activity and these are summarized in Table 8.2.

In a study for the World Bank, shown in Spotlight 8.1, Schneider (2002) estimates that the average size of the informal economy as a percentage of official gross national income in 2000 in developing countries was 41 per cent, in transition countries 38 per cent and in OECD countries, 18 per cent.

### Table 8.2
Types of activity in the informal economy

| Legality of activities | Monetary transactions | | Non-monetary transactions | |
|---|---|---|---|---|
| Illegal | Stolen goods, drug dealing, prostitution, gambling, smuggling and fraud | | Barter of drugs, stolen goods, etc; growing drugs or theft for own use | |
| | **Tax evasion** | **Tax avoidance** | **Tax evasion** | **Tax avoidance** |
| Legal | Unreported income from self-employment or legal goods and services | Employee fringe benefits | Barter of legal services and goods | All DIY and help for neighbours |

*Source*: Lippert O. and Walker M. (eds) (1997) *The Underground Economy: Global Evidences of its Size and Impact*. Vancouver BC: The Frazer Institute.

## Spotlight 8.1

### The size of the informal economy and how to reduce it

It is estimated that the informal economy in Africa averaged 42 per cent of GDP in 1999/2000 with Zimbabwe, Tanzania and Nigeria the highest at 58–59 per cent and Botswana and Cameroon the lowest at 33 per cent. In Latin America Bolivia had the highest informal economy at 67 per cent and Chile the lowest at 20 per cent. In transition countries Georgia had 67 per cent while the Czech Republic and Slovak Republic had 19 per cent. The range in Asia was from Thailand at 53 per cent to Singapore 13 per cent and Japan 11 per cent.

In European OECD countries it is estimated that 48 million people work in the informal economy, the average being 18 per cent of GDP, ranging from Greece with 29 per cent to Switzerland with 9 per cent. The UK figure is estimated to be 13 per cent. In the USA the estimate is 9 per cent.

It is in the interest of governments to at least contain but ideally reduce the size of the informal economy in order to increase their taxation income, better control the activities of organizations and provide greater protection for workers. Clearly, separate strategies are needed to deal with businesses engaged in illegal activities that need to be closed down compared with businesses engaged in legal activities that are operating in the informal economy to avoid or evade tax.

*Adapted from*: Schneider F., 'Size and measurement of the informal economy in 110 countries around the world', July 2002, accessed at www.worldbank.org on 8 Sept 2005

**Questions:** What should countries do to bring more of their economy into the formal sector? What policies have been tried and what has been most effective?

Schneider (2002), summarizing many research studies, suggests that the reasons for the large informal sector are the high and complex tax regimes including high social security payments, excessive government regulation for start-up businesses and over-regulation of labour markets.

Underground labour can include a second job carried out during or after regular working hours, or by those who are not part of the official labour market, for example because they are officially categorized as unemployed or disabled or because they are illegal immigrants. These workers are quite obviously more productive (in terms of output per unit cost of employment) than those in the official economy. They are likely to be employed more frequently by smaller organizations looking for cheap labour that are prepared to take the risk of using illegal practices to run their businesses.

## The practical difficulties faced by entrepreneurs in less-developed countries

The typical problems that are faced by entrepreneurs in less-developed countries are, in part, similar but also more extreme than those experienced by their counterparts in better-developed countries. There are also more acute problems created by the macro and micro environmental factors. Generating a vibrant business economy in a less developed country, or indeed regenerating a deprived region in a developed country is a greater challenge because the existing weak business environment is often further weakened by political, economic, infrastructure, education and market problems. Because these factors are interdependent they tend to compound the individual difficulties that are faced by entrepreneurs.

This causes a downward spiral that creates a very negative external image of the area. To reverse the downward spiral requires improvements in every area of the environment, but some of the critical difficulties, such as culture, values, education and infrastructure can take years to change.

## Access to finance

Most entrepreneurs experience problems raising finance for their operations but in less-developed countries they face more acute problems. For example, with widespread poverty it is unlikely that family and friends will be able to help with initial loans and the banks charge very high interest rates on loans, and are often inflexible in their business transactions and requirements for collateral. As with businesses in the developed countries the problem is often greatest for those entrepreneurs who have no assets and only require very small amounts of finance to start a 'survival' business. The case study at the end of the chapter on Grameen Bank shows how a social entrepreneur addressed the financial problems of some of the poorest people, seeking to set up a business.

In Pause and Reflect 8.2 it is shown that even businesses that are set up and managed as recognizable international operations can have severe problems in managing their transactions and have to resort to unconventional means.

## Pause and Reflect 8.2

### Africa crafts online

After 20 years working as an IT expert for development projects in Africa, Cordelia Salter-Nour realized that technology developments were not improving the situation of the most disadvantaged Africans. To address this she set up an online retail business for African arts and crafts, www.eShopAfrica.com. It operates under fair trade principles and its ambitions at the start were modest – to help five businesses to become sustainable. The site targets the 'snobbery market', providing detailed information and the opportunity to buy products that can be shown and discussed at dinner parties. For $1000 it is possible to buy a a coffin in the shape of a fish, aeroplane or beer bottle. Such coffins originate in Ghana, the design reflecting the way the deceased earned their living.

There have been considerable problems in starting up the business, for example, local banks could not cope with credit card payments and international banks required a bank account to be held in the West. Ms Salter-Nour solved this by using her own personal account to start off the business. A further problem is that, while she expected the USA to be a major market, because of the African roots of many Americans the country is being flooded by imports of Chinese products made to look like African products and made by workers that are paid unfair wages.

*Adapted from*: Hale B., 'African crafts go on-line', BBC News Online, 3 February 2003

**Question:** What impact on the economy does an initiative of this sort really have?

## Access to skills and education

As we have discussed earlier there is a view that successful entrepreneurs do not necessarily need to be the most formally educated. However, basic education which is still unavailable to many people in LDCs is necessary to enable the basic business activities to be completed successfully, so that the companies can become part of the legitimate business market. Indeed it might be suggested that a significant reason for the large informal economy in LDCs may be not solely to avoid taxation but simply because people operate their businesses in the informal economy because they are illiterate and cannot manage their business affairs as part of the formal economy.

## Women entrepreneurs

Women entrepreneurs experience particular problems in emerging markets due to their role in a society that is often dictated by culture and tradition. Women are unable to access education in the same way as men in many countries. The World Bank has reported that the targets for women's education have not been met and this lack of education can result in them lacking the necessary basic skills. Culture and tradition may prevent them from being taken seriously in business, moving freely around to carry out their business activities and it certainly affects their ability to access finance.

Against this background it is interesting to note that the Grameen Bank, discussed in the case study at the end of this chapter, lends primarily to women as it considers them to be more reliable in repaying a loan.

## Infrastructure weaknesses

Many of the less-developed countries have difficult geography with remote areas, difficult terrain with poor roads, and an inhospitable climate. Building a reliable financial and business support infrastructure as we have discussed earlier is essential. Many emerging countries have a poorly developed infrastructure and suffer unreliable and often poor-quality supplies of utilities, such as energy, water and power. Telecommunications and transport are often slow and unreliable and it has been suggested that mobile phones could become the most significant factor in developing the emerging market economies by enabling entrepreneurs to communicate with distant business contacts and the global market in a way that has never been possible before.

## Bribery and corruption

We have shown already that the informal economy is huge in less-developed countries but, in addition, **bribery and corruption** is rife at all levels. In Russia this will be a significant problem until the business structures, legal authority and controls are in place, as discussed in Enterprise in Action 8.4.

### Enterprise in Action 8.4

**Entrepreneurship Russian style**

Russian entrepreneurship has been born again out of the political upheavals in the country. It is characterized by a few oligarchs who, over a period of 15 years, have become unbelievably wealthy. In contrast the vast majority of entrepreneurs are fighting to survive in an environment of corruption and violence.

A few multibillionaires emerged from a small group of wheeler-dealing entrepreneurs who made money, from importing computers and cars to setting up banks. It was risky being an entrepreneur in the early days because after 70 years of communism even honest business people were regarded as thieves. Many bankers were killed by hired assassins.

A few of these oligarchs were close to the reforming communist leaders and were able to benefit from the opportunities that arose when the Russian government sold off oil and mineral assets in 1995 to try to stop the market reforms being reversed. Vladimir Potanin, a banker, acquired Norilisk Nickel, one of the world's richest raw material suppliers and Mikhael Khordorkovsky got Yukos Oil. They became fabulously rich overnight but it was their political ties that many think were critical to gaining ownership of the assets but, also, this was their greatest area of risk.

Political relationships can work two ways and Khordorkovsky appeared to fall out of favour and was taken to court on fraud and tax charges and in May 2005 was jailed for nine years. Yukos Oil was destroyed by huge tax demands in apparent political retaliation. This has sent warning signs to foreign investors who are, for the moment, more reluctant to invest in Russia.

For the many small entrepreneurs the environment is even more difficult as they are continually harassed by local mafia. Business owners are frequently killed if they do not pay up or their premises are burnt down. They are overburdened by rules imposed by the federal and local government. In the power vacuum after the fall of communism it appears that the gangsters are in league with local government officials, who change the rules to obstruct those businesses that do not pay protection money.

The gangsters appear to be filling that vacuum but there is an optimistic view that says they will gradually learn how to run legitimate businesses as the market develops and follow the example of some genuine entrepreneurs who have created excellent businesses in the local community that demonstrate how the new economy could work.

*Adapted from*: Gregory M., 'Corruption and extortion face Russian firms', BBC News Online, 23 June 2005; and Fraser H., 'Russia's oligarchs: their risky routes to riches', BBC News Online, 27 July 2004

**Question:** How can genuine entrepreneurs survive in this environment?

## War and terrorism

The disruption to businesses because of war and terrorism is well reported, particularly in developed countries. However, for developing countries it is not necessarily the disruption to goods and services organizations that is the biggest problem because enterprising individuals find new ways to serve their market and run their organizations. However, the disruption to tourism, on which many of these countries, such as Egypt and Bali, depend, can be catastrophic, as there is little individual organizations can do to generate visitors.

## Quality and service perceptions

In countries that do not have a large domestic market demand it is necessary for entrepreneurial organizations that have the ambition to grow to become involved in international trade. Later in this chapter we discuss the alternative routes to internationalization for small organizations but here our concern is that whatever the route the goods and services from the country take they must compete with those goods and services supplied from other countries, even though they may be cheaper or unique. For entrepreneurs from emerging markets this poses problems of the customers' perceptions of the quality of their goods and service. What is acceptable in a local emerging market may not be acceptable to consumers in a developed country.

## Access to markets and some dangers for community enterprises

The problem is one of both reality and perception. First, the goods and service standards in the country and company may not be of the necessary standard and a key role of governments is to support industries to improve quality standards. Second, irrespective of the actual quality consumers may have a perception of the country that the goods and services might not be of an acceptable standard. The only way this perception will change is if the company can re-educate customers and convince them of its ability to supply high-quality goods and services.

It is unlikely that an early-stage independent business in an emerging market has the resources to promote its goods and convince international customers of its quality of goods and services. There are three alternative approaches for entrepreneurial organizations, as now discussed.

### Becoming a contract manufacturer

In low labour cost countries contract manufacturers are used by multinational companies (MNCs), such as Nike and Gap, to produce their clothing products. Their customers use the Nike and Gap brand to provide the quality assurance that they require to reduce the risk of buying a poorly manufactured product. The contract manufacturers then have to make to the quality standards determined by Nike and Gap. In practice contract manufacturing should benefit the local economy by setting new quality standards.

There are some risks attendant to contract manufacturing. The principal risk for the supplier is that in return for predictable orders and income streams it will be under constant pressure to contain or reduce costs from its MNC customer. Ultimately if it is unable to compete on costs the MNC may simply transfer manufacture to another supplier, or even country, and there is unlikely to be much it will be able to do to prevent this.

### Network marketing

For small entrepreneurial organizations from an emerging market that do not wish to become locked into a subcontracting business and seek to have more control over their markets an alternative approach is to form a network that collectively markets their products. Networks are often facilitated by local trade associations, government support agencies or the buyer.

### Internet marketing

The most significant development to assist smaller entrepreneurial organizations in emerging markets to develop international trade has been the development of the Internet. As well as enabling international trade transactions it provides the opportunity for organizations to present their products and services more professionally to their international customers and obtain feedback on the quality of the supplies.

The Internet can also help to facilitate networking and support supply chain management.

## Low price competition

While it is not our intention here to debate at length the issues of fair trade and free trade, it is important to recognize the significant impact of global trading practices on entrepreneurial organizations in emerging markets. A specific issue centres on farming and the production of food and drink products in emerging markets, which is often the most important sector. The problems arise when global commodity prices fall dramatically, often due to dumping or subsidies, or simply because the huge scale of their operations make it possible for MNCs from developed countries to offer prices that are below the cost of producing the crops in developing countries, until at least the farmers have been able to improve efficiencies and increase the scale of their operations. Sudden falls in commodity prices have a catastrophic effect on the lives of millions of small-scale producers, their families, workers and their local communities, forcing them into crippling debt or causing them to lose their land and homes. Even quite large businesses can suffer from unfair practices, as shown in Pause and Reflect 8.3. These practices are justified to customers by aggressive supermarket buyers because it allows them to charge low prices. Others argue that such ruthless practices simply increase the profits of the most powerful supermarket chains.

## Pause and Reflect 8.3

### UK supermarkets' unethical behaviour?

UK supermarkets have long been criticized for their unethical business practices in their dealing with farmers. Sixty-five per cent of South African grape farmers were estimated to be operating at a loss in August 2005. While part of the pressure was caused by the strong rand and bad weather they blamed British supermarket price wars as a major reason for the high level of financial hardship and bankruptcies. While the supermarkets demand high standards of production they are not prepared to pay the price it costs to achieve this. Just before his grape farm, family-owned since 1920, was forced into bankruptcy by the low prices a farmer at Orange River went to the UK and was shocked to see the exorbitant prices consumers were being charged, compared to the prices the super-markets were paying the farmers. Five years ago his price was equivalent to £5 per 4.5 kilo box, whereas he was now getting £2 per box. On production of around 175 000 boxes a year his losses were considerable.

Buy one, get one free promotions or sudden discounts result in farmers being paid even less because, often, the promotions and what price the supermarket will pay are only decided by the supermarket after the grapes have left the farm.

So while the UK consumer possibly benefits from low prices and supermarket shareholders benefit from high profits, it is South Africa's poorest people who suffer. They live in near-poverty, earning less than the South African minimum wage of £4 per day. The campaigning charity, Action Aid, and the South Africa's Women in Farms trade union want supermarkets to abide by the ethical codes that most of them have signed up to.

Not all supermarkets are the same. Marks & Spencer and Waitrose behave ethically and pay realistic prices to their suppliers. Asian supermarkets also pay realistic prices. Of course their shoppers also have to pay a realistic price but they do this knowing that, as a result, the workers on the farms have an acceptable standard of living.

*Adapted from:* Emmett S., 'South African grape farmers face squeeze', BBC News Online, 12 August 2005

**Question:** Should supermarkets behave ethically towards suppliers or should their responsibility be merely to get the best price to benefit their customers and shareholders?


## Fairtrade

Nicholls and Opal (2005) discuss the principles of **fair trade** and the organization, www.fairtrade.org, was developed to promote ethical consumption, including:

- direct purchasing from producers;
- transparent and long-term trading partnerships;
- cooperation not competition;
- agreed minimum prices to cover the costs of production, usually set higher than market minimums;
- focus on development and technical assistance via the payment to suppliers of an agreed social premium (often 10 per cent or more of the cost price of goods);
- provision of market information; and
- sustainable and environmentally responsible production.

By September 2004 Fairtrade claimed to have certified 422 producer groups in 49 countries, who were selling to hundreds of Fairtrade-registered importers, licensees and retailers in 19 countries. Fairtrade turnover is expected to reach £1 billion by 2007.

## The nature and development of international entrepreneurship

Before leaving the discussion of multicultural entrepreneurship it is useful to consider international business opportunities and the entrepreneurial options that are available to exploit them.

## The impact of globalization

Traditionally, organizations have not needed to become international traders until their business has grown substantially as their domestic market is usually large enough to provide sufficient demand. International trading has always posed perceived risks (Barker and Kaynack, 1992) to small organizations including:

- too much red tape;
- transportation difficulties;
- lack of trained personnel;
- lack of assistance and incentives;
- unfavourable conditions overseas;
- language and cultural barriers;
- lack of competitive products to meet different needs;
- slow or late payment.

Increasing globalization, however, has posed new challenges for smaller organizations. In most sectors they are being subject to increasing competition from international companies in their domestic market. For example, in 2005 UK haulage companies complained to the government that high fuel taxes meant that haulage companies from continental European countries were using lower-priced fuel purchased in Europe, where fuel taxes were lower, to deliver loads within the UK as well as into the UK.

Globalization has meant that customers around the world increasingly want to buy similar products and services, giving rise to global niche marketing. In many technology areas entrepreneurs setting up a business based on a breakthrough technology have to be 'born global' and immediately supply customers around the world. If they fail to do this competitors will copy their idea and fill the vacuum left.

## Exporting

Traditionally, the way that organizations have pursued international opportunities has been through **exporting**, which is essentially selling products across borders. This approach relies on the organization having a distinct competitive advantage for its product, such as low cost, which should be the case for organizations from low labour cost countries. Alternatively an organization's competitive advantage might be based upon its technical leadership over competing products, even though the prices it must charge might be higher than those of competitors in export markets. Usually the exporter sells through importers, dealers, distributors or retailers but not to the final consumers, except in the case of B2B sales, as this usually requires too much financial and human resource for marketing and selling. Some organizations have been able to build an export business even in commodity sectors by offering exceptional levels of customer service, and convincing customers that there is little point in looking for supplies from elsewhere (see Enterprise in Action 6.4 and Spotlight 12.2).

Organizations with very limited resources, and marketing and management expertise, for example community enterprises or suppliers of a major MNC, rely on domestic purchasing, where the customer comes to the organization's home location to purchase the products. For many organizations the disadvantages of exporting and, particularly, domestic purchasing are that the organization has little contact with the final customers and market and so often cannot respond quickly enough to changes that might adversely affect the business. However, if the purchasers behave ethically (see Pause and Reflect 8.4), the impact for the local community can be very significant.

## Pause and Reflect 8.4

### Enterprising nut partnership

For Peru, Brazil nut processing is an important economic activity reliant on the demand from major international companies, who effectively carry out domestic purchasing. In the past many community enterprises of this type have been exploited by unscrupulous buyers.

Aveda, the personal care product company, has formed a partnership with Conservation International (CI) to add sustainability to the activity by taking a nut by-product and using it in a hair care product. Aveda's interest is to source plant-based ingredients for its developing product range. The unique ingredient for Aveda is the protein Morikue. CI's objective is to help local communities create sustainable, environmentally friendly businesses and avoid damaging the natural resources upon which they depend. Activities of this type add value to the nut-processing operation.

The enterprise is based in the Tambopata–Candamo reserve zone, an area rich in biodiversity and claiming the most extensive single-site species diversity records for woody plants, birds, butterflies, mammals and dragonflies. The nut collection and processing activities directly affect conservation and natural resource management, and so Aveda supports training activities for Brazil nut collectors and has run enterprise development workshops to show how sourcing guidelines can be used to establish reliable supply chains and improve product quality, necessary for enterprises aiming to develop new markets.

Aveda has also helped to fund Profores, a business founded in 2000 to produce and market sustainable forest products, such as fruit nectars. The funding has been used to improve the quality of manufacturing and establish the required systems, necessary for quality recognition that will enable the company to develop new markets.

*Adapted from:* corporate partnerships at Conservation International at www.conservation.org

**Questions:** How important to the community are partnerships based on ethical principles and involving for profit organizations, such as Aveda? What can be achieved?

# Niche marketing

For most entrepreneurs traditional exporting is too much at arm's length as they typically want to be more closely in touch with their customers. They prefer to have intimate knowledge of the markets in which they have started to operate, so that they can use their innovative capability to create and exploit opportunities and respond to customer demands more quickly than their larger or more local competitors. For this reason entrepreneurs are usually more successful as **niche marketers**, concentrating on a limited product and service range offered to one customer segment that has common requirements despite being found in different countries.

# Alternative patterns of international development strategies

At this point it is worth emphasizing the different attitudes and approaches to international development. For example, small and medium-sized US organizations have little reason to develop internationally because their huge domestic market provides sufficient demand without the risks identified above. In many small countries and, especially emerging markets, the domestic market soon becomes too small to support an organization's continued growth and it is forced to internationalize. Japan has few natural resources and so to pay for importing essential goods, the government has had to encourage businesses to internationalize in order to build the economy.

The pattern of geographic development of organizations varies. Western and larger Asian firms have internationalized by carefully analysing and selecting the most attractive markets, often starting with those markets close by. By contrast, as we have indicated earlier, Chinese firms have typically spread by using family connections particularly where there is a large expatriate community.

## E-commerce

Globalization has been accelerated by e-commerce and its advantages of interactivity and real-time communication and transactions. It has been particularly significant for entrepreneurial organizations as it has enabled entrepreneurs to meet many of the challenges of international trade, particularly their lack of resources compared with very large competitors. It has helped with:

- global sourcing, enabling entrepreneurial organizations to use and manage remote, low-cost suppliers efficiently and with less management resource;
- enabling entrepreneurial organizations to enter new, distant markets at low cost and supply widely spread customers at a comparable cost to larger competitors, for example, a Philippines-based IBM employee left his job to set up an e-store at www.pinoydelikasi.com to sell Philippino food delicacies because his London-based mother kept asking him to send them to her and her friends; and
- obtaining immediate feedback from customers from diverse cultures and a better understanding of remote markets.

E-commerce will be vital in the development of entrepreneurial organizations in emerging markets in central and eastern Europe, Asia, Africa and South America. Africa missed the opportunities offered through the increase in global sourcing because it was not able to offer low-cost manufacturing. It is essential that it does not miss out on this next commercial revolution.

## Summary

- Around the world entrepreneurship can be categorized as necessity or opportunistic, based on the motivations of the entrepreneur.
- The prevalence of and approach to entrepreneurial activity varies considerably because of the unique contexts, culture, history and economic situation of a particular country.
- Entrepreneurs are seen as vital to economic development or regeneration.
- Many challenges face entrepreneurs, particularly in developing markets. A key factor is making the best use of international aid and investment to develop a supportive infrastructure, but the unfair trading practices of developed nations are often the most difficult barrier confronting them.
- Opportunities exist in emerging markets and both private sector and social entrepreneurs have an intimate understanding of their local situation and often have to substitute ingenuity and determination to compensate for their lack of resources to exploit them.
- Globalization forces entrepreneurs to consider international trading earlier, and recent developments in technology and changes in approach are assisting entrepreneurs in emerging and developed markets.

## Chapter questions

1. Using appropriate examples show how different cultures have developed different attitudes and approaches to encouraging and supporting entrepreneurship.
2. Explain how the country context affects the nature, role and economic contribution of entrepreneurship.
3. You are an experienced adviser to small businesses in a developed country and have been invited to speak at a conference to discuss entrepreneurship in developing countries. You have been asked to identify the most important challenges that entrepreneurs in developing countries are likely to face and suggest some practical ways that they might adopt to overcome the problems. Create an appropriate presentation on the subject.
4. Through the use of examples show how entrepreneurs can be highly innovative in less developed countries. What do you

think an entrepreneur from a developed country might learn (in knowledge, skills and attitudes) from your examples?

5. How might international aid, charitable donations and ethical business principles, such as Fairtrade, be used to support entrepreneurship in a less developed country?

## Case study

### The Grameen Bank of Bangladesh

Muhammad Yunus was born in Chittagong, Bangladesh, one of 14 children. As with many entrepreneurs the themes and motivations for his later life probably were set in childhood. His father owned and operated a jewellery store above which the family lived. His mother taught him life values that included the values of charity. He was a bright child and, after starting a packaging business in Bangladesh, won a Fulbright scholarship and attended Vanderbilt University in the USA, where he was encouraged to question traditional economic theory and adopt a more pragmatic and social perspective. He returned home to take up a post as an economist at Chittagong University.

On a field trip with students in 1974 he talked to a woman in a poor village who was making bamboo stools and learned that she had to borrow the equivalent of 15p to buy raw bamboo for each stool made and had to pay the middleman as much as 10 per cent a week, leaving her with only a 1p profit margin. If she had been able to borrow at better interest rates she would be able to build a reserve of money and lift herself above the subsistence level. From his own pocket he lent £17 to 42 basket weavers and found that not only did this help them to survive but generated a new personal initiative to pull them out of poverty.

He carried on giving similar micro loans and in 1983 founded Grameen Bank on the principles of trust and solidarity. By 2005 the bank had almost 1200 branches, 12 500 staff and 2.1 million borrowers in 39 000 villages. Ninety-four per cent of the loans are made to women and 98 per cent are paid back, higher than for any other banking system. The average loan is $160. Despite high illiteracy levels among women (78 per cent) economic activity has significantly increased. The model has been copied in many countries throughout the world.

There are critics that argue that the micro lenders tend not to provide loans to those that most need them and the interest rates are 30–50 per cent higher than with commercial banks. They argue that the borrowers do not make the most use of the money because they lack the basic business skills and the small size of the loans only allows the financing of trading and not manufacturing. Furthermore they suggest that although women are the recipients of the loans it is the men who take control of the money once it is received.

Grameen does not offer a global solution to poverty but it does provide some practical short-term help for some of the world's poor. Despite the criticisms, Grameen continues to develop and, for example, is helping to finance community projects to provide renewable energy, purchase solar panels and mobile phone equipment and encourage the greater use of the Internet.

Grameen Bank stays focused on its aims of building social, not legal, contracts and combines social and business principles. It recognizes that credit is the last hope of those faced with absolute poverty, which is why Muhammad Yunus believes that the right to credit should be a fundamental human right. There is debate about whether this type of capitalism should be used to alleviate poverty but the

World Bank has acknowledged that this business approach has enabled millions of individuals to work their way out of poverty with dignity.

*Adapted from:* Bangladesh's Micro-Loans, Article 22, BBC World Service accessed online 6 Sept 2005; and M Yunus, Banker to the Poor, Public Affairs 2003

### Questions

1. Identify the challenges facing the very poorest people in less-developed countries who must create their own work opportunities.
2. What are the arguments for and against micro credit?
3. What do you consider to be the essential characteristics of a social entrepreneur, such as Muhammad Yunus?

## References and further reading

Barker S. and Kaynack E. (1992) An empirical investigation of the differences between initiating and continuing exporters. *European Journal of Marketing* **26**(3).

Beck T. and Demirguc-Kunt A. (2004) SMEs, Growth and Poverty: Public Policy for the Private Sector. Note No. 268, The World Bank Group, February.

Bolderson C. (2005) Africa's entrepreneurial vision. BBC News Online, 11 October.

Doole I. and Lowe R. (2004) *International Marketing Strategy: Analysis, Development and Implementation*, 4th edn. London: Thomson Learning.

Global Entrepreneurship Monitor (2004) accessed at www.gemconsortium.org on 18 September 2005.

Hart S.L. and London T. (2005) Developing native capability: why multinational corporations can learn from the base of the pyramid. Stanford Social Innovation Review, Summer, accessed at www.ssireview.org

Lippert O. and Walker M. (eds) (1997) *The Underground Economy: Global Evidences of its Size and Impact*. Vancouver BC: The Frazer Institute.

Nicholls A. and Opal C. (2005) *Fairtrade: Market-Driven Ethical Consumption*. London: Sage.

Ng D. (2000) Succession in the bamboo network. In: S. Birley and D.F. Muzyka (eds), *Mastering Entrepreneurship*. Edinburgh: FT Pitman.

Nueno P. (2000) The dragon breathes enterprising fire. In: S. Birley and D.F. Muzyka (eds), *Mastering Entrepreneurship*. Edinburgh: FT Pitman.

Prahalad C.K. and Hart S.L. (2002) The fortune at the bottom of the pyramid. *Strategy and Business* **26**(54): 67.

Redding G. (2000) Three styles of Asian capitalism. In: S. Birley and D.F. Muzyka (eds), *Mastering Entrepreneurship*. Edinburgh: FT Pitman.

Schneider F. (2005) Size and measurement of the informal economy in 110 countries around the world, July 2002 accessed at www.worldbank.org on 8 September 2005.

Twaalfhoven B. and Muzyka D.F. (eds) (2000) In: S. Birley and D.F. Muzyka (eds), *Mastering Entrepreneurship*. Edinburgh: FT Pitman.

## Key words

bribery and corruption

cash crops

culture

exporting

fair trade

high displacement

informal economy

international aid

less developed countries

low displacement

multiplier effect

necessity entrepreneurship

niche marketers

opportunity entrepreneurs

pyramid of wealth

# Integrated personal development activity

In the second part of this book we have discussed how environmental issues can support enterprise and innovation for both individuals and organizations, and a number of contexts in which enterprise and innovation arise. The purpose of this integrated personal development activity is to help the reader apply and evaluate some of the concepts that have been introduced so far in two different contexts. They should then reflect on the knowledge, skills and attitudes required in both situations, and analyse the extent to which these entrepreneurial attributes are transferable between contexts.

## Learning objectives

By the end of this section the reader will be able to:

- apply and evaluate a concept in different contexts;
- reflect on the extent to which entrepreneurial attributes are transferable between contexts;
- use research and analytical skills to construct a balanced argument and form conclusions, grounded in theory.

## The task

1. Choose a concept or issue from the first two parts of the book, and decide on two different contexts in which the concept/issue arises.
2. Drawing on the theory from the literature, and application from the business press, online sources, and your own experience, compare and contrast the similarities and differences between the two, evaluating the extent to which the theoretical arguments are supported or otherwise by real-world examples.
3. Consider the knowledge, skills and attitudes exhibited in both situations, and analyse whether they are transferable between different contexts. You may use further practical examples to support your arguments.

## Getting started

In order to get you started on the first two tasks, we include some suggestions based on the first eight chapters of this book.

In the tables below we have highlighted some of the concepts and issues raised so far, and the chapters in which they are primarily discussed. We have also listed some of the contexts in which they arise. These lists are indicative only; you may prefer to choose others. However, they constitute a starting point upon which you could base your research and analysis. Choose either a concept or an issue (therefore one topic from either Table 1 or Table 2), and apply it to two different contexts (Table 3). For example, you may choose to look at technological and non-technological innovation in a dynamic private sector company and a charity; or you may choose to analyse female entrepreneurship in America and Asia.

You should draw on both relevant theory and practical examples to address the question that you have chosen, and build a convincing argument, leading to conclusions that are grounded in the theory that you have used.

### Researching existing literature

You will need to conduct independent research as the book itself only provides an introduction to the concepts and issues. This will help you in developing your skills in sourcing and evaluating information. You should take a critical approach to the literature, as it is a representation of a particular viewpoint or argument, and you may find some of it more relevant or useful than others.

### Table 1

| Concept | Chapter |
|---|---|
| Definitions of entrepreneurship/changing conceptual perspectives | 1 |
| Characteristics of enterprise | 1 |
| Individual propensity to entrepreneurship | 1 |
| Role of government | 1, 5 |
| Personality traits/characteristics of entrepreneurs | 1, 2 |
| Invention | 1 |
| Entrepreneurial actions, what entrepreneurs do | 2 |
| Motivations of entrepreneurs | 2 |
| Types of entrepreneur | 2, 7 |
| The entrepreneurial administrative continuum | 2 |
| Categories of innovation | 3 |
| Incremental and discontinuous innovation | 3 |
| Creative destruction | 3 |
| The innovation process | 3 |
| Management of innovation | 3 |
| Entrepreneurial learning (individuals) | 4 |
| Entrepreneurial learning (organizations) | 4 |
| Entrepreneurial capacity and capability | 2, 4 |
| Entrepreneurial decision-making | 2, 4 |
| Entrepreneurial learning | 2, 4 |
| Signal and 3R learning | 4 |
| 3R learning and innovation | 4 |
| Push and pull factors | 5 |
| Technological and non-technological innovation | 3, 6 |

**Table 2**

| Issue | Chapter |
|---|---|
| The role of education in enterprise | 4 |
| Learning from critical incidents | 4 |
| Leadership and the creation of an entrepreneurial climate | 4 |
| Decision-making in entrepreneurial organizations | 4 |
| Learning capability and entrepreneurial strategy | 4 |
| Female entrepreneurship | 5 |
| Young entrepreneurship | 5 |
| Ethnic minority entrepreneurship | 5 |
| Grey entrepreneurship | 5 |
| Family businesses | 5 |
| Enterprise culture | 5 |
| Environmental change and entrepreneurial strategy | 6 |
| Intrapreneurship | 6 |
| Corporate social responsibility | 7 |
| Social and community enterprise | 7 |
| Voluntary and community sector enterprise | 7 |
| Role of entrepreneurship in social regeneration | 7 |
| Role of entrepreneurship in economic development | 8 |
| Role of entrepreneurship in emerging markets | 8 |
| The nature and development of international entrepreneurship | 8 |

**Table 3**

| Context | Chapter |
|---|---|
| Different sizes of business, different industries, private, public not-for-profit sectors/environments | 1, 6, 7 |
| Different genders, ethnicity, ages | 5 |
| Different types of business (family owned, privately owned, publicly owned) | 5, 6 |
| Different business models (e.g. traditional, e-business) | 6 |
| Different environmental conditions | 6 |
| Different markets, competitive conditions | 6 |
| Different economies (e.g. emerging economies, developed economies) | 8 |
| Different cultures, countries | 8 |

## Identifying practical examples

The next stage is to source practical examples, locally, nationally or internationally, and to consider whether 'real-life' mirrors theory. This will help you in taking a critical approach to the literature, and in analysing the concepts and issues.

## Conclusions and impact

The third stage is to draw conclusions from your research – considering the broader impact of the concepts and issues, offering opinions and drawing conclusions based on the knowledge you have gained. This will help you in developing reasoning skills.

You should also consider whether there are any lessons to be learned from the different contexts, and whether any of the attitudes, knowledge or skills exhibited are transferable between them.

# Commercialization

In the first part of this book we discussed the concepts of enterprise, entrepreneurship and innovation and emphasized the importance of the skills, knowledge and attitudes of individual entrepreneurs in creating innovative organizations. In Part II of the book we discussed the various contexts in which this enterprise occurs, including the personal and business environments, and the drivers of entrepreneurship and innovation.

In Part III we turn to commercialization and the practical aspects of bringing the idea to the market. We build upon the application of these entrepreneurship and innovation concepts and contexts by discussing the identification of these innovation opportunities and the creation of solutions to exploit them. In doing this we recognize that entrepreneurship is about creating long-term sustainable businesses from these initial ideas by adopting an innovative approach, planning for long-term success, acquiring the necessary resources to create the business and then developing the strategies to overcome the barriers to growth and success.

In Chapter 9 we discuss the identification of the opportunity that will fill a market gap and an idea that will deliver a solution that will provide new or better value for customers than is currently offered by competitors. We then discuss how a solution can be developed through innovation in every aspect of the product, service and process offer.

In Chapter 10 we go on to discuss how plans should be developed for each stage of the organization's development from the initial idea to becoming a sustainable business. To do this a business model is required to sustain and grow the business by creating new and improved revenue streams. Planning is undertaken to assess the feasibility of the idea, organize external financial support and manage the internal business activity.

In Chapter 11 we explore the process of getting started and creating an organization. This involves assembling the necessary financial and human resources, finding a suitable location and obtaining legal protection. We then go on to discuss the development of the team and how revenue should be generated through marketing activity.

In Chapter 12 we discuss the barriers and challenges that face an organization and the strategies that are needed at start-up, for fast growth and to deal with underperformance. We end by considering competitive advantage in an entrepreneurial organization and return to the importance of learning as the basis for future enterprise, entrepreneurship and innovation.

## CHAPTER 9

# Opportunity identification and solution development

By the end of this chapter the reader will be able to:

- understand the sources of opportunity;
- compare the thinking and analytical techniques that can be used to identify market opportunities;
- appreciate the importance of challenging assumptions that determine how the sector operates;
- understand the stages in the new product development process and be able to apply them to new ideas and opportunities;
- appreciate the nature of the solutions that might be created in terms of products, services, processes and ideas; and
- recognize the alternative commercial approaches to exploiting an opportunity.

## Introduction

Having discussed the contexts in which entrepreneurship and innovation occur, we now turn to the practical steps of proactively identifying the opportunities that the entrepreneur or enterprising organization might pursue and discussing the various alternative solutions that might be developed to exploit them, such as new products, services, processes and ideas. In doing this we emphasize that while there might be good potential sources of opportunity that are generated by changes in the environment or through invention, it is only when customers are convinced about the benefits of the solution that they are offered that the opportunity might be considered to be viable as a business venture.

We emphasize that opportunity identification is not simply concerned with invention and the development of completely new products or services. The response to the opportunities that are identified might take the form of many small improvements in the processes used by an organization or throughout the whole supply chain. Alternatively, the response required might involve a completely new way of thinking about and exploiting a market.

We start off by discussing the sources of opportunities and how these might be identified and look at how, with the benefit of hindsight, this has been done in the past. We then go on to discuss the knowledge, market understanding and thinking processes that might be used to identify opportunities from breakthrough ideas through to more modest incremental improvements. True breakthrough opportunities challenge the assumptions, standards and values on which the sector has operated, by fundamentally changing the ways things are done. While it is often individuals or organizations that are outside the sector that develop the new ideas, it is possible for those working in the sector to more systematically analyse a particular situation in order to challenge their own assumptions about what customers might want.

In constructing an offer to exploit the opportunity it is necessary to recognize the nature of the possible business solutions that might be developed in terms of the combination of ideas, products, services, and business support processes that make up the complete package of benefits to customers in order to provide greater value than before. Once a number of opportunities and possible solutions have been identified successful innovators follow a systematic new product (or service) development process to decide which ideas are worth pursuing to the later stages of concept testing, prototyping, and market testing. However, to follow a systematic process can be very time consuming and potentially expensive and so, finally, we consider the ways in which entrepreneurial businesses can reduce the length of the development process.

## The identification of opportunities

The starting point in the commercialization process of ideas is identifying where a gap in the market might exist or where changes in the market might act as a catalyst for developing a new solution that customers will need. Muzyka (2000) explains that opportunities come in many ways, shapes and forms and entrepreneurs, while not needing to have the idea themselves must structure a business around the idea. In this chapter, therefore, we first consider some sources of innovation before discussing the drivers that might encourage entrepreneurs to create a new business.

## Sources of innovation

Many opportunities for innovation and entrepreneurship come from applying technology or bringing new ideas into the functional areas of a business to create change within an established market. Two views about the **source of innovation** come from Ansoff and McDonnell (1990) and from Drucker (1985). Ansoff and McDonnell emphasized the effect of shock events on innovation. Opportunities for the organization and threats to the organization emerge from the environment and are not within the control of the organization. They suggested that shock events arrive suddenly, pose novel problems and raise the prospect of major business loss. Two examples of this are the effect of 9/11 on the airlines, and of Napster and other pirate websites on the music recording industry. When faced with sudden and unexpected events the organizations that are more innovative than competitors in their response to the opportunities and threats are the ones more likely to succeed.

Drucker (1985) identified the same factor but also suggested others such as:

- the unexpected event that triggers off a new demand (for example, interest in renewable forms of energy because of potential shortages or the high price of oil) or climatic effects (for example, demands for construction following the Asian tsunami and hurricanes);
- an incongruity between what is available and what is needed by consumers (for example, the creation and growth of telephone and Internet banking);
- a process need to fulfil a major new demand by consumers (for example, security software for e-commerce);

- a change in the industry structure, for example the increased deregulation of financial markets leading to many new businesses, or in the energy and farming sector (see Pause and Reflect 9.1);

- a change in demographics (for example, the increasing number of elderly people in developed countries boosting demand for certain categories of new products);

- a change in the perception or mood of the community (for example, green marketing and interest in organically farmed foods); or

- the development of new knowledge (for example in bioscience leading to the growth in research into and promise of new products and in biotechnology regarding the development of personal identification for passports and identity cards).

## Pause and Reflect 9.1

### County council bids to lead in biofuels

The county of Kent, 'the Garden of England', could become the leaders in the creation of fuel from crops as an alternative to fossil fuels if their proposal for a 'Global Centre for Non-Food Crops', being considered by the UN in New York, the Food and Agricultural Organization in Rome and the World Bank, is approved.

The plan to take a lead in a proposed move from a carbon to a carbohydrate economy, led by the leader of the county council, Sir Sandy Bruce-Lockhart after discussion with Countess Sondes of the Lees Court Estate in Kent, a long-time champion of non-food crops, has already been approved by the UK government. It aims to match land potential with industrial demand.

Already there are many initiatives to develop biofuels worldwide. So why Kent? Kent has a strong agricultural base with research facilities and industrial links too and, most importantly, no one else is doing it!

*Adapted from*: Sapsted D., 'Garden of England may become global hothouse for fuel crops', *The Daily Telegraph*, 26 September 2005

**Question:** What are likely to be the challenges for Kent County Council if this project is approved?

## Looking for opportunities in the market

So far we have presented some conceptual and perhaps rational methods for looking for opportunities in the market. However, innovation does not necessarily follow rules and the way that entrepreneurs and enterprising organizations identify and develop opportunities is often very subjective and personal as well as objective and rational. Inevitably this means that entrepreneurs often see opportunities where others do not and view the opportunities differently from others. The opportunity for an entrepreneur might not be in a high profile product but in peripheral support activities, such as consultancy, software or training.

## Mature markets, not necessarily growth markets

Conventional wisdom might suggest that high-growth markets offer the best chance of success. Indeed, stock market analysts often pick 'winners' from these growth sectors, which are typically well-researched and documented in the business press, and often overlook the new-starts and early-stage businesses that are growing steadily in more mature, less glamorous markets. These mature markets are usually dominated by well established suppliers, products and services. Competition is largely predictable, prices are often static and customer expectations and demand appear to change little.

However, many of the examples that we have given in this book relate to innovation by entrepreneurs who bring new ideas to uninteresting markets, capture the customers' interest and subsequently achieve spectacular growth.

## Seemingly impossible markets

The highest compliment that can be given to a salesperson is that 'he or she could sell sand in the desert or refrigerators at the North Pole' but there are in actuality many examples of entrepreneurial businesses exploiting opportunities that seem very unlikely. For example, a tiny UK soup manufacturer, New Covent Garden Soup Company, was able to develop a market in the USA for its soups made from fresh ingredients against fierce competition from the locally based multinational soup manufacturers.

## Exploiting the obvious

Frequently, potential entrepreneurs believe that an opportunity that is clear and obvious to them must be equally clear and obvious to many other individuals and organizations, but this is often not the case. The same opportunity is not always obvious to everyone and, often, a simple idea can be introduced without immediate competition. Although not a major player in the ice cream market Grand Metropolitan developed an entrepreneurial business, Haagen Dazs, to offer a new, premium-priced product using innovative marketing, including sexy advertising in glossy magazines and endorsements from celebrities to create an adult market for ice cream. Usually competitors in the UK, such as Walls, had traditionally produced largely children's and family oriented ice cream products and it was some time before they offered a competitive product.

## Creating customer value

One of the rules that governs entrepreneurship is that innovations must create added value for the customers. Of course, **customer value** can be interpreted in many different ways and different organizations will create different value propositions to exploit the same market opportunity.

### Offering low-cost alternatives

In identifying opportunities, simply offering a lower-cost 'me-too' alternative to existing products or services is not considered to be a sustainable strategy, because of the likelihood of competitor reaction. A small business that undercuts the market is likely to attract a response from larger and more powerful competitors, who will be better resourced to win a price war. Low-price copies of most products and services will quickly become available from organizations from emerging markets and so threaten unsophisticated offers.

Being able to introduce a new product, service or process at a lower cost than a current product from a competitor might win over customers, but it is not always necessary, and in the longer term may not be as important as building in other dimensions of added customer value.

### Low-price products and services, with 'no frills'

Some low-cost businesses have secured a viable market position; value food retailers, such as Lidl, Aldi and Netto are examples of the exploitation of a market opportunity, in which a customer segment is seeking value in the form of basic products of acceptable quality at everyday low prices. Innovation in these organizations is focused on lowering the costs of supplies, reducing overheads and maximizing the impact of limited marketing.

Pause and Reflect 9.2 shows how the 'no frills' model is being applied to many sectors.

---

## Pause and Reflect 9.2

### easyJet – one business model fits all

easyJet is a low-fare airline that operates many routes within the Europe market. Stelios Haji-Ioannou set up the company backed by £500 million from his father. easyJet grew rapidly during the late 1990s by undercutting flights that offered a full customer service package.

The key to the easyJet strategy is maximizing the income generated from each flight by carrying as many passengers as possible on each journey. The company achieves this by offering very low prices to the first passengers to book a particular flight. The price for seats on the flight is then increased for passengers booking closer to the departure date. Yield management software is used to manage the complex calculations that ensure that the revenue for each flight is maximized by balancing the price and predicted number of passengers that are likely to travel on that particular flight.

As easyJet grew, Stelios was not content to manage the company in steady state and turned his attention to other projects. In 2002 he relinquished his role as chief executive and, still only 35, he was looking to transfer his price- and cost-cutting, yield management business model to other sectors and create an 'easy-everything' empire of companies. The car rental service was already established. An early and loss-making attempt to create easyInternetcafe was revived.

Stelios decided to establish other businesses, using a similar low-cost model with hotels, ocean cruises and cinemas. The cinema concept, for example, is based on the fact that the films have to be shown, the staff employed and the cinema heated on a Tuesday afternoon when, perhaps, only one or two customers would choose to go and pay the full price. Many more would go if they only had to pay 20p and would probably also buy a drink and popcorn.

*Source*: Robin Lowe from public sources

**Question:** How easy is it to transfer one entrepreneurial idea to different sectors?

---

## Premium-priced value added products

In general new products that offer extra value for customers can carry a premium price. There are many examples of value added product introductions that were priced higher than the competitive products that they were aiming to replace. Dyson launched bagless vacuum cleaners at a price that carried a significant premium to its competitors. It was able to gain a high market share because of a product innovation for which customers were prepared to pay considerably more for real benefits. Users of mobile phones, too, have been prepared to pay more for the convenience that they offer over fixed-line telephones.

## Finding a unique edge

Even if there is competition, exploitation of one of the elements of the total offering that is made to customers can provide a unique competitive edge. For example, Starbucks run coffee bars, which are part of what is essentially a commodity market. Although they have considerable competition they provide a differentiated product offer that is valued by customers, even though customers have to pay a relatively high price for a relatively basic service.

It is important to focus on the customer needs, and Barrow *et al.* (2005: 143) suggest that it is important to concentrate on answering the question 'How can we make money for our customers rather than how can customers make money for us?'

## The triggers to the creation of new business

Bolton and Thompson (2000) note that in identifying the **triggers to the creation of a new business** there are a number of recurring themes, as follows.

### Frustration with existing products and services

There are many examples of entrepreneurs, such as James Dyson (see Enterprise in Action 9.1), frustrated that the products that were available to them were not effective, not available or did not suit their purpose.

### Exploiting a hobby

Many entrepreneurs, such as Bill Gates of Microsoft, have started their businesses essentially as hobbies.

## Enterprise in Action 9.1

**Persistence pays off for James Dyson**

James Dyson was converting his old house and became frustrated with the poor performance of the cleaner. It would not remove all the dust he was creating and so he set out to design a better product. The idea originally came in 1979 but it was not until 1993 that Dyson introduced his 'no loss of suction' vacuum cleaner. The machine dispensed with a bag and used his patented dual cyclone technology. In a number of other ways the product challenged convention as the cleaners were brightly coloured, had a highly functional design with a number of unique features and, rather than keeping the dirt hidden, it was clearly visible. Dyson was out of work after the business he worked for was sold. A former employer, Jeremy Fry, loaned him £25 000 to add to the £25 000 he raised by selling his vegetable garden and getting an additional overdraft secured on his home. Dyson risked everything and produced 5000 different prototypes during the years of development. He approached the established manufacturers with his idea but they turned him down and so he had to set up his own business.

Dyson's management style was also rather different. He banned smoking and ties and had little time for memos and e-mails, which he considered to be a way of avoiding responsibility. He was the high-profile face of the company. Despite charging a price that was almost twice that of many competitors, the company grew fast and within a decade had 40 per cent of the UK market. At the start of the 2000s the company moved production to Korea and started to attack international markets, gaining 20 per cent of the US market and 11 per cent of the Japanese market.

*Source*: Robin Lowe from public sources; and Bolton and Thompson (2000: 92)

**Question:** We all get frustrated with poorly performing products. What are the skills and attitudes that are needed to turn frustration into a new business?

### Starting young with a simple idea

Many of the best-known organizations started from a very modest base, often while the entrepreneur was very young, even while at school. Hewlett Packard made a feature of this in their advertising when they showed an image of the garage where the founders started their business. Michael Dell exploited a fairly basic retailing opportunity and simply got used to running his own business. As their companies grow, entrepreneurs spot new opportunities, continually innovate and offer new products, often in unrelated areas. Enterprise in Action 9.2 shows how Julian Richer started young with little real idea what he wanted to do.

## Enterprise in Action 9.2

### Richer information at Richer Sounds

Julian Richer, founder of the hi-fi chain Richer Sounds, opened the first of his 50 stores in 1978 when he was 19. He had no burning ambition to start a hi-fi business but hi-fi was a booming sector in the 1970s and 'reasonably sexy'. He would probably have preferred to start a property development business but he was too young to sign contracts or run a car sales business, and too young to drive a car. He concedes there is more money in property development and too much competition in hi-fi.

### Customer service

Richer places a lot of emphasis on customer service and measurement. Small businesses have a potential advantage as there is less of a gap between the customers and the management, compared to larger businesses. This should make it easier for small businesses to give good service but often they do not. Richer continually asks the customers to communicate with the business to comment on how it is doing. He believes that even the simplest questionnaire can provide useful information and should be addressed to a named person in the company.

*Adapted from*: exclusive Julian Richer interview, www.startups.co.uk, sourced 14 August 2005

**Question:** Does it matter if you do not have a 'cause' to pursue but still want to start your own business?

*Responding to a personal crisis*

Many entrepreneurs start a business in response to a personal crisis. For example, a successful woman sales executive for a pharmaceutical firm returned home one day to find her husband in bed with another man, thus leading to the break-up of her marriage. Her response was to throw all her energy into setting up a nail manicure business. It had originally been her hobby, but developed into a part-time business to help pay the way through university. The business was very successful and she sold it off very profitably when she felt she had got over the bad experience and wanted a career change. Dee Dawson (see Enterprise in Action 9.3) responded to a family crisis by setting up a business.

---

## Enterprise in Action 9.3

### Dee Dawson – mother, necessity and invention

Dee Dawson was expecting her fifth baby and on holiday with her family in France. Her husband popped home to check on the business, which was an extremely successful computer firm and found his staff had run off with the business, wiping his files and codes, and leaving him and his wife broke as he had given personal guarantees on cars and the lease of premises. He was too shocked and depressed to cope.

Dee had an MBA and had just completed seven years' training to be a doctor. She decided to set up a residential clinic for anorexic children. She was not passionate about anorexia, but just thought there was a market opportunity at the time, that there was a need for dedicated residential care, and that the health authorities and medical insurance companies would be willing to pay if she could convince them of her credibility. A friend that she had met on medical training was a leading child psychiatrist and so was willing to put her name to the project. She persuaded the medical insurance companies to recognize the clinic and then rang the Anorexia Association and said she had opened a clinic that day; thereafter they sent her their first patient. She then contacted the television programme London Tonight and appeared on television to promote the clinic. In six months she had six patients and all her family were living in one room in the house but they survived. Her reason for opening the clinic was that she felt that she had little left to lose at that time.

*Adapted from*: Handy C. (1999: 97–103) *The New Alchemists*. London: Hutchinson

**Question:** To what degree do you believe in necessity being the mother of invention?

---

## Generating new ideas

Individuals think creatively and build knowledge from their own experience and expertise that will lead to potentially commercializable opportunities. However, an organization can work against the creative capability. Baron and Shane (2005: 219) note that established firms innovate but have some disadvantages:

> ***Core rigidities*** They are good at doing the things they are used to doing, but not new things, so the organization is rigid rather than flexible.
>
> ***Tyranny of the current market*** Because they listen to customers they find it difficult to come up with new ideas. Customers ask for improvements on existing products, not products for new markets.
>
> ***User myopia*** Customers only see their own narrow needs or solutions and may not be able to articulate or explain the required solutions of others, or indeed their own needs in a different situation.

## The vital role of information

The starting point is to use **market information** to identify new possibilities. However, Baron and Shane (2005: 217) warn that traditional methods of market research work best in established markets where the market information, preferences and behaviour of customers is known, whereas when the entrepreneur is creating a new market it may be necessary to use some traditional customer surveys and focus group techniques; but simply extrapolating the past may not work and more blue sky approaches are needed, such as using expert opinion or some of the methods covered in the next few pages.

## Using someone else's ideas

At the most simplistic level the idea that acts as the stimulus for the individual to exploit could be their own or it could be someone else's. We are not, at this point, condoning stealing someone else's ideas if they intend commercializing an idea themselves even though some of the best-known entrepreneurs have 'stolen' someone else's idea. However, it is important to recognize that having an idea is often the simple part of the enterprise process and, as we have discussed earlier, all of us have ideas but few of us exploit them commercially – this is the difficult part. Often someone else's idea is interesting but not commercially exploitable; however, it can act as a prompt and start a potential entrepreneur thinking about how the idea can be built upon, developed into a real market opportunity and lead to the creation of a potentially viable business model.

## Observation in a familiar area

The normal starting point is for the entrepreneur to use his or her knowledge and experience to make observations about the market gaps and opportunities. The knowledge that is built through work, participation in hobbies and leisure activities, or simply reflecting on normal life experiences can provide the basis for the identification of new ideas.

Doole and Lowe (2004) explain that Fisherman's Friend cough lozenges were initially developed by a pharmacist in Fleetwood, UK, for local sailors and trawlermen who were working in severe Icelandic conditions and that the lozenges were sold locally. When Doreen Lofthouse became managing director, she observed that it was not just local but visiting sailors and trawlermen who bought the lozenges, and so she started to export the products. Now exports account for 95 per cent of the turnover and the product is available in 100 countries.

### . . . and in a less familiar area

There are some, but not very many, examples of individuals being successful in a market about which they had no working knowledge. Having said that, it is possible to learn very quickly about an unfamiliar market and bring to it new thinking or to have an idea established in another sector. Richard Branson has brought the Virgin brand values to a succession of unrelated markets with which he was initially unfamiliar.

### Niche opportunities

Observation of what is happening in a situation can lead to a niche business opportunity. The long queue of cars at traffic lights on commuter routes on Friday evening, each one occupied by one person only thinking of getting home to their loved one presents a great opportunity for an entrepreneur to sell bunches of flowers. However, even here the prices charged in this situation probably cannot be set as high as at the flower shop outside the maternity hospital! Ticket touts know that fans will pay a high price to be at a big sports event or concert.

There must be many times when we have all made comments about existing products such as 'That is so difficult to use, I could do that better myself', and 'Why do they do it that way; they could do it like this'. The starting point in responding to this is thinking about meeting customer needs 'better' than the existing supplier. Through routine use customers get used to coping with a badly designed product to the point that they might no longer believe that a 'better' product could be made. The task is to take a very objective view of the product, and define in detail what a customer could mean by 'better' by systematically evaluating all the possible criteria that relate to the use of the product. Once this has been done it is possible to challenge the belief that 'because customers are not complaining it must be satisfactory' and focus on providing the product and service that is 'better' in terms of the most important criteria in the eyes of the customer.

## Removing unnecessary features

Many products are 'over-engineered', either being made to too high a specification for their purpose or with too many features for some customers. There is a high cost of providing certain aspects of a product or service but this is often difficult to quantify. The myth in many organizations is that it would cost extra to remove unnecessary functions. Moreover, what is often quite difficult for an employee to understand is which aspects of a product or service are really valued by their customers and for what reasons.

For example, there was a belief that a hot meal should be provided free on all airline flights. In practice this was extremely expensive and removal of this service by the low-cost airlines has not damaged their business.

## Do better what the employer does

Many employees perceive the limitations of their employers' products and services and are only too aware of what their customers complain about and what problems the organization fails to address. Organizations very often have a set of beliefs about their products and services that have grown up over the years and are part of the mythology of the organization. They often ignore continual customer complaints or criticisms about a product or service. Often, too, within the organization a belief is built up that customers need a product or service to do certain things; however, in practice they do not, with the result that the product or service is 'over-engineered' and built to an unnecessarily high specification. Extra features might be built into a product, incurring extra cost, that simply are not necessary.

Many entrepreneurs have used this knowledge to set up a business doing what their employer does, but better. Through detailed knowledge of their market such entrepreneurs are able to assist customers in identifying simple additions to the product that could be made in the product-manufacturing process at little or no extra cost but which would add considerable customer value.

We have discussed earlier the point that opportunities are not seen the same way by everyone. Perhaps one of the main reasons for this is that different individuals bring different observations, knowledge and experience to any opportunity.

### Making connections

A particular dimension of identifying opportunities is the 'art' of making connections. Individuals always have experience of different business contexts – one or more work situations, leisure activities, holiday experiences and so on and quite often the ideas, tools and techniques that have been used in one situation can be transferred into a new situation – or new business opportunity – where they have never been used before. Often these two different business contexts will appear to have nothing in common but the technique might just work in both. This is the case in Pause and Reflect 9.2, in which it is explained how Stelios Haji-Ioannou applied the same technique to easyJet, easyHotel, easyCinema, easyCar and others, too.

In Enterprise in Action 9.4 is shown an example of opportunity spotting by making connections between two unrelated businesses.

---

## Enterprise in Action 9.4

### Plastic from corn

Environmental change offers opportunities and global warming provides one such opportunity. In this case the opportunity requires two well established companies to work in partnership and share their expertise, and to facilitate this they have set up a new venture.

The US government has chosen to respond to the threat of global warming by supporting new technology rather than reducing consumption and emissions. Chemicals giant Dow, and Cargill, one of the world's largest grain producers, have set up a factory to turn corn into biodegradable plastic after many years of research into the replacement of oil-based plastics. Their slogan is '100 years to grow a bushel and 100 million years to make a barrel'.

The difficulty that they now face, however, is how to explain the leap to customers. People have problems understanding the product because it appears the same but is radically different. Because it is from a renewable resource and is compostable, customers expect it to be inferior and fall apart on the shelf.

*Adapted from*: Russell A., 'Corn niblets could save America from its oil dependency', 30 July 2005

**Question:** What are the difficulties in establishing credibility for an entrepreneurial organization diversifying into a totally new market?

# Exploiting structural changes in sectors and large organizations

Opportunities for new products, services and processes arise when there is a change in the structure of a market or in a large organization.

# Subsegmentation of markets

All through this section we have focused upon adding value as perceived by the customer. Therefore the most important element in the opportunity search is the identification of a market gap. Most of the innovations considered in this book fill a market gap. Because of the proliferation of products and competitors it is unlikely that a huge market opportunity will be obvious to an innovator as, today, most customer needs are filled, at least to some extent. However, by articulating customer needs precisely and understanding what customers really need or want, rather than what they will 'make do' with, it is possible to identify market gaps. **Subsegmentation** is one example of filling a market gap.

While the major market segments are served, customers in the subsegments of the market are not getting products and services that they consider to be ideal. Over the last 20 years the car market, which arguably was already mature, has been the subject of subsegmentation by carmakers. A whole range of niche products have been produced to address market gaps. These include the Renault Espace, Renault Megane, Range Rover and Smart Car. In a similar way Prêt á Manger and Underground have exploited the market opportunities for better-quality, yet still fast, sandwiches.

For those who are working and cannot book at surgeries during normal surgery hours but are prepared to pay, GPs have set up surgeries in supermarkets and other convenient locations, allowing patients to drop in.

Because markets generally are crowded with products and services the key to identifying the market gap is defining and explaining to customers exactly how the new offering meets their own specific needs and how the new product or service differs from the existing products. This process is called positioning and is dealt with in greater detail in the next section.

## Sectors with particular potential for entrepreneurs

A number of sectors that have low entry barriers and low set-up costs tend to be attractive ones for entrepreneurship. These include, for example, the leisure and tourism industries. Sectors evolve over time and pass through different phases in their attractiveness to entrepreneurs. Food retailing has gone through years of consolidation, with many corner shops going out of business as supermarkets and hypermarkets have proliferated. Now, however, a gradual backlash is appearing as customers become frustrated with bland food filled with additives and salt, often grown in unnatural conditions. Specialist high-quality food manufacturers, retailers and farmers' markets seem to be expanding.

## Organization structure opportunities

The business model adopted by a large organization or changes to its structure, can offer opportunities. While we discuss these below we refer to them again in the following chapters.

> *Franchising* tends to be a relatively low risk and low cost entry option and offers the prospect of owner management without the entrepreneur having to come up with an idea and develop a business model to exploit it. Over 1000 franchise opportunities are listed at www.franchise.org. There are some clear benefits in starting a business through a franchise, for example a proven business model, reliable suppliers and supporting promotion but there are also some disadvantages, such as the relative lack of independence,

freedom to manage the franchise and scope for innovation on the part of the franchisee.

*Subcontracting* enables smaller suppliers to supply products and services to a major company to a defined specification at an agreed price. While the promise of regular orders can be attractive to the small supplier, the risk of supplying one or two customers only can be high.

*Break up of an organization* Large organizations restructure their operations from time to time because of market changes, mergers and acquisitions, and this provides opportunities for management buy-outs and management buy-ins, which are discussed in the next chapter.

### Looking at what others have left behind

If a major organization decides to stop supplying a business sector there are often opportunities for small businesses to step in and supply established products that are no longer available. Quite often when large organizations downsize their operations they often continue to require the services that they used to supply themselves and obtain them by subcontracting to small suppliers.

## Creativity and thinking techniques

We now turn to methods that might be used to generate ideas. Barrow *et al.* (2005) say that some weird ideas exist for managing creativity, commenting that, from their research, successful management practice can include opposites, such as:

- Find some people and make sure they don't fight, or . . . make sure they do fight!
- Think of some sound and practical things to do and do them or . . . find some ridiculous and impractical things to do!
- Take your past successes and replicate them or . . . forget them!
- Hire people you do need or . . . hire people you do not need!

Baron and Shane (2005: 65) discuss the importance of intelligence in creativity and suggest that entrepreneurs need to balance three components to achieve successful intelligence: (1) creative intelligence to come up with new ideas, (2) practical intelligence to identify ways to develop these ideas and (3) analytical intelligence to evaluate the ideas and determine whether they are worth pursuing. They go on to explain, in taking a broader view suggested by Sternberg and Lubart (1995), that creativity emerges from the confluence of:

- intellectual abilities, relating to problem interpretation and persuasion skills to convince others of the new ideas;
- a broad and rich base of relevant knowledge;
- an appropriate style of thinking – novel thinking and escaping the 'rut';
- personality traits, and the willingness to take risks and tolerate ambiguity;
- intrinsic, task-focused motivation so that creative people gain rewards from doing their work;
- a supportive environment that supports creative ideas.

## Asking customers or potential customers

Asking customers or potential customers about possible new product ideas is the most obvious route to generating ideas but it requires real understanding on the part of the innovator to interpret customer requirements.

The problem with asking customers for new product ideas is that they often, in the first instance, do not ask for a new product because they do not really know what is possible – therefore they cannot ask for it. They try to articulate their future requirements in terms of what is currently available, rather than what might be possible in the future. Some leading customers, especially if they are close to more 'blue sky research' thinking, are able to visualize the future and what products will be needed.

## Considering adjacent markets

Here the objective is to consider whether an opportunity in one market might lead, with some modification, into another. For example, a more robust version of the mobile phone is necessary for use where it might be easily damaged, for example, in the construction industry. Equally, there is a market for short-term mobile phone hire. The technology used in home entertainment, such as video cameras and television monitors, is used for security applications.

## Analysing competitor products

It is possible to learn a great deal by analysing competitor products as this might also provide opportunities for improvement. For example, the Japanese earthmoving equipment manufacturer Komatsu analysed the products of the US supplier Caterpillar, which was the market leader. Komatsu realized that many Caterpillar products were over-engineered and therefore unnecessarily expensive for the market it was targeting. Komatsu produced cheaper but soundly performing products for specific uses and gained considerable market share from Caterpillar.

## Analysing customer needs and behaviour

Observations of customers using products and services together with an analysis of their buying motivations can reveal new insights into the ways customers respond to products. Provided they are willing to allocate sufficient time, individual entrepreneurs can gain similar insights and so help to avoid costly mistakes in the future. For example, observing customer traffic in a shopping centre or street can help in choosing an appropriate location for a retail outlet. Studying the hits on a website will provide considerable information about how the website should be configured to retain the interest of those visiting it.

## Brainstorming

Brainstorming is a commonly used technique for idea generation but the results will not be as good as they might be if it is not carried out systematically. All suggestions or ideas should be allowed in brainstorming as they may be modified and eventually lead to workable ideas but, if there are no rules, crazy ideas are likely to be dismissed without proper discussion. Also, if the boss is present at a brainstorming session, it is necessary to ensure that he or she will not stop crazy ideas being suggested or inhibit other ideas being discussed in favour of their own. Brainstorming can be made more productive by setting some basic guidelines, such as initially listing all the ideas generated by the group of individuals without additional comment, then taking time to group ideas, build on them and ensure that even the most outrageous suggestions are considered in case there is anything of value that will build on the other ideas proposed.

## Forced relationships

The objective here is to force together two existing concepts to create a new third product or service idea. The computer workstation combines a desk and a computer, an electric piano combines a traditional piano and electronic sound system, and many combinations are available of a DVD recorder and television, and television, radio and alarm clock.

## Morphological analysis

This is a technique designed to deal with a complex problem by breaking it down into a series of steps and then considering different ways of taking each step. It is effectively about a way of determining the different ways of getting from A to B. Spotlight 9.1 considers the various ways (the routes to market) in which the buyers of personal computers have been

---

### Spotlight 9.1

**Morphological analysis in computer distribution**

When the first personal computers were developed in the late 1970s they were quite difficult for everyone but computer enthusiasts to use. They were also prone to difficulties and needed a high level of technical support. Consequently, in those early days, the computers were supplied through local or regional, typically IBM distributors, which had expertise in computing and could provide high levels of specialist technical support. When computer operating systems became more user-friendly and users became more knowledgeable, so the high level of specialist support became unnecessary and computers were supplied by new specialist retailers. Computer components then became more freely available so new assemblers or businesses that simply badged assembled computers were set up and they typically supplied direct via mail order, via firms such as Gateway and Evesham, and through retail outlets, for example Time Computers.

As the computer games market developed so computers became available through department stores, supermarkets and electrical stores, such as Dixon's and Curry's.

Now companies such as Dell supply computers using the Internet, supported by telephone sales, and it is now possible to obtain a computer made to the purchaser's specific requirements. Other companies will supply parts so that the home user can build their own computer. A number of organizations, such as banks, became aware that it was in their interest to encourage online transactions and so provided customers with a computer either free or at discounted rates.

So which is the next route from A to B? In practice, of course, consumers do not necessarily want to own a computer, especially as it will probably have to be replaced in 3 or 4 years at considerable cost as greater computing power becomes required. What consumers want is computing power as a utility in a similar way to electricity. Unless they had no alternative, most electricity customers would not dream of going to the expense of buying their own electricity generator.

*Source*: Robin Lowe

**Question:** Can you apply this technique to a situation that you are familiar with?

able to obtain the product over time from a computer manufacturer. As each new potential route has been developed it has resulted in many new business start ups.

## Challenging industry assumptions

Firms in mature business sectors often become reactive, drawing in resources to respond to short-term competitive activities and have no time or resources to think about the sorts of products and services that are needed for the future. Without this creativity these firms fall back on imitating competitors, believing the competitors' actions to be right for the market, rather than really exploiting the changes taking place in their customers' needs and wants. Their innovations often become limited to small changes that result from benchmarking against competitors.

Kim and Mabourgne (1997) explain that high-growth firms leave the competition to fight among themselves and, instead, seek to offer customers a quantum leap in value. The question that should be posed is not what is needed to beat the competition but rather what is needed to win over the mass of customers. The implications of this are that it is necessary to challenge the conventional wisdom and assumptions of the industry about the basis on which firms compete and what customers value. An additional bonus from challenging the way the industry does things is that, if the firm thinks globally, this can also lead to large cost savings as unnecessary operations are cut out. If the benefits really lead to a step change in value they will be perceived as such by customers all round the world. In Spotlight 9.2 is illustrated a structured approach to **challenging assumptions**.

---

### Spotlight 9.2

**Challenging industry assumptions to identify new opportunities**

One of the assumptions made in the golf industry was that all golf club heads should be of the same size. However, against a background of intense me-too competition, Callaway Golf, the US golf club manufacturer, launched its Big Bertha, a club with a larger head, which made playing golf more rewarding and more fun for the player. The result was a rapid increase in revenue for the company.

In starting to change the way the firm thinks about spotting opportunities, it should address the following questions:

- What factors that your industry takes for granted should be eliminated?
- What factors that your industry competes on should be reduced well below the standard?
- What factors that your industry competes on should be raised well above the standard?
- What factors should be created that your industry has never offered?

By finding answers to these questions a firm can create new markets and new expectations for customers in existing markets. Typically it is smaller firms that are not weighed down by industry traditions and standards that challenge conventional wisdom. If ideas are sufficiently innovative and appealing they will create new niche opportunities.

*Adapted from*: Kim W.C. and Mabourgne R. (1997) The strategic logic of high growth, *Harvard Business Review* 75

**Question:** Apply the technique to a sector with which you are familiar.

# Creating innovation solutions: products, services and processes

Having identified an opportunity we now turn to developing the idea, product, service or process that will provide the solution for customers.

## Customer benefits

The starting point is to consider what people actually buy. Customers buy benefits rather than product features. A new idea, product, service or process must provide something that customers need, want and will value. The benefits might be something that will save them time and hassle, entertain them, solve a problem or, perhaps, enhance their feeling of status among their friends.

However, many organizations and entrepreneurs erroneously believe that the secret to satisfying all their customers is to focus on packing a product with features, introducing a technologically advanced new product, service or process and including many (often rarely used) functions or unnecessarily intricate designs. The danger can be that entrepreneurs, designers, development managers and innovative organizations 'fall in love' with the technology and create the new product to demonstrate their superior technical knowledge and capability rather than work out and give exactly what the customer might want.

### Customer segmentation

Many new products claim to be right for everyone. The problem with the 'one product fits all' approach is that it ignores the fact that, within a mass market, there are a number of groups of customers (segments) with some similar but also different requirements. As we have discussed earlier, an entrepreneurial organization might choose to target either the mass market or one segment, as a niche supplier, but whichever approach is adopted it must meet the customer's specific needs.

Usually, the key to ensuring a match between the offer and the benefits sought by customers is recognizing that different segments want different things. The approach is first to identify a number of groups of customers (segments) that have a similar need or expectation of the product. For a personal computer, this might include the technology 'geeks', small-business users, gamers, children using it for homework, and so on. The organization would choose the segments it wishes to target on the basis of its ability to service the segment better than its competitors. To do this it then would have to profile the target segments by getting as much information as possible about their characteristics, beliefs, needs and lifestyles. It can then position its offer to be attractive to the target segment and different from the competitors' offers by innovating in various aspects of the total product offer to make it quite distinctive.

Even if the benefits are obvious, many customers will still be reluctant to buy a new product or service, until they are convinced that they have a reason to buy it and it is a good use of their money, so the product offer must also have marketing support as we now explain.

## Innovation throughout the total offer

Over the years increased competition to provide a solution for an identified opportunity has led to a proliferation of products and services and increased choice for the customer. The aim for the majority of suppliers is to differentiate their product or service from that of their competitors through innovation in some aspect of the product or service, or the activities supporting it, in order to gain competitive advantage. For the remaining suppliers who wish to copy competitor products and services the challenge is how to use innovation to gain competitive advantage by reducing costs, so that profitability can be maintained even at lower prices.

### The total product offer and areas for innovation

Building upon these ideas it is useful to think of a product or service innovation not just in terms of creating new core product benefits to the customer but rather in terms of improving some or all of the elements of the product offer.

Kotler (1997) proposed a framework for the **total product offer**, as shown in Figure 9.1. Each of the elements of the total product offer provides the opportunity for innovators to increase value by better meeting consumer needs and wants and this can be achieved through breakthrough or incremental improvements.

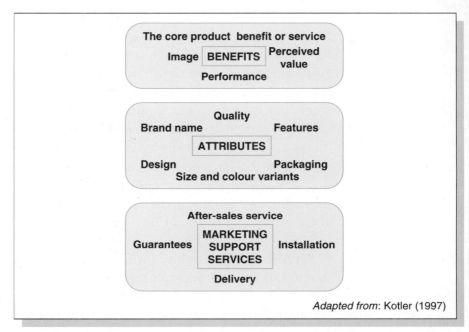

The core product  benefit or service

Image | BENEFITS | Perceived value

Performance

Quality

Brand name                    Features

ATTRIBUTES

Design                              Packaging

Size and colour variants

After-sales service

Guarantees | MARKETING SUPPORT SERVICES | Installation

Delivery

*Adapted from*: Kotler (1997)

**Figure 9.1**
Three levels of
product offer.

Goffin and Mitchell (2005: 105) refer to work by Kano *et al.* (1996), who have explained how the features of a product affect customer satisfaction, categorizing them as:

> *basic features* these are the core attributes, without which the product would be unacceptable;
> *performance features* these provide a real benefit to the customer, such as fuel economy in a car or battery life in a mobile phone; and
> *excitement features or delighters* these give unexpected value to the customer that seems out of proportion to the objective value, for example, remote controls for television operation.

In the model, product benefits are the elements that consumers perceive to meet their core needs and provide satisfaction through performance and image. Product attributes are the elements closely associated with the core product, such as features, specifications, design, branding and packaging, which provide reinforcement of the core product benefits. The marketing support services are the additional elements to the core product, which include delivery, after-sales service and guarantees. In commodity markets many of the core benefits of a product are similar, no matter which competitor provides the product. It therefore becomes necessary to differentiate the offering through innovation in one or more of the other elements of the total product offer. The core benefit of a motorcycle or a tee shirt is fairly obvious but you may wish to consider the

**Figure 9.2**
Product innovation
opportunity
checklist.

It is essential to evaluate the total product offering by answering the following six questions for each market:

- For what purpose has the product been developed and how will the product be used?
- What distinctive physical properties does the product have?
- What benefits is the consumer expected to gain?
- How is the product positioned and what image do consumers perceive it to have?
- Which consumer segments of the total market are expected to buy the product, on what occasions and for what purposes?

ways that different suppliers differentiate the product by using innovations throughout the total product offer. As you will find, new products may include a single innovation or a combination of many. Having introduced the concept of the total product offer and the opportunity for innovation in every element, it is useful to consider the questions highlighted in Figure 9.2.

## Moments of truth

Barrow *et al.* (2005: 143) explain that the quality of the offering is not just what you do but how you do it, and refer to Jan Carlson of Scandinavian Airways (SAS), who introduced the concept of '**moments of truth**' when the customer experiences the reality of who you are and what you do. The customer expects from the organization reliability, responsiveness, competence, courtesy, creditability and security that the offer will be delivered.

## Design

Design plays a particularly important role in innovation as good design embraces all aspects of:

- customer needs and values;
- the total product offer as elements for potential improvement;
- all the processes involved in getting the idea to the final customer.

A decision that must be made in design is whether to challenge conventional thinking or conform to customer expectations of design. A characteristic of French-designed cars, Citroen and Renault, is that they frequently incorporate an innovative design that bucks the trend. Others, such as the VW Golf, have maintained the integrity of their 'classic designs' over many years by introducing new models that have simply had facelifts. Because of differences in personal perception many very innovative designs manage only limited appeal. The mark of true innovation is a cutting edge design that becomes iconic, such as the Coke bottle, the Shell logo or a Harley Davidson bike. Design should be regarded as a holistic activity. In this book we provide a number of examples of design, not just of products but of services, process and business models.

## New service innovation

So far we have been discussing products but while many of the characteristics of the **service innovation** process are similar there are some significant differences that exist too. Before discussing them, however, it is worth commenting that innovation in services should be considered in two dimensions:

1. where the service is part of the total product offer, as discussed above, for example the free three-year warranty on a car or a very efficient return-to-factory and repair service for a personal computer;
2. where the service exists in its own right and is not part of a product offering, for example, hairdressing or travel services.

Confusingly, many service organizations, such as banks, refer to their service offerings such as mortgages and insurance offerings as products but here we are using the term 'product' to refer to physical goods, such as a can of baked beans or a refrigerator, and 'services' to offerings with very little physical content, such as hairdressing or training. In practice, as we have seen with the earlier discussion many but not all 'offerings' include both product and service elements.

## New service offerings

While the objective in providing new service offerings is similar to product innovation in that it is to ensure that customers obtain value in the service, there are some additional challenges too, as follows.

- Services, by definition, are intangible and so part of the innovation might be to add a powerful physical recognition of the supplier, hence both easyJet and Orange mobile phones have a strong and memorable colour. In Enterprise in Action 9.5 an example is given of challenging assumptions in a service and recognizing the importance of the customer experience.

    ■  It is often difficult to match supply and demand for services which, unlike products, do not allow for storage so innovation might be needed to try to achieve a balance. Examples include yield management systems in low-cost airlines.

    ■  Because it is the customer experience that determines the success of a service, innovation is needed to 'manage' the process that customers are taken through to ensure they have the best possible experience. Some restaurants find ways of 'helping' customers to occupy time spent waiting to be served.

---

### Enterprise in Action 9.5

**The new circus act**

Created by a group of street performers in 1984 Cirque du Soleil now employs 3000 people and its spectacular shows have been seen by 50 million people in almost 100 cities.

Cirque has achieved astonishing success by creating a new industry sector. At the time the business was created the circus industry was shrinking rapidly. The traditional circus format with the pedestrian animal acts and slapstick comedy routines of the clowns appeared to be in a time warp and unable to compete with the newer forms of entertainment.

What Cirque did was to eliminate some of the costly and problematic elements, such as the animals, and replace them with technology, performance arts and musical theatre. Moreover, Cirque no longer targeted children with a low-priced offering but instead appealed to adults with premium-priced entertainment.

*Adapted from*: Crainer S., 'Plenty more seas to fish', *The Observer*, 6 February 2005

**Question:** What assumptions were challenged in this example?

---

In providing services to support products the challenge is to identify the various aspects and limitations of service delivery and think creatively and innovatively about how the elements might be improved. Customers are constantly let down by poor and inadequate service and a lack of attention to the needs and expectations of customers. The best service organizations, especially those in commodity markets, where it is easy for customers to transfer to an alternative supplier, must work hard to ensure that their service never falls short of customer expectations.

## Retailing

Retailing is a service which, in one form or another, provides one of the largest categories of self-employment. However, it is also characterized by price competition and high failure rates, particularly among new starts. Many new start ups in retailing are 'me-too', offering nothing different and no additional customer value over what is already available from established retailers. The secret to retailing is considered to be location, location, location and, too often, poorly located shops selling me-too products close with depressing regularity.

E-commerce has been seen as providing a major opportunity for retailing innovations over the last few years as it offers customer convenience and accessibility to both mass market and niche products. In the early days of the electronic retailing boom there were many failures and it became clear that simply providing a new route to market will not work unless the retailer has something of real benefit to offer the customer. Substantial cost savings and a more exciting experience probably explains why eBay has been so successful.

## New process innovation

The opportunities for business starts based on new process development are enormous because opportunities occur throughout the complete supply chain, for example:

- research and development processes;
- design;
- manufacturing processes, ranging from the extraction of raw materials, conversion to a material that can be fabricated into components, to assembly into a finished product;
- business service processes, warehousing and logistics or administrative processes;
- new routes to the customer that involve marketing, communication and distribution;
- manufacturing support processes, such as consultancy, marketing research and advertising. Examples include Siebel Systems for customer relationship management and SAP for operations management and inventory systems.

## New market innovation

The final area of innovation that we discuss in this chapter is the exploitation of new markets. The most obvious area for market development is international development. Businesses may introduce a product, service or process that becomes a success in the company's home market. The idea may be considered to be innovative and have scope for development in other countries. The traditional way of developing internationally has been to use agents and distributors but, increasingly, firms are exploiting new international market opportunities through the use of alternative market entry strategies, such as joint ventures, alliances or licensing. A number of small firms have also used networks to exploit opportunities by working with other companies selling complementary products and services.

In recent years e-commerce has offered a new route to international market development, as we saw in the last chapter.

## Checking on the organization's capability to deliver the opportunity

Before completing this section it is important to re-emphasize that success comes from effective and efficient exploitation of an opportunity. There must be a market and the organization must be capable of delivering a solution either alone or through a partnership. We return to assessing the feasibility of the idea in the next chapter, but even at this stage the organization must have a clear idea of how it needs to reconfigure its operation, and add capabilities and techniques. One way of doing this is to use SWOT analysis (Figure 9.3) but in a slightly different way – as TOWS – to assess this.

Identifying strengths, weaknesses, opportunities and threats is a common analytical technique for assessing an organization's current position and future prospects. It can also be used to help assess whether an organization is capable of delivering a particular opportunity. The starting point is to identify the threats to the organization as it exploits the new opportunity and think about what it would take for the organization

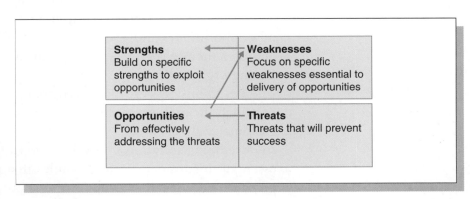

**Figure 9.3**
SWOT to TOWS
analysis.

to manage these threats effectively and exploit the opportunities. To do this the organization should then identify its weaknesses and strive to transform these into strengths. For example, the threat to success might be that competitors will compete on price for a domestically produced product. The solution and main financial opportunity might be to outsource or manufacture in Asia, in which case an organization that has little skill in managing outsourcing and supply chain management would consider this a weakness, but an area of potential opportunity that could be made a strength.

This was a problem that faced Dyson (see Enterprise in Action 9.1). Initially, the competitive advantage of Dyson in exploiting the market for vacuum cleaners was the technological invention and the knowledge applied to the manufacturing process. The opportunity initially was for the company to manufacture the products in the UK. In the early years of the product, Dyson could charge relatively high prices and was able to manufacture in a relatively high cost area in the UK, but manufacturing in the UK was not really the main opportunity and, as Dyson increased its volume of sales and came under price pressure from competitors with copies and their own developments, it transferred manufacture of its established, volume products to a lower manufacturing cost base in Asia and uses its UK base for development and early-stage manufacturing.

## Summary

- Opportunities can be identified in many situations. Entrepreneurs often exploit ideas when the market is mature or where there appears little scope for commercial success.

- There are many triggers to creating new business and entrepreneurship is often initiated by a single and often trivial event. Entrepreneurial organizations may then pursue the opportunity for many years before bringing it to fruition.

- There are many systematic and creative ways of identifying new opportunities and, even for those without a commercializable idea themselves, there are still ways of setting up an enterprising organization.

- The key to business creativity is to challenge the assumptions on which the sector operates and seek new ways of delivering customer value.

- In developing solutions that will exploit the opportunity it is essential to consider all the variables that make up the total product or service offer as opportunities arise both in the core aspects of the offer and in the support services, such as a new method of promoting or distributing the product or service.

■ To exploit the idea efficiently and effectively it is necessary for the organization to identify the threats and opportunities and reconfigure its operation where necessary to build strengths in the key areas of knowledge, capability and skills.

## Chapter questions

1. As a specialist consultant to the industry write a report identifying some potential sources of business opportunity for a major investor in the home entertainment industry.

2. If you were establishing a new product and service development process in an organization what methods would you suggest to encourage staff to identify new ideas?

3. What advantages do small firms have over large ones in exploiting market opportunities?

4. The process of exploiting an opportunity from the initial idea to commercialization can be expensive and time-consuming. How can a new or smaller organization reduce the time and costs involved?

5. How might environments that encourage networking (e.g. business incubators) support small firms in exploiting opportunities?

## Case study

### Prêt á Manger trying a new recipe

Selling sandwiches (and coffee) does not seem on the face of it to be a promising area with which to start a discussion on opportunity identification. It would, perhaps, have been even less promising when Julian Metcalfe set up Prêt á Manger in 1986. His second café opened five years later. His idea, which came to him in the 1980s, was that people were too busy making money to stick around eating lunch in cafés – they simply wanted to grab their food and drink and go. They wanted good quality sandwiches that they could take back to their office to eat in front of their computer.

Metcalfe's philosophy for the shops is 'Retail is Detail' and he emphasizes that if Prêt sells carrot juice, it must be the best carrot juice, and if it sells sausage rolls they must be the best too. The location, décor and service all have to be right, too. He believes that, where it is needed, changing the lighting and layout in one store could increase the revenue by 30 per cent. Feeling that Prêt á Manger was going well, and, perhaps, wanting a new personal challenge, Metcalfe appointed a chief executive and deputy chief executive, and focused for the next five years on a new venture, developing a chain of Sushi restaurants in Soho, Chelsea and Canary Wharf.

In 2001 McDonalds bought one third of the company and by 2003 there were 150 cafés worldwide but things had not gone altogether smoothly for Prêt. Although in 2002 the British business showed healthy profits the overseas expansion had led the company into making an overall loss. Twenty-two cafés had been opened in the USA in one year and Metcalfe believed that the expansion had been done too quickly. There were plans to open a café in Beijing, but why do that before opening one in Bromley in the UK? The chief executive and deputy chief executive left the company very soon afterwards.

When he returned to work more intensively for Prêt again Metcalfe realized that the cafés had become outdated. He said the old look was like the inside of a washing machine, with stainless steel tables and high stools. Customers had changed too. Now they are concerned with their own health. They care about what they eat, how they eat and where they eat. David Collins, the Dublin-born designer, who created the 'look' for Eat, a competitor to Prêt, comments that 'Now people wanted not only good and healthy fast food but also wanted to get out of the office for half an hour'. The 'look' for Eat, founded by Niall and Faith MacArthur, is a white kitchen, with white walls, white tiles and no clutter. Fifty Eat cafés have been opened to date.

Design seems to be important. Starbucks is still popular but no longer leading edge – it has a rather dated look too. And there are a number of other competitors in the market. In response to a decline in business and criticism about unhealthy eating, McDonalds and KFC offer real competition as does the rapidly expanding Subway sandwich chain. Even Marks & Spencer has introduced its Café Revive in many of its stores. Many other ideas are being tried, such as Internet cafés and music download services.

*Source*: adapted from various public sources, including C. Broughton, Bread Winners, *The Independent*, 29 February 2004

### Questions

1.  Using the opportunity identification approaches highlighted in the chapter, including subsegmentation, challenging assumptions and observation, suggest some possible niche business opportunities in the market for informal eating and drinking.
2.  Taking one of your ideas, explain the segment of customers you would target and what new concept you would offer them. Then show how you would design a product and service offer that would use innovation in all aspects of the business.

## References and further reading

Ansoff I.H. and McDonnell E. (1990) *Implanting Strategic Management*. London: Prentice Hall International.

Baron R.A. and Shane S.A. (2005) *Entrepreneurship: A Process Perspective*. Mason OH: Thomson South-Western.

Barrow C., Burke G., Molian D. and Brown R. (2005) *Enterprise Development, The Challenges of Starting, Growing and Selling a Business*. London: Thomson Learning.

Bolton B. and Thompson J. (2000) *Entrepreneurs, Talent, Temperament, Technique*. Oxford: Butterworth-Heinemann.

Doole I. and Lowe R. (2004) *International Marketing Strategy: Analysis, Development and Implementation*, 4th edn. London: Thomson Learning.

Drucker P. (1985) *Innovation and Entrepreneurship*. New York: Harper and Row.

Goffin K. and Mitchell R. (2005) *Innovation Management*. Palgrave: Macmillan.

Handy C. (1999) *The New Alchemists*. London: Hutchinson.

Kano N., Saraku N., Takahashi F. and Tsuji S. (1996) Attractive quality and must-be quality. In: J. Hromi (ed.), *The Best in Quality*, Vol 7, Ch 10. Milwaukee: ASQC, pp. 165–186.

Kim W.C. and Mabourgne R. (1997) The strategic logic of high growth. *Harvard Business Review* **75**:103–112.

Kotler P. (1997) *Marketing Management, Analysis, Planning, Implementation and Control*. Harlow: Prentice Hall.

Muzyka D.F. (2000) In: S. Birley and D.F. Muzyka (eds), *Mastering Entrepreneurship*. Edinburgh: FT Pitman.

Sternberg R.J. and Lubart T.I. (1995) *Defying the Crowd, Cultivating Creativity in a Culture of Conformity*. New York: Free Press.

Tushman M.L. and Anderson P. (2004) *Managing Strategic Innovation and Change*, 2nd edn. New York: Oxford University Press.

Wickham P.A. (2004) *Strategic Entrepreneurship*, 3rd edn. London: FT/Prentice Hall.

## Key words

challenging assumptions

customer value

market information

moments of truth

service innovation

source of innovation

subsegmentation

total product offer

triggers to the creation of a new business

## CHAPTER 10

# Enterprise planning and risk management

## Learning objectives

By the end of this chapter the reader will be able to:

- appreciate the stages in developing a business from initial idea to a sustainable business;
- assess the factors that will influence the choice of business model;
- evaluate the risks associated with the pursuit of new opportunities;
- assess the feasibility of commercial success for the new product or service; and
- explain the purpose of a business plan, its preparation, framework and key components.

## Introduction

In the previous chapter we discussed the first stage of the commercialization process by focusing on the identification of an opportunity and the development of a business solution to exploit it, by creating a new product, service or process. The natural inclination of an entrepreneur is to immediately want to make things happen by gathering the necessary resources and concentrating on getting the idea to market. Before doing that, however, it is worth re-emphasizing that the long-term objective is to create a sustainable business from the idea, not simply to quickly get a few customers to try to prove that the idea will work. While a key characteristic of an entrepreneur is adaptability and the ability to quickly respond to problems, it can be argued that it is preferable to avoid some future pitfalls by thinking and planning ahead wherever possible.

Creating a sustainable business from the idea requires confidence in the commercial prospects for the idea and this comes from assessing the feasibility of delivering it viably to the market and evaluating the risks associated with starting and building the venture.

It is also useful to develop an overall strategy that will determine the shape of the organization now and in the future, define its capabilities and what its activities and income streams will look like, and what its overall goals, objectives and standards will be. A more detailed plan will indicate precisely how, in the early stages, the organization intends to win customers in the market and manage and control its resources.

In this chapter, therefore, we begin by mapping out the various developmental stages of the business and explain how a strategy and plan can assist the transition of the organization between the stages. We then discuss the development of a business model that defines the organization's activities, income and cost streams. The next section deals with the feasibility assessment of the business model in the market and then goes on to discuss the evaluation of risk that occurs when acquiring and managing resources, and setting up a new organization. We then emphasize that feasibility study and planning continue to be important as the organization grows and that it should be part of a dynamic learning process rather than merely the production of an output that satisfies only the limited interests of some outside stakeholders.

In the section on planning we begin by considering the purpose and value of planning, which for some entrepreneurs might seem to be a time-consuming and unnecessary exercise for a start up business. In the last section we explain the essential components of the business plan and discuss its preparation. It is worth noting at this point that while we discuss the preparation of business plans later, it is not our intention to provide a detailed 'how to' guide to start up planning as there are some excellent books and software that comprehensively deal with this aspect of entrepreneurship. Instead we focus on the key areas of business start up and on the essential decisions that are required.

## The developmental stages of the business

The experiences of working in start up or early-stage business often seem to be characterized by a succession of crises interspersed with

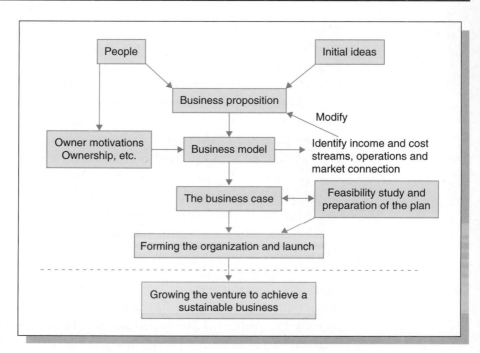

**Figure 10.1**
The start up stages.

fleeting moments of success as the long-awaited breakthrough occurs accompanied by the extremes of emotions – euphoria with a successful event and deep despair at an unexpected failure. It is only usually with hindsight that it is possible to observe distinct phases through which the start up or early-stage business has progressed. However, in order to plan, assess and manage risk it is useful to consider the organization in distinct stages, as shown in Figure 10.1.

## Stage 1: The business proposition

The first stage of the business was described in the last chapter and is the definition of the **business proposition**. This emerges from the identification of the initial opportunity by the entrepreneur or entrepreneurial team and the subsequent development of the idea to exploit it, in the form of the business solution. Through obtaining market information from an understanding of the market context, customer demand and expectations, and the likely competitor response the potential size of the market can be determined. Against this background the entrepreneur or team then use their knowledge, skills and competencies to develop the product, service or process proposition.

## Stage 2: Defining the business model

In stage 2 the **business model** is defined. As we discuss in the next section this follows from decisions made about exactly what the business will look like, what activities it will undertake itself and, accordingly, what its income and cost streams will be.

## Stage 3: Preparing the business case

An early task in the process is to prepare a clearly thought out **business case** that explains how the venture will be formed, funded and owned, operated and managed. The business case is essential if the entrepreneur wishes to persuade investors or banks to finance some or all of the necessary resources for the venture. This is fairly obviously the case for a new start up but preparing a business case is essential for new ventures within an existing organization too, where senior management support for investment is just as critical if finance is to be secured and resources acquired. The business case is normally presented formally and justified within a business plan. While the feasibility of the venture in the market will be the main focus of the business case, investors do not have a crystal ball that will enable them to make better predictions of likely success than the entrepreneur. Therefore they place considerable emphasis on the capability of the management team, particularly its enthusiasm, experience, competence and astuteness in dealing with unexpected problems.

## Stage 4: Forming the organization and launch

Having prepared the plans that justify the **formation and launch** of the organization the next stage is to get started. This involves obtaining the resources and activating the various operations of the business, including finance, production and distribution, marketing, sales and people management. While much of the focus of this chapter is on making decisions and planning the business before start up, the launch strategy is a critical stage in the start up process, especially if a high profile launch is essential, timing is crucial and resources are limited. The venture can be given a significant boost or may suffer a setback, which may take a long time to recover from. In some market sectors, stakeholders are unforgiving and, if the business launch fails, there may not be a second opportunity.

## Stage 5: Growing the venture to sustainability

The success of an early-stage venture is achieved through the combination of an entrepreneur, an idea and a realistic business model that will effectively exploit the opportunity but a surprisingly difficult task is to repeat the success and continue to build the organization. As we shall see, **building a sustainable business** requires a succession of product and service developments and improvements in the management and operation of the venture, in order to overcome the barriers to growth and ensure future success. Although this is the final part of the start up process and, perhaps, well into the future, it is necessary to build into the business model and business plan the capacity and capability for the organization to develop and grow from the start.

Enterprise in Action 10.1 provides an opportunity to consider the planning issues in a new start up business.

### Enterprise in Action 10.1

#### Consultancy start up

After gaining a good science degree you joined a company that provided consultancy to medium-sized businesses of 50–200 employees to help them improve their quality management systems. After working as a consultant there for five years you have decided to follow the dream you have had since being at university to become self-employed. With increasing energy prices you are convinced that there is an opportunity to offer consultancy to the firms that you have been working with to help them reduce their energy costs. You have made an appointment with the bank manager to discuss a loan and are trying to prepare answers to the questions that you are likely to be asked. You want to give the impression that your plans are already advanced and, if the bank manager requires you to provide a written business plan, you could submit one within a few days.

*Source*: Robin Lowe

**Question:** What are the questions from the bank manager you would expect to have to answer in your business plan?

Many successful entrepreneurs have the capability, interest and ambition to play a 'hands-on', operational role in the early stages of the process of enterprise. However, many become bored with the often less exciting later stages of building and growing the venture into a sustainable business. There are many other reasons why initially highly successful organizations are unable to overcome the barriers to growth and fail to become sustainable businesses and we discuss these factors in Chapter 12.

## Creating a sustainable business model

The key challenge at the start of the process of commercializing the idea is to decide how a particular idea might be exploited. As there are many ways of exploiting a market opportunity, the decisions that are taken may be rational, logical and justifiable but they usually also reflect the owner's personal views, experience and capabilities. A conventional business model may be safe and offer predictable returns. A more innovative model has the potential to offer above average rewards, but is often more risky because less information is available to assess the model, the problems cannot be anticipated and the outcomes are more unpredictable.

Entrepreneurs are usually prepared to take a risk based on imperfect information and implement their model quickly, believing they can act fast to change things and obtain the high returns before competitors catch up. Sometimes being first mover is essential as it prevents others competing, as shown in Enterprise in Action 10.2.

---

### Enterprise in Action 10.2

**Autoglass in the driving seat**

Autoglass is a glass distributor that has secured a very strong position in Europe. Its business is repairing or replacing damaged windscreens but it does not sell directly to motorists. Its customers are the car insurance companies, and the windscreen repair service is included in the insurance premium for the car. Autoglass therefore must satisfy both consumer and customer. Motorists want a quick service to get them moving again and this requires an effective network of depots and mobile repair staff. The insurance companies want an effective business partner to complete the necessary paperwork and operate the systems and processes efficiently, and for the motorists to be satisfied – as dissatisfied motorists are unlikely to renew their insurance policies. So long as Autoglass delivers the service effectively the insurance companies are unlikely to switch to an untried supplier.

*Adapted from*: Barrow C. *et al.* (2005) *Enterprise Development, The Challenges of Starting, Growing and Selling a Business*, Thomson

**Question:** What are the requirements of an 'ideal' business model?

---

## Defining the business model

At the outset it is necessary to define the business model at least in outline terms. The key factors in the business model are listed below.

- *What the organization will do and what tasks it will carry out.* For example, will it be a research and development company, a specialized consultancy company, a marketer of the final product or an online direct seller of the product?

- *How the organization will connect with the market.* It is essential to assess the alternative **routes to market** and how the connections with the market will be made. For example, an invention can be converted into a product that will be sold or the invention can be licensed to another producer. The route to market may be largely through e-commerce, traditional distribution through wholesalers and retailers or a combination of online and 'off-line' routes. The organization will need to decide for example, if it wishes to sell its offering directly to customers or approach the market in partnership with other organizations, for instance as might occur in a media or artists' network. The consumer may be different from the customer or, in B2B markets, a number of individuals will be part of the buying team, so it is necessary to decide who should be contacted.

- *What the offer is, how it is positioned and communicated to the customers.* For example, what benefits and value the customers might expect, how the offer and its benefits can be differentiated from similar offers from competitors and what methods are used to promote the offer and obtain feedback on customer response to it.

- *What the income streams will be.* There are many possible **income streams**. For example, the company might generate income by license fees, daily rate consultancy, payment for developing a new product, sales from selling a product or service, or being paid a proportion of the savings or increased profit that result from using a new process. For an e-business, income can be generated through sponsorship, advertising and 'click-through' fees.

- *How the organization arranges its resources and what the cost streams will be.* We shall discuss later the choices that the firm might have relating to how it will carry out the necessary value-adding business activities. For example, the company might decide to carry out tasks in-house or subcontract work resulting in very different associated cost streams. The company might outsource manufacturing but employ in-house staff for design, development and marketing. This will also have significant impact on the investment costs of setting up. If capital equipment is required, there are a number of ways of financing it and this will have a significant effect on overall cost streams and cash flow.

- *The organization's role within the value chain.* A key feature of the business model will be how the new venture will contribute to the **value chain** of the product or service and the nature of collaboration with or degree of independence from third parties to deliver value to the customer. For example, the suppliers to an independent retailer may have limited influence or impact on its operations, whereas the actions of a franchisee will probably be dominated by the demands of the franchisor.

- *How surpluses will be generated for further investment.* All these considerations are important in determining how **profit or surpluses** will be generated to pay the current investors or to further invest in the business. At a simple level this is the difference between income and cost streams. However, it is the medium- and long-term financial dynamics that are important as the business model must be flexible and robust enough to routinely deliver surpluses so that the organization is able to undertake further investment programmes to improve its efficiency and effectiveness in a changing competitive market.

## Factors affecting the design of the business model

There are a number of factors that will influence the choice and design of the business model that is ultimately adopted for the business and it is useful to group them under the following series of headings.

- Market factors
- Organizational issues
- Entrepreneurial personality and organization culture issues
- Flexibility to respond to organizational growth
- Risk factors.

### Market factors

#### Fit with the market

The business model must give the venture competitive advantage in the market. If a new-start adopts a conventional model it must operate the model more effectively and efficiently than do the competitors. A potential innovation opportunity is to develop a business model that challenges the assumptions about the way the market works and deliberately does not fit with the present ways of doing business in the sector. Over the years there have been a number of breakpoints in business models that have given the customers added value and the venture a competitive edge; some examples are included in Table 10.1.

Chaston (2000: 154) gives the example of Ray Kroc, the founder of McDonalds, who realized in the 1950s that the middle classes were migrating from the city centres to the suburbs. He noticed the rapid service and inexpensive food of the McDonalds brothers' restaurant in California and acquired franchising rights. The business model he developed was designed to fit with the market opportunity that was emerging. In Pause and Reflect 10.1 eBay, one of the most distinctive and spectacularly successful recent business models is discussed.

## Pause and Reflect 10.1

### eBay – a revolutionary business model for the Internet

In 1999 Meg Whitman founded eBay, the Internet auction site. It has expanded to become the online marketplace for the trading of a diverse range of goods and services among a globally spread community of individuals and organizations. eBay takes a fee to insert the advertisement and a fee based on the final value of the good sold. It is the most popular shopping destination on the Internet and people spend more time on the site than on any other. By mid-2005 it had 65 million active users and in the second quarter of 2005 its profits had jumped to $292 m on $1.1 bn revenue. An assessment system enables buyers and sellers to rate each other and, apart from a few high-profile cases, fraudsters have been controlled.

The site has been so effective that many individuals and companies now rely on eBay to reach their customers and it is believed that tens of thousands of people have given up their jobs to run businesses trading on eBay full-time, with many more employed people who use eBay to run businesses in their spare time.

*Sources* – various public sources, including:'eBay ups forecast as profits jump', BBC News Online, 20 July 2005

**Question:** What are the critical success factors for a new business model?

### Table 10.1

Examples of business model breakpoints

| Business models | Examples |
| --- | --- |
| Bait and hook | Low-margin basic product with high-margin refill, e.g. razor and blades, mobile phone and air time, computer printer and cartridges |
| 'No frills' airlines | Yield management processes to maximize revenue from a flight, using flexible pricing, rather than relying on a fixed seat price at South West Air, easyJet and Ryanair |
| Online retailing | Easy purchasing online with customized recommendations at Amazon |
| Online auctions | Organizer takes percentage from advertiser and completed deal, e.g. eBay and Betfair |
| *Source*: http:digitalenterprise.org/models/models.html | |

*Flexibility to deal with changing market dynamics*

A rigid model that takes one view of the market can be problematic if the market dynamics change. For example, a model that is geared to supply one main B2B customer is risky if there is a danger that the key customer goes bankrupt or is acquired by another company that is not a customer. Nestor Healthcare, set up to provide temporary staff to the National Health Service in the UK, suffered when the NHS decided to set up an in-house agency itself but Nestor had other complementary activities in its portfolio to compensate for the decline in this income stream. Granville Technology, however, failed to respond to a rapidly changing computer market, as shown in Enterprise in Action 10.3.

---

## Enterprise in Action 10.3

### Collapse of Granville Technology

In July 2005 the UK's largest computer manufacturer, maker of Time and Tiny computers, collapsed with the loss of 1500 jobs. At its height the company was manufacturing 500 000 computers a year and sold them through 150 stores in UK high streets. It also supplied supermarkets including Asda, Tesco and Woolworths.

No accounts had been filed for two years and just before it collapsed the company was losing £2 m per month. The problem for Granville was that its business model was becoming no longer appropriate as the cost of computers fell. PCs from India were being sold for as little as $225, making it impossible to compete using products made in a higher labour cost country. Furthermore, the low retail margins that were constantly eroded by Internet sellers, such as Dell made Time's high overhead retailing operation unsustainable.

Time was set up by Tahir Moshan but he resigned as managing director in 2004. It took over Tiny Computers, which collapsed in 2002.

*Source*: adapted from Tiny PCs goes into administration, 27 July, 2005 BBC News Online, Guardian online 27 July 2005 and other public sources

**Question:** What could Granville have done to reinvent the business?

---

*Competitive response*

If a new venture is successful it will be noticed by competitors, who are likely to attack the market opportunity identified. The business model must make provision for dealing with the competitive response. Body Shop initially suffered when mainstream retailers, such as Boots in the UK, brought out products with similar ethical claims but it has since grown internationally.

## Organizational issues

In order to fully exploit the potential flexibility of a business model it is vital to consider all the possibilities. To do this it is useful to consider first the concept of the organization. Morgan (1997) identifies a number of dimensions, which are shown in Figure 10.2. It is the particular combination of these elements that enables the organization to develop a unique business model.

### Protecting the idea

Some business model options make it more difficult to protect the intellectual property that is transferred in the course of the business transactions. For example, business models that are based on partnerships may mean that it is inevitable that sensitive information is shared for the business to grow but this could lead to one partner gaining sufficient intellectual property to be able to go it alone.

### Areas of expertise

It might be more expedient for the team running the business to develop a model that builds upon their areas of expertise, skill and knowledge. For example, a team of designers may not have selling expertise and it might be more advisable to offer a consultancy service rather than selling to final consumers.

---

Organizations serve a number of purposes:

- The coordinator of actions to share complex tasks; the complementary activities are carried out by a diverse range of individuals and groups of people
- An independent agent, existing and taking actions in its own right, with an individual and separate character
- A network of contracts that are a framework of agreements based on exchange of labour for something in return
- A collection of resources, including capital, people and productive assets, such as buildings, machinery and vehicles
- A system, a coordinated collection of elements and a pattern of relationships
- A processor of information that leads to the accumulation of knowledge that in turn leads to competitive success

**Figure 10.2**
The concept of the organization.

*Unsuitable partners*

It may be unwise to build a business model that is dependent for success on one particular partner that is potentially unreliable or not fully committed to the venture because the activity in question is peripheral to the main business.

## Entrepreneurial personality and organization culture issues

The business model needs to take account of any weaknesses or the preferred way of working of the entrepreneur or entrepreneurial team and either reflect or change the way they work. It is common to hear the comment 'That is the way we have always done it', when the model should be changed to meet new circumstances.

*Areas of expertise*

Some entrepreneurs prefer to work in their comfort zone of expertise and do not easily take on responsibility for some functional areas that are core to the business model. For example, the defence of Bernie Ebbers, the chief executive involved in the £11 bn fraud at Worldcom, was that he was an entrepreneur with humble origins as a milkman and he did not get involved in the finances of the company, which he left to the 'bean counters'. His defence failed and he was jailed for 25 years.

*Unwilling or incapable of working in partnerships*

Some entrepreneurs tend not to trust people who are outside their direct control and do not easily work in partnerships and so avoid outsourced services as far as possible. Their belief is that the organization will not be as efficient as it could be, because those in the venture are more committed, will be more reliable and work faster to achieve the necessary outcomes than will subcontractors or partners.

*Leadership and management*

If the entrepreneur does not have particular strengths in leadership and management, it might be better to avoid setting up a model based on employing large numbers of production or service staff and instead use a small team with expertise in outsourcing services.

## Flexibility to respond to organizational growth

### *Early-stage flexibility*

One of the merits of small organizations is their flexibility but this is often used as an excuse for not taking decisions to clearly define the business model, in the belief that changes to the business model can be made later when they are required. However, rather than leaving the business model vague, flexibility should be built into the model. To illustrate this point many e-businesses set up at the time of the dot-com boom obtained huge investment on the expectation that they would generate revenue from advertising and sponsorship of their website. However, many failed to clearly define their business model and reliable income streams and, as a result, the majority of businesses burnt their investment cash very quickly and went bankrupt.

### *Re-engineering the business model*

As the organization develops, and changes occur, it may become necessary to re-engineer the business model. Chaston (2000: 138) debates whether this re-engineering is entrepreneurial, citing the example of IBM where two senior managers tracked the organization's credit approval system. By changing from a system that used different specialists to carry out each stage of the process to appointing one person to carry out the whole process, they reduced the time needed from 6 days to 90 minutes. By our broad definition, we would consider this to be an entrepreneurial 'moment' of process or architectural innovation.

## Risk factors

Choosing a business model can be influenced by a number of areas of risk including legal, political and competitive risks. In Enterprise in Action 10.4 it is shown how Betfair were faced with legal and competitive risks but chose to pursue their business model in spite of them.

### Enterprise in Action 10.4

#### Betfair betting exchange

New business models invariably create shock waves in a sector and often lead to legal and competitor threats. The dilemma for the entrepreneur is whether to slow down or ignore these threats in the hope or belief that they will come to nothing.

The betting industry went through a huge boom at the beginning of the 2000s with a number of entrepreneurial companies offering new propositions to different customer segments, as discussed in Enterprise in Action 6.1.

Betfair was set up an attic room in 2000 by Andrew Black and Edward Wray. Within nine months £1 million worth of bets were being placed on the website each week and in three years this had increased to £50 million per week. The company employed 200 people and had won the Queen's Award for Enterprise and Innovation. In contrast with many online betting companies Betfair is an exchange that matches up those who lay odds with those who place bets. Betfair takes a commission of up to 5 per cent on the net winnings on either side. The advantage that Betfair claims is that the prices are 20 per cent better than those of traditional bookmakers. By 2005 it had 90 per cent of the betting exchange business.

However, high-street bookmakers claimed that Betfair and other similar exchanges were illegal as they flouted the UK betting laws and the model did not identify criminal activity. Betfair denied these claims and, in 2005, the UK government in the course of preparing a new gambling bill appeared to take the side of Betfair.

While this appeared to be on the point of solving Betfair's problems, it provided another threat and opportunity. Given that Betfair had substantially expanded the market, the anticipated clarification of the legal position means that the sector would become attractive for the traditional bookmakers to set up their own exchanges. Against this background Betfair had a number of options: to sell the company, refinance it or float on the stock market, in which case it would be valued at £900 million, making the two owners £100 million each.

*Adapted from*: 'Betfair in possible £700 m float', BBC News Online, 28 March 2005

**Question:** What should the owners do and why?

## Value chain contribution

Porter (1985) introduced the concept of the value chain, and the elements of a value chain for a new idea are shown in Figure 10.3. The new venture that is based on the idea must decide which of these elements it wishes to and is able to deliver. Does it wish to:

- have the responsibility for transforming the idea into a saleable product or service and/or marketing the final product or service to the consumer?
- control each of these elements in-house?
- outsource some of the elements but still control the supply chain?
- focus on a key element of the supply chain while allowing a partner organization to market the final product?

Each of these strategies involves risk that must be assessed in a feasibility study, which is discussed later in the chapter. Critical to each approach is the decision of make or buy.

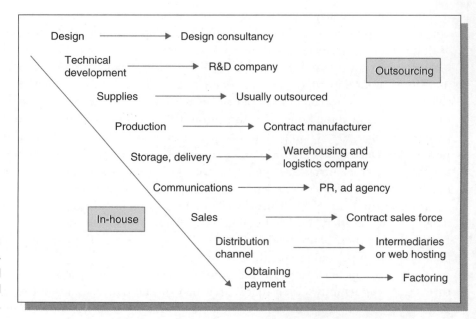

**Figure 10.3**
The value chain, in-house and outsourced provision.

## Make or buy decisions

Every link in the chain can be undertaken in-house, thus potentially adding the most value for the venture, but in this case all the costs are also incurred in-house. The venture, however, may not be the most efficient or expert supplier of these elements in the chain; for example the capital expenditure for equipment and facilities could be unjustifiably high and some of these elements could be outsourced to efficient external suppliers. If the venture wishes to maintain control of the supply chain and market the final product, outsourcing of some tasks can still be used to reduce the internal resource commitment but this will increase purchases and so have cash flow implications. This strategy increases the risk of relinquishing control of the supply chain to a more powerful partner.

Each of the supply chain elements can also provide an alternative income stream for the new venture, such as design or research capability (see Table 10.2). Alternatively, marketing and selling the final product could be left to another better resourced organization.

Market penetration is likely to be greater if the venture is able to concentrate on its core expertise but the consequence is that it would have less control over subsequent developments in the market. Knowledge of the organization's customers might be considered to be its most important asset. Tesco ran its loyalty card operation to retain customer knowledge, and you might consider if it was wise for Sainsbury to use the Nectar card from a third party to run its loyalty card scheme.

**Table 10.2**

Elements of the supply chain and possible income streams

| Some elements of the supply chain | In-house added value or possible alternative commercial income streams |
|---|---|
| ■ The intellectual property of the initial idea | ■ Licensing IP to a manufacturing or marketing company<br>■ Consultancy |
| ■ Research and development of further IP | ■ Licensing IP<br>■ Consultancy |
| ■ Design of the product or service | ■ Design consultancy<br>■ Licensing from applications of IP |
| ■ Designing the manufacturing process | ■ Process consultancy |
| ■ Development/enhancement of the product | ■ R&D consultancy<br>■ Market information research and consultancy |
| ■ Efficiency improvement in manufacturing | ■ Process consultancy<br>■ Outsourcing management |
| ■ Manufacturing the product | ■ Contract manufacture or manufacture for others |
| ■ Marketing the product | ■ Marketing externally sourced products and services |
| ■ The sales force | ■ Can be contracted out or sell externally sourced products and services |
| ■ Logistics | ■ Can be contracted out or deliver externally sourced products and services |
| ■ Retailing | ■ Physical or online retailing |

Many entrepreneurial organizations believe that in order to achieve successful commercialization they must carry out each of the tasks in the supply chain themselves – owning the IP, and designing, manufacturing, marketing and selling the product themselves. In some situations they may even wish to retail the product direct to customers, using the Internet. This approach is the most demanding as it requires the highest level of financial investment and the broadest range of expertise and management skills, and for an unproven venture it ultimately carries the highest risk of failure.

In today's competitive environment it is unlikely that a new venture can carry out each of these stages cost effectively. For example, manufacturing and some service processes, such as telephone call centres and processing of transactions can be done more cheaply in developing countries and if the venture needs to reach a mass market, online marketing alone may be inadequate. However, if retailing through major supermarkets is essential this may be difficult too. Many supermarkets would not be prepared to buy just one product (however good) from a supplier as the costs of managing the administration and logistics of a single product supplier is unlikely to be cost effective. Therefore, the venture may be forced to work through a distributor.

Entrepreneurs might find that certain of the links in the supply chain are critical in terms of adding value for the customer and protecting their intellectual property. For example, the entrepreneur might decide that manufacturing in-house is essential until the product and venture are established in order to maintain control of quality and secrecy of the manufacturing processes.

## The value chain and business model and risk

Perhaps business model and value chain decisions are ultimately decisions about what type of **risk** the entrepreneur will accept. For example, it is essential to identify reliable income streams but sometimes these may not be sufficiently attractive to win a customer's business. For instance, in many services it is preferable to charge a daily rate for the actual work done as this is usually less risky than charging a rate for a completed job, where the cost of unexpected and unplanned delays is borne by the supplier.

Entrepreneurs often appear to balance the cost and risk implications against the potential benefit differently from other managers. They are more driven to act, to be first to establish the venture and new business model, and so they value these things more highly. As a result they are prepared to run with higher levels of risk. Entrepreneurs typically are not foolhardy, however, and know that their priority is to be aware of what activities it is essential to retain control over.

## The purpose and benefits of business planning

Starting and growing a new venture and developing an appropriate business model entails the entrepreneur acquiring and applying considerable amounts of disparate information and carrying out a large number of often unfamiliar tasks. The risk in this is our limited capacity to process information and apply rational thinking (Baron and Shane, 2005). We have some weaknesses including:

- the belief is that we can complete more in a given period of time than we can;

- the fact that we find some information easier to bring to mind and so use it more often than other information that might be of equal value and more relevant; and
- the belief that we have more control over our fate than we actually have.

This means that to operate more effectively it would seem sensible for entrepreneurs to use formal processes for using information to run their business.

It is generally recognized that the **process of planning** can play a significant part in helping to reduce the risk of failure by placing greater emphasis on reflection, analysis and detailed implementation actions that are decided in advance. Planning assumes that there will be changes and so planning is particularly important, for example at times of a new start up activity, the acquisition of a new investor or growing the business. Indeed, if an organization does not intend to change anything that it is currently doing there seems to be little point in planning. Planning also infers making decisions to deal with the changes that have occurred. Planning is therefore the thinking process that involves information collection and analysis, decision-making between the options available, identifying actions to be taken, setting timescales and checking on progress. If it is to be effective in steering the venture through the various crises that it is likely to encounter planning must be an almost continuous process.

## Some arguments against formal planning

There are some arguments against formal planning. Coulter (2003: 143) summarizes the criticism of Moore (1996), Hamel and Prahalad (1994) and Mintzberg (1994), who have challenged the basic assumptions of planning as listed below:

- Formal planning may create rigidity as organizations are locked into specific goals, potentially fatal for an entrepreneur in a changing environment.
- Most environments are dynamic, and organizations cannot plan for unexpected and unpredictable events.
- Most successful organizations are the result of someone's innovative vision rather than the result of formal planning, which is based on thorough analysis that can kill creativity and innovation.

- Formal planning focuses on how to capture existing opportunities not how to reinvent the business or create a new market.
- Reinforcing current success through planning may be dangerous in a changing market.

Many writers, for example Kaplan (2003) and Coulter (2003), suggest therefore that the plan should be used as a road map rather than a rigid discipline for the business.

## The benefits of strategy development and planning

There are a number of recognized benefits of strategic development and planning, including the following.

- Planning encourages proactivity among the managers rather than reactivity, so the organization can have a greater influence on its future direction rather than simply reacting to events as they occur.
- Planning encourages a systematic process of collection of information and analysis of the factors involved in the decisions rather than using only the information that is most easily recalled.
- Planning forces organizations to define their objectives and policies more precisely, avoiding ambiguity, so they are not misinterpreted when individual decisions are taken.
- As the organization and its management becomes more complex it is essential that managers become more focused in their thinking but their actions must be complementary in delivering the strategy.
- As the environment becomes increasingly complex and unstable, planning prepares the organization to respond quickly and decisively in a coordinated and effective way.
- In a growing organization planning increases the participation of staff in decision-making and increases their motivation and loyalty.
- Day-to-day action and control can be integrated with the longer-term strategy to ensure that the objectives are achieved.
- Planning should also offer the entrepreneurial organization the opportunity to challenge assumptions in their strategic decision-making processes and reflect on and re-evaluate their operations, as discussed in Chapter 4.

# The planning process

The real purpose of planning in the organization is to address the following four fundamental questions.

1. Where are we now?
2. Where do we want to get to?
3. How will we get there?
4. How will we know when we have arrived?

## Where are we now?

Being absolutely realistic about the organization's current situation is essential because delusions about the present position and capability lead to over-optimism about what can be achieved in the future with the resources available. This is a common pitfall for an entrepreneur who is convinced of the value of the idea. There are four considerations in this section:

1. the nature and demands of the environment, including the competition and customers;
2. the range of stakeholders that have an interest in the organization and its activities, and may have the power and interest to influence its chances of success;
3. the objectives and ambitions of the entrepreneur and staff; and
4. the capabilities, strengths and weaknesses of the staff.

For a new start up organization there may be a temptation to give very little thought to the answer to this first question and the three dimensions that make up the assessment of the current situation. However, it is essential to define carefully where we are now in order to decide which business model to adopt and to work out the gap that needs to be bridged between where we are now and where we want to go to. It is also vital to identify the resources and capabilities that are needed over and above what are already available to deliver the plan. This is particularly true in terms of creating a balanced team. The entrepreneur must know what skills are needed overall to complement his or her own skills.

It is also essential to be aware of the environmental pressures that could knock the organization off course. A lack of consensus or clarity about the objectives and ambitions of the entrepreneur and the staff can lead to wrong decisions being taken. For example, an entrepreneur might be looking to create an organization with the purpose of selling it as soon as a return can be made on the investment, rather than expecting to manage the business for the long term.

## Where do we want to get to?

The 'future' must be identified through the **entrepreneur's vision** and then by setting clear and meaningful goals and objectives with the purpose of increasing the organization's focus and leading to the coherence of efforts. Financial and non-financial drivers should be included. Collins and Poras (2004) have emphasized that, in building the company's vision, the organization must be clear about its purpose or reason for being, and be able to articulate this in a phrase or sentence. They should set BHAGs – Big, Hairy, Audacious Goals – to stimulate progress. Chaston (2000: 163) explains how some entrepreneurs are excited by a unique vision that becomes their entire focus and that can lead to spectacular success. Bill Gates set out to put a computer on every desk and in every home in America.

According to Drucker (2001: 30), organizations should identify objectives in eight areas:

1. marketing
2. innovation
3. human resources
4. financial resources
5. physical resources
6. productivity
7. social responsibility
8. profit requirements.

He argues that organizations must not just think about what the business **is** about, but also what it should **be** about. They should avoid wasting energy defending yesterday's business.

Having a vision and communicating it effectively can be a significant advantage for an entrepreneurial organization if the goals stretch the capabilities of the organization. However, there is a possible downside. They must be achievable and motivating to staff – without being unrealistic, meaningless and dispiriting – in order to prevent them feeling they are always underperforming against the entrepreneur's expectations. The achievement of the goals set must also be considered as success for the entrepreneur. But Wickham (2004: 93) explains that success can mean many things and, certainly, different things to different stakeholders. Financial success was clearly not the most important factor to two of the owners discussed in Pause and Reflect 10.2.

## Pause and Reflect 10.2

### Friends Reunited but with different objectives

Friends Reunited was founded in 2000 by Julie and Steve Pankhurst, a husband-and-wife team, and Jason Porter. Friends Reunited brings together old acquaintances over the Internet. It has 12 million members and has expanded from its origins in bringing school friends together, into online genealogy and recruitment, through its acquisition of Top Dog Jobs. It has also expanded internationally through acquiring its Australian counterpart, Schoolfriends.com.

In 2004 its profits increased from £3.6 to £4.6 million on a turnover of £8.8 million. In December 2005 Friends Reunited sold out to ITV for £120 m, with the Pankhursts receiving £30 million in the deal. Despite receiving millions too in dividends, the Pankhursts still live in a semi-detached house in north London and drive a mini. By contrast Porter lives in a grand manor-house in Kent and drives luxury cars. The Pankhursts comment 'We feel a little embarrassed about our success – we are just not interested in the money'.

*Adapted from:* 'Friends Reunited hires adviser to prepare sale', *The Sunday Times*, 7 August 2005

**Question:** How important is it for entrepreneurs to define their objectives, and what types of objectives are critical?

## How will we get there?

These are the action plans that will ultimately determine whether the venture will succeed or fail. For them to work it is necessary that:

- the essential stakeholders in the venture understand the plan and are committed to it;
- it is clear who is responsible for doing what and to what timescales;
- the resources (including people and finance) are procured in timely fashion and used effectively. Moreover, Coulter (2003) emphasizes that the organization must sweat its assets, and further emphasizes that the best way to sweat assets is for the owner to roll his or her sleeves up and do the work!

## How will we know when we have arrived?

The plan rolls forward so there is a temptation for many entrepreneurial organizations to think that no concrete final goals can or need to be set. It might be thought better to set stage posts along the path with measurements to indicate whether the plan is working, for example potential customer awareness and conversion rates. The action plan should be regularly reviewed to check on progress and take corrective action when necessary. Again, using the notion of 3R learning, the question should be asked as to whether the original plans were valid in the light of what the organization is learning about its performance rather than continuing to plough the same furrow. It is this continual reflection and reassessment that distinguishes entrepreneurial ventures.

## Planning and the business plan

At this point it is worth clearly distinguishing between *planning* and *the business plan*. Whereas planning is the thinking process, the business plan is the formal written document that records the planning process at one point in time for a specific purpose. Without constant updates most plans will be out of date almost as soon as they have been completed, because of the constantly changing environment. Many entrepreneurs, therefore, have reservations about the benefit of the time that they might devote to planning what is likely to be a fast-changing entity. Many believe they plan continually and effectively – in their heads – and see little point in writing things down.

While some entrepreneurs claim that they can manage without writing down their plans, Chaston (2000: 40) point out that there are some limitations to this approach. Where the entrepreneur is not working alone and needs to convey ideas to staff and other stakeholders, such as investors, accountants or banks it is necessary to provide some justification for the decisions that have been made about how the organization will be set up and run so that they fully understand the implications for them. It is necessary to allow them to read the information and understand the link between the analysis, forecasts and assumptions that have been made and the actions that are intended.

One of the problems that we observe frequently is that the difference between a good and bad plan is that, in a good plan, there is a clear link between the implementation of the plan and the analysis. Often there is little difference in the amount of relevant information that has been collected, the understanding of the market and the objectives set, but there is a big difference in the quality of the decisions that have been made between the choices available in terms of whether the actions and timescales are realistic and whether monitoring will be in place to prevent any nasty, unexpected shocks.

Planning should ensure that, unless there is a compelling reason to change, some aspects of the business stay relatively constant, such as the medium-term objectives, otherwise decisions will be taken on a whim of the entrepreneur or member of staff and will change by the day or even hour. This can lead to contradictory instructions to staff, misunderstandings and wasted resources.

## What the plan is used for

Before proceeding to the elements that should appear in the preparation of the business plan, it is worthwhile taking one step back to consider what the plan is going to be used for and how it will be prepared, by asking the following fundamental questions.

- What is the purpose of the planning carried out by the organization and how will the plan benefit the new venture?
- What is the plan going to be used for?
- Who should be involved in the planning process?
- How should the plan be used?
- Who should write the plan?
- What should the format of the plan be?
- How should the success of the plan be assessed?

## The components of the plan

A number of writers from banks, venture capitalist companies, academic institutions and entrepreneurial firms, have proposed what should be included in the business plan for a new venture. There are also a number of business planning websites and software available that can be utilized when undertaking the process. At the end of the chapter we have referred to a number of useful websites and books to help with detailed new-venture planning. Because the authors of these books and websites have different objectives for writing their approach to planning the frameworks and priorities vary, although in general the content is very similar.

## What are the aims of the business plan?

For entrepreneurial organizations there are usually three different objectives in writing a business plan, as follows:

1. to define the business for the start up of the organization and to assess its feasibility;

2.  for the new organization to explain its proposed future business activities to external stakeholders with the purpose of obtaining investment, loans and other types of support;

3.  to manage and control the organization and staff internally through its various phases.

## Writing the plan

Before discussing what the three types of plans will be used for, how they should be used and, hence, what they should include it is useful to discuss some general points in answer to the remaining questions posed earlier.

Pre-start and close-to-start, it is likely that the entrepreneur team will write the plan as they are the only people who really understand what the organization will do, perhaps by using one of the many but similar standard formats available online or in books. Considering each element of the plan and analysing the information helps ensure integration and acts as a checklist of things to consider. Obtaining the necessary information to provide the justification of the plan might involve discussions with many people, such as potential landlords, accountants and customers, each of which has specific expertise or knowledge to contribute.

There are consultancies that offer services in business plan writing. They provide plans that are professionally written and presented to a high standard, and they can be useful in saving the entrepreneurs' time where a specific format is required, for example in obtaining specialized investment or loans. However, it is essential that the owners of the new organization have ownership of the objectives, strategies and promises implied in the plan and play a full part in the planning stages.

Whatever the purpose of the plan it should be used to direct and manage the new venture. Coulter (2003: 147) has identified the critical success factors for a business plan (see Figure 10.4).

Even if it is primarily used once to attract funding, investors will wish to refer back to the plan periodically to see how the organization has delivered on its promises. Although it may be necessary to develop plans for different purposes the fundamental business model, strategies and implementation actions must be common throughout all planning. Slightly different versions of the basic plan can be used to meet the specific demands of the different situations.

Finally, Baron and Shane (2005: 177) identify the 'seven deadly sins', as shown in Figure 10.5.

Content:
- Captures the essence of the organization
- Clear financial and business forecasts
- Detailed market research (customers, competitors and the market environment)
- Details of the key executives
- Highlights the positive factors and deals with the challenges.

Presentation:
- Relatively short and precise
- Well written and formatted
- Detailed actions and timescales
- Regularly updated
- Shows financial astuteness.

*Adapted from*: Coulter (2003: 147)

**Figure 10.4**
The critical success factors for a plan.

- Poor preparation and an unprofessional appearance
- The plan is too slick
- Rambling executive summary and long-winded explanation of the venture
- Not making it clear what stage the proposition has reached
- Not making it clear why a customer would 'buy one'
- No statement of the experience and qualifications of the team
- Financial projections are unrealistic

*Adapted from*: Baron and Shane (2005: 177)

**Figure 10.5**
The seven deadly sins of new venture business plans.

## Feasibility study and risk

## The business case and feasibility assessment

Most ventures require support from their various stakeholders, such as banks, customers, potential employees and suppliers if they are to succeed. To obtain their support the rationale and justification of the venture must be presented within the plan. The entrepreneur must be confident that the plan will work and be able to answer questions they might have. Drawing on their experience, the funders will wish to be convinced that the venture will be viable both as a business and as a personal career choice for the entrepreneur. To test this it is essential for the entrepreneur to carry out a **feasibility study** to answer the following questions.

- Is going into business in this way right for me?
- Should I spend my time working in this way?
- Is the idea credible and is it the right place and time to launch the venture for it to succeed?

As we have suggested earlier there is a great temptation to be overoptimistic in planning a new venture and so fail to assess the realistic potential and consider the obvious pitfalls. A feasibility study should provide the reality check by concentrating on the validity and the analysis of the information on which the case is built, anticipating the potential barriers and pitfalls and preparing to overcome them. It might result in changes to the plan. A rigorous feasibility study takes time to undertake but is likely to save time and cost at the implementation stage. It will identify any make-or-break issues that might stop the project going forward. In this case the entrepreneur would save the considerable amount of time necessary in writing a business plan for investors, not to mention costs of setting up and failing! It will also identify other potential problem areas that are better solved in the early stages, for example registering building plans that might involve a lengthy approval process in the local council planning department.

In the feasibility study it is also essential to assess the associated risks. No organization, particularly a new venture, is without risk and risk is an accepted element of new business creation and development. However, new and developing ventures need to recognize the risks they are taking, and manage them by developing contingency plans for when things go wrong.

Gumpert (1994) comments 'Although an unsuccessful feasibility study may appear to be a failure, it's not. The real failure would have been if you had invested your own and others' money and then lost it due to barriers you failed to research in advance'.

The focus of the feasibility study for different organizations will vary but key areas can be identified, and these are shown in Figure 10.6.

Each of these areas is important and detailed evaluation can be worthwhile from a number of points of view. For example, Coulter (2003: 98) explains that it is important to research competitors that might be in the same market and to garner as much information as possible from a range of sources to obtain an understanding of their current and likely products, services and processes, and their strengths and weaknesses and resources. It can also be useful to analyse in detail their products and services to help in understanding how they are manufactured and delivered (reverse engineering).

**Market analysis**

- Is the market defined precisely and is your forecast share realistic and big enough?
- How quickly will customers switch? Will it be fast enough to get to break-even before the cash runs out?
- Is the market stable, growing or shrinking? How many customers are there and how many can you win over?
- Who are the competitors and how will they react to your marketing?
- Do you have the right location to appeal to the customer?
- Are you critically dependent on one supplier or distributor? In what circumstances could you lose their support?

**Organizational issues**

- Is the chosen business model the most appropriate?
- Who will own the organization and do the owners have common objectives?
- Do the owners have the skills, expertise and knowledge to start up the venture? How will any gaps be filled?
- Who will manage the business and what staffing will be required?
- What technology, facilities and equipment are needed and how will it be obtained?

**Financial issues**

- Are the estimates for costs and income realistic? Can costs be trimmed without affecting customers' perceptions of value? Are sales figures supportable?
- Are the cash flows and profitability estimates realistic and can they be improved?

**Contingency plans**

- Can improvements be made to improve the projected profitability and is it possible to assess the risk of failing to generate the forecast income or of incurring extra costs?
- What are the critical success factors (CSFs)?

**Figure 10.6**
Feasibility study – some areas for assessment.

In Enterprise in Action 10.5 you are invited to consider how to obtain relevant market information in a difficult-to-assess market situation and what implications this might have for the assessment of the other areas of the venture.

## Enterprise in Action 10.5

### Car security systems

An entrepreneur has designed and developed an innovative new car alarm. The manufacturing cost is £25 but he feels that the device should be priced at around £90 in the domestic market. He sees little point in trying to sell it in developed markets, where the majority of cars are relatively new and have factory-fitted alarms or immobilizers, or in trying to license it to car manufacturers.

His idea is to sell the alarm into emerging markets where there are likely to be more, older cars but he feels he should carry out some research first to help him decide which market he should go for.

*Source*: Robin Lowe

**Question:** What advice would you give the entrepreneur and how might the research be done?

The value of the plan is dependent on forecasting accurately, and in some detail, the likely income and cost streams, but for a new venture these are usually highly unpredictable. Indeed it is often said that the one certain thing about the business plan for a new venture is that the forecasts will not be correct. Therefore it is essential to build into the plan some flexibility that allows for overhead and variable costs, cash flow and revenues being higher or lower than expected. It is worth noting that overtrading is as dangerous as not securing enough revenue, especially where the organization must wait for customers to pay their debts, which can take up to many months and preclude the purchase of further supplies. Banks may be unwilling to make further loans to the venture. There is less risk of this nature in a business that is based on cash sales, where payment is immediate.

## External plans to obtain start up investment

At start up the most obvious purpose of the plan is to provide justification for those considering investing, or providing loans or credit facilities. Indeed there would be little prospect of investment or support from third parties without the business case being presented through a written, formal business plan. In Figure 10.7 are shown the typical elements of a start up business plan.

A badly produced plan will not convince potential investors that the business is likely to be well run. The British Venture Capitalist Association has, in addition, suggested that other signs of extravagance and wasteful expenditure are likely to put off would-be investors (see Spotlight 10.1).

---

- Résumés of founders and key managers
- Statistics relating to sales and markets
- Names of potential customers and anticipated demand
- Names and information about your competitors and your assessment of them
- Financial information required to support your project
- Research and development information
- Production processes and sources of supply
- Information on requirements for factory and plant
- Magazine and newspaper articles about your business and industry
- Regulations and laws that could affect your business
- Product and process protection (patents, copyright, trademarks)

*Adapted from*: The European Venture Capitalist Association at www.evca.com

**Figure 10.7**
The elements of the start up business plan.

---

**Spotlight 10.1**

### Avoiding the appearance of extravagance

On a lighter note, the following signs of extravagance and non-productive company expenditure are likely to discourage a private equity firm from investing and so are best avoided.

- flashy, expensive cars
- company yacht/plane
- personalized number plates
- carpets with the company logo woven in
- company flagpole
- fountain in the forecourt
- 'International' in your name (unless you are!)
- fish tank in the board room
- founder's statue in reception.

*Adapted from*: British Venture Capitalist Association http://www.bvca.co.uk/

**Questions:** How important are visual signs in gaining support? What would you recommend?

---

The focus of a plan for this purpose would need to be financial. If the new venture is targeting an activity with which the investor is familiar, such as hairdressing or a restaurant, the investor will have considerable experience of similar plans and financial projections and would question unrealistic estimates of capital requirements, overheads or variable costs, or selling prices without strong evidence that this new venture will be different from its competitors and likely to be more successful. For genuinely innovative ideas or 'leading edge' technology with which investors could not be expected to be familiar, investors, being risk-averse, would require considerable evidence to be convinced that they should invest.

Business plans are also required by business support agencies to back applications for government-aided grant and loan schemes. Very often the investment in specific organizations is for a specific purpose; for example, support for a community enterprise might be specifically provided:

- to increase the employment prospects of the employees;
- to exploit new growth markets for firms locked in declining sectors;
- to increase R&D; or
- to support exporting activity in a region.

To be successful in these schemes the business plan may need to adopt a particular focus, such as identifying the number of staff to be trained, customers gained in the new growth sectors, new products being generated by the R&D activity or new export markets identified, rather than profits generated.

The emphasis in this framework is on securing outside investment, offering some guarantee of business success against the loans or investments that might be made by banks and the objective here is to demonstrate in the plan how the investors can be reassured that they will get their money back. To that end at least equal emphasis is placed upon the experience, attributes and capabilities of the owners and senior management team as upon the uniqueness or likely success of the proposed idea. Investors recognize that the new venture will not progress smoothly from the initial idea to an established, profitable organization and so when the organization hits problems they would prefer a reliable management team to be in place to deal with the crises.

The plan should reassure the investors that the new business owners have done their 'homework' in obtaining a good understanding of the market, customer demands, the power and influence of competitors and documentary evidence of the industry changes and developments from trade journals. They also expect to be reassured that the owners have a clear understanding of the legislation that affects their organization and whether their intellectual property is secure.

The setting up (facilities, equipment, etc.) and operational aspects of the plan tend to be included as financial information. Investors and banks have a clear idea of what are realistic assessments of investments, income, expenditure and cash flow management. Although the justification of the figures written into the plan might not be expected to be included formally within it, the new-venture owners and managers would be expected to have a very detailed operational plan that would support each of the financial forecasts and they would be expected to be able to answer any questions about the justification of the individual figures.

## The plan for business management

The internal operational plan for managing the business during its early and subsequent phases should be based upon a fairly standard framework. In Figure 10.8 is shown a typical structure for a business plan that includes reflection and analysis of the current situation, the principal assumptions and vision on which the plan is based, the vision, objectives and strategy for the next period, and the budgets, actions, timescales and responsibility allocations for delivery of the plan.

The emphasis on developing a plan for running the operation is to create a framework that enables progress to be checked, and deviations

- The summary or overview
- For the initial plan: the overall vision, a statement of the idea, the market opportunity, and the customer benefits
- For subsequent plans: the overall vision and the principal assumptions underlying the plan
- The situation analysis includes:
  - The assumptions about the environmental and market pressures and changes and the opportunities and threats that emerge
  - The strengths and capabilities of the management team, organization and key partner
  - The identification of any weaknesses and gaps that need to be addressed
- The short- and long-term business objectives
- The strategy
- A detailed list of actions to be undertaken in each area of operation (e.g. production, marketing), timescales and responsibilities
- Resource requirements to support the plan
- Budgets and cash flows
- Performance measures and targets
- Procedures for review, control and taking corrective action.

**Figure 10.8**
The elements of the business plan.

from the plan to be corrected. Coulter (2003: 254) advocates the use of scorecards to keep the business on track and help entrepreneurs communicate the vision to the staff. This inevitably means that the plan will need to be regularly updated as certain actions fail to achieve the results that were forecast or as new ideas and improvements are implemented.

Planning underpins the whole organization and its operations. It is true that many entrepreneurial organizations can achieve considerable short-term impact from opportunistic actions but, in a competitive market, this opportunism must still be integrated and coordinated in order to achieve the maximum long-term impact, necessary for sustainability. Planning is essential in public sector organizations that involve partnerships and stakeholder support. An example is given in Spotlight 10.2.

## Spotlight 10.2

### Learning network for a rural community

NETLinc, set up in 1998, is a project developed in the county of Lincolnshire in the UK in response to the UK government's National Grid for Learning Initiative and was set up by Microsoft and IT services provider, Ramesys. The objective was to give every child in the county a PC and connect them to the Internet. The project has created a community learning portal for children, adults in schools and libraries across the county. The system provides e-mail, filtered Internet access and firewall security, and remote monitoring and support. Each learner and teacher is profiled according to age, ability and interests and appropriate educational material and a graphical interface are provided. New developments have provided mobile learning units and taken computer equipment to more remote village halls and offices. The network also provides a link to wider e-government initiatives.

The project cost £10 million, has 367 schools and 100 000 users and NETLinc claim that 98 per cent of educational establishments connect to NETLinc daily.

*Adapted from*: Poston T., E-business success stories at www.Computerweekly.com, 23 Oct 2001;
and www.netlinc.org

**Question:** What are the most important planning elements in a situation such as this?

In the next chapter we focus on obtaining the necessary resources to support the start up plan and build the ongoing operation. The planning key here is to obtain only the resources that are necessary to establish the business according to the most realistic assessment of the future market situation.

In the final chapter we discuss enterprise strategies and here the planning contribution is to ensure that the strategy to maximize the longer-term performance of the organization is implemented efficiently. This can be achieved by using a plan similar to that shown in Figure 10.8 to build the organization's operation and continuing to manage all of the organization's resources efficiently.

## Summary

- The stages of the business have been defined and it is necessary for entrepreneurs to understand and address the requirements of each of them to enable the business to make a smooth transition between the stages and enhance its chances of success.
- It is important to create and define the business model that underpins the business, the cash flow streams, the customer offer, connection to the market and the place in the supply chain. There are advantages and disadvantages to a conventional and unconventional business model and these should be assessed.
- By identifying the value chain contribution of the venture it is possible to focus the areas of expertise and capability.
- Planning has some critics but, when used as a road map rather than a rigid, formal plan, it can:
  - secure the commitment and support of key stakeholders;
  - define the business and assess its feasibility as a sustainable business; and
  - support and manage the internal development of the organization.

## Chapter questions

1. What are the benefits of carrying out a feasibility study for a bakery that the two owners thereof propose to start in a market town in the North of England? What risks do they face and what aspects of the study would you recommend the owners to particularly concentrate on in order to address the risks?
2. Explain the difference in purpose and contents of a feasibility study, business plan for investors and internal plan to manage the new organization.
3. Explain to a sceptical entrepreneur the benefits of creating a business plan.
4. Why can timing be crucial to the decision to set up a business?
5. What assistance is provided in your area for new start up businesses? Do you consider it to be
   a. appropriate?
   b. sufficient, and why?

## Case study

### Olympic Games

When the International Olympic Committee awarded the 2012 Olympic Games to London many enterprising people could rightfully claim some of the credit. Although Lord Coe, the chairman of the London Organizing Committee and a famous Olympian himself, was praised as the main architect of the success, many others made significant contributions and were heralded as winners, from the Prime Minister, Tony Blair, who worked particularly hard in the final stages to convince the Olympic Committee members, to Princess Anne and David Beckham, who lent their unswerving support, to children from Langdon School in East Ham, East London, who were in Singapore for the announcement, to the many tireless workers that were part of the team.

### The entrepreneur

Perhaps the person who was not quite so much in the limelight at the ceremony to award the games was Keith Mills, the vice-chairman. But the insiders said that it was his steady leadership and pragmatism that was at the heart of the bid, his confident practical approach, getting on with the job and quiet determination to tackle the seemingly impossible tasks. He had done the numbers and was so confident of success in Singapore that 200 planning meetings had already been arranged for after they had won.

He was hired by Barbara Cassini, the then chairman of the bid team at a time when no-one was really interested in bidding for the games. She chose Mills because he was 'self-made' and passionate about sport. Coe adds that he is not traditional or strongly corporate, but instead is creative, seeing the world in a different way. Mills recognized that his 25 years of experience in marketing products throughout the world was appropriate for the bid. A technically excellent product had to be created and marketed domestically and internationally. Mills invented customer-loyalty schemes, selling Air

Miles to British Airways in 1987 and, later, coming up with the Nectar reward scheme. He had already amassed a fortune of £200 m by the time he was appointed.

Despite his success, Mills will not continue as chief executive of the newly formed London Organizing Committee of the Games. He recognizes that his skill is in marketing and that an executive is now needed with experience in a consumer-facing, fast-moving business based on managing logistics, perhaps retailing, to plan and implement the next stages of the preparation. The 'leg-work' for the Olympics is now beginning but Mills prefers starting companies to running them and he has already got new ambitions – to challenge for the Americas Cup sailing competition.

### The preparation for the Games

A huge area of East London needs to be cleared in order to build the Olympic village and this requires the relocation of many people and over 200 businesses. Major construction work is required to create the venues, accommodation, and training, media and support facilities and infrastructure. Entrepreneurs will exploit opportunities to provide additional services and goods that will be Olympics-related such as improved local shopping, and leisure and accommodation facilities. A month after the games were awarded the planning team had a list of 8500 jobs that would need to be done.

### The Games themselves

Fairly obviously, at what will be the biggest supported event, there will be huge challenges to coordinate all the elements necessary to make it a successful Games including competitors, visitors, service providers and media. Already 50 000 people have signed up as volunteers to help. The London bombings that immediately followed the announcement reminded everyone that ensuring security will probably become the biggest headache.

### The potential legacy

The potential legacy of the Games could be increased interest in sport and better facilities, and improvements in health of the population. The construction work will create many tens of thousands of jobs and provide pre-event training facilities and services for the foreign teams with benefits for all parts of the UK. The hope is that a neglected area of East London will benefit from the regeneration that will result and so improve the lives and prospects of the local community.

### Enterprise and planning

It is very rare that any organization has the luxury (or worry) of having seven years to plan an event, knowing that everything must be ready for peak performance during a very short period of time, and that the potential for financial failure is great, given the experience of recent Olympics.

This project requires cooperation between many different interests, public and private, large and small, those that will benefit and those that will be inconvenienced. This will result in the need for entrepreneurship and innovation as well as tight control and monitoring to avoid overspend, fraud and negative publicity, often a danger with projects such as this.

*Source*: adapted from L Armistead, Britain's real Olympic hero, *The Daily Telegraph*, 7 August 2005

### Questions

1. What are the drivers that determine the business planning process for each stage of the project? You will need to define the stages first.
2. How can the various planning challenges, discussed in the last paragraph of the case, be managed?
3. What skills did Mills bring and what will be needed in the next phase? In which aspects of the next phase of the project will entrepreneurship and innovation be needed?

# Help with business planning

## Books

Barrow C., Burke G., Molian D. and Brown, R. (2005) *Enterprise Development: The Challenges of Starting, Growing and Selling Businesses.* London: Thomson.

Hisrich R. (2004) *Small Business Solutions: How to Fix and Prevent the Thirteen Biggest Problems that Derail Business.* New York: McGraw-Hill.

Woods C. (2004) *From Acorns . . . How To Build Your Brilliant Business From Scratch.* London: Pearson Education Ltd.

Zimmerer T.W. and Scarborough N.M. (2005) *Essentials of entrepreneurship and small business management,* 4th edn. Upper Saddle River NJ: Pearson Education Ltd.

## Websites

British Chambers of Commerce
http://www.chamberonline.co.uk
DTI's Small Business service
http://www.sbs.gov.uk
London Business School
http://www.bizplans.co.uk/main.html
http://www.startups.co.uk
National Federation of Enterprise Agencies
http://www.nfea.com
UK government Business Link
http://www.businesslink.gov.uk/bdotg/action/layer?topicId=1073858805&tc=000KW020584170

# References and further reading

Baron R.A. and Shane S.A. (2005) *Entrepreneurship: A Process Perspective.* Mason OH: Thomson South-Western.

Birley S. and Muzyka D.F. (2000) *Mastering Entrepreneurship.* Edinburgh: FT Pitman.

Chaston I. (2000) *Entrepreneurial Marketing.* London: Macmillan Business.

Collins J.C. and Poras J. (2004) In: M.L. Tushman and P. Anderson (eds), *Managing Strategic Innovation and Change,* 2nd edn, Oxford University Press.

Coulter M. (2003) *Entrepreneurship in Action.* Upper Saddle River NJ: Pearson Education Ltd.

Drucker P. (2001) *The Essential Drucker.* Oxford: Butterworth-Heinemann.

Gumpert D.E. (1994) *How to Really Create a Successful Business Plan*. Boston: Magazine Publishing Inc.

Hamel G. and Prahalad C.K. (1994) *Competing for the Future*. Boston: Harvard Business School Press.

Kaplan J.M. (2003) *Patterns of Entrepreneurship*. Hoboken NJ: John Wiley and Sons.

Mintzberg H. (1994) *The Rise and Fall of Strategic Planning*. New York: Free Press.

Moore J.F. (1996) *The Death of Competition: Leadership and Strategy in the Age of Business Ecosystems*. New York: HarperCollins Publishers, Inc., pp. 230–264.

Morgan G. (1997) *Images of Organization*. Thousand Oaks CA: Sage Publications.

Porter M.E. (1985) *Competitive Advantage: Creating and Sustaining Superior Performance*. New York: The Free Press.

Wickham P.A. (2004) *Strategic Entrepreneurship*, 3rd edn. London: FT/Prentice Hall.

## Key words

| | |
|---|---|
| building a sustainable business | formation and launch |
| business case | income streams |
| business model | process of planning |
| business plan | profit or surpluses |
| business proposition | risk |
| entrepreneur's vision | routes to market |
| feasibility study | value chain |

## CHAPTER 11

# Getting started: creating the organization, obtaining resources and reaching break-even

By the end of this chapter the reader will be able to:

- identify the resources that are needed and the decisions that are required for a new venture;
- understand the requirements of forming an organization, including deciding on ownership, obtaining premises at a suitable location and legal protection for the organization and its activities;
- define the various sources of finance and the criteria that will affect the suitability of a particular source for the organization;
- develop a team of staff that will contribute to achieving a sustainable operation;
- understand the marketing and sales that are needed to win over customers and maintain their satisfaction with the organization's offerings;

- determine the critical steps and decisions needed to achieve break-even; and
- appreciate the potential pitfalls in new business starts and how they might be overcome.

## Introduction

It is easy to fall into the trap of believing that the breakthrough step occurs when a market opportunity has been identified and an idea developed that will provide a new solution for potential customers. In practice, of course, all of us spot opportunities and have ideas that we believe could be commercially viable. However, few people are able to make their ideas a commercial reality. In this chapter we discuss the important early stages of creating the organization that will achieve this.

For our purposes an organization is essentially a collection of resources brought together to achieve the principal objective of exploiting an idea, but in doing this we have emphasized throughout this book that a more important objective is to create a sustainable business. For this reason it is not enough to create an organizational vehicle that will simply get the idea to the market because it must also be capable of managing growth to achieve longer-term success. Drucker (2001: 145) identifies the challenges of entrepreneurship as focus on the market, financial foresight (and managing cash flow), and building a team before it is needed (or can be afforded), all topics for this chapter.

In this chapter we focus first upon the formation of the organization, including deciding on its ownership, its legal basis and the protection of its interests, such as its intellectual property. We then go on to discuss the decisions relating to the acquisition of premises and, for example, the problems of securing the right location and having the flexibility for expansion that might result from the growth in the organization's activities.

It is generally recognized that the critical step in the formation of a new business is obtaining the necessary financial investment to purchase the essential resources and fund the early period of development. Of equal importance is the effective management of the organization's finances in order to ensure it does not run out of cash and continues to maintain profitability.

The most critical investment of a company is in its people and, while we do not aim to discuss people management and organizational behaviour at length, we do discuss some success factors in building a team in a new venture.

Without customers there will be no demand for the idea and there will be no organization. Consequently, we discuss the use of marketing and sales in the specific situation of a new start up organization to create awareness among customers and persuade them of the benefits of the new offer to win them over. This involves communication and distribution of the offer and, where necessary, negotiating with potential partners to persuade them to become part of the extended organization.

There is always a limit to the money that people or organizations are prepared to invest or to loan to a new venture. As we have indicated it is essential for an organization to have reached break-even, where income is in balance with outgoings, before it has used up the available and potential financial resources it could attract. For this reason we discuss the management of the organization up to break-even and the potential problems it might encounter up until that point.

We follow this up with the final section, which is devoted to the major challenge for most new businesses, i.e. dealing with the constant stream of problems that must be solved, situations that must be managed and crises that require an immediate response.

## Forming the organization

Although not strictly concerned with obtaining resources we first focus on creating the organization that provides the framework for organizing and protecting the resources. At the outset it is important to recognize that the aim of entrepreneurship is to create a venture that is self-sustaining by transforming an initial idea into a commercial success from the limited resources available. Many of the best known organizations today, such as McDonalds, Vodafone and Microsoft started from humble beginnings. Many too, such as Nokia, IBM and Barnardos (Enterprise in Action 12.5) have changed substantially from their original purpose as they have responded to the changing environment.

The starting point, therefore, is to decide what kind of organization should be formed and what resources are required, by considering certain questions, which are listed in Figure 11.1.

In answering the first questions it is necessary to take the first steps in forming an organization, which are:

- deciding between the various forms of ownership of the organization;
- obtaining legal protection for the organization and any important aspects of its operation, such as the product idea or brand name; and
- acquiring premises.

**Figure 11.1**
Some key questions
for the start up and
early stages of the
business.

- What sort of venture should be created?
- Who will own the venture?
- How will the business be financed?
- How will it be managed?
- Who will make the key decisions and how will the responsibilities be shared?
- Who will have the responsibility for building the customer base and what resources are required for this?
- How will the supply chain activities (e.g. production and distribution) be delivered and who will be responsible for them?
- What other key external stakeholders with power and influence must be convinced of the benefits of the new offer?
- What will be the critical success factors for the operation, what are likely to be the challenges and barriers to success and how might they be overcome?

**Figure 11.2**
The elements of a
partnership
agreement.

- The name, location and purpose of the partnership
- The names and addresses of the partners
- The personal contributions of each partner including cash, assets and services
- The decision-making authority of each partner
- The decision areas where consensus is required
- The work responsibilities of each partner
- The duration of the partnership
- The distribution of profits or losses
- The procedure for dispute resolution and dissolution of the partnership
- The procedure for dealing with the death or disability of one partner
  *Source*: Baron and Shane (2005) and Coulter (2003)

## Alternative ownership models

For new start up organizations there are a number of alternative ownership models, as explained below.

*Sole trader* is the most popular way to start up and requires minimal formality. The proprietor has sole ownership and complete control over the way the business is run. However, the downside is that the proprietor has all the responsibility too, and (as the law does not distinguish between the business and the owner) all the liability should things go wrong. In the worst case the business fails with substantial debts and the owner could be made bankrupt too.

*Partnership* is where ownership is shared, but all the partners are jointly and severally liable should things go wrong. There is a great deal of opportunity for disagreements in partnerships as businesses grow and the circumstances of the partners change, and it is strongly advisable to draw up a partnership agreement before the business is set up. Sharing the burden, being able to draw upon someone else's ideas in making decisions, and having complementary skills are positive advantages of choosing to be a partnership. However, each partner loses some autonomy, and decision-making can be slower.

The partnership agreement is the key to anticipating and resolving potential partnership problems; some key elements of the agreement are given in Figure 11.2.

Having a partner or a financial backer usually means that the entrepreneur has to jump through hoops to keep them satisfied. In Pause and Reflect 11.1, however, it is shown that just occasionally even the most dynamic go-getting partner meets his match.

## Pause and Reflect 11.1

### Wallace, Gromit and the curse of the man from Hollywood

Nick Park created Wallace and Gromit in 1983, when he was a student at the National Film and Television School. He wrote to Peter Sallis, a star of the TV programme Last of the Summer Wine, begging him to be the voice of his plasticine model, Wallace, for his film A Grand Day Out in exchange for a £50 donation to charity. Sallis was rather puzzled and had probably forgotten all about this when, seven years later, Park phoned him to say that the film had been made. Since then Sallis has been the voice of Wallace, earning rather more than £50, and Park has arguably become the most successful UK Oscar winner with Creature Comforts (1991) beating his own A Grand Day Out, The Wrong Trousers (1994) and A Close Shave (1996). Park then turned his attention to full-length films with The Chicken Run (2000), the first of five scheduled films.

His first 85-minute movie was Wallace and Gromit: The Curse of the Were-Rabbit, released in October 2005. It was backed to the tune of £40 million by DreamWorks, makers of Shrek 2. And there was the rub. Because the plasticine models must be altered for every shot and there are 24 frames per second, up to 24 separate poses are shot for every second in the scene. About three seconds of usable film are shot every day and the film has taken five years to complete. So life moves very slowly for Park.

By contrast Jeffrey Katzenberg, chief executive of DreamWorks, lives very fast and is everything Park is not. He is a sharp dresser and fast talker, and full of confidence, and he has earned the reputation of being the most irritating little man in Hollywood. He flies in to Filton, Bristol, in his executive jet from Los Angeles to badger and cajole Park into speeding up. Park keeps his control while Katzenberg talks a lot, gives his opinions and then flies off again.

Park comments drily that '. . . it is a privilege that he takes the interest to write the cheque. I also feel grateful that he lives about 6000 miles away!'

*Adapted from:* Pearce G., 'One man and his dog have Hollywood on the run',
*The Sunday Times*, 25 September 2005

**Question:** What do you consider to be the requirements for a successful partnership?

***Limited company*** has the advantage of limiting the owner's liability to what they have invested should things go wrong, but is administratively much more complicated, with various legal requirements concerning the filing of accounts, annual general meetings, etc. It is also much more complicated to wind the business down.

*Cooperatives* are owned and democratically controlled by their members rather than investors. Members are the people that use the service or buy the products. Cooperatives fall into four general categories: consumer, producer, worker and purchasing/shared service cooperatives. They are formed by their members (Barrow *et al.*, 2005: 106) when the marketplace fails to provide needed goods or services of acceptable quality or at affordable prices. They operate in virtually every industry and range in size from large enterprises to small local businesses.

*Charitable status* The Charities Commission through its website provides advice for UK-based charities. According to the Commission, for an organization to be a charity it must fall within the law's understanding of 'charity' and be subject to the jurisdiction of the High Court according to the Charities Act. In order to fall within that definition an organization must have purposes which are exclusively charitable and must be set up for the benefit of the public. These purposes fall under four headings, the relief of poverty; the advancement of education; the advancement of religion; and other purposes beneficial to the community.

*Public ownership* There are various ownership models for community-based projects and usually there is some element of partnership in the delivery (see Spotlight 10.2).

## Ownership situations

There are a number of specific situations where particular models of ownership and formation are used, and we discuss some of these below.

*Franchise* is a system of distribution in which legally independent business owners pay fees and royalties to a company (the franchisor) in return for the right to use its trademark, sell its products and services or use its business model. In the USA it is estimated that there are 5000 franchisors with 650 000 outlets run by franchisees. A good franchise agreement can provide the owners with a strong brand name, equipment, and financial and managerial support but they must also understand the implications of the franchise agreement. Owners can be tied into legal arrangements that limit their autonomy and prevent them from making changes that are necessary. Moreover, the ongoing financial commitments to the franchisor may become onerous particularly if the franchisor sets up too many franchisees in a limited area, thus restructuring the franchisees' potential growth. For example, McDonalds was criticized by some of its franchisees who saw their revenue drop as new franchises were opened.

*Spin-outs* A specific situation for start up businesses that often has a slightly different ownership model is a spin-out from higher education institutes. The reason for highlighting this specific situation is that in many countries a considerable amount of government funding goes into supporting university research to benefit the community at large, for example, medical research. Quite frequently this research can lead to the development of ideas that have the potential to be launched commercially. As the pressure intensifies on universities to generate additional income streams to teaching and government and industry-funded research, many of the more technologically advanced universities have been encouraged by national and regional government to spin out their best commercial ideas from the university. Usually the university and the individual inventor take a share of the ownership in the business that is created.

The rationale for creating a separate spin-out business is that by operating independently from a university it is free to operate in a much more entrepreneurial way, with fewer constraints from the bureaucratic management that is necessary for a university. In practice the success rate of spin-outs has not been as high as might be expected (Lambert, 2003). One reason for this is that very often the ideas are based on leading edge, innovative technology but are a long way from being market-ready products, because they are poorly developed in terms of customer requirements, viable businesses rather than research models and efficient business operations. Quite frequently, therefore, substantial amounts of money need to be either invested in or loaned to the spin-out company and the path to commercialization can be difficult.

Quite often a preferable way of obtaining income for universities from their research is to work in partnership with existing large organizations by offering licensing arrangements, contract research or consultancy for their scientific, technical and other knowledge-based solutions.

## Management buy-out and buy-in ownership models

Most of the business models and forms of ownership that we have discussed so far, perhaps with the exception of franchising, have centred on the generation of an idea by the organization as the reason for business start. A separate situation for business ownerships is **management buy-outs** (MBOs) and **management buy-ins** (MBIs); in Pause and Reflect 11.2 is given an example of an MBO that has resisted the temptation to make a quick profit.

## Pause and Reflect 11.2

### Interfleet – taking the MBO track

When the rail industry in the UK was privatized in the early 1990s, British Rail was broken up into many operating companies. This provided the opportunity for many of the senior managers in British Rail to buy out their division or department for it to become an independent business. Consolidation usually occurs after such events as many of the independent companies are taken over by acquisitive companies. For many managers this is the opportunity to get rich quickly by selling out their MBO a few months later.

One business that bucked this trend was Interfleet Technology, which was originally the Intercity engineering division of British Rail, bought in 1994 by an MBO led by David Rollin. Rather than taking the easy option of selling out it set about developing a leading international rail consultancy business operating out of Derby and London. The business expanded quickly based on its highly experienced staff with the number of consultants increasing from 120 to 450. Export activity drove this expansion, leading to new offices being set up in Australia, the USA, Germany and Sweden. The company has carried out projects in 26 countries across the world.

*Source*: Bryan Lowe

**Question:** What drives the decision for an MBO management (a) to sell out quickly at a profit, and (b) to build a sustainable, fast-growing business?

An MBO is the purchase of a business by the existing management team. This usually occurs when a large company wishes to dispose of parts of the business or when an existing owner-manager decides to retire. This option is often preferable to the existing owner than closing the business down or selling it to a competitor. Moreover, the existing management are often best placed to develop the business, given their knowledge of the market, company operation and workforce.

For the new potential owners this may provide the opportunity for ownership and independence, which they may have long dreamed about, making a lot of money and without many of the start-up risks. MBOs, however, usually require more capital investment than start ups because they are usually substantial and valuable businesses and this may create a problem for the potential owners. MBOs are usually attractive for venture capitalists to invest in, provided a strong case is made, as some of the risk of a start up from scratch is removed, given that the management team, operations and revenue streams are already established.

An MBI occurs when an outside management team buys a stake in an existing business, usually one that is underperforming owing to ineffective existing management or where faster growth is possible if a more capable management team is in place. In return for the new managers using their experience in the firm to improve performance they share in the success through ownership.

**Table 11.1**
Some areas of legislation affecting new ventures

| Areas of legislation | Some examples |
|---|---|
| Business structure | Sole trader, partnership, limited company |
| Trading name | The name of the organization and website |
| Trading laws | Restrictions on the way the organization trades with the public |
| Terms of trading | Dealing with suppliers and other partners in the supply chain |
| Employing people | The rights of the employees and the organization |
| Intellectual property: trademarks, copyrights and patents | Protecting the organization's products and ideas |
| Insurance | Damage or loss of property or data |
| Taxation | VAT, corporation tax, staff and owner income |

# Legal protection for the organization and its stakeholders

There is a legislative framework for setting up and running a business, ensuring health and safety, employment rights and financial and accounting management. It is intended to provide protection for the various stakeholders of the venture.

Business start up books cover these areas in detail and we provide a summary of some key areas in Table 11.1.

# Intellectual property

While most of these areas are mandatory, **intellectual property** requires decisions based on commercial judgement. Intellectual property is often known as IP, and allows people to own their creativity and innovation in the same way that they can own physical property. The owner of IP can control it and be rewarded for its use, and this encourages further innovation and creativity to the benefit to the community.

In some cases IP gives rise to protection for ideas but in other areas there will have to be more elaboration of an idea before protection can arise. Often it will not be possible to protect IP and gain IP rights (or

IPRs) unless they have been applied for and granted, but some IP protection such as copyright arises automatically, without any registration, as soon as there is a record in some form of what has been created, for example the drawing of a design or a music score.

The four main types of IP are:

1. *patents* for inventions including new and improved products and processes that are capable of industrial application;
2. *trade marks* for the brand identity of goods and services allowing distinctions to be made between different traders;
3. *designs* for the appearance of the whole or a part of a product resulting from the features of, in particular, the lines, contours, colours, shape, texture or materials of the product itself or its ornamentation;
4. *copyright* for material including literary and artistic material, music, films, sound recordings and broadcasts, including software and multimedia.

However, IP is much broader than these categories as it extends to trade secrets, plant varieties, geographical indications, performers' rights and so on.

In the UK a patent for an invention is granted by government to the inventor, giving the inventor the right in law for a limited period of 20 years to stop others from making, using or selling the invention without the permission of the inventor. When a patent is granted, the invention becomes the property of the inventor, which – like any other form of property or business asset – can be bought, sold, rented or hired. Patents are territorial rights; a UK patent will only give the holder rights within the United Kingdom and rights to stop others from importing the patented products into the United Kingdom.

To qualify for the grant of a patent, an invention has to be:

- new and details should not have been previously published;
- involve an inventive step that has not been done by others;
- be capable of industrial application; and
- must not fall into an 'excluded' category, which includes literary works, scientific theories and methods for doing business.

## Disadvantages of patenting an idea

- Disclosure of the innovation enables competitors to analyse it and find a way of achieving the same objectives by getting around the patent through appropriate changes. Large firms have departments that work solely on this.

- It may be difficult to defend as the legal costs for a small firm could be huge, especially if the patent is infringed by a powerful competitor.
- It is often impossible to find out about patent infringement of processes that are carried out in the privacy of a competitor's premises and may not change the appearance of the final product.
- It is expensive to make patent applications to cover all the countries in the world where patent infringement could occur.
- In some sectors 20 years may be too short a period to recover R&D costs, whereas in fast-moving high-technology areas the period during which the patent is valuable could be insignificant as the technology moves on.

Where appropriate it may be preferable to use copyrights and trademarks, such as the golden arches of McDonalds and the 'swoosh' symbol of Nike, as they provide more effective forms of protection. Baron and Shane (2005: 278) explain that it may be best to avoid divulging essential knowledge and keeping trade secrets, such as the Colonel Sanders KFC recipe, but the danger with this approach is that if someone independently determines the formula and so long as there is no evidence of theft, there is no legal protection.

## Premises

For most small and growing businesses the decisions relating to obtaining **premises** and moving to new premises present real dilemmas. It is often suggested that businesses never have the right premises, as they are usually too small or too large and they could always be in a more visible and convenient location. The reason for this of course is that, for a growing business, there is only a short period when the building is working at its optimum capacity.

For a new venture there are three main choices:

1. *Working from home* The benefits of working from home are fairly obviously that there is no additional cost; it is convenient as there is no travelling time; and it can fit in with domestic responsibilities convenient for parents with young children. The disadvantages are quite obvious for anyone who regularly

works from home, including the distractions of domestic duties, the difficulty of 'getting away from work' and the loneliness of not being in contact with others, although this is a problem of self-employment generally. There are other considerations too, such as health and safety issues, tax implications, security, segregating the work area and even the danger of annoying the neighbours if a lot of traffic movements are involved. Customers might also be more impressed by a prestigious office address.

2.  ***Renting property*** The benefits of renting are that capital is not tied up in the building and that renting also increases flexibility for a rapidly growing business. The cost of renting properties varies enormously and, when added to rates and insurance, the costs can be become high. It is essential to balance cost with the benefits of a particular location. The disadvantages are that there may be restrictions on how the property can be used or changed and certain property landlords can be unscrupulous in adding restrictions and increasing rents.

3.  ***Buying property*** While the disadvantage of buying property is the tying up of capital, the advantage is that the mortgage repayments to purchase the premises are likely to be lower than renting costs and the venture will eventually own the premises. The owner has more flexibility over the use of the premises although there are normally still restrictions on its use and if the space is not required by the organization the property can be a source of rental income for the business.

The choice of premises depends upon a number of factors including:

- ***Location*** The major consideration of location should be based on proximity to customers and, for many retail outlets, the business location is likely to be the most critical decision of all as it may well make or break the venture. Many retailers need to be located in areas where their customers are and other early-stage organizations are dependent on 'passing trade' until they have built a reputation, at which point customers are prepared to go out of their way to visit.

- ***Space*** Given the high cost of space and the need to maintain a low level of fixed costs, new ventures should occupy only the space they need for their activities now and in the near future. The problem, of course, is that moving premises is both costly and disruptive to the organization and its customers and should be avoided if at all possible. The challenge is therefore to strike a balance between the two.

- *Cost* Ventures have to find appropriate premises that are right for their business activities and offer value for money. They can be tempted to occupy either high-cost, high-profile, ostentatious buildings that will present the 'right image' to customers or large, low-cost buildings that appear to be suitable for future expansion and that are poorly maintained and located. There is, of course, the danger that the venture may spend too much management time on property development rather than running the core business.

- *Customers* Customers are influenced by the appearance of premises and it is surprising that many organizations fail to look at their premises from the customer viewpoint, and to consider not just location, but cleanliness, decoration and so on, which are often relatively inexpensive to put right. A faded sign or weeds growing through the car park for example, may indicate a low-quality organization.

- *Grants* Local authorities often produce lists of vacant properties and premises in an area and provide grants and rent-free holidays to entice organizations to locate in less-attractive areas. While many new ventures will find this appealing and beneficial they should not be unduly influenced and, instead, should consider the other business reasons for choosing a particular location.

- *Competition* While it might seem obvious to avoid premises close to the competition, there may be some good reasons to do the opposite if the venture can benefit from a greater footfall in the area or believes it can offer a better proposition to customers and could benefit from them making a direct comparison.

For the smallest firms small, often informal, premises designed primarily to assist the venture to grow, can be found. Local authorities and other local government agencies often provide managed workspace or business incubator centres that include shared resources, such as computing infrastructure and receptionist or secretarial services. Some prestigious innovation centres and science parks offer mailboxes to allow businesses to be run from home yet have an impressive mail address and the opportunity to rent meeting- and conference-rooms by the hour.

## Obtaining the necessary finance

All new ventures require start up finance to 'pump prime' the activities that will ultimately generate sufficient revenues and surplus cash to pay for the subsequent purchases of materials, services and labour. There are few occasions when the entrepreneur has enough personal resources for it to be unnecessary to use external sources of finance of some sort, but they do exist and in Enterprise in Action 11.1 an example is given. Generally, external sources are needed and there are many to choose from. These are dealt with at length in the start up guides and websites listed. For a start up venture there are advantages and disadvantages associated with each lender. On the other side of the coin, the individual and organizational investors must weigh up the attractiveness of the proposition and the probability of high returns with the risk of underperformance of failure and the loss of the money invested.

### Enterprise in Action 11.1

**Global business and not a penny borrowed**

Jurga Zilinskienne became an entrepreneur at the age of 6 when she found some packets of seeds in the family home in Lithuania. She took them to the market and sold them but realized, given the long queues that formed, that she must be selling at too low a price. At 10 she used the family pets to get into pet breeding and also bought sweets to sell to her schoolmates.

By 16, Zilinskienne was importing clothes from the United Arab Emirates and selling them on, and a year later opened a small supermarket. After an unsuccessful marriage she moved at age 19 to the UK to study law. She did not complete the course but instead in 2001 started a translating business, Today Translations. She now has over 200 clients and a huge team of linguists. Her legal education proved of some use as 80 per cent of her business is with law firms. In 2004 her turnover was £600 000 and she was planning to double that in the following year.

Perhaps the most surprising thing about her however, is that she has only ever invested her own money into the business, £13 000, and she has never borrowed a penny form a bank – very unlike the British!

*Adapted from*: www.startups.co.uk on 18 September 2005

**Question:** What do you to consider the advantages and disadvantages of financing the business in this way?

## Personal and informal finance

*Personal funds* The majority of new ventures start with quite limited funding. The money often comes from the personal savings of the entrepreneur or a loan, or through remortgaging the entrepreneur's own home. Credit card limits have increased and provide short-term finance for working capital (Bolton and Thompson, 2000: 322). Kaplan (2003: 156) explains that many businesses are started by 'moonlighting', where an entrepreneur continues in employment while starting the new venture in his or her spare time.

*Family and friends* are a further source of funding through loans, but sometimes this is formalized so that the friends or family take a small share in the ownership and future returns, rather than expecting their money back in the short term.

*Sweat equity* Perhaps the hidden funding of a start up is '**sweat equity**' where the owners of the venture roll up their sleeves and work for lower rates of income than the work is worth. In some cases the owners work for nothing to get the business started.

The disadvantage with these sources of funding is that personal and work life become inextricably linked and put at risk the entrepreneur's personal finances and adversely affect relationships with family and friends. A further problem of using informal sources is that there is a danger that the venture will be undercapitalized. The organization works 'hand to mouth' with little money to spare for even small investments that could improve efficiency and effectiveness.

The attraction for the entrepreneur of using personal and informal sources plus bank loans is that this precludes, or at least limits, people from outside the organization having a say in its decisions and allows it to stay truly independent. If venture capitalists or business angels invest they wish to maximize their long-term returns and minimize their risk, and so wish to give their advice as to how the business should operate. While some entrepreneurs welcome this, others do not.

## External funds

There are three broad categories of external funding:

### Debt

**Debt** is funding that is derived, usually, from a bank, in the form of a loan and accrues interest. The interest charge is an ongoing expense of the organization and the capital must be repaid at set points in time. Overdrafts are essentially short-term bank loans but the interest rate can fluctuate and they can be called in at any time. They are therefore useful only for short-term needs.

Term loans are more formal arrangements with a set term of, for example, 3 or 10 years. The lender usually requires security, such as the assets that were purchased with the loan (e.g. vehicles or premises), but the entrepreneurial organization gains from the confidence in having money for the term of the loan, so long as it can keep up the repayments. The time when the loan is taken out can be important if the interest rates are fixed. Sometimes this can be advantageous, sometimes not! Governments often provide loan guarantee schemes for small businesses in order to provide favourable rates on what the lender normally considers high-risk business that should attract high interest rates.

## Grants

Grants are sometimes available and involve neither interest and capital repayment nor giving an equity stake in return, but eligibility criteria come into play, for example firms being of a particular size. It is essential that the organization does not change its strategy simply to obtain a grant.

## Equity

**Equity** in the organization is provided by the shareholders including the owner. They expect to get a return either from the annual profit or, if the profit is retained to fund expansion of the firm, by having the opportunity to sell their increasingly valuable share in the organization at some point in the future. Although there are various schemes in existence we focus here on two, which are discussed in greater detail by Muzyka and Birley (2000: 104) and Mason and Harrison (2000: 110).

*Venture capital* (*VC*) **Venture capital** firms make investments in new business opportunities on behalf of clients, for example, in the form of pension funds. VCs look for growth potential so that they can provide a good return on their clients' investment while also avoiding high-risk activities where there might be a danger of losing their clients' money. Because of the nature of their client needs, VCs operate on a medium- to long-term timescale with regard to their investment performance.

It is important to remember that, to realize the growth in their investment, VCs need to exit from their involvement in the business, by selling their share of the business to others. Often this is done when the business is sold to new owners or floated on the stock market. If the entrepreneur owner wishes to retain control it is necessary for them to buy out the VC's share of the business. VCs manage portfolios of investments, some of which do better than others, so they look for high returns from the companies they invest in to cover the potential losses and will expect 30 per cent minimum.

Spotlight 11.1 emphasizes that timing is important as the financial situation and the state of the financial markets can be important too for venture capitalist investment and exiting.

---

## Spotlight 11.1

### 3i

#### *Getting out while the going is good*

Over the five-month period to September 2005, 3i, the quoted venture capitalist, collected £6 million per day (£910 million against £577 million the previous year) as it cashed in some of its investments. The last time a similar thing had happened was at the height of the dot-com boom in 2000. Then, 3i was realizing its investments in technology businesses, whereas this time management buy outs seemed to have been a significant factor, with the sale of Travelex, a *bureau de change*, for £1 billion, and of the directories business, Yellow Brick Road, for £1.3 billion. The main reason for the good performance this time was the high level of stock markets and the excellent financial conditions for exiting from companies and investing in others.

*Adapted from*: Hope C., 'Venture capitalist 3i nets £6 m a day with more in the pipeline',

*Daily Telegraph*, 30 September 2005

**Question:** Where might the conflicts lie between the interests of venture capitalists and the organization receiving the investment?

---

VCs aim to protect their own interests and investments and usually want to influence the strategy of the entrepreneurial organization. VCs expect the owner to take advice and, to ensure this, they often select a non-executive director to serve on the board. VCs are more cautious of investing in pure start-ups as they tend to be the most risky and instead are likely to prefer MBOs and MBIs.

The costs of an investment project are high as they require an in-depth study of the organization and its market (due diligence) and so VCs rarely invest less than £1 m in an individual project. It is only appropriate, therefore, for low numbers of businesses and, as Figure 11.3 shows, it is both a good team and a good idea that are necessary to ensure high returns. It is important to remember that there is a degree of competition among those seeking funds from VCs and business angels. If there is an alternative opportunity to invest their money and obtain a higher return and/or lower risk they will take it.

***Business angels*** These are wealthy individuals who are willing to invest in more speculative projects, where others, such as VCs, 'fear to tread'. They are more informal suppliers of risk capital, are often private investors and sometimes they lose money, but sometimes they win.

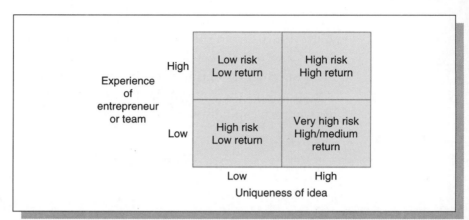

**Figure 11.3**
Risk and return for
funders.

Frequently they 'mentor' their clients too. It is difficult to estimate how much investment comes from **business angels** because it is informal. Equinox Management Consultants (2000) note that 98 per cent of business angels are male, and that many are millionaires, often previously entrepreneurs themselves with an average age of 50. They reject 90 per cent of applications at the first screening. Often their investments are located close to where they live, presumably so that they can keep an eye on them. They back people rather than propositions and are typically five times more likely to invest in start ups than are VCs.

## Problems of financing the business

In practice, most early-stage organizations will use a mix of funding arrangements to achieve the greatest efficiency. For small firms however, there can be some limitations. Due to the high transaction cost for investors of preparing and managing small investments or loans, Chaston (2000: 176) comments that small firms often have difficulty in raising relatively small amounts of money (£10 000–£50 000).

There are a number of dangers for new ventures in arranging finance. A very successful organization may grow very rapidly and this may make big demands on the cash resources to fund the expansion (equipment, operations, staff and working capital). Alternatively, a new venture must have financial arrangements that are robust enough to cope with a downturn. Problems arise as there can be a temptation to regard all sources of income in the same way but short-term funds need to be used for managing working capital fluctuation and not financing longer-term investments, such as equipment and premises that should be funded out of long-term debt finance or equity.

## Other forms of financing

Other forms of financing the business can be used, for example **invoice factoring** (see Spotlight 11.2), invoice leasing, hire purchase and leasing.

---

### Spotlight 11.2

#### Giving credit where it's due

Arguably for an early-stage business, managing cash flow can be the most critical issue and taking immediate action against late payers is vital. After 60 days the likelihood of being paid falls to 80 per cent, after 6 months to 50 per cent and, after 1 year, to 10 per cent.

On average, invoices are paid 19 days late in the UK and, like many other countries firms can charge interest, at the rate of 8 per cent above the Bank of England base rate. In practice, companies do not implement this because they do not wish to upset customers.

Small firms must be proactive, implement good credit management, and monitor their customers' credit rating. They must also invoice accurately and immediately to avoid disputes in the first place. One approach is to use factoring.

In five years Pendragon, a Hampshire-based recruitment agency, has grown from zero to a £5 million turnover. The owners, Steve Johnstone and Richard Hall, have used factoring to better manage their finances.

Factoring involves using a specialized company to collect payments and chase debts. Pendragon issues the invoices and HSBC advances 85 per cent of the money. The remainder, less their fee, which in Pendragon's case is 1 per cent of turnover, is received when the invoices are paid. Factoring has a number of advantages for Pendragon. It allows them the time to get on with their core business and they are not diverted into chasing bad debts (one or two of their customers seem to go bust every year), it smooths out their cash flow and their working capital is not tied up in debts and can be used to develop the business, making it unnecessary to refinance the business.

*Adapted from:* 'Pendragon gives credit where it's due', *Daily Telegraph*, 16 August 2005

**Question:** What are the benefits and disadvantages of factoring?

---

In practice this demonstrates that obtaining finance for the venture is tied very closely to the ongoing financial management of the organization. A highly disciplined approach to managing the finance can reduce the funds required later. Some years ago Ian MacMillan, director of the Snider Entrepreneurial Centre, emphasized this in his suggested approach to purchasing:

- Never buy new what can be bought second-hand.
- Never buy what can be rented.
- Never rent what can be borrowed.
- Never borrow what can be begged.
- Never beg what can be salvaged.

## Building and leading the team

Earlier in this book we discussed the characteristics of entrepreneurs, and highlighted, first, their approach to setting up new ventures, second, the difficulties that some have managing the routine of day-to-day activity needed to build a sustainable business, and third, their reluctance or inability to delegate responsibilities to other managers in the organization, in order to give themselves the time to focus on the next development.

In taking the embryo venture from initial idea through the early days of the venture to launch, the particular characteristics that the entrepreneur contributes are leadership and an ability to understand and focus on the details of the venture. This enables the entrepreneur to:

- take strategic and operational decisions and speed up their implementation;
- understand the whole picture, and have a detailed understanding of the market, finances and supply chain;
- be able to stretch the capability of the venture to the maximum and deliver extraordinary results;
- negotiate with suppliers, customers and partners to obtain the most favourable results for the organization;
- make connections with a network of people that can assist the organization informally or formally; and
- lead from the front on projects and take responsibility for all decisions, and also use their personal charisma to enthuse other members of staff.

Many entrepreneurs, however, fail to take the time to create a competent management and staff team that complements their own capabilities and fail to delegate tasks to the new staff, and so fail to maximize the potential of the team. To avoid these failures:

- the founder has to learn to be the leader of a team rather than a 'star' with helpers (Drucker, 1985);
- it is necessary to build a **management team** before the team is really needed, so that the team can be tested and prove their capabilities. The reason for this is that teams take time to develop relationships, trust and confidence before they can perform effectively. However, in the early days of a new venture, it may not be possible to afford to employ a full management team. The case study at the end of Chapter 2 (http://strategis.ic.gc.ca) shows how Steve Perez's staff worked

for nothing for him after he went bust, to get the new business going;

■ the critical success factor for a team is to build complementary skills and capabilities. It is necessary to determine what each member of the team is good at, and what other strengths are needed;

■ the key activities and requirements of the business, together with the gaps in the capability of the team to deliver, must be identified;

■ the team works informally at first to carry out their tasks and cover the gaps but eventually decisions must be taken regarding more formalized roles and responsibilities, and more formal identification of the gaps in capability;

■ at this stage it may be necessary to seek outside advice, either to assist training for existing staff or recruitment of new staff with complementary skills.

Cartwright and Cooper (2000: 212) emphasize the need for the entrepreneur to recognize the dynamics of team working and manage the process of building a high performance entrepreneurial team. Alongside building the internal team, building the network of external contacts is important too.

## Marketing and sales

## The nature and role of marketing in a new venture

So far in this chapter on obtaining resources, everything that we have discussed involves additional cost to the organization. Obtaining the resources to market and sell products and services also means additional cost but **marketing and selling** is the only element that generates income. In reality most businesses fail because they are unable to generate sales quickly enough in the early stages or do not succeed in sustaining the sales levels through customer repeat purchasing or winning over new customers.

As with other areas of business planning there are some benefits for the new venture in adopting a systematic, planned approach to marketing and selling, involving analysis, consideration of options, identifying priorities and identifying the tasks. While this is emphasized by Carter and Jones-Evans (2000) (see Figure 11.4), it is important to recognize that with limited resources available in a new venture and the

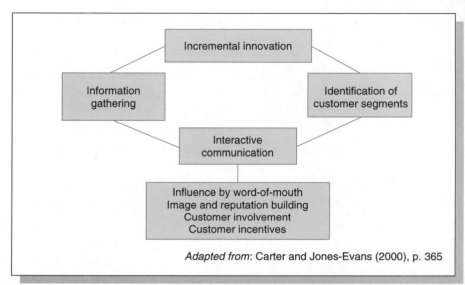

**Figure 11.4**
Creating awareness
and persuading
customers.

informality of the management, the preferred approach is incremental and interactive, rather than being based on the type of formal, rigid programmes and processes that a large firm would adopt. Such an approach allows for opportunism and many of the most successful new ventures have used highly innovative marketing and selling approaches, for example in the use of PR and advertising. Entrepreneurs, such as Richard Branson, Stelios Haji-Ioannou and Alan Sugar have used their own personality, interests and fame to build awareness in their companies. Baron and Shane (2005: 258) suggest that forming alliances with established firms is another useful ploy, citing George Foreman's alliance with Sears to sell his grilling machine.

## Marketing and selling the products and services

For most new ventures the biggest problem is to find potential customers quickly enough, explain to them the benefits of the product or service and persuade them to buy in sufficient quantity to generate the necessary revenue. Marketing embraces the whole customer- or client-oriented activity and selling focuses on building relationships and negotiating with the customer in order to maximize the revenue. While a new organization may not be able to afford staff specifically appointed to these tasks it is essential that someone takes responsibility for carrying out the tasks.

The following questions are crucial in assessing whether sales can be generated quickly.

■ ***Who exactly are the customers going to be?*** For example, there is no point wasting time selling to customers that have supply contracts from which they cannot escape without penalty. It is essential to know when the customers are 'in the market' to consider alternative offers and the EO must prepare to sell to them at that point.

■ ***How many can you switch to your offer?*** As we shall see later in the diffusion curve, only a relatively small proportion of customers want to be the first to try out groundbreaking ideas. Most customers wait to see whether the first customers to buy are satisfied with the new product or service, so it is important to focus the initial marketing and sales efforts on the most immediate prospects.

■ ***Who needs to be influenced – the customer, the retailer and/or the expert?*** As fewer distributors and retailers wield more power and dominate more and more business sectors it is becoming more important to influence the intermediaries. Also, experts in certain sectors can be very influential in recommending to customers new products, services and ideas that they believe will be of benefit.

■ ***What are the routes to the market, and what might be the barriers?*** In our discussion of the business model we highlighted the possibility of using alternative routes to the market and these need to be assessed in terms of their cost-effectiveness but also in terms of any barriers or disadvantages, such as the domination of a distribution channel by a powerful competitor or the new venture's lack of market power to control strong distribution channel members.

■ ***How will competitors respond – will you be tolerated as not significant or will you be a threat?*** Many new ventures adopt a low-profile market entry approach and operate a targeted marketing approach to customers, so that they can build early revenues before they are seen as a threat. While a high-profile market entry might lead to greater customer awareness it might also prompt a greater response from competitors.

## The extended organization

A small organization with limited resources can leverage the resources of other organizations by forming partnerships in order to market complementary products and making connections with influencers in the market. Even retailers or distributors that handle many products can be persuaded to put extra effort into promoting one organization's offering if good relationships have been built.

*Network brokers* help to facilitate networks of complementary organizations in becoming capable of selling to larger customers, whereas individually they could not. For example, a network formed from a company selling PCs together with a carpet fitter, interior designer and office furniture supplier got together to sell 'whole office' solutions to companies.

## Use of contacts

Contact can be used in all sorts of ways and charity fundraising is one example. Events such as Band Aid and Live8 involved using an extended network of celebrities, entertainment entrepreneurs and technical support staff. Sometimes, as shown in Enterprise in Action 11.2, an individual entrepreneur can mobilize a multiplicity of talents without being part of the resulting group, provided that the idea is compelling.

---

### Enterprise in Action 11.2

#### Answer to fundraising on a postcard

Daisy Bell was 20 and a psychology student when her uncle, Robin Needham, died in the South-East Asian tsunami in 2004. With two university friends she decided to raise £10 000 for Care International in his memory. Robin Needham's life's work had been spent working to help in the developing world and he was head of Care – Nepal Aids Charity. He died during a holiday in Indonesia, when trying to move people to high ground after the disaster struck.

Daisy had the idea of asking 300 artists, musicians and celebrities to fill a blank postcard with their art or doodlings. The result was a unique collection of works by people such as Sir Paul McCartney, David Hockney, Anthony Gormley and Charlotte Church. She was determined to get a contribution from Damien Hirst but her five letters were politely rejected by a secretary, before she found a connection through her sister's school and a next-door neighbour. Christie's auctioned the first 65 cards and, with the remainder auctioned online, a sum in excess of £50 000 was raised.

*Adapted from:* Iqquiden A., 'Will you help me raise tsunami cash? Answers on a postcard, please', *Daily Telegraph*, 5 September 2005

**Question:** What are the critical issues in gaining support of this type?

---

## Getting to break-even

In the section on financial management and control we emphasized the fact that cash flow management of the inflows and outflows is vital for success. The first stage of an organization can be regarded as complete when it reaches **break-even**. Then it is essential to focus on building profits that can be reinvested in further developing profitable revenue streams. The traditional advice to new ventures has been that it is important to reach break-even as quickly as possible. For organizations set up to carry out leading-edge technological research, loss-making for a number of years is inevitable because it takes time to generate new products. However, in recent years, many new ventures seem to have believed that it is essential to create a strong customer awareness and market presence through considerable marketing and sales activity rather than trying to reach break-even. Dot-com businesses, such as Amazon.com and lastminute.com seemed to justify long periods of loss-making with the promise to investors of 'profits tomorrow'. However, creditors of companies that are loss-making for long periods can become nervous, particularly when payments are delayed, as shown in Enterprise in Action 11.3.

## Enterprise in Action 11.3

### Not such a red letter day

Red Letter Days was set up by Rachel Elnaugh to sell memorable experiences, such as driving a Formula 1 car or climbing a mountain. The idea came to her when, as a 24-year-old, she could not find a suitable present for her father. The experiences are sold as gifts in major retail stores such as Boots and Debenhams. The company appeared to be growing successfully when it hired a new chairman in May 2005 ahead of a planned float on the alternative investment market, which valued the company at £20–25 million.

Only two months later, however, suppliers were reported to have lost patience with Red Letter Days over late payments. Racing track operators were reported to be owed £300 000 and a charity that provided whale and dolphin watching trips in Cornwall claimed it had not been paid for four months and had begun legal action.

The £20 million per annum turnover business went into administration in July 2005 following cash flow problems. This was rather embarrassing for Rachel Elnaugh, who was a judge on Dragons' Den, a TV show in which would-be entrepreneurs made a pitch to successful entrepreneurs for investment in their idea.

Another Dragons' Den judge, Peter Jones, teamed up with ex-Millwall football club chairman, Theo Paphitis, to buy the company's assets, which meant that more than 150 Red Letter Days employees could keep their jobs. However, it seemed unlikely that Red Letter Days' creditor suppliers would see any money.

*Adapted from:* Osbourne A., 'Red Letter sails close to the wind as suppliers play safe', *The Daily Telegraph*, 30 July 2005; and 'Gift firm thrown dragon lifeline', BBC News Online, 2 August 2005

**Question:** What are the indicators of a failing business?

## Achieving break-even

For many organizations in the early stages, accelerating and maximizing positive cash inflows is more important than making high profits as they seek to achieve break-even. Many organizations find it advantageous to quietly build a market presence without attracting the attention of larger, more powerful competitors that might apply pressure by lowering prices.

An alternative marketing strategic option is to set low prices in order to quickly build volume sales. Of course a balance must be struck, as setting unrealistically low prices in the early stages of the business simply in order to generate revenue, as against making profitable sales, can be detrimental to the business in the long run since raising prices later in a competitive market can be very difficult.

The better option for long-term benefit therefore, is to set realistic prices that the customer is prepared to pay in a competitive market and, using effective marketing and sales effort, to explain to customers the benefits and value provided by the offer and persuade them to buy. However, the financial pressure to pay outstanding invoices makes it difficult for a start up to turn away immediate, low-price sales opportunities and wait for the possibility of getting customers to buy at higher prices.

Looking at the break-even chart in Figure 11.5, it is obvious that controlling costs as tightly as possible is a key strategy in the early days by:

- minimizing or delaying capital investment;
- negotiating hard on purchases of supplies as savings here go straight on to the bottom line; and
- carrying out cost-effective marketing and selling.

### The diffusion curve

Customers demonstrate different levels of predisposition to buy new products or services and, consequently, the sales of new products and services follow the **diffusion curve** shown in Figure 11.6. A small percentage of the potential market, around 2.5 per cent, are innovators, who are always keen to try out new products or services. For a new venture the task is to quickly identify and convince the innovator customers in the sector, who will be most willing to try the new products and services. The early adopters will wait a little until they perceive there to be low risk in purchasing. They are likely to be influenced by hearing the

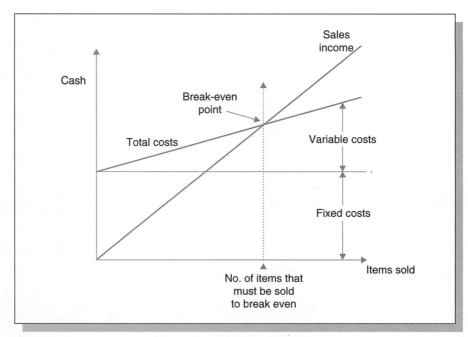

**Figure 11.5**
Break-even graph.

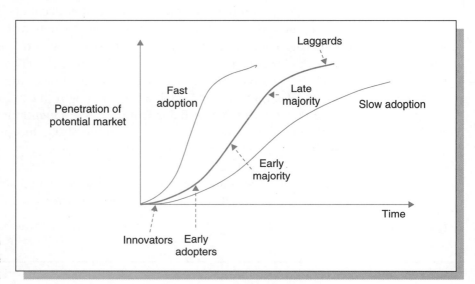

**Figure 11.6**
The diffusion curve
for a new launch.

experiences of the innovators. If the product or service performs satisfactorily they will be likely to try the new offering.

Fast adoption is likely to occur if the new product or service solves a
significant existing problem, provides substantial additional customer
value for the innovators who first try it or gains high profile through
celebrity or expert endorsement, or reaches the Internet chat-rooms.
Two of these situations are highlighted in Enterprise in Action 11.4.

Slow adoption results if the benefits of the new product are not really significant, there are deficiencies in performance against what is expected or the marketing, sales and distribution are ineffective in reaching a large audience with the result that prospective customers are not made aware of the new offering. It can be argued that it is only when the early majority decide to buy that the offer can be considered a success.

---

### Enterprise in Action 11.4

**Web success at different ends of the scale**

Londonlaunch.com was set up in Autumn 2000 by PR executive Will Broome with an initial outlay of £200 000. He spotted a gap in the market for a one-stop portal for event and party planners. It puts event organizers from office parties to awards ceremonies in touch with venues, caterers and other event service providers that are needed for the event or party to be a success. From very modest beginnings, the company has become an international operator.

Alex Tew, 21, due to start at Nottingham University in October 2005, was concerned about graduating three years later with a considerable debt. He decided to launch a website, www.milliondollarhomepage.com, in an attempt to pay for his three-year degree course. Within a month, and before he had even started university, he had earned £56 000. His website is split into 10 000 boxes, each 100 pixels in size and companies can buy one or more boxes (at $100 [£54] per box) and cover each with a logo, which when clicked on will connect with the customer's own site. Within days of the website being launched it was mentioned on chat rooms and soon Tew had 240 companies advertising and was getting 30 000 hits per day. The companies pay with a credit card and e-mail their own design in to Tew.

*Adapted from*: Poston T., E-business success stories at www.Computerweekly.com, 23 October 2001, and Savill R., 'Student solves debt fears as website earns £56 000 in a month', *The Daily Telegraph*, 24 September 2005

**Question:** What do these two stories say about the opportunities and resources needed to start an e-business?

---

In highly competitive markets where new and improved offerings are made, effective marketing and selling are needed to make even breakthrough products or services stand out from the crowd. Innovative marketing is needed to achieve the maximum customer impact with limited resources.

Both fast and slow adoption can cause cash flow problems. Fast adoption can lead to overtrading and a strongly negative cash flow resulting from the need for higher levels of funds than forecast for the purchase of materials and work in progress to support the higher level of sales, before debts can be collected from customers. Slow adoption restricts income below what was forecast while expenditure often cannot quickly be reduced below the level forecast, because it is not possible to renege on commitments made to suppliers. Slow adoption causes cash flow problems but is of greater concern if it indicates that the offer may be unsuitable for the market.

In dealing with slower than expected adoption, Bolton and Thompson (2000) suggest that there are two critical points in the early stage of the business, as shown in Figure 11.7. Cash demand increases as the venture starts trading, incurring operational and marketing costs before there is substantial income. If the offer is acceptable, income increases and the break-even point is reached. From then on the cash inflow substantially exceeds cash outflow and becomes increasingly positive and profits are generated. The period of negative cash flow is critical and it is here that the entrepreneur looks for two indicators to show that the critical points of achieving a technical and a commercial success have been reached and that the venture will ultimately prove to be successful.

Bolton and Thompson (2003: 383) suggest that the entrepreneur needs first to prove that the offer will be a technical success in the market,

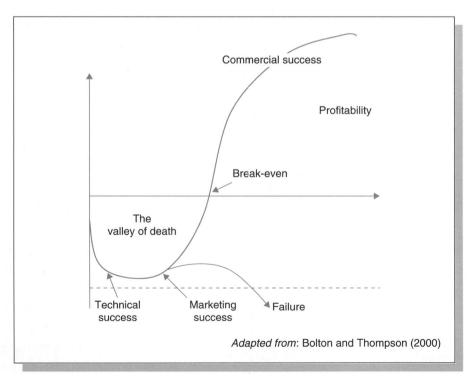

**Figure 11.7**
Cash flow at
start up.

with the product or service performing as anticipated and delivering the promised benefits when used by a (paying) customer.

It is then necessary to prove that the offer will be a marketing success, with sufficient customers (at least the early majority) being switched to this new offer and away from competitive products and services. This often requires considerable education and persuasion to overcome the customers' inertia, which can stem from their being satisfied with existing products, or being apathetic towards new products and services because of the cost and inconvenience of switching to a new, even better product or service.

For individuals intending to leave secure employment and set up a new venture it is beneficial if they can prove the proposed new venture is a technical success by gaining commitments to purchase from their first 'innovator' customers before they leave.

If the business case has been prepared and rigorously evaluated, it is unlikely that the venture will be a complete failure. However, it is also worth remembering that few new ventures are instant winners. The most likely situation is that cash flow underperforms the forecast and the performance of the new venture leaves considerable room for improvement. There are three areas where a decision might be needed:

- ▣ The offer and the way that the product or service is being marketed may be appropriate, but it may be taking longer than expected to reach break-even, in which case a 'do nothing' strategy might be appropriate.

As shown in Figure 11.8 the two other possible reasons for underperformance against forecast are that:

- ▣ The customer need and benefits have not been demonstrated effectively to customers, who need further persuasion.
- ▣ Alternatively, the need may have been demonstrated but the product or service underperforms to customer expectations and does not provide the promised benefit.

The real reasons for the underperformance need to be understood. Revision of the product specification and increasing marketing and sales effort can be expensive and should not be undertaken lightly. For ventures run by technically based staff there can be a great temptation to respond to underperformance by trying to further technically improve the product, incurring additional cost. But this may not be the cause of the problem. Sales-oriented management may believe that

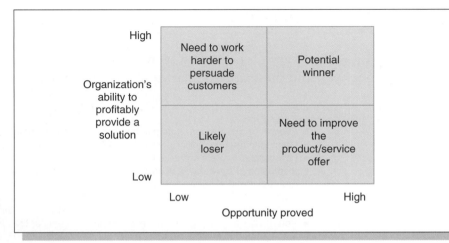

**Figure 11.8**
Decision areas for a
slow take-off.

trying harder to sell the product may be the solution, when in fact the product or service is inadequate for its purpose.

In Pause and Reflect 11.3 it is shown how a different customer offer, revision of the business model and a different approach to resource utilization proved successful at The Officers' Club.

## Pause and Reflect 11.3

### Changing the business model with The Officers' Club

For the majority of entrepreneurs the dream is a start up that funds itself but the dream comes true for only a few. Rarely does it happen first time and David Charlton is no exception. After qualifying as an accountant Charlton worked in the clothing industry for Jackson's the Tailor, now part of Arcadia Group. When parts of the business closed down, several of the factory managers set up their own business, sourcing material, manufacturing in the UK and retailing through their own shops. Charlton worked for the operation but was envious of the money the bosses made.

The trigger to Charlton becoming an entrepreneur was his brother's redundancy. In 1979 Charlton persuaded him to put his £4500 redundancy cheque into setting up an upmarket clothing business, Fiori. In 1987 Charlton bought out his brother and a venture capitalist took a 13 per cent stake in the firm.

As the recession of the 1990s took hold the company went into receivership. But in true entrepreneurial spirit Charlton tried again. A visit to the USA convinced him that discount retailers, with their fast stock turnover, were busiest, so he made the decision to go to the opposite end of the spectrum from luxury fashion and set up a discount clothing retailing business.

His suppliers were confident in his business model and were prepared to provide stock, and his landlord allowed him to pay rent one month in arrears. With only a small loan secured on his house he started up the business. He realized that he had to make money from day 1, as he had no financial cushion for security but deep discounting brought in the customers. The Officers' Club now have 180 stores in the UK.

*Adapted from*: The Officers' Club at www.startups.co.uk, accessed on 29 September 2005

**Question:** What are the key lessons from this for a determined entrepreneur?

## The start up barriers

There are obstacles that seem to conspire to prevent a successful start up and these are summarized in Figure 11.9.

- Everything takes longer than planned because entrepreneurs are optimistic
- Gaining market credibility is very difficult for an unknown new start
- Forecasts are rarely accurate but they can be under- and overestimates
- Increasing turnover by itself does not always solve the problem. Entrepreneurs are often good at selling but margins are important, too, to generate profit.
- Supplier and distributor relationships are demanding
- Getting paid is not always easy and requires a disciplined approach
- You never have the right premises; they are too small or too large
- Managing people is the biggest challenge, particularly when trying to build a good team quickly
- There will be conflicts between partners and investors, because each side has different objectives
- The pressure is relentless, both from repeated crises and the desire to perform even better

*Adapted from*: Johnson R. (2000: 164) Negotiating the start-up obstacle course. In: S. Birley and D.F. Muzyka (eds), *Mastering Entrepreneurship*, FT Pitman.

**Figure 11.9**
The start up
barriers.

## Summary

- The organizational form and location of an organization is determined partly by the owner's ambitions and also by the context for the start up.

- There is a framework of legislation for organizing the business and protecting stakeholder interests. In protecting intellectual property there is a framework of, for example, patents, copyright and trademarks, but in some cases it may not be beneficial to obtain patent protection.

- While the majority of new ventures are financed from informal and personal sources there is a range of institutional funding for larger projects. In seeking formal funding it is essential for entrepreneurs to understand the expectations of the funders.

- Building a high performing management team and staff is particularly challenging and there is a danger that the entrepreneur is unwilling or unable to devote sufficient time to managing and leading the team.

- Marketing and sales generate the revenue for the organization and this often presents challenges both in terms of winning over enough customers quickly enough and negotiating sales with a high enough margin to generate profits and funds for further investment.

■ Overall there are many start up obstacles in obtaining, organizing and managing the resources, but overcoming them is the key to success in entrepreneurship.

## Chapter questions

1. It is often said that when setting up a business the three most important things are location, location and location. Explain whether you agree and why, in the context of setting up an organic sandwich shop.

2. Many business angels choose to 'back the jockey not the horse', i.e. they are more interested in the qualities, characteristics and capability of the entrepreneur or entrepreneurial team than in the business proposition. Do you think this is appropriate and why?

3. What are the advantages and disadvantages of using a business angel to fund a growth strategy for a small business?

4. What reasons can you suggest could be the cause of a business achieving technical success and yet failing to emerge from 'death valley'?

5. Which is most important in achieving the break-even point – managing costs or generating sales?

## Case study

### Emma's start up decision

At the end of October Emma made a dramatic decision. She wanted to start the New Year working for herself. She no longer enjoyed working for the department store chain that she had joined when she left university five years ago. Her role was a buyer in the department that sourced gifts and craft items. Emma enjoyed meeting people and negotiating deals and she felt that she had good communications skills and understood what people wanted to buy. More recently, though, her department had experienced some quality problems with two of their suppliers and this coincided with some key staff leaving. Emma had become more involved with dealing with complaints from internal staff and customers as well, which seemed to be wearing her down. She could see no real end to the turmoil.

Emma had always thought she would one day run her own business and decided that this might be the time to take the plunge. A male friend from university had started a business which seemed to be doing well, although she was not sure exactly what it was – he always seemed to be too busy to spare the time for a drink and a chat. And presumably he was making lots of money as he had just bought a new sports car.

Her boyfriend, Neil, who was quite satisfied with his job as a schoolteacher in a sixth form college, appeared to be generally supportive although he had admitted to not being the slightest bit interested in, or capable of, running a business. They had recently bought a house together in the centre of a small market town in the south of England and had used up £10 000 of their joint savings on paying for the deposit and the legal fees, and had £10 000 for a 'rainy day' or getting married, whichever came the soonest. The couple had decided that getting married could wait and that the remaining £10 000 could be invested in the business. Sadly Emma and Neil had no rich relatives that could lend them any money, however, they had decided they could survive on Neil's salary for a few months until the business was profitable, although things would be tight.

Emma had always been interested in crafts and gifts and believed that she had a good eye for design, although her boss occasionally criticized her for buying 'way out' items that would only appeal to a very limited market. She believed that her contacts with suppliers all around the world and her understanding of selling prices, costs and margins could be put to good effect and, although she had no experience of marketing or selling, she felt that these were skills that she could soon pick up.

Out of their busy social life they had decided to set aside some time to decide what to do. Emma would need to give a month's notice to the company if she wanted to leave, but she could not afford to leave if she did not have a plan for the business and know how she was going to assemble the resources to run it. She knew what she wanted to sell but suddenly realized that she was not really sure what business model would be best. Her initial thought was to set up a small shop in the market square – indeed she had seen two shops empty and to let – but Neil's first contribution to the discussion rather surprised her. He rarely bothered going into the town centre because he said it was easier to buy gifts online. This prompted some lively discussion about the importance of seeing, touching and feeling the items. In the middle of the discussion the phone rang and it was Emma's university friend apologizing for never having the time before and suggesting they meet. Emma immediately agreed, thinking she could get some useful tips. Before he rang off she asked what his business actually was. His reply was 'I buy and sell stuff on eBay'. They said their goodbyes and Emma suddenly realized that she had more decisions to make than she realized.

Neil immediately adopted teacher mode and said 'the first thing we need to do is decide what questions you need to ask yourself before we try to get the answers. I have looked on the web and found that there are guides to starting up a business at www.startup.co.uk, and at www.ebay.co.uk/businesscentre/BC_Guide.pdf where the Institute of Business Advisers have teamed up with eBay'.

### Questions

1. What are the questions that need to be asked?
2. Given the context for Emma's new business, which business model should Emma choose?
3. Carry out some online research to determine what resources Emma will need and provide some rough costs, and list what she needs to do between now and the New Year.

## References and further reading

Baron R.A. and Shane S.A. (2005) *Entrepreneurship: A Process Perspective.* Mason OH: Thomson South-Western.

Barrow C., Burke G., Molian D. and Brown R. (2005) *Enterprise Development: The Challenges of Starting, Growing and Selling a Business.* London: Thomson.

Birley S. and Muzyka D.F. (2000) *Mastering Entrepreneurship*. Edinburgh: FT Pitman.

Bolton B. and Thompson J. (2000) *Entrepreneurs, Talent, Temperament, Technique*. Oxford: Butterworth-Heinemann.

Bolton B. and Thompson J. (2003) *The Entrepreneur In Focus: Achieve Your Potential*. London: Thomson Learning.

Carter S. and Jones-Evans D. (2000) *Enterprise and Small Business*. London: FT Prentice Hall.

Cartwright S. and Cooper G. (2000) Distilling a strong team. In: S. Birley and D.F. Muzyka (eds), *Mastering Entrepreneurship*. Edinburgh: FT Pitman.

Chaston I. (2000) *Entrepreneurial Marketing*. London: Macmillan Business.

Coulter M. (2003) *Entrepreneurship in Action*. Upper Saddle River NJ: Pearson Education Ltd.

Drucker P. (1985) *Innovation and Entrepreneurship*. New York: Harper and Row.

Drucker P. (2001) *The Essential Drucker*. Oxford: Butterworth-Heinemann.

Equinox Management Consultants (2000) *Informal Equity Capital for SMEs: a review of literature*, sourced at http://strategis.ic.gc.ca, 20 December 2005.

Kaplan J.M. (2003) *Patterns of Entrepreneurship*. Hoboken NJ: John Wiley and Sons.

Lambert R. (2003) Lambert Review of Business – University Collaboration, HM Treasury, at www.hm-treasury.gov.uk, accessed 5 October 2005.

Mason C. and Harrison R. (2000) Business angels are the answer to the entrepreneur's prayer. In: S. Birley and D.F. Muzyka (eds), *Mastering Entrepreneurship*. Edinburgh: FT Pitman.

Muzyka D.F. and Birley S. (2000) What venture capitalists look for. In: S. Birley and D.F. Muzyka (eds), *Mastering Entrepreneurship*. Edinburgh: FT Pitman.

The Charity Commission http://www.charity-commission.gov.uk http://www.patent.gov.uk, accessed 8/8/2005.

Wickham P.A. (2004) *Strategic Entrepreneurship*, 3rd edn. London: FT/Prentice Hall.

## Key words

| | |
|---|---|
| break-even | management buy-outs |
| business angels | management team |
| charitable status | marketing and selling |
| cooperatives | partnership |
| debt | patents |
| diffusion curve | premises |
| equity | public ownership |
| franchise | sole trader |
| intellectual property | spin-outs |
| invoice factoring | sweat equity |
| limited company | venture capital |
| management buy-ins | |

## CHAPTER 12

# Enterprise strategies and fast growth

By the end of this chapter the reader will be able to:

- appreciate the need for a strategy in an entrepreneurial organization and the need for a different strategy at key stages in the development of a business;
- identify the barriers to growth and compare the appropriateness of strategies to overcome them;
- evaluate the strategies that are used by entrepreneurial organizations at start up, and during periods of growth, consolidation and underperformance;
- develop a niche strategy to achieve fast growth;
- understand how competitive advantage is developed in entrepreneurial organizations through market positioning and building core competencies.

## Introduction

One common characteristic of the organizations discussed in this book is that the majority of them are fast changing (or need to change fast) to cope with the dynamic environment. However, the focus of their effort is often day-to-day management and frequently concerned with dealing with the current crisis. While many small firms survive and, indeed, prosper in this way, to establish a secure business and develop the capability to grow significantly requires some longer-term thinking in the form of a strategy. In the previous chapters in Part III we have discussed the steps to developing a new venture including identifying the business proposition, developing a business plan, establishing a business model, and assembling the necessary resources. In this chapter we emphasize the need for a broader and deeper understanding of strategic development and the importance of developing a strategy that is sufficiently proactive to drive the organization not only to achieve long-term success, but to be flexible enough to cope with the continual changes that occur and that need day-to-day actions in response.

We start by briefly explaining the nature and role of strategy, and justifying the importance of strategy for entrepreneurial organizations. It is important to be able to characterize the stage of development of the organization and recognize that different strategies are needed for the different life cycle stages, such as start up, rapid growth and consolidation in the mature phase of the business. It is also important to be able to develop strategies to deal with difficult trading environments that occur periodically and we discuss turnaround strategies for the organization. For both new and established organizations there are barriers to growth and organizations can become obsessed with the immediate problems. The focus on the short-term day-to-day operations means that many organizations fall into bad habits and fail to recognize that periodically they need to make major changes to the organization.

To become more successful in the longer term, entrepreneurial organizations need to reflect on their capabilities and source of competitive advantage, and work out what further knowledge and competencies might enable them to compete more effectively in the market.

Finally, we discuss the link between competitive advantage and learning and consider how entrepreneurship and innovation can be maintained in the future.

## Strategy in entrepreneurial firms

A commonly held view is that strategy is the preserve of large organizations that have an expanding customer base and substantial financial and human resources to manage. In practice, however, even a sole trader has a vision of how his or her business might look in a few years' time, and sets some longer-term goal, even if it is simply to work fewer hours for the same income. Competition inevitably appears and customer fashions change so the organization must respond by striking out in a new direction. From time to time, too, an entrepreneur decides whether or not to sell out and start afresh.

Some assessment of the various options available might be required, including which customers to prioritize and which products and services to concentrate on. The decisions taken must be implemented by deciding how to allocate the limited available resources between, perhaps, buying equipment or putting an advertisement in the local newspaper. A strategy, however flexible and informal, is needed to generate surplus funds to allow investment in some future as yet unspecified project or merely to cope with incremental growth.

There is a problem however, as there is no separate body of theory relating to enterprise strategies. Drucker (2001: 161), for example, comments that he has never come across a discussion of entrepreneurial strategies but suggests four specifically entrepreneurial strategies:

1. 'Being fustest with the mostest'
2. 'Hitting them where they ain't'
3. Focusing on an 'ecological niche'
4. Altering the economic characteristics of a product, market or an industry.

Assuming we have interpreted the first two correctly, we feel that these are not entirely comprehensive for our purpose.

The discussion of strategy in entrepreneurial organizations in most textbooks is usually a 'lite' version of corporate strategy, picking out some relevant ideas and ignoring other theories. Rather than offer a prescriptive approach to strategy development in entrepreneurial organizations, which by definition operate in very different ways, we have chosen to highlight some important issues and illustrate some key areas for strategic decision-making.

## The purpose and characteristics of strategy

Without a well defined base of entrepreneurial strategy theory it is worth starting from first principles and thinking about exactly what the purpose of a strategy might be. Mintzberg *et al.* (2003) suggest that if the potential aims or responses of intelligent opponents can seriously affect the organization's desired outcome, a strategy is needed. Most entrepreneurial organizations operate in environments where they are potentially vulnerable to competitive actions and so by this definition they need a strategy to determine the way in which they intend to compete in the market. Mintzberg and colleagues suggest that a strategy is

**Strategies can be:**

- Intended as a **plan** and a consciously intended course of action.
- Used as a **ploy** or a specific manoeuvre to outwit rivals.
- Based on a **pattern** of consistent behaviours, whether intended or not. Often, although the strategy intentions are clear they are not delivered in reality, because of a lack of consistency in the organization. Gaps then emerge and managers and staff fill them with emergent strategies that are not part of the initial intentions and sometimes take the organization away from its intended course.
- About external focus and a chosen market **position**: a unique location for the organization within its environment is achieved by matching up the organization (internal context) with the environment (external context).
- An internal focus and a **perspective**: an ingrained way of perceiving the world.

*Adapted from*: Mintzberg H., Lampel J., Quinn J.B. and Ghoshall S. (2003)

**Figure 12.1**
Five definitions of strategy.

about making plans for the future, based on a set of objectives, policies and plans that, when taken together, define the scope of the enterprise and how it intends to survive and achieve success. There must be a strategic fit of the many activities that are intertwined to provide competitive advantage and, ultimately, sustainability for the organization. They identify five definitions of **strategy** (see Figure 12.1).

In looking at these definitions it is relatively easy to match these approaches with the apparent strategies of some of the most successful entrepreneurial businesses. Both easyJet and Virgin Atlantic grew through actions specifically focused on outwitting their rivals, such as British Airways and other long established airlines. Drucker (2001) suggests that, in situations like these, large organizations have bad habits that let entrepreneurial organizations in. They include:

- the 'Not Invented Here syndrome', where large organizations only take their own developments seriously, not those of their competitors;
- 'creaming a market', with unwillingness to compete in the lower-price segments (Xerox let Japanese manufacturers of small photocopiers in to eventually dominate the market);
- a belief in setting a high specification and making a product difficult to copy but in so doing losing out to customers that want value for money, and lower-specification products;
- premium pricing, which effectively subsidizes the market entry by a newcomer that can undercut the market leader but still have plenty of margin with which to build a business; and

■ maximizing rather than optimizing. Xerox tried to compete on everything rather than selecting the segments that they could best serve.

Entrepreneurial organizations see the world differently from others and they 'do it their way' but still operate within a pattern of consistent behaviours. Sometimes it works, sometimes it does not. The behaviours in the market of many entrepreneurial organizations are less predictable than those of better established competitors. Entrepreneurial organizations, for example, create unique connections with the market, with both customers and partners. Steve Jobs at Apple has focused on developing a unique connection between the organization, its products – such as iPod – and Apple Mac and its market. In the process Jobs has built relationships with Apple's buyers such that they can now be described as 'devotees' or fans, as we saw in Enterprise in Action 3.1.

Many strategies have an internal focus and we have observed that many entrepreneurial organizations are the very personification of the entrepreneur and that the strategies they develop reflect their personal influence on, beliefs in and values regarding every aspect of the way the organization operates, as illustrated in Enterprise in Action 12.1. The reader will find a lot of evidence of the entrepreneur's influence on the strategy of entrepreneurial organizations, ranging from: a single-minded approach to maximize the benefits from limited resources; almost an obsession in trying to take customers away from more established competitors; a total focus on exploiting a specific market gap; a belief about how a new way to approach the market will succeed; to a highly autocratic way of running the organization. Some entrepreneurs are so determined to stamp their values on the organization and its products that they insist on appearing in all the advertising, too.

## Enterprise in Action 12.1

### Craigslist: to offer a public service or become a multimillionaire?

In 1995 Craig Newmark started Craigslist.organization in San Francisco to sell jobs, flats, cars and many other things to people in the form of online classified ads. The website is very basic with no pop-up ads, sponsors or sophisticated graphics, but it does provide ads that people read even if (or perhaps, because) some are sexually explicit or tasteless. There is no sales or marketing activity. Only employers who are advertising jobs are charged, not individuals. The organization's revenues are $7–10 million and it has always been profitable, unlike Amazon, which still has huge debts.

Newmark, and CEO Jim Buckmaster, have weekly offers from potential buyers of the company and they have turned down many opportunities to become multimillionaires. They believe that the website offers a public service and, moreover, their belief is that once you are financially comfortable, there is little point in having more money.

The independence of the company did seem to be threatened recently when a former employee sold a 25 per cent share of the company to eBay for a reported $15 million. However, eBay are quite happy that Craigslist.organization continues with its traditional approach to business.

*Adapted from*: D. Rushe, 'Free advertising website spurns offers to sell out', *Sunday Times*, 28 August 2005

**Question:** What do you think drives Newmark and Buckmaster's strategy?

## Strategic approaches at different stages in the lifetime of an organization

The typical and quite separate stages of an organization throughout its life cycle are shown in Figure 12.2. For entrepreneurial organizations, each of the stages requires a different strategic approach. This reveals a significant difference between the strategies of large and small organizations because large organizations are usually in a relatively steady state and their strategies usually reflect this.

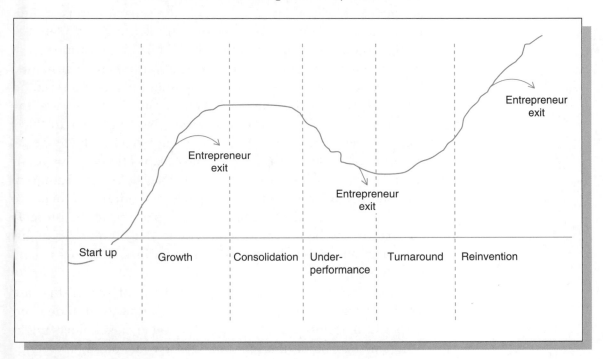

**Figure 12.2**
The life cycle stages of an entrepreneurial organization.

In the following sections of the chapter we explore the strategies that might be appropriate for each situation.

***Strategies at start up*** Strategies at start up are concerned with establishing the organization and its operations, workforce and financial basis. Strategies are needed to establish the presence of the organization in the market and to position it in the minds of the stakeholders, on which it is dependent for future success.

***Strategies to overcome the barriers to growth*** Once established, an organization is faced with a number of barriers that could curtail its growth unless suitable strategies are developed to overcome the problems arising. Typical difficulties might include shortage of investment and resources, lack of capacity and capability of the staff to take on new responsibilities, an inability of managers to respond to new challenges, an aggressive competitive response and the reluctance of the mass of potential customers to switch to the new offering.

***Strategies to achieve consolidation of the gains made*** During periods of rapid growth an organization can become overstretched. Management and staff may be expected to be totally flexible and take on too many responsibilities, and the owners often forget to encourage and support those staff carrying out difficult tasks. This can result in staff becoming tired, stressed and less effective.

Most organizations operate too closely to the capacity limits of their equipment, facilities and finance and have no contingency plans for when things go wrong, as they inevitably do. While organizations try to retain their momentum, embrace change and continue their sustained growth, there are periods when the management of the organization should **consolidate** the gains made and reflect on the situation, taking time to decide how to build up the resource base in order to 'have something in reserve' to deal with the next set of growth challenges.

***Niche strategies to achieve fast growth*** Small organizations can use their limited resources more effectively to grow quickly by concentrating on supplying one customer segment with a specialized offering. It needs to be differentiated from the offerings from competitors, and customers should perceive it to be of extraordinary value. This requires a highly focused strategy and a disciplined approach to business decision-making and development.

***Strategies to deal with underperformance*** At different points, that are often unpredictable, the organization will suffer a downturn in demand or underperform against what the owners and other stakeholders might expect. Income may be insufficient, the costs may be too high, creditor payments may become extended and drastic action may be needed to put right the problems. The organization may have strayed from its original purpose and be opting for easier but less valuable activities. Many entrepreneurial organizations reach this point and the existing management fail to take sufficiently decisive action early enough to anticipate and correct the problem. Such situations frequently result in the entrepreneurs being forced out of the organization by investors that have increased their financial stake and control in the business. This can be a painful experience for the entrepreneur, whose brainchild it was, who has struggled to set it up and steer it through the many obstacles to growth.

*Turnaround and strategies for reinvention*  Improvements in management effectiveness and business efficiency may be sufficient to turn around the organization. This might need to be accompanied by the replacement of some senior executives, staff redundancies and closure of some activities. Sometimes such incremental change proves insufficient to put right the problems of the organization, and complete reinvention may be required either with or without the existing management. It may be necessary to completely redefine the business vision and mission.

*Strategies for exit/realizing the value of the organization*  We have already referred to the fact that many venture capital organizations look for a maximum of around seven years to realize the value in their investment by selling their stake in the business. **Exit** is a valid strategy in other circumstances too. As well as an entrepreneur's personal reasons to leave the business, such as the wish to retire, to realize his or her personal investment or to move on to the next entrepreneurial venture when the venture has become established, it might be appropriate for the organization to be merged or taken over by a larger organization for it to achieve its full potential.

*Strategies for administrative management*  Many entrepreneurial organizations become so successful that they succeed in evolving into very large, established organizations. Others become so successful that competitors try to take them over to further exploit their potential success or, alternatively, to stop them becoming strong competitors in the market. While it is not our intention here to discuss generic strategies it is useful to draw attention to the different approaches to administrative and entrepreneurial strategies and management.

## The nature of strategy development in entrepreneurial organizations and the implications for decision-making

While aiming to justify our case that small organizations, as well as large, need a strategy it is clear that their strategic approaches are substantially different.

## Emergent strategies for entrepreneurial organizations

Large organizations have the resources to devote more time to formal discussion of strategy, the resources to invest in strategic development, and the advantage of having a number of management teams who bring different skills and perspectives to the debate about future possibilities. By contrast, smaller organizations are often dominated by one person and this individual has a significant influence on the vision, mission and objectives of the organization and the decisions on the future direction, too. This can be an advantage in that the entrepreneur is often very close to the customer and the market, but the decisions arrived at, although benefiting from being made quickly, can be taken on personal criteria, often on whims, that do not really stand up to scrutiny. The danger, of course, is that the strategy emerges as a series of knee-jerk responses to critical events and crises that occur from time to time with decisions being largely taken to deal with short-term problems and not to deliver long-term success.

Smaller organizations can in addition be too heavily dependent on a key customer, and this can also influence their thinking. If they have a small market share, they are less able to influence the longer-term market development than can a larger business with more significant market influence. Smaller organizations may not have the resources to diversify and, not being limited companies, cannot go to the stock market to raise funds for expansion. They do not always have the management capability, or capacity, to grow successfully, and can feel that many strategic options that are talked about in textbooks are simply not relevant to or viable for them. However, as we discussed in Chapter 10, knowing where you are now, where you want to be, and having a plan for getting there is just as relevant to a small organization wanting to build its competitive edge as it is to a large firm.

## Strategic decision-making

Small organizations usually have a simple business structure in which line management responsibilities are clear. It is relatively easy to develop a vision of what the owners and managers expect the business to be like in the future – its short- and long-term objectives, its target customers, main products and services, operations and activities – and to communicate these to the staff. Even when rapid changes occur it is still relatively easy for the managers to keep staff informed and engaged with the development of new strategies and plans and the key decisions that need to be made and implemented swiftly and effectively.

Larger, more complex organizations have complicated, geographically diverse departmental structures with matrix management in which staff often are required to report to two or more bosses. Many such organizations are slow to respond because of their bureaucratic processes, procedures and control systems. They need to consult with a range of interested stakeholders and poor coordination and communications often lead to turf wars between rival departments or managers. Because of central planning, annual budgeting and multilayer managerial approval before making investments, it is often difficult for larger organizations to make fast decisions. Sometimes, for example, if the request for new investment is not included in the annual budget it may be a year before there is an opportunity to bid for a new project investment. This provides the entrepreneurial organization with an opportunity to compete with larger organizations through speed of response and decisiveness. This speed of response can be critical, as shown in Enterprise in Action 12.2.

---

### Enterprise in Action 12.2

**Survival means a fast response**

Philip Bull and Andrew Lever supply women's clothing to high street stores in the UK and until seven years ago they designed the garments in the UK and had them made in eastern Europe.

They faced a dilemma when they were squeezed on price by customers and soon realized that if they did not make changes they would not survive. They moved their whole manufacturing operation to China, leaving a small sales office in the UK. The company turnover dropped from £10 million to £3 million but is now back to £9 million trading as 'Trade in Asia'. Bull and Lever say that if they were a large company they would be too locked into existing processes, would not have been able to respond quickly and might not have survived.

*Adapted from*: Bridge R., 'Fast moving firms can beat the big boys',

*Sunday Times*, 21 August 2005

**Question:** What are the advantages and disadvantages for smaller organizations in fast decision-making?

---

## Strategies for start up

Earlier in the book we emphasized that the business approach adopted by entrepreneurial organizations is characterized as the pursuit of an opportunity irrespective of the resources that are controlled by the organization, and we have discussed the external and internal factors that drive the process of start up.

The fundamental purpose of the strategy is to set the framework for the longer-term vision, objectives, policies and plans that were discussed earlier. For a lifestyle business the strategy might simply be about establishing a modest but reliable income with relatively little risk to the owners. For a more ambitious venture the objectives, policies and plans must be developed to achieve growth and high performance. In both these cases, which are at opposite ends of the scale of new starts however, the fundamental requirement of the strategy must be to configure the organization to define, create and deliver value for the customer (Doyle, 2000):

- Define value within the business proposition in a way that indicates clearly how customers will benefit and obtain value from the product and service offer.
- Deliver consistent value by cost-effectively using the resources to meet or exceed the customers' product and service expectations.
- Create value by efficiently acquiring and utilizing the necessary skills, competencies and supporting resources (e.g. human, financial and equipment) within a robust business model to continually improve value for the organization and increase its competitiveness over the longer term.

## Start up capability

Bolton and Thompson (2000: 58) explain the start up strategy in terms of the convergence of three dimensions: (1) the business environment; (2) the resources of the organization; and (3) the values of the organization (its culture and style of management, usually largely influenced by the entrepreneurial leader). Windows of opportunity are constantly opening up in the environment but it requires appropriate resources to be assembled and an entrepreneurial approach to be applied to exploit the opportunity.

This leads to the definition of three key areas of capability of the entrepreneurial organization: (1) opportunity recognition; (2) strategic positioning; and (3) the ability and commitment to change, as shown in Figure 12.3.

*Opportunity recognition* is not just about identifying a new customer demand or gaps in market supply, but is about defining exactly what

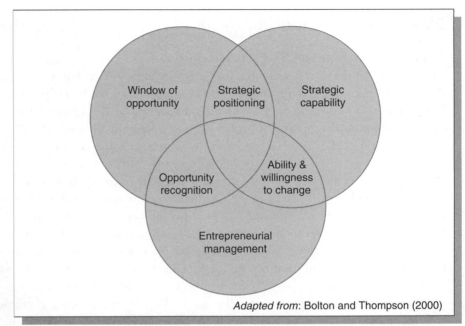

**Figure 12.3**
Entrepreneurial
strategic
development need
to change.

*Adapted from*: Bolton and Thompson (2000)

the opportunity might be for the entrepreneurial organization, what the offer or solution should be, discussed in Chapter 9, and what business model could be applied, discussed in Chapter 10, to enable the opportunity to be effectively exploited.

*Strategic positioning* is about defining the offer in a competitive market so that the value to the customer and other stakeholders is clearly identified, and seen to be differentiated from and superior to the value offered by competitors.

*The ability and commitment to change* is essential within an organization not only as the staff configure the organization to deliver the solution to customers at start up but to reconfigure the organization internally as successive new products are introduced.

Therefore, having the idea and spotting the market gap is not enough. Exploiting the window of opportunity requires distinctive strategic positioning that ideally offers a 'quantum leap' in customer benefits and then continues to build competitive advantage and increase the barriers to entry, in the process developing a secure position for the entrepreneurial organization in the supply chain. To do this the firm must be willing to change (including competencies and resources, etc.) to achieve this new strategic positioning and build its competitive advantage, as is discussed later in the chapter. An example of this is shown in Enterprise in Action 12.3.

## Enterprise in Action 12.3

### Organic growth at the Soil Association?

The Soil Association is a charity that campaigns to promote sustainable organic agriculture in the UK, by encouraging consumers to buy organic produce. It also provides certification for farms that meet its criteria, and allows them to use the Soil Association logo. It has an income of £7.4 million and employs 146 full-time and 25 part-time staff. The organic sector is the fastest growing part of the UK food and drink market, showing 10 per cent annual rise with sales of £1 bn.

The survival of the association currently depends on subscriptions and it has 25 000 subscribers. If the idea really caught the imagination of consumers, however, it could become very influential indeed, especially given the high profile of healthy eating and environmental concern. The charity has set an initial target of 100 000 subscribers within the next five years.

To increase subscriptions, however, the Soil Association must change the public's perceptions. Most people think that the Soil Association is a government body, not a membership organization and last year just a few hundred new members joined. It has no large marketing or advertising budget and instead relies on the PR that results from campaigns. Its 'Food for Life' campaign hit the headlines recently because it showed that more was spent on lunches in jails than in schools but this did not lead to an increase in membership.

At the moment the assumption is that the subscribers are contributing to a good cause. They only receive a magazine in return for their subscription. More might join if they could perceive more benefits.

*Adapted from*: Terry F., 'Green food campaign sows seed of success', *Sunday Times*, 14 November 2004

**Question:** What would you do to set the Soil Association on a path of healthy growth?

## Step change and incremental change strategies

After the organization has established an initial market position Bolton and Thompson (2000) emphasize that it must continue to build a sustainable business by:

- maintaining growth through continual small-scale innovations;
- improving management efficiency; and
- making visionary leaps forward to achieve periodic step changes in performance in the business.

This is achieved by two types of learning (see Figure 12.4). The continual improvement and reinforcement of strategic positioning is achieved by single loop learning and, particularly, learning good practice by reflecting on past successes and failures. Making visionary leaps

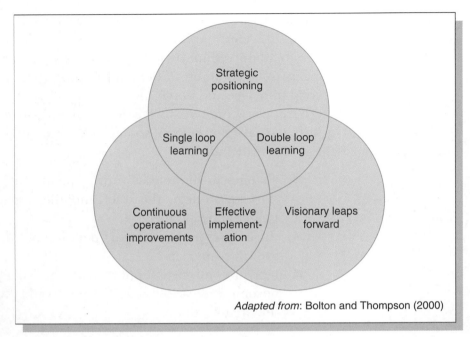

**Figure 12.4**
Entrepreneurial
strategy
development.

*Adapted from*: Bolton and Thompson (2000)

forward and establishing entirely new strategic positions is achieved by double loop learning, discussed in Chapter 4.

## The barriers to growth and turnaround strategies

The start up strategy should result in the organization gaining a sustainable and commercially viable position in the market. However, strategies are transient and their appropriateness for long-term growth is usually limited. Without periodic updates a strategy will become obsolete and no longer appropriate for the current situation. There are considerable barriers to growth and, before discussing fast-growth strategies in the next section, it is useful to identify the barriers and challenges of growth and consider the possible response of an entrepreneurial organization to situations such as where it is underperforming to expectations or is having to deal with a severe market change and is faced with a turn-around situation.

## The barriers to growth

Storey (1994) found that only around 4 per cent of SMEs grow significantly but this small number of organizations contributes 50 per cent of the increase in employment created by the SME sector. Barrow *et al.* (2005: 110) refer to evidence that shows that nearly one third of firms cease to trade within 10 years and the overall pattern of mortality appears to be common throughout European and the US economies among franchise and non-franchise businesses.

There are a number of barriers that will prevent the continued growth of the organization if strategies are not put in place to deal with them. These include:

- changes in the market environment that make the existing start up strategy, the offer and the targeted customers no longer appropriate;
- the failures in the internal operation of the organization (the growth pains); and
- lack of continued support from the stakeholders, who may become increasingly disillusioned with the performance of the organization.

## Growth challenges of management

Of particular concern to us in this section is the owner and management effectiveness in responding to the growth challenges. Ultimately the 'external' barriers, such as inadequate funding, insufficient customers and underperforming products (Hall, 1995) should be overcome by management action. It is worth saying that stakeholders, such as employees, suppliers and investors, are unlikely to dismiss a failure of the entrepreneurial organization to respond to market changes as 'unlucky' but rather criticize the management for a failure to anticipate the market changes, use the resources available to seek out new opportunities and take action to change the direction of the organization to secure its future.

The biggest challenge for the organization, therefore, is the development of a team to manage the organization through its growth challenges. Fast-growing organizations become totally obsessed by the obvious growth drivers and the need to make the next sale, get the next order delivered and get the next product offer on to the market.

For the team itself there seem to be a continual flow of daily problems that disrupt this growth, such as staff being away ill and so slowing down a new development, a spelling mistake on the packaging that holds up the production line or the delivery lorry breaking down at a critical moment, delaying an essential delivery. This is interspersed with more serious periodic crises that threaten the ambitious growth plans, such as coming close to exceeding the overdraft limit, failing to win a new customer order or the threat of an essential supplier to withdraw supplies.

There is a danger that the organization's strategy simply becomes task focused with little or no time to consolidate the gains already made and build in management flexibility, spare capacity and capability to more effectively manage the problems and crises, and prepare strategies to cope better in the future. To both develop a longer-term strategy and deal better with the day-to-day activities for the organization the managers need information, effective communication with their colleagues, contact with key stakeholders and a robust way of making high quality decisions.

Greiner (1972) provided a model (see Figure 12.5) of the problems that occur within the management team, which managers of most developing organizations will recognize. He found that many entrepreneurial organizations face a number of **crises of management** which, if not dealt with effectively, could lead to business failure. It is essential for management to recognize the signs, anticipate the problems and take action.

It is important to recognize the different phases of organizational development as separate states and know when the organization must change its management strategy, culture and guiding operating

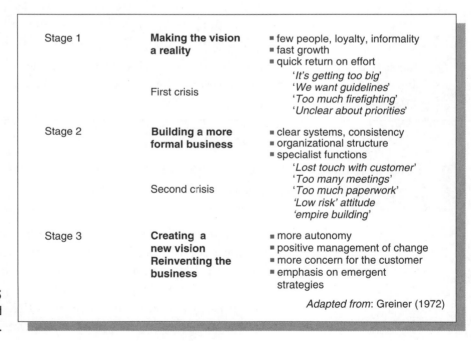

**Figure 12.5**
Evolution and revolution.

principles in order to deal with a new phase and the challenges it poses. In Enterprise in Action 12.4 it is shown how Napster has been involved in turbulent changes as it has moved to become a legitimate organization.

---

**Enterprise in Action 12.4**

### Napster seeking legitimate downloads

The name of Napster is linked with illegal music swapping. Although it was just one of many illegal sites in 1999 it was the one that gained the most publicity.

It was started by 19-year-old Shaun Fanning, a bored Boston, USA computer science student, who wrote software for his friends to download and share music. It was named Napster after Fanning's 'nappy-style' hairdo. The popularity of the illegal sites was in part due to the frustration of CD buyers who felt they were being ripped off by the record companies, which maintained very high prices for the CDs. Napster was shut down in July 2001.

In reality such sites were the forerunners in an industry breakthrough and the creation of a new business model, arguably more radical than Amazon and eBay, because the whole process of the purchase, delivery and usage of music for consumers was changed.

Now Napster has reinvented itself as a legitimate business to capitalize on its well known brand. It is marketing two formats, selling permanent downloads, which in the UK sell typically for 79p but can be as low as 39p, and by monthly subscription, where users can rent the downloads for £9.95 per month. Napster's current competitors include Virgin Digital at £9.99 per month and HMV at £14.99 per month for the subscription service. iTunes only sells permanent downloads. One potential growth problem for Napster is that a poll by Parks Associates suggested that UK customers would not pay more than £5.50 per month for the subscription service.

*Adapted from*: Flanagan B., 'Napster's a hit – but can it stave off rivals?'
*The Observer*, 4 September 2005

**Questions:** What are the advantages and disadvantages of the two models, permanent download and subscription service, and how would you advise Napster? What implications might this have for the operations?

---

## The reasons why start up strategies might no longer be appropriate

Chowdhury and Lang (1993: 8–17) refer to the boiled frog syndrome, which is particularly relevant for small firms as they are often so focused on the immediate problems that they are not aware of what is going on around them. A frog that is dropped into a boiling pan of water reacts instantly and jumps out because it is aware of the changing environment. A frog that is dropped into a pan of cold water that is gradually heated does not realize that the environment is changing dangerously and eventually dies!

There may be many reasons for a failure to meet the short-term targets set. The reasons for underperformance might include:

- poor implementation of the right strategy by a weak management team;
- the right strategy, properly implemented but taking too long because of a failure to generate turnover and recover debts, production delays, sourcing difficulties and a failure to obtain additional loans;
- the strategy no longer being appropriate for the market, because it has changed as a result of competitive action, the introduction of alternative offerings or changing customer fashion;
- operational inefficiency and poor cost control, because of lack of management experience or expertise or as a result of management 'living beyond their means';
- indecisive leadership, and weak management leading to lack of direction and control;
- lack of investment in new projects as the existing offer is no longer competitive in the market;
- unwise and inappropriate investments by the management as a panic reaction to market changes;
- failure to cope with the nature, speed and intensity of change in the sector;
- inability to manage an economic downturn, or an industry sector cycle;
- failure to anticipate and plan for legislative and technological changes;
- inability to cope with slower than expected diffusion of key products and services because switching customers proves more difficult than anticipated;
- inability to cope with changes in the route to market and distribution channels;
- becoming overdependent on one major customer or one major product;
- overfocusing on production, research and development and a lack of focus on changing customer needs and competitor actions;
- the imminent withdrawal of a major sponsor, investor or supporter.

Of course the organization may have outperformed its start up strategy objectives and exceeded its most optimistic estimates. Without corrective action this situation can also be problematic, because the organization may run out of cash, have to cut back its activities or risk being taken over. Sometimes an entrepreneur may have the objective at the start to prepare the organization for takeover and so outperformance may simply speed up this end point. In other situations where the senior managers wish to maintain ownership and control it might be useful to opt for a period of consolidation, which we discuss below, rather than seek further 'wild' expansion.

## Strategies to achieve consolidation of the gains made and the development of the management team

While most discussion in this and most other business textbooks is concerned with opportunity exploitation, growth, and business expansion, for most businesses the most difficult strategic tasks are coping with a less benign market environment and addressing underperformance in the market. Most firms, including the majority of global businesses, have faced serious problems at some stage. The same is true for entrepreneurial organizations and the true test of the organization is whether it can survive in difficult situations. During the good times the entrepreneurial organization must make sure it is well equipped for difficult times, for example, by balancing the portfolio of products and services to manage risk.

There needs to be a constant drive to improve efficiency, especially if there are in-house production operations. The capacity required during growth periods will exceed the demand during periods of downturn. Kano and Rao (1995) in studying entrepreneurial businesses during the Japanese downturn in the 1990s, emphasized the importance of improving the efficiency of production operations. Chaston (2000: 150) discusses the 3 'Ds':

- Dehumanize by replacing human involvement with automation.
- Delegate tasks to subordinates or external suppliers.
- Delete unnecessary tasks in the operation to increase long-term efficiency.

While a more prudent strategic approach in running the business might fail to achieve the full growth and revenue potential in the good times it will result in a leaner organization – perhaps with fewer staff – that is more capable of operating on a smaller scale in difficult times. By not using up scarce financial resources to try to maintain a larger operation during difficult times, spare cash might be available for investment when the market picks up. In this way a more prudently run organization might be better equipped to come out of a recession more quickly than its rivals.

If the management team is able to recognize and address the various crisis points that Greiner (1972) refers to and develop appropriate strategies to deal with them the organization will be able to consolidate its success and be able to build for the next phase of growth.

## The indicators of poor performance and the concerns of stakeholders

In the section above we identified the reasons why strategies fail or are no longer appropriate. Coulter (2003: 336) identifies the following causes of organizational decline.

- poor financial controls;
- costs too high and out of control;
- new more aggressive or unexpected competition;
- unpredicted change in customer requirements;
- failure to respond sufficiently to change;
- overexpansion or too-rapid growth;
- internal culture problems.

Of course, these reasons for decline only really become apparent with the benefit of hindsight, analysis and reflection on good and bad practice. For the stakeholders that are dependent on or have some expectations of the organization, such as employees, investors or even family, there is little concrete evidence of how the organization is performing and they must look for indicators that might give clues and early warning of the possibility of losing their job, income or investment. Coulter (2003: 335) identifies some of the early warning indicators, which might include:

- lack of a clear vision and goals;
- inadequate or negative cash flow;
- overstaffing;
- waste, inefficiency and a high level of complaints;
- fear of conflict and risk aversion;
- ineffective internal communications;
- overfocus on unnecessary, bureaucratic procedures.

The underperformance in not-for-profit areas may be more concerned with no longer fitting with the current environment situation (see Enterprise in Action 12.5).

---

### Enterprise in Action 12.5

**Barnardos finding a new way to help children**

In London in the 1860s a Dublin-born doctor, Thomas Barnardo, formed Barnardos, a charity dedicated to 'giving children back their future' by 'preventing disadvantaged children carrying over problems into adulthood or into the next generation'. By 1905 when Barnardo died the charity had 96 'Dr Barnardo Homes' fostering 8500 children.

Today in the UK, residential homes are not considered the best way to foster children, following investigations in the 1980s and 1990s that found some children had suffered neglect, discrimination, and even physical and sexual abuse in residential homes run for children.

Barnardos has changed its strategy completely and instead of running orphanages it now has 300 projects that range from schoolwork mentoring to legal counselling for domestic violence issues. However, to date it has failed to reposition and build the brand and 70 per cent of the UK population still associate the charity with orphanages. It currently spends less than 0.5 per cent of its £180 million income on publicity. It has maximized donations by using 'shock advertising', such as a baby snorting heroin rather than 'good work' stories but this also leads to complaints.

Charities face problems in getting across their message. Donors cannot try out Barnardo's services – all they see is the advertising and publicity, so getting it right is vitally important.

*Adapted from*: Modernising Barnardo's, Centaur Communications,
Brand strategy online, 4 April 2003

**Question:** Given their shortage of resources, Barnardos needs an entrepreneurial approach to get across their message. What should they do?

---

## Turnaround strategies to deal with underperformance and taking difficult decisions

Ullmann (2000: 337) suggests strategies to achieve a turnaround and emphasizes the importance of getting in new management with a new perspective, but also stresses that it is important to recruit managers who are known to the owners and to motivate them. We have indicated earlier that turning around an underperforming business requires decisive actions to reassure external stakeholders. This usually involves cost cutting and redundancies among staff. Very often too, outside investors will insist on a change of leadership to indicate a clear new direction and restore their faith in the organization. For an entrepreneurial organization this inevitably will mean the entrepreneur whose idea the business was and who built it from scratch will either have to take a back seat or be removed completely from the business.

The difficult decisions in a turnaround strategy are often portrayed as being cost cutting. A new chief executive is appointed at the crisis point specifically to turn around a business, and to undertake cost cutting, by sacking staff, because this has short-term financial benefits. Often, however, the actual short-term costs are increased given the cost of redundancy. Moreover, the removal of key staff often results in the loss of essential knowledge and expertise with the effect that rebuilding the organization can take much longer. Such actions change the culture of the entrepreneurial organization and it loses its original identity and values. Indeed a number of organizations that underperform following a period of extraordinary success find it extremely difficult to substantially improve their position for many years and many never recover at all.

To avoid this, first it is necessary for the entrepreneurial organization to react quickly and decisively to the early signs of underperformance as this can avoid the need for more substantial change later. Entrepreneurs that have weak management capability themselves need to establish a professional team, quickly learn to delegate tasks to it and leave it to run the day-to-day business.

Businesses in trouble are a potential opportunity for entrepreneurs but Ullmann (2000: 337) warns of the difficulty of assessing potential companies for turnaround because of the difficulty of obtaining reliable information, especially in the case of firms that are in receivership, as the receiver has few obligations to potential buyers.

## Fast growth, niche strategies and service

A few organizations grow quickly to become large organizations. Some achieve spectacular growth from day 1, while others start with modest growth then suddenly accelerate fast, because of some critical incident.

Successful organizations focus on the areas of activity that are the most important and become expert in them, as shown in Figure 12.6. There is little point in over-investing in activities that are unimportant for the organization's future, even if the organization performs well doing them. Successful organizations maintain their efforts in areas that are important, where they are doing well, and concentrate their efforts by using their resources for the high importance, low performance activities.

It is important to focus, too, on those activities that will deliver the best reward for the risk involved, but it may be that the portfolio will need to be balanced and include activities with different levels of reward and risk

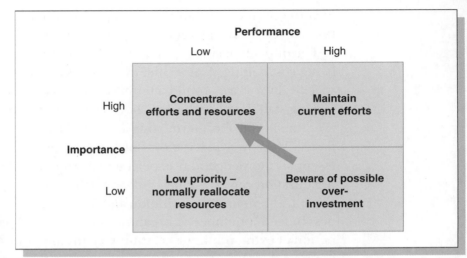

**Figure 12.6**
Performance–
importance matrix.

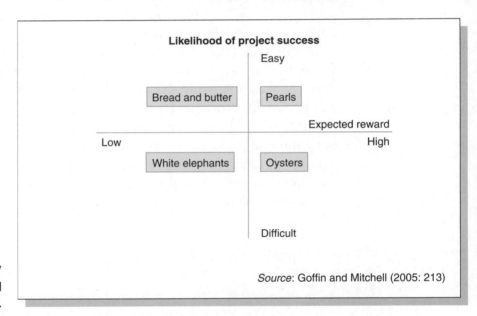

**Figure 12.7**
Risk and reward
matrix.

(Goffin and Mitchell, 2005: 213). The risk and reward matrix is shown in Figure 12.7. Bread and butter activities ensure that the fixed costs are covered; pearls are the current profit earners; oysters are the hidden or future profit earners; and white elephants are a drain on resources.

## Niche strategies

Many small entrepreneurial organizations aim to maximize the value they obtain from their resources by concentrating their efforts on supplying one main target customer segment and offering a very limited range of products and services that will suit the segment's requirements. In addition a small number of these start ups manage to achieve spectacular growth and, for example, the *Sunday Times* produces an annual league table of the UK's fastest-growth organizations and runs a website that provides more information on the characteristics and good practice lessons of the firms that achieve **fast growth**.

While not all fast-growth organizations can be described as using niche strategies, many do. The characteristics of an organization that operates a niche strategy are that they:

- focus on one particular customer segment and a limited range of products and services to service the niche;
- make sure the niche or segment is recognizable to end users and distributors;
- build barriers to entry for a mass market competitor;
- make sure the niche product or service is distinctive;
- make sure it appeals strongly to a particular segment of consumers;
- define clearly the basis of the organization's competitive advantage;
- aim for premium price positioning for the product and to certainly be above average pricing in the market.

Many niche marketing organizations are pioneers that have subsegmented an existing market to create their own small niche. By focusing all their activities on one customer segment and one niche they gain a reputation among their loyal customers and recognition among potential customers who know exactly what they do. In Spotlight 12.1 it is shown how Tie Rack started and developed its business.

## Spotlight 12.1

### Tie Rack tying up new deals for growth

Tie Rack was the archetypal niche retailer. It opened in 1981 selling mainly ties at airports and other travel locations. The definition of its business was very tight, in the same way that Amazon started by selling books to the customer segment that was prepared to buy online; and McDonalds started by selling burgers for customers that wanted food fast.

The problem is that these customer segments can be quite small for an ambitious organization and so one interesting aspect of these niche businesses is how they choose to grow their business. In contrast to Amazon and McDonalds, Tie Rack has maintained a relatively niche operation, but now has 350 stores in 27 countries placed in a wider range of locations than just travel-related. It has joined up with Frangi of Italy with the aim of becoming the world's leading accessory retailer and so the definition of its niche has broadened somewhat. Tie Rack has also set up a division, Rolling Luggage, to retail premium luggage and accessories, again at airports and main travel locations.

*Source*: www.tie-rack.co.uk

**Question:** What growth options are there for a niche retailer and what are the advantages and disadvantages of each option?

Both Amazon and McDonalds have broadened their business from their original niches to supply mass market customers on the back of their originally innovative business models.

The key to growing niche business is to build greater competitive advantage and prevent the niche business becoming an easy target for competitors. The most obvious ways of doing this are by making choices between the alternative generic strategies proposed by Porter (1985):

- *Focus:* this strategy moves away from the origins of a limited range of products towards offering a complete service for the one or two target segments.
- *Differentiation:* the aim here is to further differentiate the product and service, and to tailor it more to the needs of the segment in order to add customer value, but this needs to be done without increasing cost, which might encourage competition. The dangers are increasing the portfolio and dissipating the limited resources and effort.
- *Cost:* reducing the cost of the operations either allows more profit to be made or the price of the products and services for the target segment to be reduced. Cost reduction can increase the loyalty of the segment, but not if further differentiation and additional customer value is lost.

Cost reduction must be a continual goal of entrepreneurial organizations. The most significant benefits derive from:

- economies of scale, whereby the existing fixed assets are used to generate a larger volume of activities as the organization grows, the fixed costs so becoming a smaller proportion of the cost of each product or service sold; and
- the experience effect, whereby the cumulative experience of the same business process reduces cost (the more times it is carried out the more efficiently it will be carried out), as shown in Figure 12.8.

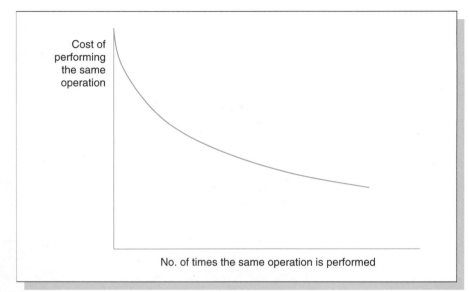

**Figure 12.8**
The learning curve.

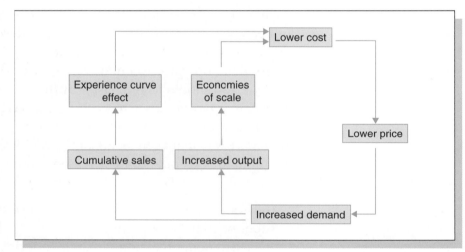

**Figure 12.9**
Virtuous circle of
cost and price.

Figures 12.9 and 12.10 (p. 416) show two alternative approaches to cost reduction, first using it to operate a low-price strategy, and second, using the lower cost to generate a higher margin to invest in a focus or differentiation strategy.

## Fast growth strategies

The advantage of a niche strategy is that it enables the organization to focus on one customer segment and gain insights into the customer

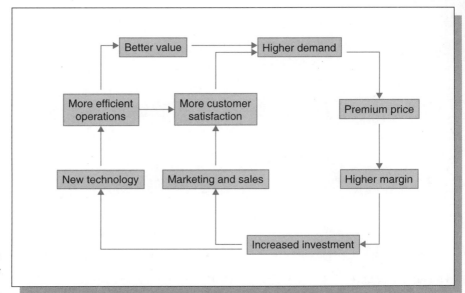

**Figure 12.10**
Virtuous circle of
value and margin.

needs, beliefs and perceptions of value. By focusing, the niche operator can become expert on every aspect of the development, delivery
and supplier management of a few products and services. This focus
enables the niche operator to build competitive advantage in its own
defined niche and should lead to fast growth.

The way that organizations achieve fast growth is by having an effective, well thought out and focused strategy, being customer-led and,
because they are well-managed, being not only efficient but also innovative throughout the organization. The reasons why organizations achieve
fast growth (Wilson and Gilligan, 2004) are because:

- ■ they offer a product or service that they can demonstrate is
  superior to the alternatives;
- ■ the customer perception is that the offering is better than that
  of the competitors, because of its functional and/or emotional appeal expressed through the brand;
- ■ they have global skills and competencies, and learn faster than
  their competitors, and so are able to develop new markets;
- ■ they have greater assets and resources focused in the key areas
  that will deliver competitive advantage;
- ■ they exploit legal advantages over competitors, wherever possible, for example by defending intellectual property;
- ■ they routinely build stakeholder value and quality advantages;
- ■ by focusing their operations they build scale economies and
  obtain experience curve benefits, so operating on a lower cost
  base;

- by identifying and concentrating on the most important business connections they build better relationships with key stakeholders; and
- they exhibit positive leadership and encourage a confident approach to management in the organization.

Bernie Ecclestone (see Enterprise in Action 12.6) showed how the effective development of a niche strategy, erecting substantial barriers to entry and adopting a well-thought-out negotiating stance proved to be extremely rewarding.

---

### Enterprise in Action 12.6

**Bernie Ecclestone: entrepreneur behind Formula 1**

Since the 1970s Bernie Ecclestone has dominated Formula 1 (F1) racing, making it a globally watched sport supported by most of the top names in the car industry. Some years after leaving school he started a business trading motorcycle parts, and raced motorcycles until he had an accident at Brands Hatch. He left racing to make a number of lucrative real estate deals before returning to manage racing drivers. In 1972 Ecclestone purchased the Brabham racing team and began his campaign for the racing teams to control F1. In 1978 he became chief executive of the Formula One Constructors Association and negotiated a television rights deal that gave 47 per cent of the revenues to the teams, 30 per cent to the FIA (the world governing body of motor sport) and 23 per cent to himself in return for putting up the prize money. Through a series of negotiations Ecclestone has managed to maintain his rights to TV revenues and also to manage the administration, set up and logistics of each Formula One Grand Prix.

His shrewd planning, management and negotiation placed him eighth on the 2004 Sunday Times rich list with an estimated personal wealth of £2343 m.

*Source:* Bernie Ecclestone, www.en.wikipedia.org on 12 July 2005

**Question:** What is it that enables an entrepreneur to dominate a niche market?

---

Ecclestone and other successful entrepreneurs demonstrate the validity of Hamel and Prahalad's (1994) view that successful organizations free themselves from the constrictions of accepted business wisdom by breaking free from:

- the latest management tools;
- industry dogma;
- industry rules; and
- a limited mindset.

# The importance of service

One of the characteristics that is common to the majority of successful entrepreneurial organizations is the focus on customer service. In situations where the entrepreneurial organization is competing with larger, better-resourced and more powerful rivals, especially in commodity markets, the only competitive advantage that the entrepreneurial organization has is to deliver efficient, personalized service. In Spotlight 12.2 it is shown how a small competitor is competing in the toughest part of a commodity market.

---

## Spotlight 12.2

### Beatson Clark: shipping air with service

Beatson Clark manufacture glass containers for the pharmaceutical, food and drinks industries. It is a highly competitive market and virtually all countries have their own indigenous producers, given the fact that the materials to make glass are inexpensive and shipping costs are high; you are shipping a lot of air in the empty bottles, too!

It is perhaps surprising therefore to learn that Beatson Clark export to over 100 countries. They have developed a very effective niche business by focusing on low-volume small bottles, which tend to be an irritation for large producers. Beatson Clark have become expert in their chosen niche by:

- offering a design service;
- focusing on quality throughout the organization;
- building close relationships with trusted distributors and customers – sometimes they are in contact 10–15 times a day;
- having a dedicated team for the safe movement and delivery of the bottles, which can be problematic; and
- monitoring all aspects of the business, including performance on every aspect of customer service.

*Source*: Isobel Doole

**Question:** Identify the requirements for a niche entrepreneurial organization.

---

# Comparing strategies for entrepreneurial and bureaucratic organizations

It is not our intention here to discuss generic strategy at length and, at the end of this chapter, we have directed the reader to texts that discuss both administrative and entrepreneurial strategies. However, it is useful to draw attention to the different objectives and approaches of larger organizations, both because these organizations can be competitors to many entrepreneurial organizations and because the most successful entrepreneurial organizations can themselves become large administratively managed enterprises.

The majority of sectors are now dominated by large, mature and powerful organizations. The strategy of many large, bureaucratic organizations is to use their competitive market power to dominate their business sector by providing their large, loyal customer base with well-established products and services. Their huge scope and resources, tried and tested activities, processes and systems, and modest innovations enable them to deliver customer satisfaction. However, because their income streams are substantial and predictable they can become complacent and even arrogant, often unwilling to change a 'winning' formula unless there is clear evidence of a decline in customer demand.

Very often these more bureaucratic organizations become very internally focused on the efficient use and control of their resources – particularly the management structures and responsibilities – and develop very formal, lengthy and inflexible planning and decision-making. Such firms can become vulnerable to environmental changes and the more entrepreneurial firms that exploit the opportunities result from these environmental changes.

In practice, the changes occur continually in all areas of the business environment and internal operations that require an immediate strategic response. Larger entrepreneurial organizations are more strategically proactive, particularly in faster-changing markets; they adopt a more interactive strategy development approach, in which their ability to respond to changes is inbuilt, by developing real-time information systems and encouraging all lower levels of management to be more entrepreneurial, enabling them to take even quite significant decisions in the specific function area or strategic business unit.

In fact many large organizations state that they need to become more like small entrepreneurial organizations and adopt their strategies, by encouraging entrepreneurship and adopting innovation as an essential component of their culture. They try to avoid a 'blame' culture and instead ensure that individuals in the organization who have the courage to innovate and take risks are not blamed for failures.

## Sustaining and building competitive advantage

Businesses are dynamic and always evolving and in order to survive and grow in an increasingly globally competitive market the entrepreneurial organization must decide the basis on which it will compete in the market now and in the future. Boston Consulting Group's annual report for 1982 explains that in the real world of business competition each survivor is uniquely superior to all others in some significant way, no matter how subtle the difference. Unless the competitor dominates his unique niche his life cycle will be very short.

Because there are many combinations of customer characteristics and requirements, costs structures, supply chains, management processes, etc., each competitor must defend its chosen niche against many other competitors that have also defined their own unique niche. Of course, to create a successful niche market the entrepreneurial organization must find sufficient customers that will value the business proposition offered. In practice, markets and the basis of **competitive advantage** change. For example, in the car industry the winners in the 1970s and 1980s were Japanese manufacturers making high quality mass-market cars that were durable and reliable. During the 1990s it was the turn of well-designed cars to fill a niche and these were marketed well. Apart from Toyota, many of the Japanese manufacturers fared badly. In the early part of the new millennium it is prestige niche market cars, such as BMW, niche entrepreneurial organizations, such as component makers, designers and service providers and those manufacturers that have offered consistently high quality, well designed cars, with a well managed supply chain, such as Toyota, that have been the winners. The traditional mass market US car makers, such as Ford and GM, have too much production capacity and too high a cost base and are struggling to survive.

## Sources of competitive advantage

Wilson and Gilligan (2004) suggest that the main sources of competitive advantage for organizations operating in any sector are as follows.

1. a superior product benefit;
2. a perceived advantage, through imagery and effective communication;
3. low-cost operations;
4. legal advantage because of patents, copyright or a protected position;
5. superior contacts and closer relationships;
6. superior knowledge of customers, markets, science or technology, and the current and potential competition;
7. scale advantages;
8. offensive attitudes, competitive toughness and a determination to win.

The small size, limited resources and lack of power and influence in the market mean that there are only a limited number of areas wherein entrepreneurial organizations can build competitive advantage, principally points 1, 5, 6 and 8.

## Building competitive advantage

Over time the sources of competitive advantage are likely to be eroded as competitors offer alternative products and services, and entrepreneurial organizations must continually work to build new sources of competitive advantage. Given the increasing ability of competitors from around the world to copy, undercut costs, generate alternative products and undertake intensive marketing and selling activity, the entrepreneurial organization must build competitive advantage that strengthens its niche market position but also builds into the organization the flexibility to deal with a changing market situation. It can do this through:

- improved market effectiveness;
- improved operational efficiency and cost reductions;
- encouraging and supporting innovations that will add customer value;
- creating intangible assets, such as company reputation, brand identity and intellectual property;
- learning new and more effective ways of running the business through building staff and management skills, knowledge and capability.

## Competitive advantage through adding stakeholder value

Underpinning the whole concept of competitive advantage are two principal considerations that the entrepreneurial organization must continually address:

- the need to focus on value-creating activities throughout the organization for all stakeholders, but particularly customers;
- the need to remove unnecessary costs in the organization by periodic re-evaluation of the internal and external value chain.

Politically inspired innovations, such as that discussed in Pause and Reflect 12.1, need to demonstrate value added if the entrepreneurial organization is to become a major, sustainable organization.

## Pause and Reflect 12.1

### NHS Direct – good health a phone call away

A number of innovations in primary care treatment have been introduced in the UK. The idea for NHS Direct, a 24-hour, nurse-led telephone advice and information service, was announced in the 1997 White Paper *The New NHS, modern, dependable*. Three months later, NHS Direct was established, at three pilot sites to provide 'easier and faster advice and information for people about health, illness and the NHS' so that they could manage many of their problems at home or know where to turn to for appropriate care. The intention was also to improve quality, increase cost-effectiveness and reduce unnecessary demand on other NHS services. The services were provided by telephone and text, and online. Another of the innovations provides a walk-in service.

The website was set up quickly without a proper understanding of user needs in detail but, following a survey of such needs, the website had to be extensively revised in 2001. Later research questioned the real impact of the new service and suggested that it was being used by the same people who already make use of existing health services, the white, healthy middle class and was underused by older people. There was also a suggestion that improving access in this way could be expensive without resulting in significant reductions in the use of other primary care services.

*Adapted from*: Nicholas D., Huntington P., Williams P. and Jordan M. (2002) NHS Direct Online: its users and their concerns. *Journal of Information Science* 28(4): 305–319; Chapman J., Zechel A., Carter Y. and Abbott S. (2004) Systematic review of recent innovations in service provision to improve access to primary care. *British Journal of General Practitioners* 54: 374–381; and NHS Direct Online at www.nhsdirect.nhs.uk

**Question:** Are these simply early problems that are to be expected as the organization grows or is there a more fundamental difficulty with politically driven innovation?

Treacy and Wiersema (1995) have explained the value disciplines that underpin the creation of a value proposition for customers. For an entrepreneurial organization this has to be done against a background of limited resources. They are:

*Operational excellence:* The organization should limit the operations it undertakes itself to those in which it can or should achieve excellence. These should be core and essential to the organization's success.

*Product leadership:* The products and services for which the organization is known must lead those of the competitors in their own particular niche. However, the basis of the leadership, such as being technically advanced, has to be relevant and essential to the customer requirements.

*Customer intimacy:* Having deep customer insights enables the organization to prioritize its innovation in order to improve its offerings in areas that will prove to be of real value for customers. Customer service is where entrepreneurial organizations have the opportunity to excel.

*Brand leadership:* In general, customers want to obtain products and services from organizations that have a strong reputation and brands. They feel more secure. Conventional brand building is expensive but many entrepreneurial organizations, such as Body Shop, Apple and Virgin initially built their reputations by word of mouth.

*Value-based marketing* Doyle (2000) explains four steps which are the cornerstones to building value that will ultimately deliver competitive advantage:

1. the development of a deep understanding of customer needs, operating procedures and decision-making processes;
2. the formulation of value propositions that meet the needs of customers and create a differential advantage;
3. building long-term relationships with customers so that a level of loyalty and trust is built based on satisfaction and confidence in the supplier;
4. an understanding that the delivery of superior value to customers requires superior knowledge, skills, systems and marketing assets.

## Competitive advantage through learning

Many entrepreneurial organizations adopt a traditional pattern for growing their business by using the easily identified, tangible assets of their business and carrying out and controlling many of the operational activities themselves. Indeed, entrepreneurial organizations are mainly valued by their tangible assets, such as facilities and equipment, and resources, such as finances and staff. However, for many entrepreneurial organizations, particularly those from developed countries, high labour costs will increasingly prohibit them from carrying out many of these operational tasks in-house, with the result that their most valuable assets will not be these physical assets.

The emergence of the information age has meant that tangible assets represent an increasingly small proportion of the total market value of the largest organizations. For example, Doyle (2000) observes that the ratio of the market value to book value of the Fortune 500 averaged 8, implying that tangible assets represent only 12 per cent of the organization's total assets. So entrepreneurs might reflect on whether this offers a lesson for the future development of entrepreneurial organizations and whether creating and extracting value from intangible assets might

**Table 12.1**

Asset types and their characteristics in the resource-based firm

| Types of assets | Characteristics |
|---|---|
| Reputational assets | ■ Name of the company and brands that convey the reputation of its products and services and fair dealings with stakeholders |
| Strategic assets | ■ Licenses, natural monopolies or other privileges that restrict competition |
| Technological assets and the capacity to innovate | ■ Proprietary technology in the form of patents, copyrights and trade secrets or special know-how in the application of technology |
| Human resources | ■ Skills and adaptability of employees |
| Organization and culture | ■ Values and social norms that shape the commitment and loyalty of employees<br>■ The architecture of the organization that enables decision-making, knowledge transfer and service delivery |

be a way of further adding value and building competitive advantage in the future.

There are five types of assets and the characteristics of these are shown in more detail in Table 12.1.

If the reader takes time to consider the process of building competitive advantage by focusing on creating and extracting value from intangible assets it becomes clear that the particular knowledge, skills and attitudes of entrepreneurs can be used to full effect.

Most importantly, however, it is entrepreneurial learning as a core competence that underpins successful entrepreneurial growth strategies. Success is a result of the early appreciation of the signals from the environment; recognition of the potential opportunities and threats; reflection on the implications for the organization of responding to these challenges; and questioning the underlying assumptions about the most appropriate response before forming conclusions about the best way forward. Then all that has to be done is to implement these themes before the competition does!

This returns us to the learning spiral described by Doole and Lowe (2005: 42). As the entrepreneurial organization gains and sustains competitive advantage, it uses its learning experiences to inform and challenge perceptions and so is able to more effectively manage the interplay between the strategies of the organization and its environment.

In doing so, the organization's aspirations in terms of development and growth also make a step change. The perception of barriers changes, and the organization is able to build the capability to maintain advantage even when faced with hostile challenges.

## Summary

- All entrepreneurial organizations should have some kind of strategy to draw together their long-term vision, aims and objectives.
- Strategies in entrepreneurial organizations are needed for the various stages of development, from start up to consolidating growth to becoming an entrepreneurial, large organization.
- Turnaround strategies are also needed for times when an existing strategy fails to deal with changes in the environment and downturns in demand.
- There are significant barriers to be overcome in the pursuit of growth, but entrepreneurial organizations can develop niche strategies to achieve fast growth.
- A key part of the strategy for entrepreneurial organizations is to define their future source of competitive advantage. Increasingly this will be founded not on tangible assets but on their reputation, resources and the learning capability of staff.

## Chapter questions

1. Define the stages of entrepreneurial organization development and explain the key skills that are required to successfully manage each stage.
2. What do you consider to be the characteristics of a fast-growth organization? What prevents many large organizations achieving above average performance?
3. A significant number of organizations achieve fast growth for short periods especially after start up but many of them fail to maintain growth rates. Why do you think this is?
4. What advantages and disadvantages do periods of consolidation have for the entrepreneur and the entrepreneurial organization?
5. Why are many owner managers not interested in growing their businesses?

## Case study

### Jokers wild!
**Question:** *How can you be certain of making a profit out of playing poker?*
**Answer:** *Make a business out of producing the playing cards.*

By the 1990s the future for small independent printers was bleak. Changes in technology and in buyer behaviour, increased global competition, and volatile raw material prices led to oversupply in print and wafer-thin margins, and the intense competition resulted in many business failures.

For entrepreneur David Moger, founder and MD of Richard Edward Ltd, the futility of winning business only to cover marginal costs was obvious – he boldly refused to actively participate in the commoditization of the market. He took a bold step – while others were seeking an exit strategy from the industry he invested heavily in new equipment that would enable his firm to develop what today is a strong position in a niche market – producing playing cards.

This strategic move into the card market was brave and insightful. It sounds easy . . . It wasn't. The strategic move was instinctive and would prove to be right, but the investment further burdened the business with debt. The company was traditional in culture and product-focused. Personal selling and relationships between the directors and key figures in the card market enabled the firm to steadily increase its share of this new market. But despite this there were four years (from 1999 to 2003) of losses and continued survival was dependent, not on the company working harder and following the traditional business model and approaches, but working smarter.

The directors were worn out by the constant battle for survival – managing the cash flow in such tight conditions is a full-time occupation. Finding new approaches to doing business – even the notion of marketing – was not something there was time or appetite for. Reducing average costs was critical to a more solid foundation, either through improved cost control or building volume to increase utilization of the plant. The watershed came in the form of the next generation. Moger's daughter, Louisa, with a background in telesales for the media and returning from a year out travelling, offered to help. She identified external sources of help, and a number of initiatives supported by the LDA (London Development Agency) were negotiated and implemented. The first introduced lean manufacturing to the business, helping to identify and eradicate waste and improve efficiency. This initiative represented a watershed in the company's fortunes and provided a more stable corporate base from which the business could continue to consolidate and then grow to become a profitable business.

Sceptical senior management had seen enough to arouse their interest in some of these change agendas. The drive to improve efficiency needed to continue but it was clear that this required supplementation by actions which would both maximize and leverage the firm's potential competitive advantage. The LDA's supply chain project came at the perfect time for Richard Edward as it provided access to the external skills that ensured the momentum for change was maintained and the necessary extra 'management time' could be imported to help see through the change process.

Detailed analysis of the external market led to the prioritization of segments and a more structured approach to business development. A differentiated offer for various segments of the market ensured that there were key account management for major clients in the games and corporate print markets but online ordering for the local bridge club, too. Sales activity was more effectively aligned against clear targets providing focus, a reallocation of effort and better management metrics.

There is plenty of evidence for the change and a more positive outlook for the future of the business. A redecorated reception area, a new improved website www.richardedward.co.uk and refreshed branding thanks to the help given by the Design Council has enabled the company to showcase its high-quality print operations as well as communicating more effectively the thousand and one uses of playing cards from the basic pack for poker players to collectables, education and promotional give-aways.

Founder David Moger is now Chairman of the company and daughter Louisa is Marketing and Sales Director . . . an entrepreneurial business in safe hands for the next generation.

*Source*: Angela Hatton

**Questions**
1. What were the internal and external reasons for the original strategy failing?
2. What were the critical factors in making the turnaround strategy work?
3. Identify the lessons in good practice for entrepreneurs in this case.

## Suggested further reading on generic strategy development and evaluation

Johnson G., Scholes K. and Whittington R. (2005) *Exploring Corporate Strategy* [text and cases], 7th edn. Harlow: Financial Times Prentice Hall.

Mintzberg H., Lampel J., Quinn J.B. and Ghoshal S. (2003) *The Strategy Process: Concepts, Contexts, Cases*, 4th edn., Harlow: Pearson Education.

## References and further reading

Baron R.A. and Shane S.A. (2005) *Entrepreneurship: A Process Perspective*. Mason OH: Thomson South-Western.

Barrow C., Burke G., Molian D. and Brown R. (2005) *Enterprise Development, The Challenges of Starting, Growing and Selling a Business*. London: Thomson.

Bolton B. and Thompson J. (2000) *Entrepreneurs, Talent, Temperament, Technique*. Oxford: Butterworth-Heinemann.

Bolton B. and Thompson J. (2003) *The Entrepreneur in Focus: Achieve Your Potential*. London: Thomson Learning.

Chaston I. (2000) *Entrepreneurial Marketing*. London: Macmillan Business.

Chowdhury S.D. and Lang J.R. (1993) Crisis, decline and turnaround: a test of competing hypotheses for short term performance improvements in small firms. *Journal of Small Business Management*, October 1993.

Coulter M. (2003) *Entrepreneurship in Action*. Upper Saddle River NJ: Pearson Education Ltd.

Crainer S. and Dearlove D. (2001) *Firestarters*. Harlow: Pearson Education Ltd.

Davidson H. (2002) *The Committed Enterprise*. Oxford: Butterworth-Heinemann.

Doole I. and Lowe R. (2005) *Strategic Marketing Decisions in Global Markets*. London: Thomson Learning.

Doyle P. and Bridgewater S. (1998) *Innovation in Marketing*. Oxford: Butterworth-Heinemann.

Doyle P. (2000) *Value-based Marketing: Marketing Strategies for Corporate Growth and Shareholder Value*. Chichester: John Wiley.

Drucker P.F. (1985) *Innovation and Entrepreneurship*. Oxford: Heinemann.

Drucker P. (1999) *Innovation and Entrepreneurship: Practice and Principles*. Oxford: Butterworth-Heinemann.

Drucker P. (2001) *The Essential Drucker*. Oxford: Butterworth-Heinemann.

Goffin K. and Mitchell R. (2005) *Innovation Management*. Palgrave: Macmillan.

Greiner L. (1972) Evolution and revolution as organizations grow. *Harvard Business Review*, July–August.

Hall G. (1995) *Surviving and Prospering in the Small Firms Sector*. London: Routledge.

Hamel G. and Prahalad C.K. (1994) *Competing for the Future*. Boston: Harvard Business School Press.

Handy C. (1999) *The New Alchemists*. London: Hutchinson.

Kano C. and Rao R.M. (1995) New management secrets from Japan. *Fortune Magazine*, 27 November, pp. 45–52.

Kao J. (1989) *Entrepreneurship, Creativity and Organization*. Englewood Cliffs NJ: Prentice Hall.

Kaplan J.M. (2003) *Patterns of Entrepreneurship*. Hoboken NJ: John Wiley and Sons.

Mintzberg H., Lampel J., Quinn J.B. and Ghoshall S. (2003) *The Strategy Process: Concepts, Contexts, Cases*. Harlow: Prentice Hall.

Porter M.E. (1985) *Competitive Advantage: Creating and Sustaining Superior Performance*. New York: The Free Press.

Storey D.J. (1994) *Understanding the Small Business Sector*. London: Routledge.

Treacy M. and Wiersema F. (1995) *The Discipline of Market Leaders*. London: HarperCollins.

Ullmann M. (2000) Routes to a successful turnaround. In: S. Birley and D.F. Muzyka (eds), *Mastering Entrepreneurship*. Edinburgh: FT Pitman.

Wickham P.A. (2004) *Strategic Entrepreneurship*, 3rd edn. London: FT/Prentice Hall.

Wilson R.M.S. and Gilligan C.T. (2004) *Strategic Marketing Management: Planning, Implementation and Control*, 3rd edn. Oxford: Butterworth-Heinemann.

## Key words

| | |
|---|---|
| barriers to growth | fast growth |
| brand leadership | operational excellence |
| commitment to change | product leadership |
| competitive advantage | strategic positioning |
| consolidate | strategy |
| crises of management | turnaround |
| customer intimacy | underperformance |
| emergent strategies | value-based marketing |
| exit | |

# Integrated personal development activity

## Introduction

In the third part of the book we discussed the actions that entrepreneurs undertake to commercialize an idea and create a sustainable organization. The purpose of this integrated learning activity is to help the reader to reflect on the knowledge, skills and attitudes that are required to set up and manage an entrepreneurial organization during its early stages.

The task for the reader is to identify the range of actions that are needed to establish an idea in the market environment or achieve a turnaround in an underperforming but potentially entrepreneurial organization, anticipate the potential barriers to achieving these outcomes and deal with the crises that might affect the organization's long-term future. In doing this the reader is required to identify the process elements of entrepreneurship and the actions and decisions that are needed for the process to be successful, and then reflect on their own entrepreneurial capabilities by assessing the degree to which their own knowledge, skills and attitudes would enable them to successfully start up or turn around a potentially entrepreneurial organization.

## Learning objectives

By the end of this section the reader will be able to:

- identify the steps and decisions needed in the process of commercializing a new idea or achieving a turnaround in an underperforming organization by taking an entrepreneurial approach;

■    reflect on how the entrepreneur's personal knowledge, skills and attitudes impact on the steps and decisions needed.

## The task

Choose either:

A.  a possible new venture (based on a new innovation of a product or service) that could be created with the potential for growth; or

B.  an existing organization, where there is a need for 'reinvention' of the organization, so that it might grow faster and improve upon its present performance. The organization might be underperforming against what could be achieved in the market, or there could be potential for substantial growth in a new market area.

As the basis for your project you should use an organization of your choice or, alternatively, one of the scenarios discussed in the book.

Your tasks are to:

1.  explain the actions that will establish a sustainable venture for (A) or a step change in performance for (B). It is important to explain the innovative and entrepreneurial approaches that you would recommend and not simply to include a general market analysis and generic business strategy;

2.  identify the challenges and barriers that you anticipate could face the entrepreneur and the critical management success factors for success in the project; and finally

3.  reflect on the knowledge, skills and attitudes that are needed by an entrepreneur to effectively carry out the commercialization activity.

## The scenarios

We have provided throughout the book a number of scenarios of organizations in different contexts that are insufficient on their own to provide you with the information that is required to carry out the task. You will, therefore, have to carry out research and information collection similar to that which you would have needed to do had you selected a company yourself.

## Getting started

In order to get you started on the first two tasks that have been set, we include some suggestions based on Chapters 9–12 in Part III. To carry out task 3 we have included some suggestions as to how you might utilize the learning from Parts I and II of the book.

To start you need to consider some basic questions, such as:

- What needs to be done?
- Who needs to do it?
- Where does it need to be done?
- Why does it need to be done?
- When does it need to be done?
- How does it need to be done?

### Task 1: Actions to establish a sustainable entrepreneurial organization

In this first task it is useful first to check how many of the various elements in Chapters 9–12 are relevant to the organization and its situation that you have chosen. However, be careful not to dismiss areas without considering their implications. For example, in the turnaround of an existing underperforming business some elements of Chapter 9 concerning the identification of opportunities may still be important, as they may prompt you to develop a solution that is more innovative than simply doing 'more of the same' rather more efficiently, which might be the administrative rather than entrepreneurial management way of dealing with the problem. Equally, for a start up you should be thinking of the growth challenges once it has been established, as some of the later barriers can be anticipated and dealt with very early in the life of the organization.

To make it easier to refer to the chapters, we have presented our suggestions in what we hope is a reasonably logical format. However, we do realize that much of entrepreneurship is about challenging the norm and so you may carry out the task using a different sequence of actions. This is quite acceptable, provided, of course, that the final outcome represents a convincing and comprehensive approach.

To make your answer convincing it is necessary to focus on an entrepreneurial approach and include innovative actions wherever possible. However, they must be realistic too so, for example, increasing customer awareness will need to be done within the limits of the organization's financial situation. For an organization with little money, creative news stories that will be picked up by the media and spread 'for free' will be more realistic than paid-for advertising.

In Table 1 below we have identified a series of actions and referred to the sections in the chapters that provide some ideas. The following list is not meant to be comprehensive as it will change according to the context for the task and organizational situation.

**Table 1**
Task 1 questions

| Some actions | Chapter |
|---|---|
| Challenging the industry assumptions | 9 |
| Define the market opportunity for which the organization could obtain the resources to exploit | 9 and 11 |
| Identify and quantify target customer segment | 10 |
| Define business model | 10 |
| Carry out feasibility study | 10 |
| Plan for investors | 10 |
| Decide on organization form, premises and legal requirements | 11 |
| Decide on amount and type of investment required | 11 |
| Overcome growth barriers | 12 |
| Strategic positioning | 12 |

## Task 2: Anticipating and dealing with the challenges and barriers

In the course of carrying out the actions to develop a new organization start up or to achieve a turnaround in the performance of an existing organization obstacles inevitably arise that, if not dealt with, will prevent the entrepreneurial approach from working. There are two approaches to dealing with challenges and barriers that arise: wait until a crisis occurs and then rush around to sort out the problem; or anticipate the potential problems and try to plan them out.

In carrying out this task it is necessary to recognize that giving equal importance to every potential problem that might be encountered would make management an impossible task. There is little point in trying to plan for unlikely events. Indeed some argue 'analysis equals paralysis'.

The entrepreneur's available time is very limited, so allocating it equally to everything that could go wrong is wasteful. While we would caution against wasting time on endless analysis we do believe that successful entrepreneurs anticipate and highlight the most important potential challenges and barriers and focus on actions and key decisions that are needed to overcome them. That is what is required in this task.

In Table 2 we have included a number of questions that indicate some of the common problems and barriers that occur and commented on some of the actions that might be taken to counter them. Again the solution to these problems should be innovative and you should consider some of the lessons learned from the experience of other organizations. Some examples of these innovative solutions are included in the chapter Spotlights. The barriers and challenges will differ considerably from situation to situation and our list is given simply to start you thinking of what might or could go wrong for your chosen organization.

## Table 2
Some barriers and challenges

| Some barriers/challenges | Possible issues |
| --- | --- |
| What is the most vulnerable part of the organization externally? | Rapidly changing technology, economic cycle, legislation changes |
| What is the most vulnerable part of the organization internally? | Undercapitalized; cash flow management; IT system; skills weaknesses |
| What might stop customers responding positively to the new 'offer'? | Are we doing enough to: understand their requirements; raise awareness; explain the benefits; make the offer distinctive |
| How might competitors respond if we are starting to appear successful, and what could we do? | Keep a low market profile with modest growth until the organization is operating efficiently and can withstand a competitor attack |

## Task 3: The knowledge, skills and attitudes of commercialization

In tasks 1 and 2 you will have identified the what, who, where, when, why and how of the actions that are needed. If you have addressed the tasks in an entrepreneurial way you will have included some innovative ideas in a number of these areas, for example, in what you are proposing, and where and how you will carry it out. In this last task it is necessary to take a step back and think about how the entrepreneur (and you, too):

■ comes up with innovative solutions;
■ chooses the particular area to focus upon;
■ knows which industry assumptions to challenge.

To do this it is necessary to review what mindset and capabilities the entrepreneur must have or develop to exploit opportunities in a more innovative way. In reading this book and carrying out the tasks included within it you should have become more sensitized to and aware of the different knowledge, skills and attitudes of entrepreneurship. In carrying out the series of tasks in this integrated learning activity you should reflect on, first, what is required of the entrepreneur to complete the actions effectively and second, which areas you feel you have or could develop expertise in. In the areas that you have no interest in developing capability in yourself, you should think perhaps about how you would delegate these tasks and how you would create a team that includes members with knowledge, skills and attitudes that complement your own, so that between you there is a complete set that you consider necessary to develop a sustainable organization. You should also consider which areas of entrepreneurship do not appeal to you or do not fit with your personality, ambitions, values and beliefs at the moment.

In thinking about these issues it is not enough to carry out a superficial evaluation of everything that you can think of that will result in

**Table 3**
Areas for consideration

|  | **Knowledge** | **Skills** | **Attitudes** |
|---|---|---|---|
| Ideal for an entrepreneur in this situation | Concepts, their application and evaluation in this context | ————————————————————➤ | |
| Your assessment of yourself | Your beliefs and values and contributions | ————————————————————➤ | |
| Gaps that would need to be filled by the entrepreneurial team | The team members need to make the following complementary contributions | ————————————————————➤ | |

you having thirty or forty areas of future actions, possible unresolved thoughts and dilemmas. You need to think deeply about a few areas of priority that are of interest to you, where you can gain some real insights into good and bad practice and learn a few valuable lessons.

To assist in carrying out this last task, in Table 3 we include some areas for consideration.

# Index